Healthy House Building for the New Millennium

A DESIGN & CONSTRUCTION GUIDE

By John Bower

TH4813
.B693
2000

Published by:
The Healthy House Institute
430 N. Sewell Road
Bloomington, IN 47408
www.hhinst.com

Illustrations by John Bower
Photography by John Bower and Lynn Bower
Book and cover design by Lynn Bower

This book originally appeared under the title of *Healthy House Building*.

Copyright © 1993, 1997, 2000 by John Bower

All rights reserved. No part of this book may be reproduced or transmitted in any form, electronic or mechanical, including photocopying, recording, or by any information storage and retrieval system, without the written permission of the author, except for brief passages in a magazine or newspaper review.

Printed on recycled paper with soy-based ink.

DISCLAIMER: Because each individual is a unique biological specimen with unique tolerances to various pollutants, no house design can possibly satisfy the needs of all people. While the Model Healthy House in this book has been designed to minimize indoor pollution levels in every way feasible, to eliminate indoor air pollution altogether would be virtually impossible. None of the information in this book should be taken as medical advice. Sensitive individuals should always consult a physician about their particular health requirements prior to doing any remodeling or construction. Anyone planning to construct a house based solely on this book is also advised to consult a qualified professional to verify that the plans comply with local building codes and geographic or climatological requirements. Neither the author nor The Healthy House Institute is responsible for any damages, losses, or injuries incurred as a result of any of the material contained in this book.

Publisher's Cataloging-in-Publication Data.
Bower, John
Healthy House Building for the New Millennium: A Design & Construction Guide.
Includes index.
1. House Construction—Handbooks, manuals, etc. 2. Housing and Health.
    3. Dwellings—Environmental engineering.
 I. Bower, John. II. Title.
TH4813.B69   2000
693'.8

Library of Congress Catalog Card Number: 99-95477
ISBN 0-9637156-8-2 $21.95 Softcover

PREFACE

■■■ I have always learned a great deal by asking a question like "If you were going to do it over today, what would you do differently." It doesn't matter what the subject is—a person's life, raising children, a big project, or writing a book—the answer is always informative and insightful.

This book follows the building of a Model Healthy House that I completed in southern Indiana. A great deal of what I did in this project, I would still do today, but there are also some things I would do differently. So each chapter in this book discusses in detail what I actually did in building the Model Healthy House. And at the end of each chapter there is an "Update" where I discuss new developments in the field of healthy house construction, and also things I would change if I were doing the project today. I think it will give you an appreciation, not only for how technology changes, but also how my thinking has evolved.

The last chapter of this book covers another project—the house my wife and I built for ourselves after the Model Healthy House was completed. It should give you additional insight as to what I have learned, and what I would do differently today. I have purposely shown how my thinking has changed over time, rather than simply discuss my current way of doing things. That's because experience has taught me that many people have read various books and articles that were written with what is now outdated advice. By discussing both the older recommendations as well as the results of new research and experience, I feel you will have a better understanding of the current state-of-the-art of healthy house building.

A decade ago, indoor air pollution was an emerging topic in the news. Yet in some circles it was still not considered a problem. Well, the topic is now coming of age, with articles appearing regularly in the mainstream media. You have probably already read about the dangers of asbestos and lead paint—indoor pollutants that have been studied for decades. They can lead to lung disease or mental retardation in children. In recent years radon and formaldehyde have been in the news as being responsible for additional health complaints. If you look through technical and medical journals, you will find evidence that fiberglass insulation can cause cancer, some new carpeting can kill mice, and there are paints that can affect brain function. A report in *Pediatrics* found that if your house is heated with wood, your children will be more likely to suffer from respiratory symptoms.

When examined closely, many components of a house have been found to have a negative effect upon your health. Sometimes those effects are major, but fortunately others are minor. The key to designing and building a healthy house is to choose the construction materials that are the most benign, and put them together in a manner that enhances your health rather than compromises it.

I got involved in this field in 1984 after my wife, Lynn, had her health severely compromised as a result of commonly used building materials. Since then I have analyzed most construction products and techniques in order to determine how to build houses in a healthy manner. I have also personally built several healthy houses and consulted on the construction of many others.

This book discusses the health aspects of most common building materials, and how to choose between them. But it is much more than a list of construction products. As it turns out, there are building *techniques* that are just as important as material selection. By following the construction of a Model Healthy House, *Healthy House Building for the New Millennium* will show you *how* to put the materials together.

While it's unlikely that you'll want a house exactly like the Model Healthy House—or the one featured in the last chapter that Lynn and I built for ourselves—the basic principles and details are easy to apply to virtually any building project. After all, houses of widely differing styles, floor plans, and sizes can easily be constructed with very similar materials, using almost identical construction techniques. So, while there are certainly a few people out there who might build a house very similar to the Model Healthy House featured on these pages, many others will apply the information to their own layout and design. You can too.

John Bower
The Healthy House Institute
Bloomington, Indiana

AVAILABLE FROM THE HEALTHY HOUSE INSTITUTE

■ *The Healthy House*: How to buy one, how to build one, how to cure a sick one

■ *Creating a Healthy Household*: the ultimate guide for healthier, safer, less-toxic living

■ *The Healthy House Answer Book*: Answers to the 133 most commonly asked questions

■ *Understanding Ventilation*: How to design, select, and install residential ventilation systems

■ *Healthy House Building for the New Millennium*: A design and construction guide

■ *Your House, Your Health*: A non-toxic building guide (VHS video)

■ *The Healthy House*: Designing, building and furnishing a non-toxic home
   (13-episode VHS video series)

ACKNOWLEDGMENTS

■■■ This project would not have been possible without the assistance and generous contributions of healthy materials by the twenty-nine corporate sponsors. In particular; I'd like to thank James Whitefield at Alumax; Jerry Glenn, Susan Van Voorhees, and Peggy Batus at American Olean Tile Co.; Jack Hoffmann and Rod Chambers at Ametek; Leon Bausch at Asko, Inc.; John Banta at Baubiologie Hardware; Quintin Rottering at Beam Industries; Bob Rasmussen and Laurie Brammer at Broan Manufacturing Co.; Mike McDonnell at Burnham Corp.; Ernest Hollas at C-Cure; Dan Murphey at Delta Faucet Co.; Dennis Harr at Denarco, Inc.; Bob Myers at Dietrich Industries, Inc.; Gary Hasenbhler at Enterpriser Lighting, Inc.; Don Johnson, Dale Johnson, and Roger Growden at Kitchens and Baths by Don Johnson; Brian Koetter at Koetter Woodworking, Inc.; John Czerwonka, Connie Conrad, and Todd Lerting at Lee/Rowan; Tom Morris, Ray Gilpin, and Ray Palazzo at Metal Sales Manufacturing Corp.; Dan Carothers at Murco Wall Products, Inc.; Raymond Valle and Tom Warner at Norandex; Sonny Bishop, Joe Rourke, and Chuck Metzger at Nordyne; Bob Henderson and Craig Henderson at Nutech Energy Systems, Inc.; Wayne Harrington at Nu-Tek Plastics, Inc.; Harold Zander at Pace Chem Industries, Inc.; Pete Miller at Polyken Technologies; Don Musilli at Pure Air Systems; Howard Hartsfield, Jerry Maibach, and Tom Bollock at Reynolds Metals Co.; Bob Block, Terry Sears, and Tom Scott at Sage Advance Corp.; Francis Hummel and Kim Bray at Stanley Door Systems; and Joe Zajac, Linda Stewart, and Karen Walters at Universal-Rundle Corp.

I owe thanks to several of my local suppliers who supported the project and helped coordinate deliveries: Larry Bastin and Dave Rose at Rose & Walker, Joe Price and Terry Davis at Wickes Lumber, and Pam Smith and John Brown at Dal-Tile.

Although I did most of the actual construction myself, I would like to acknowledge the work done on the project by E.L. Branham Contracting (excavation), Cleveland Thomas (concrete finishing), and Myers Quality Drywall (drywall finishing). Dave Michaelis of Indiana CAP Directors Association, Inc. deserves my thanks for performing a blower door test on the house.

Gratitude is extended to David Goldbeck of Ceres Press for his initial involvement in the project and his many helpful suggestions; Allan Edmands for his comments; Jeffrey Fox who shared his knowledge of photography; Al Wasco of the Housing Resource Center in Cleveland for reviewing an early version of the manuscript; Annie Berthold-Bond and Bill Sanders of Greenkeeping, Inc. whose extensive organizational and editorial work helped bring the rough manuscript into its final form; Bob Baird for a very fine job of copy editing; Penny McQueen for helping obtain the high-resolution pages for paste-up; John Railing for answering dozens of computer-oriented questions during the page layout phase of book production; Dale Risch of ProTec Publishing who loaned me the use of his darkroom and provided a great deal of information about book publishing in general; Dwight Link who helped my wife manhandle a 320 pound crate off a delivery truck one day when I was out of town; and Melanie and David Lyle for the use of some of their furniture for the finish photography.

I am indebted to Doug Hyland for his outstanding camera work, direction, and editing of *Your House; Your Health*, the accompanying video to this book; Bryce Hyland for his handling of the lighting; Roger Priest for his narration; and my sister Mari Wiese who recommended them to me.

Most of all, I would like to thank my wife Lynn who was there every day offering suggestions during the design and construction of the Model Healthy House and the writing of the manuscript. She tirelessly took hundreds of photographs, assisted in the construction, and supplied a tremendous amount of moral support during what was a hectic two-year project. Lynn gets all the credit for the cover design and the superb layout of the book.

CONTENTS

8

CONTENTS

9

CONTENTS

11

12

CONTENTS

13

ABOUT THIS BOOK

■ ■ ■ This book is for every homeowner, builder, designer, and remodeler who is interested in reducing indoor air pollution and improving health. It describes the construction of a Model Healthy House that I built in southern Indiana, but *Healthy House Building for the New Millennium* is more than a step-by-step guide. By discussing the rationale behind all of the decisions that affect indoor air quality, this book will help anyone apply the same principles to other houses, offices, schools, or any other type of building.

Portions of this book were written with construction professionals expressly in mind, but if you are a homeowner or do-it-yourselfer, this book will give you an excellent background so you can better discuss a project with your builder or designer. A few chapters were written primarily for non-professionals. For example, Chapter 4, "Selecting a Designer and Contractor," will help someone unfamiliar with home construction locate professionals who can bring their dreams into reality.

The primary focus of *Healthy House Building for the New Millennium* is how to improve indoor air quality. However, I am also concerned with how buildings fit into the larger scheme of things. Houses with minimal insulation waste fuel like gas-guzzling automobiles. Therefore, to be environmentally friendly, your house should be energy-efficient. Besides being extremely well-insulated, the Model Healthy House described in this book receives a considerable amount of free solar energy through south-facing windows and is fitted with a solar collector for heating water.

Conventional design principles are covered in *Healthy House Building for the New Millennium* only when they have a bearing on health. My discussion of design deals mostly with construction techniques, mechanical systems, and materials. Most designers of model homes emphasize the visual appearance of the house, and the structure becomes less important. This book is about health, not aesthetics, so conveying how the structure is put together is most important. I have purposely made this house plan fairly simple, so that the healthy features and energy efficient aspects are easy to visualize.

Whenever I discuss a construction material I feel residential builders may be unaccustomed to working with, I cover it in extra detail. For example, steel studs and metal roofing are used extensively in commercial buildings, but many residential carpenters remain unfamiliar with them. Therefore, I have included enough design, selection, and assembly information so a first-time user will feel comfortable working with unfamiliar materials.

In order to keep costs down, I have used a few marginally unhealthy materials, but I have only used them in a way that they do not compromise indoor air quality. These building products can, however, affect the workers who install them. Because I am a builder myself, I very much care how the construction process affects workers, so I discuss how to use such materials safely.

The Model Healthy House in this book was built to optimum standards in order to show how a pristine indoor environment can be created. The end result is a house that is suitable for most hypersensitive individuals who require a totally unpolluted indoor environment. While this is the best environment for all of us, you may prefer to make some compromises in favor of a different construction material or technique that appeals to you. After all, not everyone requires the same degree of air purity that others do. However, it is important to remember that you are bombarded with pollutants everyday at work or school, in your automobile, while jogging, and from what you eat and drink. If your house is built to maintain good indoor air quality, then you and your family can truly rejuvenate yourselves during the time spent there. Therefore, I recommend that you build the healthiest house possible. It will help you become a stronger and healthier person, one better able to handle the assaults from the pollutants we all encounter when we're away from home.

In order to help you locate healthy construction products, I approached a number of carefully selected manufacturers about sponsoring the project by contributing materials. Of course, they aren't the only companies making healthy materials. Chapter 4 will show you how to evaluate other sources. The sponsors are shown in **bold type** in the text, their addresses and telephone numbers are listed in Appendix 2, and their products are shown on the Plans. Other appendices contain sources of further information, as well as the complete set of house plans.

At the end of each chapter there is an "Update" that contains new information or research that has come to light since the Model Healthy House was completed. The "Updates" also include discussions of what I would do differently if I were building the Model Healthy House today. Finally, the last chapter covers the construction of the house my wife and I built for ourselves after the Model Healthy House was completed. It will give you additional insight as to what I might do differently today.

A healthy house needn't look exactly like the Model Healthy House nor like the one my wife and I now live in. Having built several healthy houses myself, and having worked with contractors and architects on projects across the country, I can assure you that a healthy house can be built in practically any style that appeals to your particular taste.

PART 1:
GETTING STARTED

18

Chapter 1

WHY A HEALTHY HOUSE?

■ ■ ■ To know how to build a healthy house, it is very important for you to know what makes one unhealthy. In other words, you need to understand why your house is making you sick before you try to fix it.

When you buy a new mobile home, you are given a notice that says in part: "Some of the building materials used in this home emit formaldehyde. Eye, nose and throat irritation, headache, nausea, and a variety of asthma-like symptoms, including shortness of breath, have been reported as a result of formaldehyde exposure." In my opinion, this warning should be applied to most conventionally built houses as well. It is a health risk that we all should be aware of, and one none of us should have to tolerate.

In recent decades, most of us have become more aware how polluted the air is outdoors. And to many of us it has come as something of a surprise that the air quality indoors is far worse. Many scientific studies document this: Indoor air pollution is almost always at least five to ten times more severe than outdoor air pollution; it isn't unusual for it to be a hundred to a thousand times worse. This frightening discovery is true everywhere, from rural areas to major cities. The reasons are sometimes simple, sometimes very complex, but the good news is that answers

are available for improving the air you breathe indoors. That is what this book is all about.

Modern Construction

New houses today are built with different materials than were used earlier this century. Solid lumber has, in many instances, been replaced with composite materials such as plywood and particleboard. Different techniques are also used to build today's houses. While older methods such as post-and-beam framing and log construction are still being used, most houses are now built of smaller 2x4s, and many are prefabricated in factories. Our high-tech heating systems are vastly different from the equipment our grandparents used. Natural gas and electricity are now preferred as primary heat sources over coal or wood. And many of us have the convenience of air conditioning.

Similarly, modern appliances, furnishings, and cleaning products are unlike anything available just a few short decades ago. Soap formerly was a mixture of fat and lye; today it is a complex chemical concoction. Synthetic fabrics abound over natural fibers such as cotton, wool, and linen. Unfortunately, all of these things can—and do—cause indoor air pollution. As a result, many houses are designed to be filled with contaminated air.

We often assume that if a product is sold on the open market, it must be safe. But this is far from always being the case. Take the example of tobacco, whose negative health effects have been well documented. Tobacco smoke itself is one of the top indoor air pollutants. There is also a considerable amount of evidence describing the toxicity of the solvents used by painters every day.

Analyzing the healthfulness of a material requires considerable expenditure of time and money before the scientific proof can be firmly established. In the meantime, potentially harmful products remain on store shelves and find their way into your home. Certain pesticides that were used for decades, after having been thoroughly evaluated, are no longer sold in the United States. Their danger to plants, animals, people, and the environment is now fully documented. Common construction materials are now coming under this same scrutiny. As a result, many building products will, no doubt, be removed from the market in coming years. In the meantime, they will continue to pollute your environment unless you are aware of them and are selective in using them.

The Pollutants

Much of the environmental movement of late has focused on large visible issues such as the killing of whales, the slaughtering of animals for their fur and skins, nuclear power plant emissions, factory discharges, incinerators, toxic waste sites, polluting landfills, trees dead from acid rain, etc. These are indeed very important issues, but they all tend to be concerned with the environment "out there," and are somewhat removed from our daily lives. The interior of your home is an environment you are much closer to. In fact, it is often a closed environment, a microcosm, like a terrarium with a sealed top. It is an environment that affects your health through the interaction of several different categories of pollutants: biologicals, pesticides, gases, metals, minerals, radiation, and vapors.

Biologicals

Biological pollutants include such things as dust mites, mold, mildew, *Legionella pneumophila* bacteria, pollen, etc.—all living organisms that can affect your health. Because some 41 million people in the U.S. have conventional allergies, there is a good chance that you or a family member will end up with a runny nose, itchy eyes, sinus congestion, or a headache if these biological pollutants are allowed to proliferate indoors. When you suffer from these allergic reactions, your body is in a weakened state, making you more susceptible to many other pollutants.

In addition, even more devastating health effects than allergies are attributed directly to biologicals. Legionnaire's disease, a vivid example, has certainly taken its toll in human life. Some molds can be equally deadly and an asthmatic attack resulting from an allergic reaction can prove to be quite frightening. *Practical Homeowner* magazine reported in February 1991 that there were 4,580 asthma-related deaths in this country in 1988. And the incidence is rising. Today, asthma affects some 3.7 million children, up from 2.4 million in 1980.

One of the most common things that people are allergic to is the dust mite. These microscopic creatures find carpeting to be a comfortable home, where they eat the tiny particles of dead skin that we all shed every day. If you are allergic to dust mites, you typically sneeze when their feces is stirred up in the carpeting, it becomes airborne, and you inhale it. Even if you aren't allergic to dust mites, I think it is a rather disgusting thought to be inhaling dust mite feces on a regular basis.

Mold is another biological pollutant prevalent in houses, especially where water is present, such as in humidifiers. Cambridge, Massachusetts, home inspector Jeff May is very adept at understanding how to prevent homes from making people sick. He tried weekly cleanings to keep his own furnace humidifier in good shape. Finally, he gave up and removed it because the water remained "virtually indistinguishable from pond scum." Many people have humidifiers that are never cleaned. I shudder when I think what might be growing in them.

An abundance of biologicals can affect not only your own health and well-being as an occupant, but also the structure and contents of a house. Decay organisms can be responsible for rotting wood. A house can literally collapse because of rotted beams.

Pesticides

Sometimes biologicals themselves don't have a direct effect on you personally, but toxic pest control chemicals have the capacity to destroy your health. A good example involves termites, small creatures seldom even seen. The termite workers that actually do the damage to a house can pass through a crack as small as $\frac{1}{32}$". The chemicals we have typically used to control termites have destroyed the health of many people around the world. These pest-control chemicals are literally formulated to kill, and most don't differentiate between termites and human beings. They affect all forms of life. Since termites are so small, they are easily killed with these toxic solutions. It takes considerably more to kill you because you are so much larger, but small amounts of termiticides have caused a variety of negative health effects ranging from headaches, nausea, and dizziness to Multiple Chemical Sensitivity and cancer.

In *Safety at Home,* the National Coalition Against the Misuse of Pesticides reported that consumers buy and use 285 million pounds of toxic pesticides every year. The Coalition says these chemicals "are nerve poisons, can cause cancer, respiratory problems, birth defects, genetic damage, injure wildlife, and pollute the environment and drinking water." You must move toward non-toxic methods of pest control in your house if you are to insure your family's health.

Gases

Gases are another major category of air pollutants. Gases from combustion processes have been polluting the indoor air since our ancient ancestors began building fires inside caves. None of us would consider sticking our nose up to an automobile's exhaust pipe and inhaling the gases, yet unvented furnaces and heaters are often used indoors that spill their combustion gases directly into the air we breathe. Natural gas kitchen ranges emit carbon monoxide, carbon dioxide, sulfur dioxide, and nitrogen dioxide. Even furnaces and fireplaces that are connected to a chimney or flue can be problematic. It is not uncommon for the combustion gases to backdraft, that is, flow back down the chimney—and into the living space.

Volatile organic compounds (VOCs) are gases that are emitted from a wide variety of modern materials. Many are difficult to pronounce: Cyclopentadine-ethenyl-2-ethylene, Hexamethylene triamine, Tetrachloroethylene, 4-Phenylcyclohexene, etc. Formaldehyde is probably the best known. It is a probable human carcinogen, as well as a sensitizer. Exposure to formaldehyde can sensitize you so that your body will react to very tiny amounts of it—amounts that were previously not a problem. Once sensitized, you may begin to react to a wide range of other VOCs as well. A typical house could have a hundred or more different VOCs floating around in the air. These include compounds that are neurotoxins, carcinogens, mutagens, and irritants. Consumer products advocate Debra Lynn Dadd has pointed out in her book *The Nontoxic Home* that the average house today contains more chemicals than were found in a typical chemistry lab a century ago.

Most VOCs have not been studied for their precise health effects, but it has been estimated that 25% are carcinogenic. To study how they act in combination is virtually impossible because the concentrations and specific compounds vary so much from house to house. What we do know is that, in general, we should not breathe VOCs.

Most of the VOCs from products such as fresh paint will dissipate relatively quickly, often in a matter of days. Other compounds can linger for weeks or months. Building materials such as particleboard and medium-density fiberboard will emit formaldehyde into the air for years.

Metals

Metals can also be pollutants. Although no longer on the market, lead paint can still be found on the walls of tens of millions of houses. A window painted with lead paint can, as it is raised and lowered over the years, result in a considerable amount of powdery lead-dust particles on the window sill. A child looking out such a window will invariably put his hands on the sill, then later put them into his mouth. Lead ingested in this way can result in permanent brain damage. It is often surprising to many people that children generally ingest more lead by coming in contact with lead dust that has settled on window sills and in carpeting than by chewing on lead-painted woodwork.

In 1989, a Michigan child developed a rare form of mercury poisoning after his family painted the interior of their house with what they thought was benign latex paint. Mercury had been used in the paint as a fungicide and the toxic metal evaporated into the air of the house as the paint dried. Because of swift action by the U.S. Environmental Protection Agency (EPA), mercury can no longer be used in interior latex paints. However, you can still buy exterior paint containing mercury, and other heavy metals like cadmium are still permitted in interior formulations.

The metal arsenic is a common component of chemically treated lumber used for wooden decks, porches, and railings. This lumber has a greenish tint and is often described as being "salt treated." It isn't table salt that is used, but rather an arsenic salt. Several lawsuits have resulted from individuals being made ill after working with treated lumber. One worker, whose job it was to build picnic tables, was so affected that he vomited seven to eight units of blood, nearly half of his total body supply. When tested, he and a co-worker had arsenic levels in their hair and nails that were hundreds of times higher than normal. Although manufacturers warn against using it on eating surfaces, this type of lumber is often found on picnic tables. I also have serious concerns about children playing on surfaces made of treated wood.

Minerals

Asbestos is a naturally occurring fibrous mineral that can cause a variety of lung diseases including lung cancer. While its use in construction materials has been severely curtailed, it can still be found in many older houses as a component of insulation, vinyl flooring, gaskets on doors of furnaces and wood stoves, siding, and drywall joint compound. If such materials remain intact, they cannot release any asbestos fibers, but if they become damaged or start to deteriorate, the asbestos can become airborne and be inhaled.

Fiberglass is believed by some experts to also cause lung disease, especially if the fibers are similar in size to asbestos. Fiberglass is currently classified as a man-made mineral, and a possible carcinogen. It is widely used as house insulation. Because of reported human health effects, an organization called "Victims of Fiberglass" was formed in Sacramento, California. Unfortunately, many indoor air quality experts have been disappointed with the type of information this organization has put out, saying that much of it is biased and taken out of context.

Minerals, such as calcium, that are dissolved in tap water can also become air pollutants because, when the water is used in humidifiers, the minerals can be spewed into the air. Their particle size is so small that they can be inhaled deeply into the lungs. As a result, in December 1988 the U.S. Consumer Product Safety Commission issued an alert recommending that you use demineralized or distilled water in humidifiers.

Radiation

Radiation is a well-known cause of illness. In houses, the main source of radiation is radon. Radon has been widely discussed in the media, yet many people do not fully understand its danger. It is a radioactive gas that is found in small amounts in the soil virtually everywhere on the planet. You are probably breathing some radon right now, and while it isn't good to breathe it, low levels can't be avoided totally. Problems occur when radon seeps into houses and builds up to dangerous concentrations. Breathing large amounts of radon can lead to lung cancer. The EPA has estimated that up to 20,000 lung cancer deaths a year can be attributed to radon.

Electromagnetic fields (EMFs) may be even more pervasive than radon, although their seriousness is the subject of much debate. An electromagnetic field is the invisible energy that surrounds electrical wiring and appliances. Most sources are relatively weak, but there are some areas indoors strong enough to be of concern, and it is possible to measure high levels in your house if it is located near an electrical power station or high voltage power lines.

Many people are aghast to learn that you can actually purchase products containing radioactive material. Some types of compact-fluorescent lights and some smoke detectors contain tiny amounts of what is normally considered hazardous waste. These products are claimed to be safe by the manufacturers, but I myself don't like the idea of supporting an industry that sells products that require radioactive material to operate. When safer alternatives are available, why take a chance?

Vapors

Vapors are the gaseous forms of liquids. When latex paint releases mercury, it is in the form of mercury vapor. However, the most common vapor in your house is water vapor, something that is not really a pollutant in itself. Yet, too much water vapor can result in air pollution problems. Most of the biological contaminants discussed earlier thrive and proliferate at higher humidity, and VOCs, such as formaldehyde, outgas at a more rapid rate at higher humidity. (Outgassing refers to the release of VOCs from synthetic materials.) Even in a house that seems dry, microclimates of high humidity will exist near cold surfaces. Because of this, it can be fairly dry in the center of a room, yet you may find mold growing on a cold window frame or in the corner of a closet.

A considerable amount of water vapor is generated in a house through bathing, laundering, and washing dishes. Even your exhaled breath contains moisture. If a house isn't ventilated properly, this moisture can build to excessive levels, resulting in biological pollution problems like mold and mildew that can affect both the occupants and the structure.

Increased Risk

If you are an average American, you spend about 80 to 90% of your time indoors where you are inhaling more polluted air on a daily basis than your forebears—probably more than your body was designed to process. The air in your house is literally unlike any air that has existed since the dawn of the human race. It is composed of chemical compounds that are emitted, or outgassed, by modern building materials, and by combustion gases from heating systems. To assume that you can evolve and adapt to this new kind of polluted air is wishful thinking. It takes hundreds of thousands of years and tens of thousands of generations for evolution to make major changes in a species. In the meantime, nature works through the law of the survival of the fittest. In other words, people who are overly susceptible to indoor pollution will be the first to get sick. Some won't survive.

It comes as no surprise that not everyone responds as quickly or in the same way to pollutants. We have all heard about someone who smoked two packs of cigarettes and drank a quart of hard liquor every day, and lived to be over one hundred years of age. However, people with such strong constitutions are generally the exception to the rule. Indoor air pollution probably affects us all to some degree; those who are the most susceptible will be affected first. Those at increased risk include children, the elderly, the sick, pregnant women, and unborn fetuses. In other words, we all are at risk at some time during our lives because we all start out as fetuses, grow into children, most of us will eventually reach old age, and it is a rare person who is not weakened by illness at some time during his or her life.

Our children are especially susceptible to indoor air pollution because their immune systems aren't fully developed until they are about six years old. Their livers are unable to process toxins as well as adult livers, and they have higher respiratory rates than adults so they inhale more pollution per pound of body weight. Unborn fetuses are even more vulnerable because of their developmental status. If you are pregnant, your body is supporting two people, so that also makes you more susceptible. The elderly, on the other hand, have immune systems that are on the decline, making them less able to handle pollutants than people in their middle years. When you are sick, especially with a respiratory condition, your immune system is already compromised.

Modern Illnesses

Because we have done little to clean up the air in our houses, many people are already getting ill. Some feel tired all the time. Others have a variety of different illnesses because their bodies cannot cope with the air they are breathing. Some certainly die before their time. This isn't just speculation. This is something that is happening today. According to *The Inside Story, A Guide to Indoor Air Quality*, an EPA publication, some symptoms may show up immediately while others require years of exposure. Typical immediate symptoms include dizziness, headache, sinus irritation, or fuzzy thinking. In the long term, an individual may develop emphysema, heart disease, or cancer.

In the future, people may contract brand new diseases that we haven't heard of yet. These new illnesses may be caused by pollutants themselves, or by viruses attacking weakened bodies. One illness that was unheard of a few short decades ago is a condition called Multiple Chemical Sensitivity.

Multiple Chemical Sensitivity

Multiple Chemical Sensitivity (MCS) is something that people generally aren't born with. Rather, it usually develops after a person is exposed to various forms of pollution. People can get this illness by being exposed to a large amount of pollution at one time, or after experiencing low levels over a long period. Individuals with MCS become hypersensitive to a wide variety of synthetic pollutants such as exhaust gases and artificial fragrances. Often, they cannot tolerate synthetic clothing, plastic materials, paints, adhesives, or printing inks. Some people with MCS exhibit such a wide variety of symptoms to so many different substances that they are sometimes called "universal reactors." In other words, they seem to react to everything.

William J. Rea, MD, is a Dallas, Texas, specialist who has been working with MCS patients for over 20 years. He suggests that "avoidance of as many pollutants as possible is the first step in prevention and treatment." Unfortunately, we are being exposed to an atmosphere that is more chemically laden each day. The result is that you are more likely to develop a condition like MCS than ever before, and this is not a small problem. Over 17,000 patients have passed through the doors of Dr. Rea's clinic. The Wichita, KS based American Academy of Environmental Medicine currently has over 500 physician members who are treating MCS patients across the country.

There are two analogies that are often used to describe individuals with MCS. The first involves canaries. Coal miners used to take canaries underground with them because they knew that the birds were very sensitive to bad air in the mines. When the birds quit singing and fell off their perches, the men knew it was time to return to the surface for fresh air. The birds represented a sort of early warning system, a way to judge air pollution levels before the miners themselves were seriously affected. People with MCS can be viewed as our society's "canaries." When we see how seriously they are bothered by the pollutants surrounding us all, we should take note and realize that we too may soon be affected.

A rain barrel analogy is used to describe why some people develop MCS, but others don't. The immune system is viewed as a barrel. When we are born, it is empty, but each time we are exposed to pollution it fills up a little. The barrel has a small hole in the bottom to allow the rain water to drain out. Some of us have "barrels" with small drain holes that don't drain very quickly. If your "barrel" ever gets completely full and overflows, it represents an immune system that is overwhelmed, one that can no longer contend with the loads imposed on it. Because we are all biologically unique, each of our "barrels" has a different capacity. Some of us can live our entire lives without ever having the barrel overflow, while other barrels may fill quickly. If your "barrel" is full, your immune system can no longer cope, and MCS may develop. One of the best treatments is to remove some of the water from your "barrel," to lower the loading of pollutants on your body. This can often be done by living in cleaner air, eating less polluted food, or by building up the immune system so it can better cope with the pollution.

24

We, as a society, have a great fear of life threatening diseases. When the air in your house is contaminated with radon or asbestos, it can certainly result in cancer, but there are many other conditions that are related to indoor air pollution. The everyday symptoms that you experience from time to time are often attributed to the air indoors. Things like conventional allergies, asthma, joint pain, anxiety, and depression are typical examples. People with MCS have been known to exhibit a wide variety of symptoms. Virtually every complaint possible, both physical and psychological, has been recorded. Because of mental symptoms like depression and anxiety, such individuals are often said to be suffering from psychosomatic disease. In other words, they are told that their condition is all in their head. Actually, the brain is a very sensitive organ and it is easily affected by pollutants, especially volatile organic compounds (VOCs) and pesticides, many of which have well documented neurotoxic effects. While the cause is physical, the result can be psychological.

A 1989 report titled *Indoor Air Pollution in Massachusetts* stated that "Indoor air pollution is a growing problem in the U.S. and accounts for 50% of all illness." According to Senator George Mitchell (D-ME), "We now have clear evidence that the effects of indoor air pollutants result in substantial costs to society in the form of reduced productivity, sick time, health care costs, and disability costs estimated in the tens of billions of dollars." It is clear we have a problem.

Solutions

While the air in most houses is unhealthy, a general trend is afoot to clean up our environment. With people becoming more aware of the health of the planet, and how we have been destroying it, they have begun to live their lives differently. Recycling is now routine in many households. Many families use less-polluting waxes, cleansers, soaps, detergents, and polishes. Supermarkets are beginning to offer organically raised food. Automobile exhaust is less polluting and gasoline mileage figures are increasing. Yet many of our homes still remain polluted.

As people realize how bad the indoor environment has become, they are beginning to demand that builders, designers, and contractors do things differently. They are demanding that their houses be built in a manner that promotes health, rather than diminishes it. An annual survey in *Professional Builder* magazine regularly finds that the vast majority of new home buyers are willing to pay extra for a healthier house. While healthy house construction promises to be a major trend in the future, and is in fact a trend that is already well on its way, many people simply do not know where to start.

The best way to curb indoor pollution is to build your house in the first place with materials that do not contribute to the problem. It is considerably easier to build without asbestos, lead paint, pesticides, and formaldehyde than it is to clean up a problem house after the fact. With a properly designed ventilation system, you can be supplied with fresh air regularly. This will also help reduce indoor moisture levels and keep biological pollutants in check.

It is quite easy to build an unhealthy house— it is being done every day. To build a healthy house really isn't difficult either, although it may seem so at first. The techniques are already well-established. It just takes a little planning and forethought. The purpose of this book is to acquaint you with the concepts, materials, and methods that are used in healthy house construction. As you read through the remaining chapters, you will see that it is surprisingly easy to build or remodel a house so it will not make you sick.

Update

Over the years, there has been a steadily increasing awareness of indoor air pollution issues. In the last few decades many scientific papers have been written on the subject yet for a long time stories in the mainstream media were uncommon. Today, the technical knowledge has gotten increasingly sophisticated, and the information is starting to trickle down to renters and homeowners. Articles dealing with healthy (and unhealthy) construction are becoming regular features in leading consumer publications. Part of this tread has to do with increased consumer interest, but it is also because people are continuing to get sick in their houses. In other words, indoor air pollution is affecting the health of more and more families.

Consider the situation in Cleveland, Ohio. Since 1993 there have been at least 34 cases of pulmonary hemorrhage and hemosiderosis among local infants. This is a condition that involves bleeding in the lungs, and it has resulted in at least 10 deaths in the Cleveland area. The outbreak has been linked to a particular black mold, *stachybotrys atra*, and a style of heating system ductwork that is common in Cleveland. Molds have been affecting people's health for years, and as a Canada Mortgage and Housing Corp. publication states: "People should not live in moldy houses!" While lesser symptoms are more common, the Cleveland situations shows that the ultimate symptom, death, is certainly possible.

Indoor air pollution from something as seemingly innocent as candles has also made the news in recent years. It seems that some candles, particularly the scented or aromatic varieties, can release a considerable amount of soot that can become deposited on all the walls and ceilings of a house. It's even been found inside a refrigerator! Before candles were determined to be the culprit, there were several lawsuits directed toward heating/cooling contractors, because the heating systems were thought to be the source of the soot. While dark staining in houses can have a variety of causes (mold being a common cause), scented candles are most problematic when the fragrances used are not suitable for combustion. Of course, there are other contributing factors, some obvious (like the number of candles), but others less so (like the length of the wick). This is no insignificant problem—cleanup in some houses has cost thousands of dollars.

Since first being described in the 1950s, the diagnosis of Multiple Chemical Sensitivity (MCS) has been attacked by skeptics. In fact, less than a decade ago it was, in some circles, still not considered a valid medical condition. That situation has changed considerably in recent years. In fact, people with MCS are now getting disability payments from Social Security; many Gulf War veterans exhibit a variety of MCS symptoms; articles discussing MCS now appear regularly in mainstream newspapers and magazines. While MCS was once considered unusual, most Americans now know someone personally who is affected. Current estimates suggest that only 1-3% of us have MCS to a severe degree—but that translates into several million people. And many more of us probably have MCS to a lesser degree. This is a condition that can radically change your life, and it is something that a healthy house can help you avoid.

Chapter 2

NEW CONCEPTS IN HOUSE CONSTRUCTION

■■■ When you decide to build a new house, or renovate an existing one, you will be concerned with the style of the house, room layout, shape, color, traffic plan, etc. These are the things that make your house comfortable, livable, and attractive. The purpose of this book is to add the criterion of health. The traditional issues will remain important, but the goal is to implement them in a healthy manner.

To give you a better understanding of how to build houses that are healthier, I'd like to explain a few new and helpful concepts that have emerged in recent years. They will make it easier for you to understand the design and construction process I have used in this book.

The Holistic House

Over the years, many members of the medical profession have tended to specialize. There are doctors who concentrate on the lungs, others only deal with the brain, and some are devoted to the skin. As a result, their concentration of knowledge is in one narrow field, and they aren't always very aware of developments in other specialties, or of how the different specialties interact. House construction has

followed a similar path. Plumbers know about plumbing systems and heating contractors know about furnace systems, but neither may fully understand what the other is doing. Just as we are seeing a need for a more holistic approach to medicine, we need to start looking at houses in a holistic manner. Just as the human body is a collection of systems that function as a whole, so is a house. We should not look at a house as an assemblage of lumber, pipes, and wires. It is a large integrated system consisting of several smaller systems. How all the components are assembled ends up being just as important as which pieces are selected.

Indoor air pollutants enter the living space in a variety of ways. Some are released directly by surfaces that are visible. For example, fresh paints and carpeting release VOCs. Other pollutants enter the living space from the outdoors or from inside wall cavities.

If insulation remains where it was installed, hidden inside the wall or ceiling, it can't affect you as an occupant. However, most houses have innumerable small hidden air leaks, so particles or gases from the insulation can filter into the living space. Radon enters the living space from the soil through similar gaps and cracks in the foundation. You can solve these problems in a couple of ways. For example, you could select totally non-toxic insulation and only build where there is no radon. But non-toxic insulation can be expensive, so it may not be affordable, and radon is a potential problem virtually anywhere. If you analyze how the different components of a house interact and assemble them in certain ways, you can easily prevent radon and insulation from entering the living space. This leads to the idea of an airtight house. If a house is built in an airtight manner, pollutants generated outside the living space, remain outside the living space. I'll go into this in much more depth in Chapter 11.

The concept of ventilation systems in houses is actually a fairly new idea. In the past we were told to have plenty of windows for fresh air, but who has their windows open in the winter? And if they are open, it doesn't always mean that air will pass through them. On a windy day, you may receive plenty of fresh air, but on a calm day there may be none. This feast-or-famine approach isn't the best way for you to bring fresh air indoors. Mechanical ventilation using a fan is a much more reliable technique, but it must be done correctly. If it isn't, it can interact with the furnace or other systems in the house and cause some serious problems. See Chapter 15 for a discussion of ventilation systems.

So it is not just the materials that go into a house that cause indoor air pollution. Your house is more than a collection of components, it functions as an integrated whole, and the different components tend to interact. If they interact in inappropriate ways, pollution results. As you read on, you will begin to understand how a house functions, how it breathes, and how it really is more than an assemblage of pieces. Doctor Frankenstein put some pieces together incorrectly and created a monster. You can do the same with a house and create a building that can damage your health or even kill you. Or, with an understanding of how the various pieces interact, you can create a house that will enhance your health.

And of course, the building itself could be 100% inert, and you could fill it with toxic furnishings and maintain it with noxious household cleaners. What we put into a healthy house is as important as the structure. While this book deals with the structure

itself, Appendix 1 lists sources that you will find useful in furnishing and maintaining a healthy house.

Outgassing

Outgassing has emerged as one of the important buzz words in indoor air pollution circles. It refers to gases that are emitted by synthetic materials as they age or degrade. Particleboard outgasses formaldehyde from its glue. New carpeting outgasses over one hundred different VOCs. These come from the carpet material itself, the coloring, dyes, stain resistant treatments, etc. In addition, carpet pads and carpet adhesives also outgas a variety of different VOCs.

In the past, no one even considered the fact that there might be any negative health effects related to outgassing. When we sat in a new automobile, we deeply inhaled the new car smell believing it to be a symbol of something pleasurable and satisfying. You could even buy aerosol cans to replenish the odor as it dissipated over the first several months of the car's life. More recently, we have come to understand that many of the synthetic chemicals given off by new materials are harmful to us.

Some manufacturers are reformulating their products so that consumers and installers are exposed to fewer VOCs than in the past. These low-VOC products are now beginning to appear on shelves in your local building supply center. Some states are even starting to regulate the VOC content of paints and adhesives. These new regulations will definitely improve indoor air quality, but surprisingly, the regulations weren't promulgated specifically for that purpose. They were designed to combat smog. Areas like California, New Jersey, and New York City that now require low-VOC paints have notoriously high levels of outdoor pollution. VOCs tend to be a significant component of smog, and the laws were passed to improve the quality of the outdoor air.

The Time Factor

While it is best to choose products that don't outgas VOCs, 100% inert materials aren't always available. Fortunately, there are ways you can use some of these products relatively safely. This is because outgassing decreases with time. A newly manufactured product that is subject to outgassing will only contain a limited quantity of VOCs that will eventually all be released. Most of them will be emitted fairly quickly. If the material can be stored somewhere, such as in a garage, until the outgassing period has ended, then it can be brought indoors and installed.

If the odor of fresh paint is intolerable, you could take a vacation for a week or two until the majority of the outgassing has dissipated. Some paints tend to lose their odor relatively quickly, in a matter of a few days. However, your sense of smell may not be acute enough to tell you when the outgassing period has truly ended. I have worked with people who have an extremely acute sense of smell and can detect paint odors as long as a year after the walls have been coated.

Unfortunately, time will not solve all of your outgassing problems. Something like medium-density fiberboard (often used in kitchen cabinets and for closet shelves) contains a very large percentage of formaldehyde-based glue. This reservoir of glue is so potent that formaldehyde will be released in significant amounts for years to come. Such products' "half-life" can span up to six years. In this case, half life refers to the amount of time it will take for half of the formaldehyde to be released. For example, it can take six years to lose half of the initial amount of formaldehyde, six more years to lose half of the remainder, and during every six years thereafter, only half of the remaining formaldehyde will dissipate.

The half-life of formaldehyde and other VOCs is affected by a number of factors, but humidity and temperature are the most significant. Higher temperatures and higher humidities mean a shorter half-life. For example, a new mobile home (which contains a great deal of formaldehyde) located in Florida will outgas formaldehyde at a faster rate than one in a cold, dry climate. If a mobile home is located in a northern climate, the overall indoor formaldehyde levels may be lower, but they will last for more years.

One of the problems with VOCs is the fact that they haven't been studied sufficiently to determine how long they take to outgas completely. Nor have enough data been accumulated to know which VOCs are the worst offenders. Therefore, while you can reduce your risk by allowing a product to outgas awhile before exposing yourself to it, no one can say for certain just when a product can be considered totally safe and inert.

The "Bake-Out"

Some scientists are suggesting that you "bake out" a new building in order to reduce the levels of VOCs. This suggestion is based on the fact that VOCs outgas quicker at higher temperatures. If you simultaneously raise the temperature inside a new house to 90 degrees and provide extra ventilation, it is believed the VOCs can be removed rather quickly. The high temperature causes rapid outgassing and the increased ventilation gets the gases out of the building before they can be reabsorbed. According to the scientists who are working in this area, the process is supposed to take at least three days to be effective.

Not all researchers are in agreement that a bake-out will actually work. They point out that it won't be particularly effective with manufactured wood products such as particleboard since those materials contain such a large reservoir of formaldehyde that it takes years to lower the formaldehyde levels significantly.

In my experience, heating up an entire building and "baking" for three days does a good job in releasing some VOCs, but not others. For example, most furnaces and baseboard heaters are painted, and while the paint may have no discernible odor when they are cool, the first few times they are heated up, the high temperature can cause the finish to outgas. I have seen some baseboard heaters that have had a fairly strong paint odor even after two or three months of use, but others are relatively inert after an hour or so.

When you go into a new building that has had the temperature raised to 90 degrees, you will usually be able to detect a strong odor as some of the VOCs are released from the components of the building. Something is obviously happening. I have had several

29

hypersensitive clients try a bake-out to make their home more tolerable, but the people I have worked with have not found that it has helped enough. In my opinion, a bake-out seems to be a simplistic solution to a very complex problem, a technique that just doesn't seem to live up to its expectations.

If you are considering a bake-out, it is important to know that high indoor temperatures can harm some furnishings. Your musical instruments, phonograph records, candles, etc. could easily be damaged. The bake-out process may also cause some chemicals to be released that would remain inert at normal temperatures.

Baking out products during the manufacturing process seems to hold more promise. Factory-applied baked-on finishes on metal siding, roofing, and cabinets are usually much more inert than other finishes. This is because manufacturing plants can design a specific bake-out technique for specific VOCs and apply it to their specific product before it is shipped out to consumers. Already, some companies are reformulating their products and manufacturing processes so that they release lower levels of formaldehyde and other VOCs, but it is an area in which more work needs to be done.

Even if you can use the time factor or a bake-out to reduce indoor levels of VOCs, you must keep in mind that the chemicals are being released into the outdoor air. This in turn contributes to outdoor air pollution.

Selecting the Site

Deciding exactly where you will build your healthy house is one of the first decisions that must be made. It is also one of the most important. However, the criteria used to select a healthy site are different from the criteria most home buyers and Realtors are accustomed to using. For example, real estate people place a higher value on a corner lot than one in the middle of a block. From a health standpoint, a corner lot is less desirable because it will be exposed to exhaust gases from traffic on two sides.

If you build a house in an area that has very poor outdoor air quality, it will be difficult to maintain good indoor air quality. The reason is simple: if the air is bad outside, that same air will be brought in via a ventilation system. It is certainly feasible to use air filters indoors to improve the quality of air that enters your house, but it is far easier to start with clean outdoor air in the first place. If there is only an occasional outdoor air problem, then a fairly simple air filtration system will suffice, but if it is always smoggy outdoors, a major (and often expensive) filtration package may be in order. The Model Healthy House is located in an unpolluted section of southern Indiana, but, as in many parts of the country, there can occasionally be some wood smoke in the area during the winter. Therefore, I have incorporated an air filter into the design of the ventilation system to handle any pollutants that occasionally show up in the outdoor air.

While living in a house surrounded by pristine outdoor air is highly desirable, employment, schools, or family may dictate that you remain in an area that is less than perfect. In that case, an efficient air filtration system may be high on your priority list. If you are considering a move to a less polluted locale, you should make a list of the pros and cons of where you are and compare it to a similar list for where you are planning to go. Then you can compare both lists to see if a move is in your best interest. You should also consider doing what you can to reduce outdoor pollution wherever you live. For example, encourage the farmer down the road to switch to organic methods, or ask the electric utility company to mow rather than spray chemicals under its power lines.

Site Analysis

The first step in analyzing a piece of property for building your house involves walking around to see what is in the area. When visiting a site, you should look for potential pollution sources. These include natural features as well as man-made structures. A stream that periodically floods its banks could mean a wet foundation; a swamp or field of ragweed could be a source of mold or pollen. A gasoline station or factory could pollute the surrounding neighborhood. Farm fields, orchards, or manicured lawns could be routinely sprayed with pesticides or fertilizers. A

30

neighboring house with a creosote blackened chimney could be a sign of unwanted wood smoke in the winter. Children living near high voltage power lines have been found to be more likely to get leukemia.

You should also consider traffic patterns. Busy streets or highways will mean exhaust gases. Less-traveled gravel roads can be very dusty when there is traffic. A house located near the back of a subdivision will have less traffic than one near the entrance. Based on a variety of studies, the National Institute of Occupational Health and Safety regards diesel exhaust as "a potential occupational carcinogen," a good reason not to live next to a busy highway.

You should consider the prevailing wind direction. Since the wind isn't always blowing, this might be good information to get from neighbors. The best house location will be downwind of the cleanest air and upwind of any pollution sources. Check out the neighborhood for things like landfills, orchards, or power lines rights-of-way that may be routinely sprayed with herbicides.

Once you have selected a building site, you will need to decide exactly where on the parcel the house will be located. With a very small lot, there may not be many choices, but with several acres, there could be several possible locations. You should pick high ground to get the most benefit from the wind and for good drainage. Try to pick a site where trees won't need to be cut down. Trees provide shade and have the ability to produce oxygen.

Consider using native plants or a ground cover of some type for landscaping rather than a manicured lawn to avoid chemical lawn treatments and exhaust gases from lawn mowers (or use an electric mower). There is even a name for doing the lawn this way: Xeriscaping. It refers to creative landscaping for water and energy efficiency. For example, cacti and yucca plants can be appropriate in a hot dry climate, and ferns grow well in the woods. Prairie grass may be a good choice if you live on the plains. Your county agricultural extension agent can help you select plantings that require low maintenance and are native to your area.

It has been my experience that there is no part of the country that has perfect air quality at all times of the year. The Southwest was promoted as being good for asthmatics, then newcomers brought in pollen-bearing plants. I know a woman who moved to Hawaii for clean air only to discover that part of the year some areas smelled of volcanic sulfur. In spite of such problems, you can find relatively clean pockets of good air in nearly every state. It just takes some driving around, looking at various areas, asking questions, and applying some health-related criteria to find the best spot. I suggest that you learn what is within a two- or three-mile radius of a building site before making a final decision. And don't rule out a site just because there is a pollution source less than a mile away. Every site is unique, and prevailing winds, hills, or woodlands can provide protection for a spot even though the air is polluted just down the road.

Subdivision Restrictions

If you plan to build your healthy house in a subdivision, be sure to check to see if there are any restrictions that are tied to the deed or are related to an owner's association. In the past, such restrictions were designed primarily to exclude ethnic or racial minority groups, but today may specify what kind of roofing and siding are allowed, the type of landscaping, or even the size of the house. I know of one subdivision that as recently as 1989 actually required houses to use a specific brand of roofing that contained asbestos. It may be easier to search for another lot than to try to fight a restriction. However, if a site is otherwise perfect, you may be able to point out the health advantages of a change in policy and have a positive impact on the entire neighborhood.

Airtight Construction

Very often when I first start talking to someone about airtight construction, they invariably think I am talking about a cause of indoor air pollution. Actually, there are many airtight houses that do have serious air quality problems, but I consider airtight construction part of the solution. Not THE solution, but PART OF the solution. I feel that when a house is built with healthy materials, in an airtight manner, and with a mechanical ventilation system, you will end up with more fresh air, and a healthier indoor environment, than in a conventional loosely built house.

There are three reasons why airtight construction is a good idea. First, an airtight house is an energy-efficient house. Second, by building an airtight structure, you can easily separate the insulation from the living space so it can't affect the health of the occupants. Third, with an airtight house the outdoor air is separated from the indoor air. If there is an outdoor pollution alert, the ventilation system can be temporarily shut off and the living space will remain pollution free. I'll go into the specifics of airtight construction in much more detail in Part 3.

Principles of Healthy House Construction

For several years I have recommended the use of three basic principles in building or remodeling for health: ELIMINATE, SEPARATE, and VENTILATE. I originally came up with these principles in 1987 and they have stood the test of time quite well. They have been adopted by many designers and builders, and have been incorporated in other publications in both the U.S. and Canada. Once understood, you can use them along with all of the conventional design principles in order to create a healthy house of any size, shape, or style.

Principle 1: Eliminate

The most important thing to do in building or remodeling a house is to eliminate toxic materials as often as possible. Simply reject them from your list of potential building products. If there are no polluting materials used in the construction or renovation of a house, the air quality will be far superior.

For example, I consider carpeting to be a very problematic building material. So you simply eliminate carpeting from your house. But you may not like the appearance of the bare subfloor. The next step is to substitute a healthy material for the unhealthy one. After eliminating the carpeting, you might substitute

ceramic tile or hardwood. If cost is a consideration, and it often is, you might consider a relatively inexpensive colored or textured concrete floor slab accented with cotton area rugs.

The principle of Eliminate is often considered the most important of the three. This is because it is easier to build with healthy materials than it is to clean up the air in an already polluted house. Think about the tons of radioactive waste from nuclear power plants around the country that still need to be disposed of. If we had developed cleaner solar-generated electricity in the first place, we wouldn't have such a big mess to contend with. Although they are no longer in use, lead paint and asbestos will be toxic legacies forever. It can cost thousands of dollars to remove lead paint from a house, considerably more money than a healthier paint would have cost originally.

What to Eliminate

If you are planning to build a new house, or remodel an existing one, and you want to utilize healthy materials, I would say that the three most important things to eliminate would be carpeting, manufactured wood products, and combustion appliances. I call them the Big Three.

I don't like carpeting for a variety of reasons. First of all, the VOCs released from new carpeting have been implicated in a wide variety of health complaints. Second, carpeting contains millions of microorganisms, as well as pesticides, mold spores, soil particles, and animal waste that you track indoors on your shoes. Conventional vacuum cleaners blow this conglomeration called house dust all around the room. Shampooing carpet has been linked to Kawasaki Syndrome in children. This is a disease, characterized by a high fever, that occurs predominantly in children under five years of age. In addition, most of the carpeting on the market today is made from non-renewable synthetic materials.

Manufactured wood products should be eliminated because most contain glues that release formaldehyde. Even though some of these materials are somewhat better than others, personally I prefer to avoid all manufactured wood products because formaldehyde is such a powerful chemical.

32

Because combustion appliances (natural gas water heaters, oil furnaces, wood stoves, etc.) all have the capacity to release burned combustion gases into the air, I don't use them in the houses I build. Natural gas or oil leaks are also common occurrences in basements, crawl spaces, and utility rooms. I prefer electric and solar methods of heating houses, heating water, and cooking.

There are literally hundreds of different materials used in houses that can affect indoor air quality, but most of the construction products currently on the market are somewhat less problematic than the Big Three. That doesn't mean that everything else is benign; it just means that they generally aren't quite as serious.

Principle 2: Separate

The second principle of healthy construction involves separating some unhealthy materials from the air you breathe. This can be done when it is not economically, or logistically, feasible to eliminate a polluting material, or substitute a healthy one.

Lead paint is a perfect example. You may discover that removing the lead paint from your walls will require a ten-thousand-dollar expenditure that you simply can't afford. While removal may be the best solution, a second best choice may be quite acceptable. Many experts recommend that you cover up the lead paint so that it is no longer exposed to the occupants. Walls can be covered with new drywall and wood trim, or doors can be coated with a special encapsulating paint. It might also be possible for you to perform a combination of procedures. You might have the woodwork stripped of all lead paint and then use an encapsulant on the walls.

If you separate problematic materials from the living space, then they can't pollute that space. Even though it may not be a good idea to have a jar of formaldehyde sitting on a shelf in your house, it can't affect your health if the lid is screwed on tightly. The formaldehyde is separated from the living space by the glass jar and the metal lid. In a similar way, the air in the attic may be somewhat polluted, but if it doesn't leak into the living space, it should be of little concern because it can't get to you and affect your health.

With lead paint and asbestos, encapsulants have become popular and lower-cost alternatives to trying to totally remove the contaminant. Encapsulation is separation carried to its extreme, it means 100% containment. Sometimes encapsulation is a good idea, but for some materials a perfect seal is not always necessary.

Insulation is a material that I highly recommend separating from the living space. With negative health effects associated with most of the insulating products on the market today, I feel that an airtight barrier between the insulation and the occupied living space is an excellent idea. I don't feel that it is necessary to totally encapsulate the insulation however. If it is exposed to your attic, I don't see that as a problem as long as you don't live in the attic. However, if ductwork runs through such an attic, then the seams in the ducts must be carefully sealed in order to keep them from being contaminated. Also, if your attic is to be converted to living space during a remodeling project, then the insulation must be kept out of the new space, and you should take care to avoid polluting the rest of the house during the construction process.

Principle 3: Ventilate

The third principle of healthy design involves ventilation. If ventilation is used alone to clean up the air in a house built of unhealthy materials, large amounts of fresh air may be needed, but if used in conjunction with the first two principles, smaller, more reasonable, amounts of ventilation will usually be sufficient.

Ventilation is important because we all need fresh air to breathe continuously. In the past, we have relied on natural forces such as the wind to randomly infiltrate our houses and supply us with fresh air. But the wind isn't blowing every day, and infiltration can often actually contribute to indoor pollution. Operable windows are always nice to have, but they are not a substitute for a mechanical ventilation system. The concept of "natural" ventilation isn't necessarily a bad one, but it can be highly unreliable.

Although the principles of Eliminate and Separate are usually more effective at reducing indoor air pollution, ventilation can be used to dilute the pollutants that do enter the living space of the house. For example, ventilation can be used to reduce indoor radon concentrations. In many houses, radon enters the living space from the soil through cracks or gaps in the foundation. If it is impractical to caulk and seal all of the radon pathways, then providing a basement with extra ventilation will reduce the radon concentration by diluting the contaminated basement air with fresh outdoor air.

I will cover the disadvantages of relying on Mother Nature to supply a house with fresh air naturally in Chapter 11, and the details of mechanical ventilation in Chapter 15, but basically there are two ways to correctly provide for ventilation in houses. First, a whole house, or general ventilation system running continuously can provide a small amount of fresh air to all the rooms of the house; it can remove small amounts of stale air from all of the rooms of a house; or it can do both at the same time. General ventilation systems are designed to supply the entire house with fresh air. Although they are not yet common in houses, they will probably be required by future building codes.

You are probably already familiar with a second way of ventilating houses. It is often called spot ventilation since it is meant to ventilate only a certain spot in the house. Kitchen range hoods and bathroom exhaust fans are designed to remove pollutants from kitchens and bath rooms where they are generated so the pollutants can't travel through the house and contaminate other rooms. Spot ventilation usually doesn't provide any fresh air to the bedrooms and living areas where you spend the most time.

Compromises

When I tell people to eliminate carpeting, manufactured wood products, and combustion appliances, I often hear a response such as "But I don't want to live without those things. How can I use them in a healthy manner?" It is an understandable question, and actually one that comes up quite often because, after all, there are definite advantages to using them. Carpeting is comfortable to walk on, attractive, and

cheaper than hardwood and ceramic tile. Plywood and particleboard are also often cheaper and easier to work with than solid lumber. Combustion appliances generally result in lower utility bills, and many people prefer cooking over an open flame.

While my personal choice is to use materials that are as non-toxic as possible, you may prefer to make some compromises. If you insist on using carpeting, you can minimize your exposure to VOCs by purchasing wool or cotton carpet, or by rolling new synthetic carpet out in a garage or warehouse for several weeks so the bulk of the outgassing can take place before installation. You should install carpet with tack strips whenever possible, rather than adhesives, and a central vacuum with an outdoor exhaust should be used to keep the carpet clean.

While they still release formaldehyde, the manufactured wood products used for exterior sheathing or roof decking contain a more benign glue, and since they are not directly exposed to the living space, can serve as a reasonable compromise for many people. For the more potent formaldehyde-containing materials that are used indoors, paints and sealants can definitely reduce emissions, although not always enough for hypersensitive people.

If you prefer cooking over an open flame, you should have a powerful exhaust hood above your range and use it regularly. The fan will operate more efficiently and be less likely to cause an air pressure problem affecting the operation of your furnace if you crack open a kitchen window when using it. Fireplaces and wood stoves that bring combustion air in from the outdoors are better choices than those that pull the needed air from the living space, and natural gas fireplaces and furnaces with totally sealed combustion chambers are also less polluting.

Sheet vinyl flooring would be another example of a compromise. While it is a much better choice than carpet, my first recommendation would be to not use it. But if it must be considered for economic reasons, I would let it outgas in a garage before bringing it indoors, and I would install it without adhesives if possible. (The baseboard molding around the perimeter of the room can be used to hold it in place.) If adhesives must be used, you should select a water-based product.

An important thing to remember about compromises is that they are not perfect solutions. And they do add up. The more little compromises you make, the more likely that indoor air pollution will become a problem. On the other hand, you may decide that a couple of minor compromises may be quite acceptable.

Miscellaneous Considerations

Of course, there are many different kinds of considerations that can be used in creating a healthy house. These concepts can affect our feeling of well being but may have little to do with indoor air quality. They include such things as natural light vs. artificial light, and the use of comfortable, relaxing colors. Air that is neither too warm nor too cool, neither too humid nor too dry is also important, as is noise control. Scientists now talk about noise pollution and its negative effect on our health.

There are also a variety of environmental considerations related to the construction industry that have little to do with indoor air quality. For example, materials should be used efficiently. In his *Guide to Resource Efficient Building Elements*, Missoula, Montana, builder Steve Loken lists dozens of construction products that utilize natural materials in the most efficient way possible. This is important because we cannot continue to build houses in the same wasteful way we have in the past. Many of the materials listed in Loken's book are actually quite good from a human health standpoint, but some are not the best choices possible. For example, it is very commendable that cellulose insulation is made from recycled newspapers, but some people have reported negative health effects after having it installed in their house. Cellulose insulation is very fine and powdery, and during installation it can easily seep into the living space where it can be inhaled by the occupants. Since it is contaminated with printing inks and flame retardants, cellulose insulation is not good to breathe. I have heard of cases where heating ducts or kitchen cabinets were accidentally filled with insulation by careless installers. Particleboard is another product that utilizes raw materials in a resourceful way, but as

I have already said, it contains a potent formaldehyde containing resin.

We also need to concentrate on using construction materials that can be harvested or otherwise obtained in a sustainable or conscientious manner. Doing so helps protect rain forests or other sensitive parts of the planet. To view a major strip mine from an airplane is to see how we are permanently disrupting our fragile ecosystems.

In addition, we should consider building houses of components that were manufactured in a healthful manner. The production of asbestos-containing products destroyed the lives of many miners and manufacturing employees over the years.

While this book is primarily concerned with indoor air quality, I have incorporated as many environmental considerations as possible into the design. However, few products meet all possible criteria, so whenever a compromise was necessary, I chose the materials that were the healthiest for the occupants.

Update

I continue to get a lot of questions asking about what I call "simplistic solutions to complex situations." Everyone wants an easy way to solve the problem of poor indoor air quality. Well, I'd like that too and, in some cases, there are relatively simple solutions. But in many cases, the solution isn't easy. For example, I've spoken to a number of people over the years who started feeling sick after moving into a new house or apartment. After talking to them for a while it was obvious to me that they were reacting to a combination of all the new materials, as well as a lack of ventilation. In many cases, it was also apparent that one or more of the occupants was already, or was in the process of becoming, hypersensitive to a variety of indoor air contaminants.

In such cases, the first thing I'm asked is: "Isn't there some kind of filter I can get?" Filters are marvelous inventions, but filtration is actually a subcategory of my principle of Ventilation. To clean up the air in a polluted house with filtration alone would be very difficult. For example, you would need a fairly large filter system capable of processing a great deal of air over and over very quickly. That's because you would be trying to clean the indoor air while, at the same time, all the new materials (e.g. carpet, cabinets, etc.) continue to release various VOCs. So, you have to try to filter them out faster than they are being released. Portable filters simply don't have the capacity, so a whole-house filtration system would be necessary. This can be expensive. There will need to be a tremendous amount of air movement through the filter—and the house—and, in the end, it will still be an imperfect solution. I'm certainly not against filters. As I said, they're marvelous inventions. It's just that, in many cases, they aren't the best solution. The most effective solution generally involves Elimination, Separation, and Ventilation.

If a person who is experiencing an indoor pollution problem has spoken to other experts before talking to me, they will likely have been told to try a bake-out, or to get an ozone generator, or to get a bunch of air-purifying house plants. (Filters as well as ozone and house plants are discussed in Chapter 15.) They might also have been told to put a sealant on the cabinets, walls, or carpeting. These solutions are all going to be imperfect. With hypersensitive people, it's unlikely that they will help enough, and they may make the situation worse.

The solution to a given indoor air quality problem almost always involves Elimination, Separation, and Ventilation. The principles can certainly be used independently, but they are usually most effective when used in combination with each other—in a holistic approach.

Chapter 3

SELECTING A DESIGNER AND CONTRACTOR

■■■ This chapter is for homeowners who are planning to have a new house built, considering a room addition, or are thinking about some general remodeling, but don't know precisely where to start. It contains a preview of what you can expect, and guidance in selecting the best professionals to get the work done.

A builder or designer who is involved with new house construction or remodeling on a regular basis will have a good understanding of all of the steps involved. They will also be familiar with all the different kinds of stumbling blocks, the day-to-day difficulties, and the delays that can plague any major project. Unfortunately, homeowners are often unfamiliar with much of the process, so when something doesn't go quite according to plan, they may be unprepared for the consequences. Homeowners may also become frustrated with their contractor who simply says that "these things happen."

Who Should Be in Charge?

Often, a homeowner places the entire project in someone else's hands and waits for it to be completed. I feel this approach is wrong. If you plan to live in the house, then you have a role to play in its creation. That doesn't mean you should be on the job every day ordering people about, or that you should be in charge of the day-to-day construction process. It does mean, however, that you get actively involved in the planning stage so that the house will reflect your true needs. It also means that you should visit the construction site on a regular basis to see how the project is progressing. If you are chemically sensitive or allergic, you should test various materials to see how you tolerate them, and you should have the last word on substitutions of materials.

I heard a story once about an architect who designed a magnificent house that was going to be a statement of some sort. When the clients saw the completed plans, they said that all they wanted was a house, they didn't want to live in a statement. In another case, workers ran some people off a construction site without realizing that it was their house. I have had several hypersensitive clients who wanted me to select a paint for them. That is something I can't do because, with sensitive people, there is no universally tolerated paint. Paints must be tested personally.

When you take an active role in a building or remodeling project, it can be a very rewarding experience. You will end up with a house that is truly yours, one that reflects your personality, life-style, and health needs. Since it is your house and you are paying the bills, the designer, the contractor, and all of the workmen are actually your employees. You hired them to do a job, but keep in mind the fact that it is your house and you are the one who must be pleased with the result. Don't let yourself be talked into something you don't want. But, at the same time, don't be afraid to delegate authority to a builder who has a good understanding of your particular needs.

Are You Ready?

I designed a municipal sewer project once that involved digging a large pit in front of two houses so that an underground tunnel could be bored between them. In a preconstruction meeting, the homeowners seemed very relaxed. They had seen sewer trenches before and it didn't seem like it was going to be a big deal to them. I could tell that they weren't prepared. I proceeded to tell them that this was an especially deep sewer and that larger equipment would be needed than they might be familiar with. When I told them there would be a hole in their front yard much larger than their house, they started getting a realistic picture. I said that it would be an incredibly big mess for a couple of weeks, but that when everything was completed, the driveway would be replaced, a new lawn would be planted, and that everything would return to normal. By having a realistic understanding of what would happen, they were prepared for the devastation and knew that it would be temporary.

When building a new house, you may need to be prepared to see trees accidentally knocked down. You should be ready for large trucks and excavators. You should know that the unexpected may very well happen. And if it is the rainy season, you should anticipate a great deal of mud. If you are planning a major remodeling project, be ready to live amidst noise and dust.

Creating any house, healthy or unhealthy, is a big project, involving dozens of people: designers, municipal planners, zoning commissioners, building inspectors, bankers, Realtors, general contractors, excavators, utility workers, carpenters, electricians,

painters, landscapers, and several other tradesmen. Coordinating this many people is difficult under the best of circumstances, but when you throw in the unexpected thunderstorm, a trucker's strike, and occasional illness, the process is rarely as smooth as everyone would like.

A house is the largest single purchase most of us will ever make in our lifetimes. Buying a house can be emotionally draining, and having one built can be even more so. If you plan to be involved with many of the steps along the way, driving to and from the designer's or builder's office and the construction site, it can also be physically demanding. And of course, houses cost money, and since most of us are limited as to how much we can spend, there will be pressure to save money wherever possible.

You should also keep in mind that the project will take time to complete—a large house can take a year or more to finish. Are you ready for such an undertaking? The answer to that question will depend a great deal on how much preplanning you do and what kind of relationship you have with your designer and builder.

Despite all the difficulties, houses are built and remodeled every day, and they are usually completed to the satisfaction of all parties involved. My point is not to discourage you from starting a project, but to prepare you for some of the trials and tribulations, and to reassure you that you aren't the first person to go through the process.

Preplanning

Some basic questions arise that call for answers before you begin the actual design and construction process. How big a house do you need? How many bedrooms? How many bathrooms? A formal dining room or an eat-in kitchen? Should any provisions be made for hobbies? What style do you prefer (ranch, split-level, Colonial, Cape Cod)? You should also consider materials (cedar or fiberglass shingles, paint, or stain), construction features (crawl space or basement, wood or brick) mechanical equipment (washer and dryer, dishwasher, water heater), and storage needs.

If you are involved in a minor renovation project, sometimes there are fewer questions to ask—but not always. Do any walls need to be moved? What color of paint would you like? Will there be a new floor covering? In some ways, a remodeling project can be trickier than building anew because, with remodeling, the house is usually occupied during construction.

You probably already know the answers to many of these questions, but may not have ever verbalized them. They should all be put down on paper so there will be no surprises for such a costly project. Dozens of books and magazines on the market can give you ideas, and you can probably make a list of your likes and dislikes by simply walking around your current home or those of your friends and neighbors.

Include on your list any special features that may be required. For example, a sauna may be something that you have always wanted, or a special area for canning all that organically raised food from your garden. A kosher family will have special kitchen requirements, an invalid may require wheelchair access. A home office or guest apartment may be other special features you would like.

Who Will Design the House?

It is the designer's responsibility to put enough information on paper in the form of drawings, notes, and written specifications so that the builder will know precisely how to proceed. The individual who does this could be an architect licensed by your state, a graduate of an architectural technical school, or a self-taught draftsman. Many builders do their own design work, and I know of homeowners who are quite adept at producing drawings themselves.

Whoever designs the house should be familiar with local building codes, zoning requirements, as well as healthy features, and should have an understanding of what specific homeowner needs must be addressed. If you locate a designer who has never designed a healthy house, don't automatically rule him or her out. Just because a designer has never done so, doesn't mean that he/she can't. Give a prospective designer a copy of this book and see how receptive he or she is to the concept of healthy construction. This book is written with enough depth to give a designer the guidance necessary to make your dream house a healthy one.

In general, a designer should be someone who you can get along with on a personal level, one you aren't intimidated by. He or she should be flexible and open to new ideas. Once you locate someone with these attributes, it is always a good idea to ask for references to determine the kind of relationship that person has had with past clients.

Design for Health

Since you are reading this book, you are, no doubt, interested in going beyond basic planning, and incorporating the health implications into your decision-making process. This is the time to set some priorities. How important are the health features? Would you rather have formaldehyde-free kitchen cabinets that you will use every day, or an extra bathroom that might only be used once a month? Do you want a non-toxic hardwood floor in the living room or would you rather have a guest bedroom? Some decisions will be relatively easy, but others will be difficult. An extra bathroom or guest bedroom may be very important, but if you are like most of us, you may not be able to afford it all. When you talk to someone who has had their health destroyed by the air in their house, they often have different priorities. They often wish that they had made healthier choices when they originally built or remodeled their house.

The most important health decisions you will make have to do with floor coverings, the heating and air conditioning system, mechanical ventilation, and kitchen cabinets. They all play a big role in indoor air quality, and they are fairly expensive components of a house. By addressing these issues and their costs early, you will have a more realistic idea of how your budget will be affected. If it is necessary to downsize a house to make the mortgage payments affordable, this needs to be taken into consideration very early in the design process.

Fortunately, either/or choices aren't always necessary. For example, choosing a low-tox paint

39

over a conventional one can be a relatively easy decision. But it is one of many decisions that need to be made, and they need to be made as early as possible if the rest of the process is to go smoothly. But don't feel bad if you can't figure everything out immediately. Some choices will evolve as you work with your designer and builder. The important thing is to start the process early.

The Way Many Houses Are Designed

Many houses are incompletely designed. For example, it may be assumed that the walls will be constructed of wood 2x4s, that the shingles will be fiberglass, and the subfloor will be plywood, even though none of these materials are shown on the plans. When these choices aren't specified on the drawings, the carpenters will do things as they have done them on previous houses. In other words, certain design aspects are being placed in the hands of the construction crew.

A good example of workmen doing the design involves the heating system. Often a floor plan will show the furnace location, but it won't give the size or even the manufacturer's name. It may not even show the locations of registers or return-air grilles, duct sizes, or materials. This design is too often left up to the heating contractor who installs the equipment. A homeowner has the right to choose what equipment is desired, and where and how it will be installed.

Many house plans consist of only 3 or 4 pages. I have seen some sketched on a yellow pad. Their purpose is to convey how the finished building will look. A complete and well-detailed set of plans may contain 20 or 30 sheets, sometimes many more for a large, complex house.

Incomplete design isn't necessarily a bad thing. With the high cost of houses today, it can result in a definite monetary savings. However, if you are interested in doing something that a contractor may be unfamiliar with, then the design needs to be more complete. That is why I have gone into extra detail in this book, describing carefully any areas that I feel designers and builders would find helpful. That is why the set of plans in Appendix 4 is more complete than typically.

Who Will Build the House?

In some ways the selection of a builder is more important than the choice of a designer. Once the plans have been finalized, the designer may visit the job site only a handful of times. If a builder is unsupervised, he/she may not pay very close attention to the plans. He/she may do things only as he/she is accustomed to doing, or workers may make unnecessary mistakes. I know of one instance where unsupervised painters used the wrong paint in the house of someone who had sensitivities to VOCs. The painters were recent Russian immigrants who couldn't yet speak English, so they couldn't read the labels on the cans. It is possible to pay a designer an additional fee to spend extra time inspecting the day-to-day progress, but it is generally cheaper and more productive to hire a contractor who will follow the plans to the letter and provide a competent foreman.

A contractor should be just as open to new ideas and as flexible as your designer. He/she should be conscientious and do quality work. If you can't locate a builder with experience in healthy house construction, you might look for someone who specializes in superinsulated houses. This is because a correctly constructed superinsulated house requires special hidden detailing in order to make it superbly energy-efficient. These builders are used to airtight construction, and they are usually very familiar with the design and installation of ventilation systems.

As with selecting a designer, don't rule out a builder just because he/she hasn't built a healthy house in the past. Give him/her a copy of this book and see if the concepts are intriguing. Most competent builders could use this book to either duplicate the Model Healthy House or apply the basic principles to other designs.

Do-It-Yourselfers

I was a do-it-yourselfer long before I became a builder, so I often encourage people who want to save some money by doing their own work. However, if you are considering this option, you must be realistic. Most do-it-yourselfers start out small, then progress to larger projects. If you have successfully built a storage barn in the backyard, you may feel ready for a minor remodeling job. But without additional experience, you probably aren't skilled enough to build an entire house.

You may also consider acting as your own general contractor. This means you would coordinate the entire building process. You would hire an excavator to dig the foundation, a mason to build the foundation, a framing crew, plumbers, electricians, and so on. Unless you have done this before, I generally don't recommend this approach. A general contractor needs to have a good working knowledge of all the trades and how their work interacts. You may feel that if you hire competent tradesmen, they will automatically coordinate their work with each other. This isn't always the case. If something doesn't fit and everyone claims that they did their work correctly, you could be in a financial bind and need to have some work redone.

Bankers are reluctant to loan money to do-it-yourselfers and individuals who want to act as their own general contractor. Yet it is done. The "This Old House" series on public television often involves homeowners in their projects. I often say that if you feel up to the challenge, do as much as you can. It can be very rewarding.

Remodeling

Healthy remodeling can be accomplished by using the three basic healthy design principles of Eliminate, Separate, and Ventilate. After all, the same laws of physics apply to remodeled houses as to new structures. If you are planning something as simple as repainting a room, then Chapter 21 will provide you with most of the information you need. With a major remodeling job, like a room addition, most of the chapters in this book will prove helpful. You simply need to look at the addition as if it were a new house being attached to your existing home.

In general, contractors specializing in remodeling work are often more resourceful that those who deal only in new construction. This is because every remodeling job is different. Each new job is a challenge to figure out the logistics and the small details that will make the project proceed smoothly. Many remodelers thrive on these challenges; they enjoy doing something new every day. Therefore, they can be especially receptive to the idea of healthy construction. However, it is still important to ask for references in order to locate someone who will be easy to deal with and will carry out a remodeling job to your complete satisfaction.

Precautions with Remodeling

Remodeling presents a special problem because people are often living in the house during the construction process. A sensitive occupant or a highly susceptible one like an infant can be exposed to all the same dust, VOCs, and construction debris as the healthy adult workmen. In order to minimize any negative health effects, it is often possible to separate the construction area from the rest of the house with some type of temporary barrier. A 2x4 framework covered with plastic sheeting or builders foil can be placed in a doorway or even across an entire room until the remodeling is complete. In some cases it will be necessary for a sensitive individual to find temporary housing elsewhere until the work is done. I have known people who have simply camped out in a tent in their backyard for the duration.

Since most existing houses were not built with health considerations in mind, your remodeling project may center around remedying that. In other words, you may be interested in making the house healthier rather than making any changes to the floor plan. Again, the principles discussed in this book will all apply. It is just a matter of understanding what features are unhealthy in the existing house and modifying them.

Prefab and Kit Houses

Quite often I'm asked if there are healthy prefabricated or kit houses available. Unfortunately, there aren't any I am aware of. I worked as a draftsman for one of the country's largest prefab house builders a couple of summers while in college, and I know that they are capable of building healthy houses. To date, they haven't, but that doesn't mean they won't in the future. Such companies react to market demands. If they see that more and more people want healthy houses, I am sure that they will start producing them. There is no reason that a kit house, or a prefab, or even a mobile home can't be built in a healthy manner. Manufacturers just haven't yet caught on that health can be an excellent marketing tool.

Special Precautions

The weather can easily wreak havoc with a construction project. While houses are often built in the winter, or during the rainy season, this is not recommended—especially for sensitive people. If building materials get wet, they can be in danger of mold contamination even before the house is complete. In cold weather, antifreeze admixtures must be used in mortar or concrete, and unheated building are often heated with unvented kerosene space heaters that can contaminate building products that will be exposed to the interior. It is better to schedule a building project for good weather.

I highly recommend placing "No Smoking" signs around the job site. I have not seen any statistics to prove it, but it seems as if a high percentage of builders and tradesmen are smokers. The no smoking policy is less important outside the house, with roofers for example, but once the house is enclosed, it is not a good idea for anyone to be smoking indoors. It is too easy for raw building materials to absorb the tobacco odor.

A job site sign placed in a prominent location is also advisable. This is especially important if the house is being built for a sensitive occupant. The following simple sign was placed in front of a house that appeared in *Fine Homebuilding* magazine:

NOTICE
CHEMICAL SENSITIVITY
ABSOLUTELY NO MATERIALS
ARE TO BE USED OR STORED
IN THIS BUILDING WITHOUT
PRIOR APPROVAL OF
ALLEN, DRERUP, WHITE, SUPERVISOR

If necessary, a sign with a longer description of the project may be in order. You may want to give a brief summary of what a healthy house is, or say that it is being built for medical reasons, whatever seems appropriate. The purpose of such a sign is twofold. First of all, it will inform everyone that there are certain rules or restrictions that must be followed. And second, perhaps more importantly, it will educate everyone who reads it. I have found that the more workers know about what is going on, the more excited they get about the project and the more conscientious they are.

Update

One of the most commonly asked questions I get is "Where do I start to find a builder or designer?" If you have any friends who have been through a construction project recently, you might ask them how easy the designer was to get along with, how receptive the builder was to new ideas, or how carefully the subcontractors carried out any unusual requests. If you belong to a heath-oriented self-help group, you might ask the other members if they have had any particularly good experiences with builders or designers on a project lately.

As I mentioned earlier, designers or builders specializing in superinsulated houses can often be good choices. There is an organization called the **Energy Efficient Building Association (EEBA)** that can give you a list of members in your geographic area. EEBA has members throughout the U.S. and Canada. While not all EEBA members are qualified to work with very chemically sensitive people, they are generally familiar with the basics of tight construction, sealed ductwork, mechanical ventilation, and the importance of avoiding combustion by-products. If you can clearly spell out your special needs in the area of material selection, they might easily do an excellent job for you. (The addresses of the organizations mentioned in the section are listed in Appendix 3.)

The **American Lung Association** has a Health House Project which involves incorporating various healthier approaches in building houses. A number of contractors around the country have built demonstration houses, and others are incorporating health-oriented features into all the houses they build. While some of the projects wouldn't be suitable for hypersensitive people, they are definitely much healthier than average. If you are hypersensitive to a variety of indoor air pollutants, it would be much easier for a builder of a Lung Association sponsored house to make a few modifications to what they have already learned to do, than to educate a builder from scratch.

There are growing numbers of "green" builders and designers. Their focus is often on issues surrounding the health of the planet, sustainability, recycling, etc. Some are also interested in the health of the occupants, but others don't place as much emphasis on indoor air quality as they should, and many aren't familiar with the needs of hypersensitive people at all. It is actually quite easy to claim that a building material is green. For example, a manufacturer might say that their product is green because they make it from recycled material, or that they recycle their waste, or that they have an energy-efficient manufacturing process, or that they don't pollute the environment. They very well may produce a green product, but they may totally ignore the fact that it's not healthy for the occupants. Many green products are, in fact, healthy, but many aren't—so be careful of green claims.

There are a number of regional organizations whose main focus is on green building but who also have members interested in indoor air quality. In New England, the **Northeast Sustainable Energy Association (NESEA)** has many members who are interested in healthy construction. In Georgia, the **Southface Energy Institute** might be helpful because they offer some very good training programs to both professionals and consumers, and in the Pacific Northwest, you might contact the **Northwest Eco Building Guild** which has a directory of members listing their areas of specialization.

In reference to subcontractors, I've most often been asked about locating a heating/cooling contractor who is familiar with minimizing combustion by-products, and is knowledgeable about the importance of sealed duct systems. If you're in a medium-sized or larger city, a good place to start would be to contact the local Community Action Program (CAP). These organizations are set up primarily to do weatherization work on low-income housing. When you weatherize or tighten a house, you often affect how the heating system operates. So the people who work for these organizations are usually very familiar with heathy—and unhealthy—heating systems. They are typically very much aware of problems that occur as a result of leaky ducts and poor chimney function. While Community Action Programs mostly deal with low-income housing, many of their contractors operate independent businesses, so they can work for anyone—not just low-income clients. So if you are looking for a heating/cooling contractor, give your local CAP a call and see if they can give you a referral. The **Advanced Energy Corp.** in North Carolina offers an excellent school for heating/cooling contractors, so they can give you a referral in that part of the country.

A question that occasionally comes up—but, fortunately, not often—is "My designer (or builder) won't do what I've asked. Now I'm afraid my house won't be healthy. What do I do?" This can be a tough situation. It's sometimes the result of not doing your homework in the first place, in other words, not checking out a designer or builder well enough prior to beginning a project. But it can also be due to the fact that you were the victim of an overzealous individual who thought he/she could handle the project—but couldn't. It may also be due to misunderstandings or, in rare cases it might be due to incompetence or fraud. It's difficult to advise someone in such a situation without having a good knowledge of the particulars of a situation. I generally suggest first speaking with a person who is familiar with the project, but not closely tied to the parties involved—perhaps the municipal building inspector, a real-estate professional, or your banker. Explain what your concerns are, and get their opinion of the situation, then see if they can offer any advice. While we live in a very litigious society, I generally don't recommend consulting with a lawyer right away. While there have been situations where lawsuits were necessary, this isn't common. Most of the time, a situation can be resolved fairly easily to the satisfaction of everyone involved.

When you're looking for a designer or builder, and aren't sure whether or not they're going to be receptive to incorporating healthy features, it's unlikely that they will read this entire book while you're still in the preliminary talking stages. Something that can work out well is to loan them a copy of the video *Your House, Your Health* that takes you on a walk-through tour of the Model Healthy House after it was completed. Most builders will be willing to watch a video in the evening at

home, then they will have a much better understanding of what you're interested in doing, and you can see how receptive they will be to building in a healthy manner. Many builders have found it useful to loan the video to their subcontractors before they arrive on the job—to familiarize them with the concepts involved. Please see the last pages of this book for a description of *Your House, Your Health* and other publications offered by The Healthy House Institute.

Chapter 4

LOCATING AND PURCHASING HEALTHY MATERIALS

■ ■ ■ One of my priorities in this project was to use healthy materials that were cost-effective and easy to locate. Many of the products I used in the construction of the Model Healthy House are available locally throughout the country. Some are rather specialized, but they, too, are readily available through the mail.

Many Americans regularly order a wide variety of products from catalogs—clothing, food, gifts, furniture, etc. Therefore I felt comfortable using a few products not found on the shelves of every local building supply center. But before you start ordering healthy construction materials, you must know what to look for and what to avoid.

This chapter will provide you with some basic, general guidelines in selecting healthy building materials. I will cover the finer, more specific points later in the book in Parts 2–5. If you are chemically sensitive, you may need to go beyond the basics and choose products that are as inert as possible, and compatible with your particular metabolism.

Defining Healthy Materials

There is a growing body of evidence that poor indoor air quality is negatively affecting us all. Yet it is still difficult to define precisely what makes some materials unhealthy. Virtually anything can be toxic in certain situations. Table salt is necessary for survival, but if you consume too much, it can lead to hypertension. Most people can drink milk, but some are lactose-intolerant.

Regarding materials such as asbestos, lead, and radon, there is sufficient scientific documentation to convince anyone of the need to avoid exposures whenever possible. However, such evidence is not yet available for all pollutants. For example, some people say that manufactured wood products containing formaldehyde really aren't that bad. I don't agree. I advocate the concept of "prudent avoidance." This means that you should avoid pollutant sources whenever practical. In many cases it is easy to do.

Generically Healthy Products

Many construction materials are quite inert. I call them generically healthy. For example, metal products like siding, roofing, cabinets, shelving, etc. are often inert if they have baked-on finishes. Stainless steel is inert and requires no finish at all to protect it from rust or corrosion. Usually, ceramic or stone products such as roof and floor tiles, slate, and porcelain bathroom fixtures are generically healthy because they don't tend to outgas anything. However, you should check to see if the glazed surface of tiles contains lead.

Wood and Wood Products

Although outgassing usually refers to the gases emitted by synthetic products, it is a term sometimes applied to naturally occurring materials as well. Softwood framing lumber is said to outgas low levels of terpenes (turpentine-like compounds), chemicals that can negatively affect some hypersensitive individuals. For most people, solid wood is a healthy material, but since each species of wood has a unique odor, sensitive people may find some woods more benign than others. Maple, beech, birch, and tulip poplar are often the best tolerated.

The wood products industry primarily uses two different kinds of glue in their manufacturing processes. All construction-grade plywood (both interior and exterior grades), oriented strand board, and other structural products use a waterproof phenol-formaldehyde (PF) resin. Most particleboard, medium-density fiberboard, and cabinet-grade plywood uses a cheaper non-waterproof urea-formaldehyde (UF) resin. UF resins outgas about ten times more formaldehyde than PF resins. So the UF-containing products are the more potent formaldehyde emitters, and they are the ones that are typically used indoors for kitchen cabinets, shelving, and wall paneling. If you must use manufactured wood products, stick with those made with phenol-formaldehyde glue.

The Medite Division of SierraPine Ltd. in Roseville, CA produces medium density fiberboard (a denser product than particle board) with a glue that contains no formaldehyde. This is a much healthier choice than conventional particleboard, but some sensitive people have trouble tolerating these products because of the tiny amount of formaldehyde found naturally in softwood lumber, and the naturally occurring terpenes.

Most of the chemically pressure treated lumber on the market today contains arsenic and chromium, and should be avoided whenever possible. I have found that when an insect-resistant wood is required, redwood is often quite well tolerated by sensitive people. Cypress is another possibility. Cedar

is also naturally insect-resistant, but its strong odor is often intolerable to sensitive people.

Plastics

Soft plastic materials like vinyl flooring and wall coverings are subject to more outgassing than hard plastics. This is because chemical additives called plasticizers are incorporated into the plastic resins to make them flexible. Plasticizers are fairly toxic chemicals and some are carcinogenic. That new car smell is composed of plasticizers outgassing. This smell is strongest when a car is new, but the chemicals continue to outgas in smaller amounts for months—actually until the upholstery gets brittle and cracks. Hard plastics, though not perfect choices, are subject to less outgassing.

The Fleece Factor

Highly textured products such as carpeting, draperies, and coarse wall covering fabrics are subject to what is known as the fleece factor because of their large surface area. A Danish study concluded that such materials are capable of emitting larger quantities of VOCs, especially when new, and they are a lush medium in which microorganisms can proliferate.

VOCs: My Argument Against Them

I have heard it said that the VOCs found in the indoor air are not in high enough concentrations to affect human health. Twenty years ago I might have agreed, but today, after several years of personal experience and research, I feel that VOCs are an unnecessary component of indoor air and levels should be reduced whenever possible. Over the next few years there will no doubt be many specific compounds that scientists will prove to be benign, but at the same time, some are going to be found to be worse than we could have imagined. The research required to differentiate the good VOCs from the bad ones could cost billions of dollars and take decades. I suggest that it is much easier, and cheaper, for you to reduce all VOCs to a minimum wherever possible.

46

Carpet manufacturers have been saying for years that there is no proof that the VOCs released from synthetic carpeting cause negative health effects. Of course, they didn't offer to spend the money to find out either. Then in mid-1992 physiologist Rosalind Anderson performed a very simple experiment in her New England laboratory. She exposed mice to air blown across some samples of carpeting. The mice gasped, turned blue, lost their balance, had lung hemorrhages, and suffered paralysis. Many then died. This inexpensive experiment has many people reexamining the impact of VOCs on health.

Low Outgassing Materials

Many new synthetic materials, such as carpeting, carpet padding, vinyl flooring, adhesives, paints, etc. release VOCs. While not all VOCs are odorous, many are, so a good way to choose low-VOC products is to select materials that have little or no odor. If you don't have a particularly good sense of smell, take someone who does with you when you go shopping for building materials.

As I mentioned earlier, odorous materials can be stored in a garage for several weeks or months until most of the smell dissipates. This can certainly reduce your exposure to VOCs. However, this may not mean zero risk. When the Anderson lab tested carpet on mice, some of the samples that killed the mice were as much as twelve years old. This is why, in general, I prefer using building products that simply do not have the capacity to outgas. Throughout the construction of the Model Healthy House, I used low outgassing materials wherever possible. There are many such products on the market today even though they are not advertised as such. These are the generically healthy materials I just mentioned. They have always been good choices for healthy houses and some have been in use for hundreds of years.

Paints, Adhesives, Caulking

Paints, stains, clear finishes, adhesives, caulking, etc. are all materials purchased in a liquid or semi-liquid form that dry into a solid or semi-solid form. They are all subject to outgassing when wet, and some can remain odorous for extended periods of time. The water-based products on the market today are far lower in VOC content than the older solvent-based formulations. Thus, simply using water-soluble products is an easy way to reduce VOC exposure. A few zero-VOC materials are now starting to appear on the market.

As VOCs are implicated more and more in causing illnesses, and manufacturers bring out low-VOC formulas, it is important to realize that what is low to one manufacturer may be high to another. This is a fast-changing field, so you will need to read product labels or call manufacturers and ask for the current VOC content. Then you can compare products and choose accordingly.

There are other ingredients besides VOCs that have been implicated in causing health problems. Liquid or semi-liquid products often contain biocides as preservatives, or antifreeze compounds. Until a few years ago, 25% of paint manufacturers used toxic mercury compounds in their products. Because of the wide variety of minor ingredients, a number of small manufacturers have begun making products for chemically sensitive people that are low-outgassing, low-biocide, or have minimal additives. Generally, these kinds of products are better choices than their off-the-shelf counterparts, and they are readily available through the mail.

Material Safety Data Sheets

A Material Safety Data Sheet (MSDS) is a form on which a manufacturer provides information about the harmful ingredients in a product. Required by law, an MSDS contains basic information like the product name, boiling point, flammability, etc. You can get an MSDS for virtually any building product on the market. They may be available through local building supply stores but sometimes you will need to contact a manufacturer to obtain one.

An MSDS also lists hazardous ingredients and health effects. However, an MSDS does not always list *all* potentially hazardous ingredients—some formulas are considered proprietary or trade secrets. In such cases, specific health-related information will be given to a physician in the event of a medical emergency, but it is not listed on the MSDS. Also, when the percentage of a hazardous ingredient is below a certain level, it may not be listed. It is not unusual for an MSDS to have incomplete or misleading information.

When a hazardous ingredient is listed on an MSDS, the amount that will cause negative effects may be listed as a TLV (Threshold Limit Value), PEL (Permissible Exposure Limit), or LD_{50} (the Lethal Dose that kills 50% of lab animals). TLVs can be described in different ways: based on exposures over an eight-hour workday, a fifteen-minute exposure, or an instantaneous exposure. The smaller the TLV, PEL, or LD_{50}, the more hazardous the substance. For example, the TLV for grain alcohol is 1,000 ppm (parts per million), turpentine 100 ppm, and formaldehyde 1 ppm. Since a product that contains only a tiny percentage of a hazardous substance may not be as dangerous as one that contains a great deal of a slightly less hazardous substance, you should look at the percentages of the ingredients as well as toxicity.

Unfortunately, TLVs, PELs, and LD_{50}s have not been established for many hazardous ingredients. When this is the case, an MSDS can give you a false sense of security, because you will have no idea how hazardous the substance really is.

The health effects section of an MSDS will list short-term (acute) or long-term (chronic) health effects, based on different routes of exposure (inhalation, ingestion, absorption through the skin, eye contact). All of the information on an MSDS is meant to be applicable to healthy adult workers during an eight-hour day. More susceptible people, such as children, the elderly, the sick, or people exposed to a substance for twenty-four hours a day, can be affected much more readily or severely. Chemically sensitive individuals, many of whom react to extremely low levels of hazardous substances, are not addressed on an MSDS at all.

An MSDS will often list the vapor pressure, vapor density, percentage of volatiles, and evaporation rate of a substance. These can be uses to gauge the outgassing rate, but they can be difficult to analyze.

Despite some rather serious drawbacks, an MSDS can be a good starting point in researching the healthfulness of a product. While they contain some valuable data, the information can be difficult to interpret. A good pamphlet to use in deciphering an MSDS is *How to Read a Material Safety Data Sheet* (see Appendix 3).

Salvaged Materials

I have worked with a number of people who have used salvaged construction products in their houses. Some of these materials came from houses that had been torn down. Others were overruns, slightly damaged materials, or discontinued styles from local building supply stores. An advantage to such products is reduced cost. Sometimes, their quality is equal to that of brand new products.

I know of one new house that has old interior doors in it. Each door is 75 to 100 years old and each is different. The doors are solid and well-made, and they were stripped commercially of their old lead paint and refinished with a low-tox finish. The owners love the charm of the varied styles, and they were considerably cheaper than brand new solid wood doors. Salvage yards in many major cities offer such finds. Look in the yellow pages of the phone book. You might even be able to find matching doors from an old historic hotel, complete with room numbers.

Since salvaged materials are older than new materials, they can be more inert because they have had a long head start on outgassing. Look for doors, wood trim, cabinets, and flooring. For a unique decor, antique sinks, toilets, and bathtubs can often be attractive, durable, and low-cost alternatives.

Using Unhealthy Materials

Sometimes it is impossible to locate a healthy substitute for an unhealthy construction material. Fortunately, there are ways you can use such materials in a healthy house. In fact, I used fiberglass insulation in the Model Healthy House. It is a product that has received a great deal of negative health-related publicity. I only use these types of materials when I am convinced that they will not have any effect on the air within the living space.

When you analyze how pollutants move into, out of, and through a building (see Chapters 11 and 13), you will see that it is possible to use potentially unhealthy materials like fiberglass insulation in a healthy manner.

Insulation is cited by some people as a major problem in houses. In fact, I know of many cases where occupants have been made very ill, some permanently, by insulation. Urea-formaldehyde foam insulation was one of the worst products in this regard, so much so that it was banned by the Consumer Product Safety Commission. Even though the ban has been overturned in the courts on a technicality, it has virtually disappeared from the market.

In most cases, I have found that insulating materials like fiberglass and cellulose remain inside the walls or roof system, where they have little effect on the air in the living space. The most serious problems with them have occurred during installation or remodeling when small particles of insulation wafted their way throughout the house. In new construction it is possible to separate insulation quite well from the living space, as I will discuss in more depth later. When adding insulation to an existing house during remodeling, it is just a matter of taking extra care to keep the material out of the living space.

Unhealthy materials, however, can seriously affect the workers who install them. In the case of fiberglass, there are some basic precautions that workers must follow in order to protect their personal health. In doing so, the health risks can be greatly minimized. Actually, insulation installers are at much greater risk than either workers in fiberglass manufacturing plants or people living in houses insulated with fiberglass.

Of course, a healthier insulation would certainly be preferable over an unhealthy material. Air-Krete is a cement-like insulation that is quite inert when compared to fiberglass and cellulose. However, it is not widely available, and it is quite expensive. If I could find it locally, and it were cheaper, I would definitely consider using it. I do recommend it occasionally, but in most cases, I can't justify the extra expense. Most of my clients are on a budget, and it is usually more cost effective to spend the extra money elsewhere. For example, I feel that with proper precautions fiberglass insulation can be used in a healthy manner at a reasonable cost, and that the extra

money would be better spent on selecting a low-tox flooring. You'll get far more benefit for the same money with a wood or ceramic tile floor than with a non-toxic insulation.

Special Orders

Most builders consider materials that aren't available from the local lumber yard to be special orders. In general, builders are not accustomed to dealing with products they can't purchase immediately. If you want to use any unusual materials in your new house or in your remodeling project, you should specify your exact requirements. Give your contractor the model number, type of paint, or style of window, along with the manufacturer's name and phone number. This information is often incorporated into the plans, but the specifications can also be written out on separate 8½" x 11" sheets of paper. This is very common on large commercial projects where the specifications can run into several hundred pages. Remember, this is your project, so you must take control. Be specific, and make sure special instructions are put in writing.

Ordering in Advance

For any material or product that is not available locally, I recommend ordering well in advance to avoid any unnecessary delays. Such materials must be stored somewhere until it is time to use them. If your contractor has a shop or warehouse, they can be stored there, or you might have a garage that is suitable. Storing excess materials on the job site can be risky because of the danger of theft. Be sure to choose a storage area that is dry so that mold contamination won't be a problem.

I experienced no unusual delays when ordering products for the Model Healthy House. All the suppliers had ample materials in stock, and shipping was prompt. However, it is still prudent to order early rather than late to avoid unnecessary delays when workers are waiting for a vital shipment. It is also important to estimate accurately and order enough material so that you won't run out.

What Does It Cost?

One of the most frequently asked questions I here is "How much more does a healthy house cost?" The answer isn't always as simple. Some healthy features don't cost any more than regular features, some can be cheaper, and some are more expensive. The overall cost increase depends on the specific features selected.

If you are building a fairly expensive house, there may be little cost increase to incorporate healthy materials because you may already be using ceramic tile and wood floors rather than less expensive wall-to-wall carpeting. In a lower-cost house, the addition of ceramic tile floors can add significantly to the overall cost. However, there are usually low-cost options available. For example, a colored concrete floor can be quite attractive when accented with natural-fiber area rugs. You might also consider ceramic tile "seconds." The minor imperfections are rarely noticeable. A #3 grade hardwood flooring is less expensive than a clear grade, and many people value the character of the color variations.

In an article published in the Spring 1992 edition of *Northeast Sun*, architects Mary Kraus and Bruce Coldham compared the costs of various healthy construction strategies to conventional building practices. They found that the significant added cost of gypsum plaster ($6,000) yielded only slight health benefits over conventional painted drywall. A floor of solid pine boards, however, was not only cheaper than carpeting and padding over particleboard, but it yielded a fairly substantial health benefit. Radon mitigation fell between the extremes and, at $600, would seem to be something that most homeowners could afford.

As a rule of thumb, I generally tell people that, while there may be no cost increase at all, a healthy house can cost as much as 25% more than a conventional house, depending on its features. However, in most cases I think that a 10-15% increase is a good average range to go by. If houses in a certain part of the country are selling for $50 per square foot, then it should be possible to build a reasonably healthy house for $55-57 per square foot.

This book will help a builder who is apprehensive about healthy house construction understand the costs involved. A builder who is unfamiliar with health aspects may be a little unsure how to bid such a project. In order to cover unforeseen expenses, he may tend to increase his estimate. By reading through the applicable chapters of this book, he or she should have a more realistic idea of what goes into a healthy house and be able to estimate costs more accurately.

If the cost increase of healthy materials means that a house is no longer affordable, I often recommend reevaluating your needs and consider building a smaller house. With 10% fewer square feet, a healthy house is often within a budget. I have talked with people who said they didn't think they could afford a healthy house, but when they downsized their plan a little, it fit within their budget. Downsizing doesn't have to mean a cramped house if careful attention to room layouts and traffic patterns makes more efficient use of space. We often build houses larger than we need so they will have better resale value. It makes more sense to build for your immediate needs rather than the next owner's. Keep in mind that the health aspects of your house can enhance its value and make it easier to sell when that time comes.

When comparing house prices, it is important to remember that they vary considerably in different parts of the country. It is also important not to compare apples and oranges. A custom-built house will generally cost more per square foot than a tract house because of the extra time and labor necessary. When construction crews are building similar houses every day, they are much more efficient than if they are doing things differently from house to house.

In order to incorporate as many healthy features as possible, the Model Healthy House in this project is slightly more expensive than other healthy houses I have been involved with. Its cost increase is 20-25% more than other custom built-houses in this area, but it was also downsized in order to make it more affordable.

Health Care vs. Mortgage

I find it sad when people tell me that they have decided not to incorporate healthy features into their project because of cost. We would never consider building a house without doors on the bedrooms just because doors cost money. We rarely reject having a garage or a second bathroom because of its expense. Yet some of us are willing to sacrifice our health for a few dollars even though health is one of our most basic needs.

Both houses and health care cost money. What if you save a little money by using unhealthy materials when you build your house, but your house makes you sick? You don't actually save any money because you spend it at the doctor's, or on high health insurance premiums. Most of the people I have talked to, if given the choice, would rather spend a little more on their mortgage payment each month than pay their doctor when they get sick. If you get cancer as a result of the air in your house, your health-care expenses could easily exceed the cost of the entire house. Healthy houses can save money in the long run.

If you are already sick and need a healthy house to regain your personal health, you may be able to deduct the cost of health-related features on your income tax. If prescribed by your doctor, they may be considered legitimate medical expenses. Since tax laws continually change, this should be discussed with your accountant or tax preparer. If this is a possibility, you should keep careful records of all expenses.

A Special Note for Sensitive People

As I stated earlier in this chapter, almost anything can be toxic in a given situation. This is especially true for chemically sensitive people. They often react to very low levels of air pollution, to air that by many standards would be considered clean. For these hypersensitive people, it is necessary to select construction materials more carefully. In fact, I usually recommend testing all of the products that are directly exposed to the living space in order to determine an individual's tolerability. This is especially important for paints and other finishes.

For very sensitive people, testing should generally be done under a doctor's supervision.

One method that seems to yield good results is to place a sample next to your bed and see how you sleep with it nearby. When testing paints, a two- or three-square-foot piece of aluminum foil can be coated, allowed to dry until odor free, then tested. A good night's sleep generally means that a sample is tolerable. Be sure to date and label each sample so you won't forget how old it is and exactly what paint was used.

Update

Regarding costs, there is a growing body of evidence showing that if you build a very well insulated, tightly constructed house, the extra money spent on insulation will be offset by a smaller, less costly heating/air-conditioning system. In addition, some banks offer something called an energy-efficient mortgage. Because they know that your utility bills will be lower, they realize you will have more disposable income, therefore they are willing to lend you a little more money. As you will learn in the following chapters, I feel that tight construction is extremely important, so with proper planning, you should be able to use the cost advantages of tightness and energy efficiency to make a healthy house more affordable. Many of the Health Houses sponsored by the American Lung Association have done just that—they spend a little extra on energy efficiency and use the savings for health features. Often the total cost to the homeowner is the same as a conventional house.

It would be beyond the scope of this book to discuss all of the possible building materials available that are healthy. So in this book, I have discussed only the most widely available products and, except in a few instances, have only included sources for those materials actually used in the Model Healthy House featured herein. However, I realize that, for a variety of reasons, many people will be interested in in-depth information about other materials besides those covered on these pages. The book that will be the most useful in this regard is the one I wrote titled *The Healthy House, How to buy one, How to build one, How to cure a sick one.*

51

It discusses virtually every building material and technique currently in use, plus it lists hundreds of address of suppliers. It's an excellent companion to

this volume. Please see the last few pages of this book for a description of it and other books published by The Healthy House Institute.

PART 2:
THE STRUCTURE

Chapter 5

FOUNDATIONS

■■■ Besides holding up the house, a foundation is also a connection between the soil and living space. How this connection is made is important for the health of the occupants and the durability of the house. The foundation must prevent problems due to moisture, radon, and termites, and also be energy-efficient. In short, a foundation must protect the house and its occupants from the negative effects of the ground.

Moisture Control

Moisture control is important because moisture's effects upon foundations can mean mold growth or rot. Mold is a common allergen and a health problem for millions of people. Wood rot that results from excessive moisture can lead to costly repairs.

One of the most significant moisture sources that must be controlled is rainwater. For all foundation types, rain pouring off a roof needs to be channeled away from the building—usually via gutters, down spouts, and splash blocks. In addition, the ground around all houses should slope away to keep the water exiting from the downspouts from soaking into the soil around the structure.

There are two forms of moisture in the soil that must be addressed in foundation design: water and dampness. Both can be handled by good design practices. If a building is in an area where the ground water extends above the footings of a foundation, then a system of drainage pipes or tiles should be installed to divert that water away from the building. This is important for all foundation types. A perforated drain pipe is usually located near the bottom of the footing, and the area above it is backfilled with gravel. Any water in the vicinity, since it is a liquid, will easily travel down through the gravel into the tile and away from the structure. Synthetic drainage mats now on the market can be substituted for the gravel.

Dampness is the slight moisture found in many soils. It can migrate horizontally through concrete or masonry foundation walls, or up through a concrete slab. Dampness can also rise up through a concrete footing into the foundation wall and then evaporate into a crawl space or basement. This is often called "rising damp." Cement-based foundation dampproof coatings are less odorous than asphalt or synthetic coatings, but since they are generally quite well separated from the living space, foundation coatings rarely cause problems for the occupants of a house. Plastic sheeting is often used as a barrier in foundation construction, but it too is usually well separated from the living space.

There are a variety of strategies for controlling moisture in foundations. The specific techniques will vary from house to house because of differing foundation types, climates, and soil conditions. Generally, moisture control involves using a piping and drainage system to divert water away from the building, as well as coatings or barriers to prevent dampness from passing into the structure. I will cover the basics of moisture control when I discuss the specific foundation types later in this chapter. More complete information can be found in the *Moisture Control Handbook* listed in Appendix 3.

Radon Control

Radon is a radioactive gas found in small quantities in the soil virtually everywhere. Radon is invisible, you can't smell it, and you can't taste it, but it should be avoided because it is a known cause of lung cancer. If a great deal of radon is present in the soil, the gas can contaminate the air in your house by passing from the soil, through the foundation, and into the living space.

While it is possible to measure radon concentrations in the soil, such measurements are not always good indicators of indoor radon levels. This is because all houses are different, and they interact with the ground differently. The only way to know for sure how much radon is in a particular house is to actually measure it. This is easy to do with an existing house, but if you are planning to build a new house you must wait until the house is finished before you can determine if it has excessive indoor radon levels.

In new construction, it makes sense to take some inexpensive precautionary measures when building the foundation. In an existing house, indoor radon levels can be reduced by blocking its entry points (caulking and sealing holes in the foundation), diverting it to the outdoors (through a series of pipes), or diluting it (increased ventilation). Since every house is unique, the best radon control method will vary from house to house. Often a combination of approaches will be the most cost-effective. The EPA

offers several publications (see Appendix 3) that discuss in detail a variety of specific techniques.

How Much Radon Is Too Much?

Since radon is a carcinogen, it would be preferable if we could avoid it altogether. However, since radon is found nearly everywhere, this can't be done. We all breathe some radon all the time. The goal is to breathe as little as possible.

The concentration of radon in the air is usually measured in units of picoCuries per liter (pC/l). If 1,000 people were exposed to a level of 2 pC/l in their house over a lifetime, one of them would probably get lung cancer. At a level of 20 pC/l, about eight would get lung cancer. The EPA has suggested that if levels are above 4 pC/l, you should consider remedial measures. The risk of dying from radon-induced lung cancer at this level is about the same as your lifetime risk of drowning. For further information on what risk is posed by different levels of radon, see the brochure *A Citizens Guide to Radon*, published by the EPA which is listed in Appendix 3.

Testing for Radon

Radon can be measured in a few days with a short-term test, or over several months with a long-term test. Short-term testing is more common because it is less expensive, but long-term testing is more accurate. Inexpensive ($10-25) short-term test canisters can be found in building supply or discount stores (Figure 5-1). I usually get them from a nearby university that offers the service. If you can't find a source for test kits locally, ask your local health department for a referral.

To perform a radon test, simply follow the instructions supplied with the kit. The usual method is to open the canister and place it in a central indoor location for 1 to 3 days. The opening and closing times are recorded on a form, and the canister is mailed to a testing lab for evaluation. The kits usually contain a mailing envelope. The most common kits contain a few ounces of activated carbon that absorbs radon as long as the canister is open. By measuring the radon in the canister and knowing

Figure 5-1.
Short term radon test canister.

how long it was open, the lab can determine what the indoor radon concentration is. Results are usually returned by mail within a week or two.

If a short-term test reveals a radon level above 4 pC/l, the EPA recommends that you either do a second short-term test to validate that the first test was accurate or have a professional perform a more expensive long-term test. Again, your local health department should be able to help you find a nearby radon testing service. A long-term test will give you a better idea what your year-round average exposure will be. This is helpful to know because the levels in most houses vary somewhat from season to season. If a house has a radon level of 5.0 pC/l in the winter, but only 1.2 pC/l during the rest of the year, the average year-round level would probably be below the EPA's 4 pC/l action level.

Termite Control

Often the news that a house is infested with termites will scare a homeowner into calling an exterminator to spray the foundation with chemical poisons. A well-built foundation, not chemical poisons, should be the first line of defense against termites. Even though the termiticides used today are slightly less toxic than those used a few years ago, these chemicals can still have a devastating effect on human health.

There are several different species of termites in the U.S., but the most common is the subterranean type. Subterranean termites live in the ground because they require the moisture of the soil to keep their bodies from drying out. When they leave the ground to eat the wood in a house, they have two ways to protect their bodies from losing too much moisture. The easiest way is to climb up inside hollow concrete blocks to get to the wood. If such a path isn't available, they will build mud tubes. If they are either inside a block wall or a mud tube, they are safely protected from the dry air. Once such an enclosed pathway has been established, they will travel back and forth between the soil and the wood.

Common Termite Control Strategies

Termites have usually been controlled with toxic chemicals that poison the soil around a house, but metal shields are often recommended as an alternative (Figure 5-2). The location of metal shields is the same for all foundation types—between the concrete or masonry foundation and any wooden framing members. What many people don't realize is that termites can easily get around the shields and still attack the wood. They simply travel as far as they can in a hidden and protected way, then build mud tubes around the shields to reach the wood. What the shields do for the homeowner is not prevent a termite infestation, but rather force the termites into building their tubes out in the open where they can be more easily spotted during a regular inspection. While shields are an acceptable way of dealing with termites, it should be remembered that termites can travel through very small cracks. If the seams between the pieces of the metal shields are not tightly fitted and sealed, the termites might be able to squeeze by the shields in a hidden location without building any tubes. If this happens, the termites could attack the house without being detected by a quick inspection.

Some of the newer methods of insulating foundations with foam board materials can provide pathways for subterranean termites that are difficult to block with metal shields. Many designers don't worry about this and rely on chemical treatments instead. It would be far healthier to take the time to design an adequate shielding system. However, I don't consider termite shields a permanent solution because, sooner or later, you could get an infestation anyway, and then you would still need to select a low-tox treatment method.

Drywood and dampwood species of termites can be found in the southern and western United States. They do not need to live in the soil and they can attack any portion of a house. Therefore, the metal shields are ineffective against them. Shields are also ineffective against carpenter ants.

If a house is built of a material that termites can't eat, then no particular control is necessary. For example, a house constructed entirely of concrete, masonry, or steel will be immune to the ravages of termites, as will a building made of redwood or cedar. Chemically treated lumber won't be attacked by termites either, but the negative health effects associated with most treated wood make it something to avoid in healthy house construction. Some highly toxic treatments, like creosote and pentachlorophenol, are no longer used in residential construction because of the health hazards associated with them. The widely used

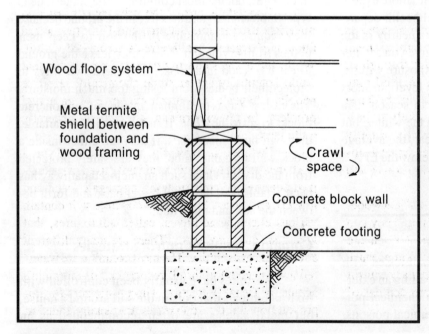

Wood floor system

Metal termite shield between foundation and wood framing

Crawl space

Concrete block wall

Concrete footing

Figure 5-2.
Termite shields must be installed consciously to be effective.

waterborne salts, many of which contain arsenic and chromium, are also coming under fire for the same reason. For chemically sensitive people, cedar is probably not a viable option either because it is so odorous.

One less-toxic chemical alternative that is effective against termites is the recently introduced wood treatment called Tim-Bor, made by U.S. Borax. It can be used in both new and existing houses, but Tim-Bor is water soluble, so it cannot be used on wood exposed to weather or to soil dampness. Besides insects, it is toxic to plants and fish, so must be applied with care so that it doesn't kill your lawn, get into streams, or pollute sewage treatment plants.

Alternative Termite Control Strategies

A variety of non-chemical control methods are available for combating a termite infestation in an existing wood framed house. However, they aren't always as effective as chemical controls. For dampwood or drywood termites, electrical probes can be used to electrocute them, or liquid nitrogen can be used to freeze them to death. For subterranean termites, a species of nematode is being marketed as a biological control method. Nematodes are microscopic worms that can be mixed with water and injected into a termite nest. They get inside the termites' bodies and eat them.

Sand of a certain grain size can be used as backfill around a building to deter subterranean termites because when they try to dig through it, their tunnels cave in. However, this method may not be effective if the sand gets damp, because tunnels through damp sand are less likely to collapse. This method of control can be costly to apply to an existing house because of the expense involved in excavating the soil around a house and replacing it with sand.

Unlike termites, carpenter ants don't eat wood; they simply tunnel through it for nesting. They can enter a house virtually anywhere. Carpenter ants are usually associated with damp or rotted wood because it is easier for them to excavate, so the primary control strategy involves reducing the moisture content of wood—keeping it dry.

I highly recommend *Common-Sense Pest Control* (see Appendix 1) for a complete discussion of less-toxic control methods for all insect pests.

Energy Savings

Many people think of energy efficiency as applying only to walls and ceilings, but floors and foundations need to be well-insulated, too. Heat leaks out of a house in all directions—up, down, and sideways. If you insulate your walls and ceiling but forget about the floor or foundation, you haven't done a complete job. Energy efficiency also has an effect on controlling moisture problems. If a foundation is uninsulated, it will be cool, and any moisture in the air can condense on those cool surfaces, resulting in mold growth. While insulation alone can't always solve a moisture problem, it is often part of the answer.

Different foundation types require different approaches to energy efficiency. *The Superinsulated Home Book* listed in Appendix 3 is a good reference for more in-depth information.

Concrete

Concrete is one of the primary construction materials used in foundations, and I'm often asked about any negative health effects associated with it. While there are some ingredients in concrete that could potentially bother some chemically sensitive people, I haven't seen much evidence of an actual problem. In my experience, concrete is generally quite inert.

Concrete is typically a mixture of Type I Portland cement (other types are only used in specialized commercial construction), aggregate (sand and gravel), and water. Sometimes concrete will contain various chemical additives, called admixtures, that give it specific properties. There are many different admixtures in use today. The most common are water-reducing agents for shrink resistance, air-entraining agents for freeze protection, and plasticizers for improved flowability. Admixtures are usually added in such small quantities (a few percent by weight) that they are not a health problem. I have had a couple of chemically sensitive people report being bothered by concrete when it is warmed by the sun. This may be the result of outgassing from the admixtures, or it might be due to something that was spilled on the concrete, perhaps a solvent or a cleaning product. This kind of outgassing could be a consideration with a concrete patio where a homeowner might spend a lot of time, but it is not likely to be a problem with a concrete foundation.

Solid concrete walls are usually constructed by pouring concrete between wood or metal forms. Once the concrete has hardened, the forms are removed. Forms are usually coated with a release oil so the concrete won't stick to them. I have seen fuel oil used for this purpose. Since concrete is absorbent, the oil can soak right into it, leaving the concrete with a persistent odor. Release oil isn't always necessary if forms are waxed or painted, or if they are cleaned promptly after they are removed. Contamination from release oil is much more severe than contamination from the use of admixtures. In commercial construction, concrete may be sprayed with a chemical curing agent to help it achieve its maximum strength. This could bother sensitive people, but curing agents are rarely used in residential construction.

Since radon occurs naturally in some rocks, many people are concerned that the sand and gravel used in concrete could release radon. There are certainly cases of this occurring. In fact, there are houses built with radioactive materials from uranium or phosphate mining operations. However, concrete is not a significant source of radon in new construction. Most radon enters homes from the soil, not from concrete.

Concrete has been used successfully for hundreds of years without release oil, admixtures, and curing agents. Many of these products are proprietary mixtures for which manufacturers won't release complete ingredient lists, so it is difficult to determine which products actually are the least toxic. I find that it is easier to use regular concrete with no admixtures or curing agents, and forms with no release oils, than to specify nontoxic substitutes. In most cases, it is easy to do so.

Selecting a Foundation Type

Any foundation type can be built in a reasonably healthy manner. It is often more a matter of suiting the foundation to the site. For example, a steep hillside may lend itself to a pier foundation. In warm climates, concrete slabs with little insulation are popular and cost-effective. In colder climates, basements often make more sense. In the middle latitudes of the U.S., foundation types are divided fairly equally between slab-on-grade, crawl space, and basement, depending on personal preference (Figure 5-3). There are both advantages and drawbacks to all foundation types, so no particular style is correct for all situations or climates. Good foundation design simply requires common sense: You should build a solid, energy-efficient, dry foundation that will allow for a way to keep radon and termites out of the house.

The first step in the process of selecting a foundation is actually related to one of the last steps in the construction process. You need to determine what type of finished flooring will be used. This is because some floor coverings are easier to install on specific foundation types. For instance, ceramic tile will adhere easily to a concrete slab-on-grade, but it is simpler to nail tongue-and-groove wood flooring to a wooden subfloor over a basement or crawl space.

The specific details of a particular foundation design will vary from one part of the country to the next because of differing climatic and geological conditions. The *Builders Foundation Handbook* and the *Building Foundation Design Handbook* (listed in Appendix 3) both contain very good information about all aspects of foundation construction in a variety of climates. Following is a discussion of the basics.

Pier Foundations

Pier foundations are the least common type; however, they can be one of the best choices from a health point of view. Pier foundations are the easiest to build in a healthy manner because the house and the ground are so well-separated from each other. They

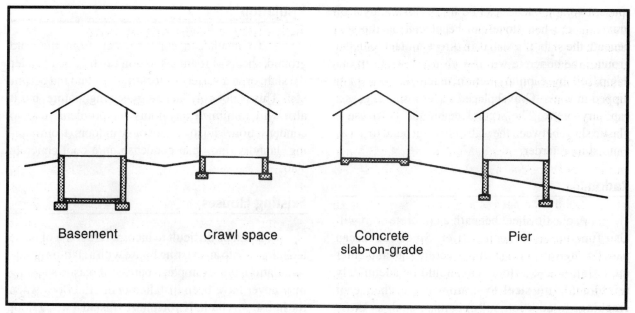

Figure 5-3._Basic foundation types._

have traditionally been a good choice in hot, humid climates, but they can work well in any locale.

The primary drawback to a pier foundation is that it can appear out of place in most subdivisions. However, on the right building site a pier foundation can look very dramatic. I built an office for myself several years ago using a pier foundation. Located on a hillside in the woods, it fits into the landscape quite well.

A pier foundation needs a drainage system if there is a high water table, but since there is minimal contact with the soil, no other moisture control measures are necessary. No radon control is required either. With the space between the ground and the house open to the air, any ground moisture or radon can dissipate harmlessly into the atmosphere.

In new construction, metal termite shields can be placed on the top of each pier. Since the only points of contact with the ground are the piers, they can easily be inspected for signs of termite tubes. If necessary, spot treating the ground where there is an infestation can be done with nematodes. With a pier foundation, the floor system should be well-insulated and contain a diffusion retarder just like the walls of a house. If there are any exposed plumbing lines and heating

ducts they should also be insulated, but no additional precautions are necessary.

Slab-on-Grade Foundations

Concrete slab-on-grade foundations are popular in warm climates because they can be built at less cost than the other types. In cold climates, this type of foundation is sometimes associated with cold floors, dampness, and mold growth. This is because many concrete slab foundations have been built without proper moisture prevention strategies or enough insulation. If constructed correctly, slab-on-grade foundations can be trouble-free. The Model Healthy House has this type of foundation, and it is neither moldy nor damp.

Moisture

If ground water is present in the soil around a slab foundation, a series of drainage tiles should be installed around the perimeter of the building to divert the water away. To prevent dampness in the soil from migrating up through a concrete slab into the living

61

space, two approaches can be used. First, a layer of gravel or crushed stone can be placed on the soil beneath the slab. If a slab is in direct contact with the ground, the concrete will absorb moisture from the damp soil by capillary action much like a napkin dipped in water. Gravel placed under a slab acts as a capillary break. The second technique is to use a plastic sheet between the slab and the ground to act as a moisture retarder.

Radon

A plastic sheet beneath a concrete slab will also function as a radon barrier. Since radon can pass through any cracks in a concrete slab and enter the living space, a floor slab should be adequately reinforced with steel to minimize the chance of cracking. In addition, all openings, such as those around plumbing or electrical lines, need to be sealed with caulking. The goal is to have a perfect barrier between the living space and the soil. Since we live in an imperfect world, a radon removal tube should be installed in the gravel layer under the slab. I'll describe this in more detail later in conjunction with the Model Healthy House.

Termites

Several termite control strategies were discussed earlier, but there are some points that pertain specifically to concrete slab construction. Since it is relatively warm under the center of a concrete slab in the winter, that is where subterranean termites often build their nests. Because of this, all of the wood-framed walls in contact with the slab are vulnerable to termites, and they should all have metal termite shields under them. This is something that is not always easy to do effectively. The use of steel reinforcing in a concrete slab will minimize any cracking that could become pathways for subterranean termites to travel through. However, termites can still chew their way through openings in a slab that were caulked for radon control. A house built with concrete, masonry, or metal walls, rather than wood, will be immune from subterranean termite attack and will not require any control strategies.

Insulation

To insulate a concrete slab from the cold ground, sheets of foam insulation can be placed under the slab, or in a variety of locations around the perimeter. This is not only an energy-saving feature, but it also will minimize any moisture problems due to condensation. Moisture generated indoors (from bathing, laundry, etc.) can condense on a cool concrete slab.

Existing Houses

It can be difficult to incorporate some of these techniques into an existing house with a slab-on-grade foundation. For example, a barrier of plastic sheeting may never have been installed under the floor when the house was built. If you plan to install a wood floor on top of the slab, you can place plastic sheeting between the wood and the concrete. Another option would be to rely on air conditioning or dehumidifiers to lower the indoor humidity levels.

Insulation and drainage tiles can usually be added to the perimeter of an existing house, but the necessary excavation might be costly. Cracks in a floor slab can be pathways for both radon and termites. The best option for the termites would be one of the alternative approaches I discussed earlier, perhaps termite-eating nematodes. One way radon can be controlled is to bore holes in the slab and run pipes from the holes to the outdoors. Suction fans connected to the pipes will pull radon from under the slab and exhaust it into the atmosphere before it can have a chance to enter the house. If the ground under the house has been treated with toxic termite chemicals, a radon suction fan will vent any outgassing from them into the atmosphere along with the radon, thus preventing the noxious chemicals from entering the living space.

Crawl Space Foundations

A crawl space can be a convenient place to run furnace ductwork, plumbing lines, and electrical wiring. Since the air in a crawl space can contain radon, mold spores, and moisture, crawl spaces need to be thought of as being outdoors and well-separated from the living space in order to be healthy. Crawl spaces are probably not a good idea in hot, humid climates because the warm, moist air can enter the cooler crawl space and condense on the walls.

Moisture

Moisture control is complicated by the fact that a crawl space is sort of a no-man's-land. It isn't heated or air conditioned, but isn't exactly at outdoor temperatures either. In the winter it is warmer inside the crawl space than it is outdoors, especially if the heating ducts are located there. In the summer it is cooler. What this means is that moisture control strategies can vary, depending on the season. Because of this, crawl spaces are more difficult to design properly than other foundations.

As with other foundation types, drainage tiles should be used to divert any ground water away from a crawl space. In addition, the floor of a crawl space should be covered with some kind of barrier to prevent soil dampness from evaporating. Plastic sheeting is the usual choice, but sometimes concrete is used. The walls of a crawl space, being in contact with the soil, should be coated with a damp-proofing material. Some experts are now recommending that either a plastic barrier be placed beneath footings, or a dampproof coating be applied to the top of footings. This minimizes rising damp.

Ventilation

Most building codes require that crawl spaces be ventilated. This is to allow any moisture that does happen to enter the crawl space to escape to the outdoors. Ventilation is often provided by 8" x 16" aluminum grilles spaced every so many feet around the foundation. The vents should contain insect screening to keep bugs out of the crawl space. Many homeowners close these vents in the winter in the interest of saving energy and to keep the plumbing lines from freezing. While this may protect the plumbing and save on the heating bills, it can trap moisture within the crawl space and lead to mold growth.

In the summer, the air in a crawl space will be cooler than the outdoor air. If the vents are left open, soil moisture can escape; however, humid air from the outdoors, or from the living space, can enter and condense on the cool crawl space walls. This can be a serious problem in very warm and damp climates. Some experts have suggested that crawl spaces in hot, humid climates not be ventilated in order to better control moisture. However, this is in violation of some current building codes and it means that a much better job needs to be done to prevent moisture from entering in the first place.

Radon

The first method of dealing with radon in a crawl space is to isolate the crawl space from the soil. Covering a bare dirt floor is important to prevent radon from entering the crawl space directly. The same large sheets of polyethylene plastic used for moisture control will also act as a radon barrier. They should be carefully sealed to each other and to the perimeter walls with tape. Some builders prefer covering the floor with concrete because it is more durable.

Another way of dealing with radon in a crawl space is to seal the floor system, thus forming a barrier between the living space and the crawl space. In new construction this can be done by placing a well-sealed layer of builder's foil or plastic sheeting between the subfloor and the finish floor and caulking all electrical, plumbing, and heating system penetrations in the floor.

Ventilating a crawl space throughout the year will help radon escape to the atmosphere rather than enter the house. It is also possible to install a suction fan and pull radon from the soil beneath the plastic sheeting and vent it into the atmosphere.

Termites

The primary termite control strategy in crawl spaces is to use the metal shields discussed earlier. It is also important to have the floor of the crawl space at least 18" from any wood framing members. This is because termites can build their mud tubes out in the open, away from the foundation walls, but the tubes aren't sturdy enough to rise as high as 18". Termite killing chemicals used around a crawl space will not easily be able to migrate into the living space if the house is constructed in an airtight manner, and any ductwork in the crawl space has had all of the joints well sealed.

Insulation

Many builders insulate the walls of crawl spaces with foam insulating boards. This improves energy efficiency only if a crawl space is unvented. In a vented crawl space, outdoor air entering through the vents negates the purpose of the insulation. Since health concerns related to moisture and radon dictate a vented crawl space, a more effective place for insulation is between the floor joists. With the penetrations in the floor caulked and sealed, the insulation will be separated from the occupants in the living space. One problem with insulating the floor is that the crawl space will tend to be colder in the winter. Therefore, any plumbing lines located in a cold crawl space will need to be insulated to prevent them from freezing. Heating ducts in the crawl space should also be insulated to prevent heat loss and waste of energy.

Existing Houses

Many of the same techniques used in new construction can be incorporated into an existing crawl space. Plastic sheeting (from building supply stores) can be rolled out on the floor of a crawl space. Be sure to overlap all seams by about a foot or tape them securely. You should also tape the plastic around the perimeter to the foundation walls.

If ground water is present, a drainage tile can either be installed around the outside, or the inside, of the foundation. Exterior excavation can be done by machine, but it may result in destroyed shrubbery, sidewalks, and driveways. Interior excavation is less disruptive, but must usually be done by hand. Dampproof coatings can be more effective on the outside of a wall, but they often result in some moisture control when applied to the interior surface.

Floor insulation and foundation vents can usually be added to an existing house with a crawl space

without a great deal of difficulty. It is also relatively easy to seal the joints in the ductwork with tape or mastic, insulate the ductwork, and caulk electrical and plumbing penetrations in the floor system at the same time.

Basement Foundations

Basements should be considered living spaces that need to be heated, air conditioned, and ventilated along with the rest of the house. Since they have so much surface area in contact with the ground, healthy basements require a considerable amount of care in both design and construction.

Many people build basements because they consider it an inexpensive way to gain extra space. However, the costs involved in building a healthy, finished, dry, properly insulated basement can sometimes exceed that of constructing main floor space. Given the choice, most homeowners would rather have above-ground living space than basement space, if the costs are similar.

Moisture

For a basement to be healthy, it must be kept dry. If not, mold can attack anything stored there, including books, clothing, furniture, etc. Moisture control strategies include those discussed with the other foundation types: drainage tiles to divert liquid water away from the structure, dampproof coatings on the exterior, plastic sheeting under the floor slab, and either plastic sheeting under the footings, or a dampproof coating on top of them. Moisture control must be carried out more conscientiously in basement construction than with other foundation types because the basement is living space.

Radon

If a basement is constructed in an airtight manner, there will be no pathways for radon to enter. Poured concrete walls are more airtight than masonry walls, but it is still important to caulk all electrical and plumbing penetrations. In most cases it is a good idea to install a radon removal tube under the floor slab just in case any excess radon does find its way into the living space. This is the same type of system that I discuss later with the Model Healthy House. Sometimes, the radon removal system and a drainage system can be combined. For example, a suction fan can be attached to a tight fitting cover on a sump pump. Since drainage lines are rarely completely filled with water, the suction fan will pull radon through them and vent it outdoors.

Termites

The termite controls for basements are similar to other foundation types. Keep them out through crack resistant construction, use metal shields to force them to build their mud tubes in visible locations, and use building materials like concrete and steel that they can't eat. If a house must be chemically treated, a radon suction fan will help prevent the chemicals from migrating into the living space.

Insulation

Basements should be insulated for energy efficiency. In new construction, this can be easily done on the outside of the foundation wall with a foam insulating board. A basement can also be insulated on the inside of the foundation. A typical method involves building a conventional wood- (or metal-) framed wall just inside the concrete or masonry basement wall, filling the cavity with insulation, and covering it with drywall. It is absolutely essential to control moisture in the basement before doing this, or else you might trap moisture within the wall and end up with mold and rot. Such a wall should have a moisture retarder to prevent moisture generated in the living space from penetrating the wall and condensing on the cool foundation. It should also be constructed in an airtight manner, as I did with the above-ground walls in the Model Healthy House (see Part 3).

You should heat the basement in the winter to minimize problems associated with moisture condensing on cool surfaces. If the basement walls are well-insulated, moisture condensation on the walls will be less likely. It is also important to exchange the air in a basement continuously with the furnace system or a ventilation system, to keep the air from becoming stagnant. Air conditioning or dehumidifying in the summer will also help to remove moisture from the basement air.

Existing Houses

If you have an existing basement that is excessively damp, you should first determine where the moisture is coming from and prevent it from entering the basement. A minor dampness problem can often be solved by using a dehumidifier, but if the soil around the basement is saturated with water it may be necessary to install a drainage tile around the foundation. Such a tile should direct the water to a storm sewer, drainage ditch, or sump pump. If the soil surrounding the basement is damp, but not saturated, the walls can be coated with a dampproofing material. While dampproofing can be applied to the inside of a basement wall, it will usually be more effective if it is on the outside of the wall.

With an existing house, installing a drainage tile or an exterior dampproofing could involve the considerable expense of digging a trench around the entire foundation. Solving a moisture problem in an existing basement can sometimes be very costly, and each house can require slightly different techniques, so it is best to get more than one opinion about a solution before starting any repairs.

There are a number of ways to handle radon in an existing house. For example, radon can be kept out of a basement by sealing cracks and electrical or plumbing penetrations, or it can be diverted to the atmosphere by installing a suction fan connected to a pipe installed through the floor slab.

The Model Healthy House Foundation

After analyzing all of the factors involved in choosing a foundation, including cost, I decided to construct a concrete slab-on-grade foundation system for the Model Healthy House. One of the main influences was the fact that I wanted to use ceramic tile for a floor covering. Ceramic tile will yield one of the most inert floors possible. Ceramic tile can be adhered easily to concrete, so a slab-on-grade is a good economic choice. Although a hardwood floor can be fastened to a slab, it is easier and less expensive to attach it to a wooden subfloor of some type. Therefore, a wood floor is usually more cost-effective over a basement or crawl space than over a concrete slab..

Placing the House on the Lot

I built the Model Healthy House on a 3.62-acre parcel in southern Indiana (see Sheet 2 of the Plans in Appendix 4). The land is wooded and the area is relatively unpolluted. A small country cemetery borders the property to the south and a paved road runs along the east and north sides. The nearest two houses are 700 feet to the south (beyond the cemetery) and 500 feet to the west. There was an existing septic system on the property, so I located the house on ground high enough so that a sewer could flow by gravity from the house into the septic tank.

Using some white strips of cloth tied to trees or to temporary wooden stakes, I roughly spotted the corners of the 28' x 56' house where I felt it fit nicely among the trees. I positioned the house so it wouldn't be too near large trees so their the roots wouldn't interfere with the foundation. I then walked around the site, looking at it from different angles, and located the garage and driveway. Then I changed my mind and relocated everything. By the third try, I was satisfied that all was in the right place. One of my requirements was that the house be on an east-west axis so that the majority of the windows faced south. This insured that the house received as much free solar heat as possible in the winter.

The house ended up roughly in the center of the lot, with the garage and drive to the north. The driveway meets the road at the northwest corner of the property near the neighbor's drive. Thus, the house is relatively far from the road, so automobile exhaust at the house will be minimal.

The existing house to the west is heated electrically, so there is no polluting chimney. The existing

Figure 5-4._Simple rectangular foundation layout._

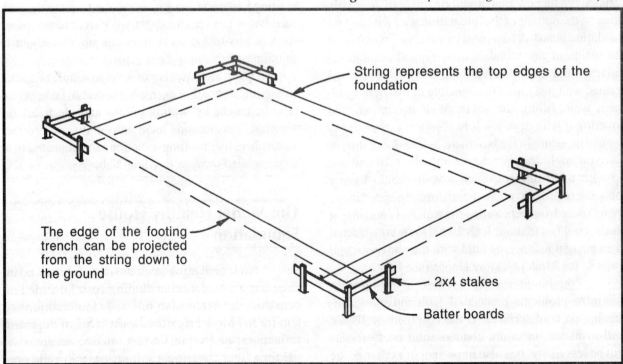

String represents the top edges of the foundation

The edge of the footing trench can be projected from the string down to the ground

2x4 stakes

Batter boards

66

Figure 5-5.
Foundation corner construction.

house to the south is heated with wood and it could be a concern in the winter, especially at night when the smoke tends to hang near the ground. The air filtration system I selected for the Model Healthy House will be able to handle any such smoke. If necessary, the ventilation system can be shut off in the event that the outdoor air is temporarily polluted.

With the house location decided, I cut down the trees that were in the way. Then I hired a bulldozer to remove the stumps and scrape away the upper layer of topsoil. A concrete slab should not be placed over loose topsoil because it generally won't provide a firm enough base. If the ground were to settle unevenly, the concrete could crack.

Once the area was cleared, I accurately located the corners of the house with stakes and batter boards. This allowed me to create a layout of strings to precisely mark the top surface of the foundation. I later measured all aspects of the foundation from these strings. A simple rectangular layout is shown in Figure 5-4. The tops of the batter boards must all be level and in the same plane. I accurately located the strings so that all distances were correct and all corners were square. With the house all strung and squared up, I used the same procedure on the garage. I placed the 24'

x 24' detached garage 17' away from the house to minimize the chance of any exhaust gases contaminating the house.

Once the strings were up, I used them to mark the width of the footing on the ground so that a trench could be dug. According to Sheets 6 and 7 of the Plans, the size of the footing is 16" wide and 8" deep. The bottom of the footing was located 32" below the level of the string. The result is 8" of foundation above the ground and 24" below ground. The 24" depth is set by the local building code as the frost depth. In colder climates it would need to be deeper.

Constructing Footings and Foundation Walls

Once the trenches for the footings were dug, I placed steel guide stakes at four- to six-foot intervals in the bottom of the trench so that their tops were precisely 24" below the string. This marked the top of the 8" thick footing. Sometimes wooden stakes are used for this purpose, but they can be an invitation to termites. Stakes cut from a ½" (#4) steel reinforcing bar (rebar) are a better choice. In order to minimize cracking of the footing, I strung two long lengths of #4 rebar in all of the trenches. It was wired to the steel

67

Figure 5-6.
Laying concrete block foundation walls.

stakes so that it would be midway between the top and bottom of the footing. Rebar gives the concrete considerably more strength.

Next, I filled the trenches with concrete up to the level of the guide stakes. I ordered the concrete without any admixtures. The concrete was delivered in large trucks, dumped into the trenches, pulled into place with a rake until relatively level, then smoothed with a hand trowel. The steel guide stakes make leveling easy. The next day the concrete was hard enough for me to begin laying concrete block.

Concrete block construction is fairly straightforward. It involves masons building a wall using the sizes of block shown on the Plans. The blocks are held in place with a mortar mixture typically containing Type I Portland cement, powdered lime, clean washed sand, and water. Sometimes the cement and lime are packaged together in bags called "masonry cement." In cold weather, when freezing can affect the water in the mix, an antifreeze admixture may be added. It is doubtful if admixtures in mortar will have an effect on the occupants' health since they are added in such small amounts. However, sensitive people may wish to have masonry work done in warm weather so that antifreeze isn't needed. In the Model Healthy House,

I used standard masonry cement (Type N) for the mortar in the concrete block foundation.

Masonry construction always begins at the corners. With a plumb bob, the intersections of the layout strings (house corners) are projected down and marked on the footing. These marks are then connected with a chalk line. Enough masonry corner blocks are laid in place to reach the level of the layout strings. Special care should be taken to get the corners plumb and square with evenly spaced, level rows because the rest of the foundation is based on the corners (Figure 5-5). The uppermost corner blocks are aligned precisely with the layout strings. Once my corners were complete, I filled in the rows of block between them (Figure 5-6).

I embedded L-shaped anchor bolts in the concrete block foundation wall to a depth of 16", as required by the local building code. The cores of the blocks around the anchor bolts were filled with mortar to hold the bolts in place. I later used the anchor bolts to attach the house walls to the foundation. An anchor bolt is needed at each house corner, next to doors, and they should be spaced no more than 6' apart. Anchor bolts usually extend about 2½" above the foundation so that a 1½" piece of lumber can be bolted in place.

In this case, I built the walls with steel framing, which is very thin, so the bolts didn't need to extend nearly as high. I left about 1" of the threads exposed on each bolt.

Installing the Foundation Drain

Next, I laid a 4" perforated plastic drain around the outer perimeter of the block wall and covered it with crushed stone to a level that was just below the surface of the ground. The stone was then covered with red rosin paper before the top layer of soil was placed. Available in rolls at most lumber yards, the rosin paper keeps the fine soil particles out of the stone so it doesn't get clogged. According to Sheets 2 and 4 of the Plans, at the northwest corner of the house, I ran a 4" non-perforated pipe by gravity into a nearby drainage swale. The purpose of this drainage system is to divert any standing water in the ground away from the foundation. If there is a high water table in an area, the drainage system takes on greater importance, and it would be a good idea to locate it near the bottom edge of the footing rather than on the top of the footing as I have done. There are various drainage boards on the market that can be substituted for the stone backfill. Their purpose is to provide a pathway for any water to travel down into the footing drain.

Installing the Plumbing Lines

Once the foundation walls were in place, I installed the below-grade plumbing lines, including the pipes for both the water supply and sewage drains. This is a relatively standard procedure. In most cases, the plumber will work with a floor plan and calculate all of the dimensions for the various pipes. I took the trouble to show all of the required information on Sheet 4 of the Plans. This includes the layout, pipe sizes, material, and their locations.

The plumbing drain lines extend to the outside of the foundation where they then run to the septic tank. There are a variety of regulations that must be followed in installing a plumbing system. The regulations are designed to prevent any water contamination and to insure that the system will function correctly. These requirements are familiar to all licensed plumbers.

The only water supply line under the slab is the main line coming from the water utility com-

Figure 5-7.
Plastic forms create voids in the concrete slab for bathtub drains.

69

Figure 5-8.
*Foam caps over toilet drains
create voids in concrete floor slab
for a toilet mounting flange.*

pany. It must be deep enough to protect it from freezing in the winter. I used extra-heavy Schedule 80 PVC plastic pipe to ensure that it would never develop a leak. Some plumbers will locate most of the water supply lines under the slab because the installation is easier, but if a leak should ever develop under the slab, it would be very costly to repair. To be on the cautious side, I decided to place the hot and cold supply lines above grade within the walls of the house where they would be easier to get to, should a leak ever develop.

The slight outgassing of plastic piping materials can occasionally be bothersome to some hypersensitive people, but when placed below a concrete slab, they are well-separated from the living space and they cannot outgas into the air of the house. The utility's water main running along the road is plastic and I didn't see the addition of the 1" PVC supply line into the house as a major additional contribution to drinking-water contamination. In any case, the water filtering system I installed will remove any pollutants added to the water by the plastic piping.

The glues and cleaners used to connect plastic pipe fittings are fairly noxious, but they air out very quickly. Health considerations are more of a concern for plumbers who are directly in contact with them than for homeowners. I only use such materials with plenty of ventilation in order to dilute the dangerous gases. The piping within the living space will be discussed in Chapter 16.

The drain connections for the two bathtubs in the Model Healthy House needed to be below the surface of the concrete slab. Here I used plastic forms that created a void in the concrete. Such forms usually result in an open hole in the slab that would easily allow radon to enter the house. To prevent this, I secured a piece of foam insulation board to the bottom of the form with 100% silicone caulking and caulked the drain pipe exiting the form (Figure 5-7). I have found 100% silicone caulking to be very long-lasting. Once cured, it has no odor, so I use it a lot in healthy house construction.

When I later hooked up the bathtub drains (Chapter 16), I cut out the top of the form and caulked the perimeter of it to the concrete slab. The end result is a sealed void containing the bathtub drain. I created a similar void in the concrete around the toilet drains with a performed foam cap (Figure 5-8). During the finishing stages of the house, after the ceramic tile was in place, I dug the foam away with a utility knife and

70

attached a plastic water closet flange for mounting the toilet. After the foam was carved away and the flange was glued in place, I resealed the pipe to the concrete with a can of single-component poylurethane aerosol-foam insulation so there were no gaps for radon to pass through (see Chapter 24).

Radon Removal

I elected to install a 4" radon removal tube under the concrete floor slab. It consists of a plastic pipe that has small perforations along its length, connected to a non-perforated pipe that runs up through

Figure 5-9.
Radon removal tube in place.

Figure 5-10.
Below-slab piping complete.

the slab and vents outside the house (Figure 5-9). The perforated pipe is the same material that is used for drainage around the outer perimeter of the foundation. While the Model Healthy House is located in a part of southern Indiana that isn't known for high levels of radon, there is no accurate way to predict indoor radon levels. An inexpensive radon test can only be performed after the house is built. If such a test shows indoor radon levels to be high, I will hook a suction fan up to end of the tube. The fan will draw the radon-laden air out from under the concrete slab and exhaust it to the outdoors where it will dissipate harmlessly into the atmosphere. This is a highly effective method of handling radon, known as sub-slab depressurization.

At this stage of construction, I had no idea whether or not radon would eventually be a problem. But since the piping system would only add a couple of hundred dollars to the cost of the house, I considered it cheap insurance. If the piping wasn't installed now and then it turned out to be necessary later, it would be much more costly to do after the fact. Most builders are willing to spend a little extra up front on the chance that a radon removal system might be needed once the house is complete.

Crushed Stone

Once the below slab piping for both radon and plumbing was in place (Figure 5-10), I leveled out the crushed stone fill (gravel is an acceptable alternative) around the perimeter, and the insulation was installed. The stone has several purposes. First, it is easy to move around and create a level surface. Second, it will allow any ground water to drain away, insuring that the slab will remain dry. Third, it will allow a radon removal system to function by making it easy for a suction fan to move air between the pieces of stone.

Insulation

I used approximately three times as much foundation insulation as is common in this section of the country as a part of my superinsulation package. The extra insulation cost a little more at this stage, but it will help to ensure very low utility bills for the life of the house. Extruded polystyrene (XPS) foam insulation is readily available everywhere under several brand names. This is one of the few types of insulation that is suitable for use underground or in damp locations. Expanded poly-

Figure 5-11.
Extruded polystyrene under-slab insulation.

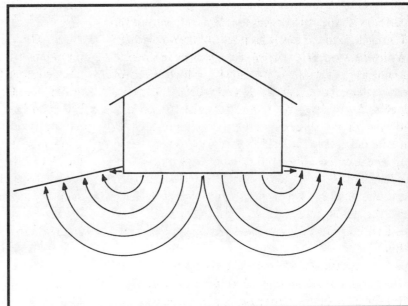

Figure 5-12.
Heat loss pathways beneath a concrete floor slab.

styrene (sometimes called beadboard or EPS), although it has a similar sounding name, is not believed to be as moisture-resistant. The only other product on the market that can be used successfully below-grade is a product called Foamglas made by Pittsburgh Corning. Foamglas smells strongly like rotten eggs because of the hydrogen sulfide used in its manufacture, it is three times as expensive as XPS and, being a commercial product, it is generally not available to residential contractors.

XPS is one of the materials that has been implicated in destroying the ozone layer because of the CFC (chlorofluorocarbon) chemical used in its manufacture. Fortunately, manufacturers are changing their formulations and HCFCs (halogenated chlorofluorocarbons) are now being used. While they still have a very small effect on the ozone layer, they are many times more benign than CFCs.

It is possible that the HCFCs outgassing from the foam insulation could bother some sensitive people, but in most installations the insulation is well-separated from the living space. I haven't found outgassing of the insulation to be a problem, in fact, many sensitive individuals can tolerate XPS quite well. Since my choice of insulation was quite

limited, I chose XPS over Foamglas as the lesser of two evils.

XPS is sold in a variety of thicknesses. I used a double layer of 2" material. The Plans called for 4" around the perimeter, just inside the upper row of 4" concrete block. This is the most important location to insulate well because it is where the slab is closest to the outdoors. This is where the most heat loss will occur. In addition, I used 4" of XPS under the slab for a distance inward of 6' (Figure 5-11). The center of the slab has no XPS under it because it is already insulated by the earth beneath the house. Figure 5-12 shows the pathways by which heat travels when leaving a concrete floor slab. Even though soil isn't a very good insulator compared to XPS, the heat loss pathways from the center of the slab to the outdoors are quite long, so the center is actually insulated better than the edges. Where the XPS needed to be cut around plumbing lines, I found a serrated steak knife quite helpful.

Once I had all the insulation in place, the remainder of the stone was leveled out. I left a trench in the stone fill running down the middle of the house (Figure 5-13). This was to provide a space for extra concrete that would support the load-bearing wall that

Figure 5-13.
The trench in the stone fill allows for a thickened concrete slab that will support a load-bearing wall.

Figure 5-14.
Insulation detail at end of trench.

was later built in that location. At the ends of the trench, I installed the XPS so that there were no areas around the perimeter left uninsulated (Figure 5-14).

I covered the crushed stone with a layer of polyethylene sheeting, overlapping the seams by about one foot. Most builders use a thickness of 4 mil, but 6

mil is sturdier. The poly acts as a diffusion retarder, to prevent both radon and ground moisture from entering the house. It was spread in place and run up the sides at the perimeter. Once the concrete slab was completed, I trimmed away any extra material at the edges with a utility knife.

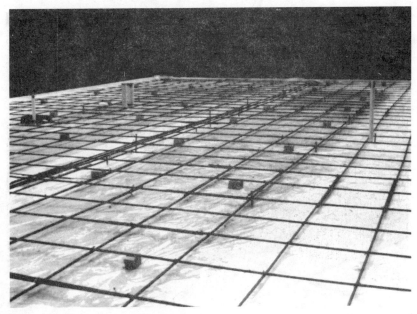

Figure 5-15.
Steel reinforcing for the concrete floor slab.

Figure 5-16.
Rough leveling of the concrete floor slab.

Crack Prevention

It is important to prevent cracking in the concrete floor slab in order to eliminate pathways for pollutants like radon and moisture to enter the living space. This is an important health consideration. Crack prevention is also important from an aesthetics standpoint. In a house with carpeting, a cracked slab wouldn't be visible, but with our healthy ceramic tile floor, it could be very unsightly.

One of the most important things to do to prevent a floor slab from cracking is to provide a good

75

Figure 5-17.
Using a bull float to smooth the concrete floor slab.

base for the concrete. This involves removing any loose topsoil and using a compacted crushed stone or gravel base. Pea gravel or #11 crushed stone (my choice) are both self-compacting, so they don't require the use of mechanical compaction equipment. Any uncompacted soil or fill material will mean that the slab will eventually settle and such settlement could mean a crack.

The next thing to do is to reinforce the slab. Most builders use welded-wire reinforcing fabric for this purpose. It works reasonably well, but it really isn't the best product for the job. I chose to use a heavier rebar reinforcing. The Plans called for ½" diameter (#4) rebar to be placed at 18" on center in about the middle of the 4" thick slab (Figure 5-15). To prevent cracks, it is also important to use a good quality concrete. I chose concrete with a 4,000-pound-per-square-inch compressive strength, and used the minimum amount of water. Concrete mixed with extra water can be subject to shrinkage cracking as it cures. In order to further minimize the chance of shrinkage cracks, I elected to use a reinforcing fiber admixture in the concrete. This consists of very small plastic fibers that are mixed in directly with the concrete when it is delivered. They aren't meant to act as structural reinforcing like steel, but they do help to stop shrinkage cracks from forming.

The precautions I took to prevent the concrete house slab from cracking may seem excessive to some builders and may not all be necessary in every part of the country. However, it should be remembered that even when all these measures are taken, there could still be the remote possibility of a small crack forming in the slab. That is why I took all steps possible.

Placing the Concrete Slab

When the premixed concrete was delivered to the site, it was first leveled roughly with a length of 2x4 (Figure 5-16). Next it was smoothed with a large trowel known as a bull float. This evens out the surface and causes some of the fine aggregate to rise to the top, resulting in a stronger surface (Figure 5-17). As the concrete started to harden, it was troweled to give it a smooth and hard surface. This can be done by hand, but for such a large area, a motorized trowel is easier and faster (Figure 5-18). Since the weather was very hot, I misted water on the surface for 24 hours to keep the concrete from drying too rapidly.

76

Figure 5-18.
Finishing the concrete floor slab with a motorized trowel.

Figure 5-19.
Wooden forms for the garage floor slab.

The Garage Foundation

The garage is not attached to the house so that any odors from a hot automobile (gasoline, oil, rubber) or from materials stored in the garage will be well-separated from the living space. Many garages contain lawn and garden chemicals, cans of paint, gas cans, lawn mowers, and a variety of other products. Odors from all these can migrate into a house attached to a garage. A detached garage is much healthier. If you have an existing house with an attached garage, it may be possible to isolate the garage from the house.

Figure 5-20.
Welded wire reinforcing and poly moisture barrier in place prior to placing concrete at garage.

This can be done by making the wall between the garage and the living space airtight. For example, caulk any gaps in the wallboard, along the floor, or between the wall and ceiling, and use energy-saving gaskets under the electrical covers. The goal is to seal any holes that could allow pollutants to pass through the wall into the house.

In the Model Healthy House, the garage foundation does not have a separate concrete block wall or a separate concrete footing. Instead, I poured what is called a one-piece monolithic foundation (Sheet 24 of the Plans). This is a less costly approach. It was done because the garage was not to be heated, so insulation wasn't required. A system of forms is used for a foundation of this type. Some contractors have metal forms, but I built mine out of plywood and 2x4s. While the plywood does contain a formaldehyde-based glue, the forms were removed once the concrete was hard and they did not contaminate the concrete. Forms need to be braced very securely to prevent the weight of the wet concrete from causing them to bow outward (Figure 5-19). It is often common practice to spray oil or some type of other type release agent on the forms to prevent the concrete from sticking to them, but this can leave the concrete with a long-lasting odor. If the forms are removed the next day and cleaned quickly, release agents should not be necessary.

Since a garage isn't considered living space, radon control is less important, so a minor crack can be tolerated. Therefore, I didn't use the heavy $\frac{1}{2}$" (#4) rebar reinforcing. Instead, it was reinforced with 6" x 6" welded-wire fabric. However, the thicker portion around the perimeter does contain two #4 rebars. As in the house foundation, crushed stone provided a good base and a poly barrier was placed under the slab to keep moisture from rising up from the ground (Figure 5-20). This type of uninsulated slab construction is very common in houses and would be an acceptable healthy foundation in warm climates.

Before the concrete started to harden, I embedded several $\frac{1}{2}$" diameter, 8" long anchor bolts around the perimeter. The anchor bolts were later used for holding the garage walls in place.

Porch Walls

The last job for the foundation of the Model Healthy House was to build the two stone walls by the house and garage entry porches (see Sheet 11 of the

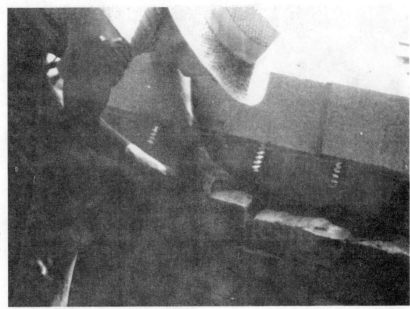

Figure 5-21.
Building a stone porch wall.

Figure 5-22.
Completed porch wall.

Plans). These walls both have a footing that is 20" wide because they support a wider 12" concrete block below grade. At ground level, I laid a 4" concrete block wall, 3 courses high, on top of the 12" block. This left me with a 4" wide ledge on each side for the facing stone. I selected sandstone from a local quarry

that was broken into pieces about 4" thick. Brick could easily have been substituted for the sandstone.

When I laid the 4" concrete block, I inserted small metal ties in the mortar joints. These were then worked into the joints between the stones to help anchor them to the block. With a mason's hammer, I

79

Figure 5-23.
Completed foundation.

was able to chip away at the stones to get them into rectangular shapes so that they could be laid together tightly. In order to get a dry-laid look, I bedded only the backs of the stones in mortar (Figure 5-21). The result looks like a wall that was laid up without any mortar. The larger capstones had to be bedded more securely because of their exposure to weather and abuse. The finished walls are attractive and functional. They are handy for setting packages on while unlocking the door, or for sitting on (Figure 5-22).

Grading the Land

Once the house and garage foundations were complete, I graded the land so that rainwater would drain away from the house. This generally involves a bulldozer of some sort. Because there were so many trees around the house I didn't want to damage, I had to hire an operator with a fairly small piece of equipment. It took a little longer, but no trees were destroyed. Some raking and final shaping by hand were then necessary, and the bare ground was seeded with grass seed suitable for shady areas.

I had the crushed stone delivered for the driveway the same day the grading was done so it too could be leveled and smoothed by the bulldozer. After constructing the sidewalk between the house and garage, and laying the concrete stepping stones between the house porch and the redwood deck, I was ready to begin the actual framing (Figure 5-23).

Update

On the subject of chemically treated lumber, most of the material that is available is CCA treated. CCA stands for Copper-chromated-arsenate, meaning it contains copper, chromium, and arsenic. Though not as widely available, you can also purchase lumber in some parts of the country, that is treated with a somewhat less-toxic preservative called ACQ. It contains ammonia, copper, and quaternary ammonia, and it does not have the same greenish tint that CCA lumber has.

I've heard of a few good alternatives to conventional form oil since the Model Healthy House was completed. First of all, there are now some commercially available water-based form oils that are less noxious than the usual oil-based varieties. Second, I've talked to builders who have used an off-the-shelf

80

cooking oil successfully with chemically sensitive clients. While this can be expensive, it is certainly a creative solution. For other sensitive people, I've also heard of contractors spraying a diluted dish soap or household cleaner on the forms as a release oil. These solutions seem to work fine, but there is one drawback—if the forms are already contaminated with conventional form oil that was used on previous jobs, the concrete may still become contaminated. So they work best with new, uncontaminated forms. The alternative solution I like the best is to simply line the forms with plastic sheeting prior to filling them with concrete. Once the concrete has hardened and the forms are removed, the plastic it simply peeled off. This protects the concrete from contaminated forms, it releases easily, it is fairly easy to install, and contractors generally don't mind doing it.

One question I've often been routinely asked has to do with a concrete slab in the winter: "Isn't it cold to walk on?" Well, the answer is yes and no. Being well-insulated, the floor slab in the Model Healthy House is certainly warmer than it would be if it were uninsulated. While it isn't as quite as warm as the 68°-70° F air in the room, even if it were, it would still be cooler than body temperature (98.6° F), so it would feel cool to walk on. One way around this would be to embed heating coils in the slab. These radiantly heated floors are becoming popular as a substitute for forced-air heating or baseboard heaters. One of their big advantages is warm floors in the winter. Personally, I don't mind slightly cool floors. For about 9 years, my wife, Lynn, and I lived in a house with an insulated slab covered with ceramic tile that was almost identical to that of the Model Healthy House. During the winter, I often walked around barefoot, and didn't find it uncomfortable at all. Lynn, on the other hand, didn't like the coolness on her feet, so she generally wore slippers. Of course, we had a number of area rugs (for example, in front of the kitchen sink, bathroom lavatory, and bathtub) so our feet were insulated from the slab in those locations by the rugs. Which leads me to an important point. We learned that very thick rugs insulated the floor a bit too well—there was a cooler area under the rug that had a higher relative humidity which resulted in some minor mold growth. This was only a problem with our thick Oriental rug, but not with our thinner woven rugs. This would not be a concern with a radiantly heated floor.

82

Chapter 6

FRAMING

■■■ The frame of a house sits on top of the foundation and surrounds the living space. It is usually covered on the outside with some type of siding and on the inside with drywall, plaster, or some type of wall paneling. Insulation is generally placed within the cavities formed by the individual framing members in order to make the entire assembly energy-efficient.

Framing Alternatives

Most houses built in the U.S. today are framed with wood studs, joists, and rafters. Houses are also built out of concrete and masonry, although these materials are more often used in commercial buildings like schools and offices. Steel framing, also popular in commercial work, is another option for residential construction.

Wood Framing

The use of wood framing is well established in the residential construction industry. Builders and designers are familiar with it. It is readily available, easy to assemble, and easy to insulate. If you ask a

builder to construct a house out of wood, he will know exactly how to proceed, where to buy the material, what sizes are necessary, and how much it will cost. I enjoy working with wood framing. But it isn't my first choice for a healthy house.

When you purchase framing lumber, you will most likely be buying spruce, pine, fir, or hemlock. These are softwood trees. They are also known as conifers because they bear cones. Most softwood trees are evergreens and have needles. Hardwood trees like oak, maple, and walnut are rarely used to produce framing lumber because they grow slowly and are more costly.

Some people are bothered by the aroma of softwood trees. They can react to Christmas trees or softwood framing lumber. Many of the chemical compounds making up this natural fragrance are terpenes, the same chemical compounds found in turpentine, a solvent derived from softwood trees. But even though terpenes are a problem for some people, I feel that the biggest drawback to using wood framing is that most wood-framed houses will sooner or later be attacked by termites. I hope that some day effective, long lasting, non-toxic termite-control methods will be in widespread use, but today most pest-control operators use toxic chemicals. Some banks and lending institutions actually require that these noxious chemicals be used before they will approve a mortgage.

Termites and Wood Framing

In the northern extremes of the United States and in Canada, the most common species of termites can't survive the winter, so they are not considered a threat to wood-framed houses. In those areas, if the occupants are not sensitive to the odor of terpenes, then wood can be used for framing without the need for chemical treatments.

In moderately cold climates where subterranean termites are not considered a severe pest, and if the inhabitants are not sensitive to softwood framing lumber, a wood frame with metal termite shields may be a reasonable compromise. Such a house should be inspected annually to insure that termites have not built any mud tubes around the shields. This inspection can be done by a pest control company, or the homeowner can learn to do it himself. If a small infestation is found, a low-tox treatment can be used.

In the warm climates of the western and southern U.S., there are other species of termites besides the more common subterranean type found elsewhere. They include the drywood or dampwood species. Unlike subterranean termites, these can easily get up into a roof structure. They can be so invasive that when a house is infested, it must be enclosed in a plastic tent and the entire structure fumigated. In order to avoid termiticides in these climates, a house can be framed entirely out of a material that termites won't eat.

Termites won't eat chemically treated lumber, and it is often used in climates where termites are a severe pest. The greenish colored pressure-treated lumber that is widely available contains toxic arsenic and chromium compounds. Less hazardous boron-based treatment methods may be a reasonable substitute, but the healthiest framing materials are those that are inherently insect resistant. Naturally resistant redwood would be effective, but it is generally too expensive for framing an entire building.

It is possible to use a combination of materials in framing a house. For example, in climates where termites aren't a problem but the occupants are bothered by softwood lumber, wood framing could be used for the load-bearing portion of a house. This typically consists of the insulated walls, the roof system, and the floor (unless the floor is a concrete slab). By using the airtight construction techniques I discuss in Part 3, all this framing can be isolated from the living space. Then the interior partition walls within the occupied space can be framed with a material less offending to sensitive individuals such as masonry or steel.

Concrete and Masonry Framing

Most concrete and masonry materials (like brick, concrete block, and mortar) are fairly benign. The main health considerations in using these products would be the admixtures sometimes added to mortar or to concrete, or the release oils used on concrete formwork.

While concrete is a very hard, dense material, it is still porous and must have some type of coating to make it impervious to water. Concrete block is even more porous, sometimes so much so that a small amount of air can blow through it. When a masonry-framed house becomes depressurized, outdoor air can be pulled through the porous walls into the interior. In order to build an airtight house out of masonry, it must have a coating to make it impervious to both air and water.

Steel Framing

Steel framing has been used for many years in commercial construction projects. Designers of schools, shopping centers, and hospitals often specify it. But steel framing may at first seem an unusual building material for houses even though homeowners living in steel-framed houses don't often realize that the frame is steel rather than wood. This is because the finished house doesn't look any different than any other house. Despite several decades of use, the average residential builder may be only vaguely familiar with steel framing. While it isn't found at every building supply store, most large cities have one or more distributors.

When most people hear me mention steel framing, they often envision the heavy steel I-beams used in skyscrapers. Such material is entirely too heavy for most residential applications. The material that is appropriate for residential construction is called light-weight steel framing. It actually weighs less than wood framing and is made from galvanized (zinc-plated) sheet metal, so it is rust-resistant. Some insurance companies offer a discount on steel-framed houses because the framing is fireproof.

Steel studs are C-shaped in cross section and are manufactured in a wide variety of sizes. They have

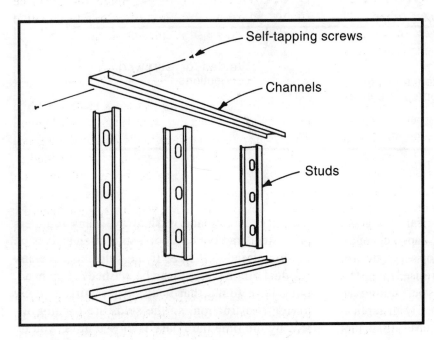

Figure 6-1.
Light-weight steel wall framing.

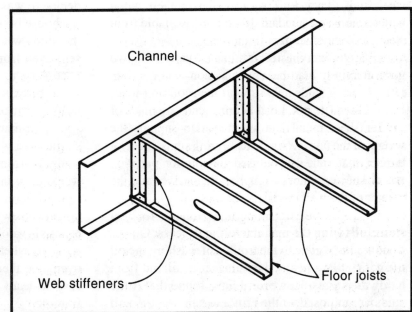

Figure 6-2.
Light-weight steel floor framing.

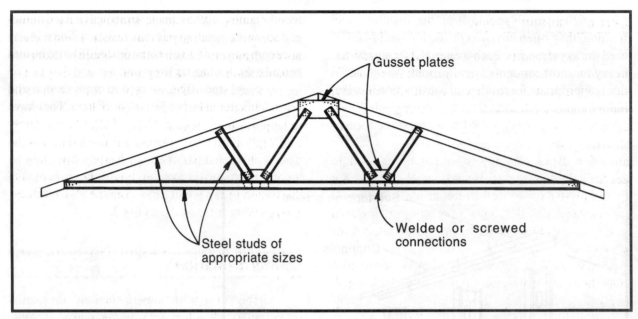

Figure 6-3.*Light-weight steel roof truss.*

holes pre-punched in them for electrical wiring and plumbing lines and they fit into U-shaped channels (also called tracks or runners) at the top and bottom of a wall (Figure 6-1). The larger sizes are used for rafters and joists (Figure 6-2). Light-weight steel framing can be used to replace wood framing in nearly all applications. Roof trusses can easily be made up using smaller steel studs. They look very similar to their wood counterparts and standard designs are available from steel stud manufacturers (Figure 6-3).

Light-weight steel framing is available in two general types: load-bearing and non-load-bearing. Load-bearing studs help support the roof, non-load-bearing studs do not. Load-bearing studs are made of thicker sheet metal and are meant to support the weight of the house. Non-load-bearing studs, made of thinner material, can be used for interior partition walls. They only need to support themselves and the weight of the wall covering material.

A thin oil film sometimes adheres to steel studs following the manufacturing process. On occasion, I have gone to the trouble of washing the oil off with TSP, a heavy duty cleaner available from hardware stores. However, I have found that if the studs are exposed to the rain and sun, the oil will tend to evaporate and wash away. Many suppliers store steel framing outdoors, so it often arrives on the job already oil-free. If the studs do have any residual oil on them, it can be washed off by hand, but I have found that it dissipates fairly quickly during construction, so the studs are usually oil-free by the time the house is closed up. If you do decide to wash the studs, keep in mind the fact that if a house is constructed in an airtight manner, then the studs within the insulated walls will be well-separated from the living space, so it will only be necessary to wash the studs that the occupants could be exposed to—those within uninsulated interior partition walls.

In many ways, a steel-framed house is very similar to a wood-framed house. Both have vertical studs, horizontal members at the top and bottom of walls, wind bracing at corners, and so on. There are some differences, the biggest of which is that self-tapping screws are used in steel framing, as opposed to nails in wood framing. A few different tools are also required when working with steel. Once builders overcome their initial apprehension, it is relatively easy to learn how to work with light-weight steel framing.

86

Cost of Framing Options

One of the first questions asked about alternatives to wood framing is "How much does it cost?"

The cost of masonry construction can vary. For example, a house built solely of unpainted concrete blocks can provide a fairly inexpensive form of shelter. However, concrete block walls are not very attractive. Brick or stone construction, while more aesthetically pleasing, is also more costly. If you want to add plaster or drywall to the inside surface of a masonry wall, it will require more labor and material to add the wood or metal furring strips needed for attachment.

When figuring costs, it is important to consider the expense of heating and cooling a building. A house that is cheap to build but costly to heat isn't very cost-effective in the long run. Houses built of masonry and concrete are not always easy to insulate, although some innovative systems have been introduced in recent years. In moderate climates where less insulation is needed, this may not be a problem, but it can be a major drawback in very cold climates.

In the past, the cost of steel framing scared off many builders. But with the rising price of wood in recent years, steel framing has become cost-competitive. A load-bearing steel stud is often similar in cost to a comparable piece of wood, and the lighter-weight non-load-bearing studs are usually somewhat cheaper than wood. In some parts of the U.S., all steel studs may be cheaper than lumber. Because steel framing is not subject to warpage, studs can be spaced 24" on center rather than the 16" centers common with wood framing. This means less material and reduced cost.

The various screws and fasteners used with steel framing are definitely more expensive than nails, and a little more labor is sometimes required to assemble the various components. When all costs are considered, a steel-framed house can cost a little more than a wood-framed one, but not much more.

Passive Solar Heating

Passive solar design involves placing windows on the south side of a house and building a roof overhang that will shade the windows in the summer and allow the sun to enter in the winter. There is really not much more to it. Such features should be taken into consideration when framing a house, and they can be incorporated with whatever type of framing material is used. Passive solar heating is one of the easiest ways to help warm a house, and best of all, it's absolutely free. Only a little extra planning is needed during the design phase and passive solar heating can often be incorporated into an existing house. For a complete discussion of the possibilities, see the *Passive Solar Energy* book listed in Appendix 3.

"Superinsulation"

The concept of "superinsulation" originated in the 1970s. It refers to a house that's so well-insulated, it requires little heat in the winter. Superinsulated houses often have annual heating bills that compare to most people's monthly bills. There are a variety of ways to build a house with such low-energy requirements (see *The Superinsulated Home Book* in Appendix 3). The method I chose for the Model Healthy House is to actually build two exterior walls, space them a few inches apart, and fill the entire cavity with insulation. This double-wall approach can be used with either wood or steel framing. Superinsulation also requires that a house be built in an airtight manner and that it have a mechanical ventilation system. I'll discuss both subjects in depth later.

Framing the Model Healthy House

I used a light-weight steel framing system in the Model Healthy House primarily to avoid toxic termiticides, and secondarily to avoid the odors of softwood framing lumber that can bother some sensitive individuals. The roof of the Model Healthy House, however, was framed out of wood. The larger steel members necessary for the roof were somewhat more expensive than wood rafters, so I opted for this hybrid approach as a cost-saving measure. Since the subterranean termites found in most of the U.S. can't climb as high as the roof, neither termite shields nor toxic chemicals are necessary to protect it. Because I made the house airtight, the roof framing is completely separated from the living space so that any terpenes from the softwood lumber can't affect sensitive occupants. In those parts of the country where other species of termites can infest any portion of a house, the roof system can also be framed out of steel.

Designing with Steel Framing

When buying wood studs, you simply ask for a 2x4 or a 2x6 and specify a length. Steel studs are a little more complicated because they come not only in different sizes, but also in different flange widths, and the steel itself is available in various thicknesses, or "gauges."

A Variety of Sizes

The steel framing for the Model Healthy House was manufactured and supplied by **Dietrich Industries, Inc.**, one of the country's largest producers. They stock load-bearing studs in sizes ranging from

$2\frac{1}{2}$" with a $1\frac{3}{8}$" flange all the way up to 14" with a $2\frac{1}{2}$" flange. The thinnest are 20-gauge (.0375" thick) while the heaviest are 12-gauge (.1094" thick) (Figure 6-4). The larger studs can be used for floor joists, rafters, and window headers. With so many different sizes available, it is possible to select studs that will closely match the loads imposed on them. If oversized material is used, it will, no doubt, be far stronger than necessary, but it will also be more expensive.

I have found that if one's design calculations call for two different gauges to be used, it is often best to specify only the thicker material. This helps avoid mix-ups on the job site where workmen could mistakenly use a lighter-gauge material in a critical location. For example, if most studs are to be $3\frac{5}{8}$" 18-gauge, but a few could be $3\frac{5}{8}$" 20-gauge, they could easily be switched. Specifying the heavier 18-gauge studs throughout would eliminate any potential problems.

Heat Loss with Steel Studs

Where winter temperatures aren't cold enough to make superinsulation cost-effective, the insulated

Figure 6-4. *Light-weight steel studs are available in a variety of sizes. Larger members are used for window and door headers, floor joists, and rafters.*

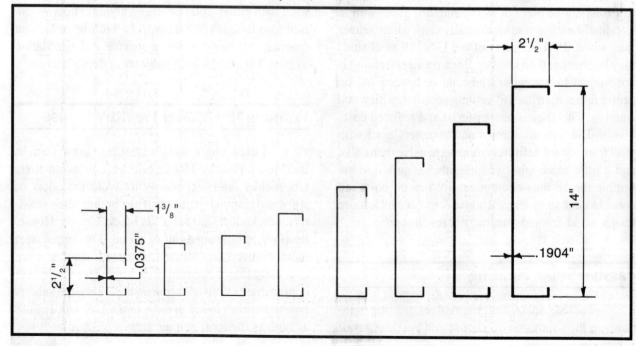

DIETRICH

Combined Load Tables–3⅝″ Studs
Maximum Allowable Axial Load In KIPS (1000 lbs. per stud)
EXTERIOR–15 PSF–Wind Load

Stud Height (ft.)	CSW 14 Gage		CSW 16 Gage		CSW 18 Gage		CSW 20 Gage		CSJ 14 Gage		CSJ 16 Gage		CSJ 18 Gage		CSJ 20 Gage		CSN 14 Gage		CSN 16 Gage		CSN 18 Gage		CSN 20 Gage	
	S	M	S	M	S	M	S	M	S	M	S	M	S	M	S	M	S	M	S	M	S	M	S	M
12″ on center																								
8	8.845	8.809	7.054	6.799	4.685	4.394	3.294	3.054	7.988	7.339	6.368	5.563	4.192	3.689	3.071	2.608	7.540	6.634	6.043	4.949	3.936	3.333	2.848	2.335
9	8.288	8.224	6.590	6.364	4.484	4.249	3.107	2.920	7.480	6.857	5.991	5.217	4.021	3.574	2.695	2.379	7.051	6.190	5.702	4.665	3.716	3.234	2.437	2.092
10	7.515	7.515	6.070	5.859	4.205	4.053	2.677	2.545	6.799	6.275	5.526	4.846	3.569	3.260	2.252	2.033	6.501	5.691	5.251	4.360	3.180	2.836	2.029	1.783
12	6.107	6.113	4.912	4.819	3.230	3.007	1.928	1.794	5.481	5.171	4.228	3.943	2.642	2.381	1.518	1.364	4.994	4.661	3.818	3.486	2.287	2.013	1.340	1.163
14	5.042	4.718	3.762	3.525	2.137	2.078	1.189	1.134	4.212	3.827	3.159	2.877	1.691	1.584			3.703	3.352	2.787	2.508	1.410	1.309		
16	3.626	3.467	2.650	2.521					2.973	2.792							2.584	2.403	1.905					
16″ on center																								
8	9.230	8.809	7.426	6.799	4.806	4.394	3.299	3.004	8.421	7.339	6.765	5.563	4.334	3.689	2.855	2.458	8.081	6.634	6.420	4.949	3.994	3.333	2.598	2.160
9	8.663	8.224	7.608	6.364	4.512	4.199	2.817	2.620	7.914	6.857	6.291	5.217	3.814	3.374	2.400	2.079	7.540	6.190	5.990	4.665	3.421	2.934	2.147	1.817
10	7.941	7.515	6.389	5.859	3.894	3.653	2.361	2.195	7.257	6.275	5.711	4.846	3.238	2.910	1.936	1.708	6.922	5.691	5.233	4.360	2.835	2.486	1.722	1.483
12	6.148	5.988	4.623	4.419	2.786	2.582	1.510	1.419	5.261	4.871	3.950	3.593	2.211	1.981	1.145	1.014	4.718	4.261	3.515	3.136	1.845	1.638		
14	4.623	4.293	3.371	3.125	1.717	1.628			3.810	3.452	2.781	2.502					3.330	2.977						
16	3.241	3.067																						
24″ on center																								
8	9.831	8.809	7.859	6.799	4.697	4.194	2.795	2.529	9.045	7.339	7.172	5.563	3.923	3.364	2.346	2.008	8.634	6.634	6.768	4.949	3.465	2.883	2.099	1.735
9	9.977	8.224	7.681	6.364	3.950	3.599	2.249	2.070	8.999	6.857	6.601	5.142	3.246	2.824	1.811	1.554	8.114	6.190	5.937	4.490	2.794	2.384	1.596	1.342
10	8.269	7.515	6.447	5.434	3.223	2.978	1.709	1.595	7.542	6.050	5.443	4.346	2.569	2.285	1.290	1.133	6.722	5.291	4.845	3.785	2.159	1.886	1.105	0.958
12	5.591	5.238	4.000	3.694	1.986	1.807			4.678	4.171	3.325	2.943					4.085	3.586	2.896	2.536				
14	3.884	3.568																						

Figure 6-5. *Dietrich Industries, Inc. design table for exterior load-bearing studs.*

double wall of the Model Healthy House wouldn't be necessary. A single wall of 6" steel studs may be a reasonable compromise. However, it is important to remember that steel is an excellent conductor of heat. This means that when outdoor temperatures fall, there can be rapid heat loss through the steel from the indoors to the outdoors, resulting in cold vertical strips on the interior wall wherever there are studs. Cold spots mean localized areas of high humidity and possibly mold growth. Mold growth can be seen as vertical shadows on the wall over each stud. This problem is easy to avoid by using a foam sheathing material that will protect the frame from the low outdoor temperatures. Another approach is to use a double-wall system like I did in the Model Healthy House. With a double wall, the interior and the exterior walls aren't connected, so there is no direct path through which the heat can flow.

Calculations: Load-Bearing Framing

Any stud of a given size, whether wood or metal, will support a certain downward weight and a certain wind load. In most residential applications, wood studs are stronger than they need to be, so it isn't necessary to do any loading calculations. Since steel studs are available in so many sizes, some figuring is required to insure that the pieces will be strong enough to support the building, but not so heavy as to be wasteful. The calculations required will be familiar to most architects and engineers. Any actual design work of this type should be done by a qualified person, but I will illustrate the process here.

Wind Loading

The maximum wind loading varies in different parts of the country. The figure for any particular area can be found in the local building code. This information is usually on file with the building inspector at the area planning commission. In the locale where the Model Healthy House was built, the design factor for wind loading is 15 pounds per square foot (psf). This means that the strongest winds expected in southern Indiana will exert 15 pounds of pressure on every square foot of a house's exterior wall. The wind speed in such a situation would be 80 mph. Winds of 125 mph would exert 40 psf on a building.

Axial Loading

In the manual describing their products, **Dietrich Industries, Inc.** has a number of tables listing the allowable loads that can be imposed on their various studs. These are called axial loads. This refers to the amount of downward force that can be applied to the vertical axis of the stud—in other words, the amount of weight a stud will hold up.

Load Tables

Three-and five-eighth-inch studs are one of the most common sizes, so that is the size I used. They will generally support the loads found in most single-story residences, but it is important to do a few calculations and check some tables to make sure they will be strong enough for a particular application. The tables in Figure 6-5 are taken from a **Dietrich Industries, Inc.** manual and list the maximum allowable loading on 3⅝" studs in a 15 psf wind. The CSJ studs I selected have a 1⅝" wide flange. CSJ is a designation **Dietrich Industries, Inc.** uses for a 1⅝" flange width. Other manufacturers use different designations. I had estimated that the lightest-weight studs (20-gauge) would be sufficient even if placed 24" on center. I then used the appropriate tables and performed a few simple calculations to see if 20-gauge CSJ studs would be strong enough.

The tables differentiate between studs mechanically braced with either a rigid sheathing or drywall attached (the S column) and those simply mechanically braced (the M column). A rigid facing material stiffens the wall so it can support more weight. In the Model Healthy House, I used the M column because I didn't plan to use any sheathing on the outside of the house. Looking at the table in the appropriate box you can see that the maximum allowable load for such a stud 8' high is 2.008 kips, or 2,008 pounds. This means that each stud is capable of supporting slightly over one ton. The exterior wall studs on both the north and south walls of the Model Healthy House are actually less than 8' high, so in

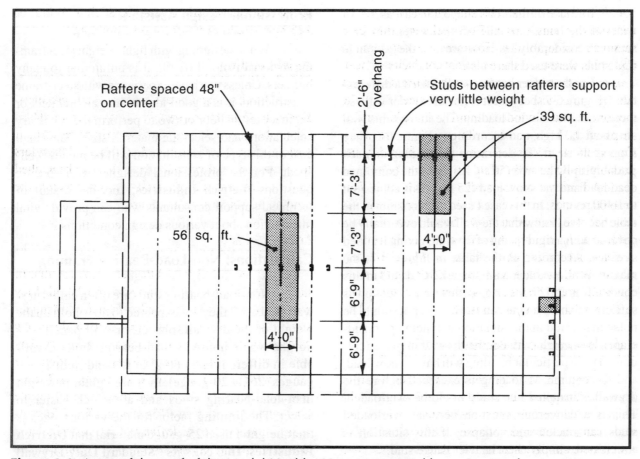

Figure 6-6. *Areas of the roof of the Model Healthy House supported by various studs.*

reality they would support slightly more. The next step involves calculating just how much weight will be on the studs in this particular house. If it is more than 2,008 pounds, a heavier stud will be required.

Calculating the Actual Axial Load

The actual weight that our studs will be called on to support is the weight of the entire roof system including the rafters, metal roofing, drywall, and insulation (this is called the "dead load"), plus the weight of any snow in the winter. In our area, according to the building code, the snow load is 20 psf. In southern Florida there is no snow load and in northern Maine it could be as much as 80 psf. Figure 6-6 shows the house layout with various sections shaded to delineate the amount of roof area supported by differ-

ent load-bearing studs. A single exterior stud along the north wall supports an area 9' 9" by 4' 0" or 39 square feet.

The weight of all of the materials in the roof structure in this 39 square feet is about 5 pounds per square foot. Fiberglass shingles over a plywood roof deck would be about 2.5 psf heavier; a slate roof would be perhaps 7 psf heavier. In this case, the total weight on the stud will be 25 lb. (dead load of 5 pounds plus the snow load of 20 pounds) multiplied by the area, 39 sq. ft., for a total 975 pounds. This is less than the maximum allowable loading of 2,008 pounds in the table, so a 20-gauge CSJ 3⅝" stud is more than sufficient to hold up the house when spaced 24" on center with no sheathing. The studs along the south wall actually support slightly less weight, so I used the same size there.

91

Because of their odd shape, the east and west walls of the house are taller in the center, but they support considerably less roof area, so the 20-gauge CSJ studs were used there also.

For the center bearing-wall, I used a different table (Figure 6-7) because it is not an exterior wall, so there is not a lot of wind loading. The studs in this wall are about 11' high, and according to Figure 6-6, they support 56 sq. ft. To determine the loading on each stud, multiply the area (56 sq. ft.) times the combined dead load and the snow load (25 lb.). This comes out to 1,400 pounds. In this case I used the S column in the table because I knew that the wall would eventually be covered with a rigid facing of drywall, giving it added strength. According to the table in Figure 6-7, the maximum allowable loading for a 12' CSJ stud in this condition is 2,027 lbs. Again, my size selection is sufficient to hold up the house. However, it should be noted that a stud in this situation will hold up considerably less weight without the drywall in place (column M). If a particular building will have a snow load, and the column M loading is exceeded before the drywall is installed, the studs would be overloaded. This is a dangerous situation because overloaded studs can buckle and collapse. If this situation is anticipated, simply use a heavier gauge stud.

Rafters, Floor Joists, and Headers

Similar calculations and tables are used when selecting steel rafters, floor joists, or door and window headers. The weight that is supported by a floor joist, divided by the length of the joist, yields a number in pounds per lineal foot. This can be compared to the appropriate table to select a joist size.

For our window headers, the loading isn't uniform. The design calls for "point loads" under each rafter, meaning that weight is concentrated at certain points on the header. If these point loads are too high, the web of the header can buckle. This is called "web crippling" (Figure 6-8). Maximum web-crippling loads are available from other design tables. In order to compensate, stiffeners can be used to make the web stronger (Figure 6-9). In this design, I used 6" 18-gauge CSJ studs for headers to be strong enough so that no web stiffeners were needed.

Professional Design Assistance

While designing with light-weight steel framing material is not difficult, it is unfamiliar to many builders. Unless you have experience with steel-frame construction, it is a good idea to hire an architect or engineer for an hour or two to perform the necessary calculations and select the material sizes. The small cost of this type of consultation will be money well-spent. For the professional designer with specific questions **Dietrich Industries, Inc.** has a staff of technical support consultants who can provide vital information about various design conditions.

Calculations: Non-Load-Bearing Framing

Non-load-bearing studs are often called dry-wall studs. All they are expected to do is hold up the weight of the drywall, plaster, or wall paneling—not the whole house as load-bearing studs. Available in different sizes (1⅝" to 6") and in different gauges (26- to 20-gauge), they are lighter in weight than load-bearing studs and are much easier to select. The limiting factor for the various sizes is their height. I used 25-gauge material that **Dietrich Industries, Inc.** calls its "Standard Duty Drywall Studs" (STN).

The **Dietrich Industries, Inc.** table in Figure 6-10 shows the various heights allowed for different sized studs at different spacings. The $1/120$, $1/240$, and $1/360$ columns indicate the amount of deflection a wall will tolerate. With $1/240$ and 24" stud spacing, the deflection will be $24/240$ or 0.1", if a 5 psf load is applied to the entire wall. At $1/360$, the deflection would be a little less ($24/360$, or about 0.07"). Walls with a brittle plaster finish should be stiffer than those with a drywall finish. In our case, I used 2½" and 3⅝" studs in most cases. According to the table, at $1/120$ and 24" on center, 2½" studs are sufficiently strong for a wall up to 11.1' high and 3⅝" studs are suitable for walls up to 14.7' high.

Working with Steel Framing

In order to illustrate how light-weight steel framing isn't difficult to work with, I will cover in

DIETRICH

Combined Load Tables–3⅝″ Studs
Maximum Allowable Axial Load In KIPS (1000 lbs. per stud)
INTERIOR–5 PSF–Wind Load

12″ on center

Stud Height (ft.)	CSW 14ga S	CSW 14ga M	CSW 16ga S	CSW 16ga M	CSW 18ga S	CSW 18ga M	CSW 20ga S	CSW 20ga M	CSJ 14ga S	CSJ 14ga M	CSJ 16ga S	CSJ 16ga M	CSJ 18ga S	CSJ 18ga M	CSJ 20ga S	CSJ 20ga M	CSN 14ga S	CSN 14ga M	CSN 16ga S	CSN 16ga M	CSN 18ga S	CSN 18ga M	CSN 20ga S	CSN 20ga M
8	8.845	8.809	7.054	6.799	4.685	4.394	3.294	3.054	7.988	7.339	6.368	5.563	4.192	3.689	3.071	2.608	7.540	6.634	6.043	4.949	3.936	3.333	2.848	2.335
9	8.288	8.224	6.590	6.364	4.484	4.249	3.182	2.970	7.480	6.857	5.991	5.217	4.021	3.574	2.920	2.529	7.051	6.190	5.702	4.665	3.766	3.234	2.712	2.267
10	7.515	7.515	6.070	5.859	4.280	4.078	3.052	2.870	6.799	6.275	5.526	4.846	3.819	3.435	2.777	2.433	6.501	5.691	5.251	4.360	3.580	3.111	2.579	2.183
12	6.107	6.113	5.012	4.894	4.030	3.657	2.878	2.619	5.481	5.171	4.503	4.118	3.567	3.081	2.568	2.189	5.169	4.711	4.243	3.736	3.312	2.788	2.315	1.963
14	5.467	4.968	4.512	4.075	3.262	3.128	2.239	2.134	4.862	4.227	4.009	3.452	2.791	2.609	1.923	1.704	4.503	3.852	3.712	3.133	2.510	2.309	1.736	1.512
16	4.376	4.067	3.650	3.346	2.598	2.452	1.708	1.600	3.848	3.467	3.192	2.843	2.145	1.979	1.381	1.270	3.534	3.153	2.855	2.579	1.886	1.723	1.216	1.112
18	3.565	3.364	2.869	2.747	1.962	1.873	1.250	1.187	3.084	2.869	2.420	2.284	1.610	1.495	0.989	0.936	2.738	2.578	2.145	2.013	1.382	1.296	0.876	0.805
20	2.900	2.816	2.230	2.148	1.481	1.432	0.900	0.881	2.408	2.325	1.857	1.777	1.195	1.126			2.125	2.023	1.640	1.564	1.012	0.973		

16″ on center

Stud Height (ft.)	CSW 14ga S	CSW 14ga M	CSW 16ga S	CSW 16ga M	CSW 18ga S	CSW 18ga M	CSW 20ga S	CSW 20ga M	CSJ 14ga S	CSJ 14ga M	CSJ 16ga S	CSJ 16ga M	CSJ 18ga S	CSJ 18ga M	CSJ 20ga S	CSJ 20ga M	CSN 14ga S	CSN 14ga M	CSN 16ga S	CSN 16ga M	CSN 18ga S	CSN 18ga M	CSN 20ga S	CSN 20ga M
8	9.230	8.809	7.426	6.799	4.806	4.394	3.374	3.054	8.421	7.339	6.765	5.563	4.334	3.689	3.105	2.608	8.081	6.634	6.420	4.949	4.044	3.333	2.873	2.335
9	8.663	8.224	7.608	6.364	4.612	4.249	3.242	2.970	7.914	6.857	6.291	5.217	4.114	3.574	3.000	2.529	7.540	6.190	5.990	4.665	3.846	3.234	2.772	2.267
10	7.941	7.515	6.389	5.859	4.394	4.078	3.111	2.870	7.257	6.275	5.786	4.846	3.913	3.435	2.836	2.433	6.922	5.691	5.508	4.360	3.660	3.111	2.622	2.183
12	6.323	6.113	5.198	4.894	4.086	3.657	2.810	2.594	5.736	5.171	4.700	4.118	3.611	3.081	2.370	2.089	5.418	4.711	4.415	3.736	3.220	2.788	2.135	1.838
14	5.573	4.968	4.596	4.075	3.117	2.978	2.131	1.934	4.960	4.227	4.081	3.452	2.619	2.409	1.725	1.529	4.580	3.852	3.667	3.133	2.300	2.084	1.530	1.337
16	4.441	4.067	3.558	3.321	2.390	2.227	1.514	1.400	3.856	3.467	3.016	2.743	1.953	1.779	1.262	1.095	3.428	3.153	2.667	2.429	1.685	1.523	1.056	0.937
18	3.505	3.339	2.681	2.547	1.739	1.648	1.045	0.967	2.919	2.744	2.250	2.109	1.406	1.320			2.566	2.403	1.968	1.838	1.197	1.121		
20	2.702	2.616	2.054	1.973	1.277	1.232			2.231	2.125	1.702	1.602					1.943	1.848	1.480	1.414				

24″ on center

Stud Height (ft.)	CSW 14ga S	CSW 14ga M	CSW 16ga S	CSW 16ga M	CSW 18ga S	CSW 18ga M	CSW 20ga S	CSW 20ga M	CSJ 14ga S	CSJ 14ga M	CSJ 16ga S	CSJ 16ga M	CSJ 18ga S	CSJ 18ga M	CSJ 20ga S	CSJ 20ga M	CSN 14ga S	CSN 14ga M	CSN 16ga S	CSN 16ga M	CSN 18ga S	CSN 18ga M	CSN 20ga S	CSN 20ga M
8	9.831	8.809	7.859	6.799	4.972	4.394	3.420	3.054	9.045	7.339	7.172	5.563	4.398	3.689	3.143	2.608	8.634	6.634	6.768	4.949	4.090	3.333	2.899	2.335
9	9.977	8.224	7.856	6.364	4.750	4.249	3.324	2.970	9.049	6.857	7.051	5.217	4.246	3.574	3.036	2.529	8.514	6.190	6.587	4.665	3.944	3.234	2.796	2.267
10	8.444	7.515	7.297	5.859	4.523	4.078	3.184	2.870	8.367	6.275	6.543	4.846	4.019	3.435	2.765	2.383	7.847	5.691	6.095	4.360	3.734	3.111	2.505	2.108
12	6.691	6.113	5.475	4.894	3.861	3.507	2.451	2.244	6.103	5.171	4.950	4.118	3.213	2.831	2.027	1.268	5.735	4.711	4.546	3.736	2.832	2.463	1.806	1.538
14	5.734	4.968	4.419	4.000	2.834	2.578	1.747	1.584	4.866	4.227	3.724	3.302	2.315	2.034	1.204		4.327	3.802	3.308	2.908	1.977	1.734	1.201	1.037
16	4.238	3.942	3.218	2.971	1.974	1.827	1.050		3.507	3.217	2.679	2.418	1.568	1.429			3.084	2.803	2.362	2.129	1.198			
18	3.142	2.989	2.359	2.222		1.298			2.592	2.419	1.939	1.784					2.250	2.103						
20	2.393	2.291																						

Figure 6-7. Dietrich Industries, Inc. design table for interior load-bearing studs.

93

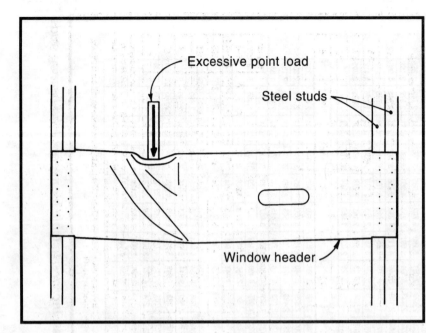

Figure 6-8.
Web crippling resulting from excessive point load.

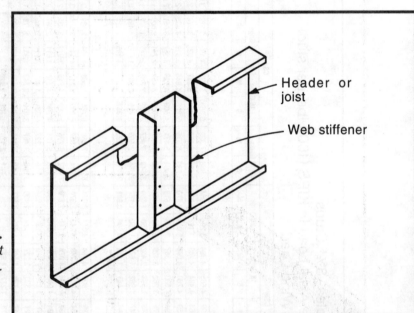

Figure 6-9.
Web stiffeners are used to support greater point loads.

some depth the various tools, techniques and details necessary for assembly.

In the Model Healthy House, the framing was done in two stages. The Phase 1 framing covered in this chapter consisted of all of the exterior walls, the center load-bearing wall, and the roof system. When this framing was complete, the ventilation ducts, wiring, and plumbing were installed in any walls that were to be insulated. The insulation was then put in place and covered with foil-backed drywall. Then the structure was ready for Phase 2, in which the remainder of the interior non-load-bearing walls were built

94

DIETRICH

Maximum Allowable Clear Span Height in Feet[2 & 3]

Stud Size (in.)	Studs Spacing 12" on center			Studs Spacing 16" on center			Studs Spacing 24" on center		
	L/120	L/240	L/360	L/120	L/240	L/360	L/120	L/240	L/360
1⅝	10.0	8.0	7.0	9.1	7.2	6.3	8.3	6.3	5.5
2½	13.9	11.1	9.7	12.7	10.1	8.8	11.1	8.8	7.7
3⅝	18.6	14.7	12.9	16.9	13.4	11.7	14.7	11.7	10.2
4	20.1	15.9	13.9	18.2	14.5	12.6	15.7	12.6	11.0
6	·	·	·	·	·	·	·	·	·

Physical Structural Properties[1]

Stud Size (in.)	Weight (lbs./ft.)	Cross Section Area (sq.in.)	About Major Axis				About Minor Axis			m (in.)	X_o	$\frac{J}{1000}$ x	C_w	r_o (in.)	B BETA	Resisting Moment (x-x) (in.-lbs.)
			$\bar{X}$ (in.)	I_x (in⁴)	S_x (in³)	R_x (in.)	I_y (in⁴)	S_y (in³)	R_y (in.)							
1⅝	.273	.067	.539	.036	.045	0.738	.014	.019	.452	.653	−1.101	.007	.010	1.373	.357	805
2½	.327	.069	.521	.093	.075	1.162	.014	.020	.455	.591	−.965	.009	.025	1.470	.569	1451
3⅝	.395	.089	.404	.227	.125	1.594	.019	.022	.456	.530	−.839	.011	.057	1.700	.755	2432
4	.418	.096	.375	.287	.143	1.729	.020	.023	.452	.513	−.805	.012	.071	1.791	.798	2767
6"	.540	.132	.273	.765	.255	2.410	.073	.024	.420	.439	−.666	.016	.179	2.336	.919	·

NOTES: Design based on minimum thickness.
*This member exceeds the Allowable Web Depth to thickness ratio of 200.

(1) Yield strength is 33 KSI.

(2) Limiting heights are calculated using a 5 psf uniform load perpendicular to studs and based on stud properties alone. Use of composite action with collateral materials will increase height limits. Stress calculations are based on capacity of studs alone. Where stresses are due to wind loading, the allowable unit stresses have been increased one-third in compliance with the AISI Specification.

(3) Limiting heights based on stress, shear and deflection. Web crippling is assumed negligible due to stiffening provided by connection to track.

Standard Duty Drywall Studs (STN-25 Ga.)

Dietrich Big "D" standard duty (25 gage) drywall studs are fabricated in standard sizes and stock lengths from corrosion resistant galvanized steel. Custom sizes and cut to length sizes are available upon request. Knockouts for piping, electrical installation and horizontal bracing are located over the entire length of the stud.

Figure 6-10. *Dietrich Industries, Inc. design table for non-load-bearing studs.*

and the rest of the house was wired, plumbed, dry-walled, and finished in a conventional manner. The reason for a two-stage approach was to show in a simplified way how to construct an airtight house. For builders unfamiliar with airtight construction, a two-phase approach makes airtightness easy to visualize.

Cutting Steel Framing

When marking the steel for cutting or layout, I found the galvanized surface difficult to mark with a pencil, but a fine-point permanent felt marker worked quite well. I have also had good luck in using a china

Figure 6-11.
Cutting load-bearing studs.

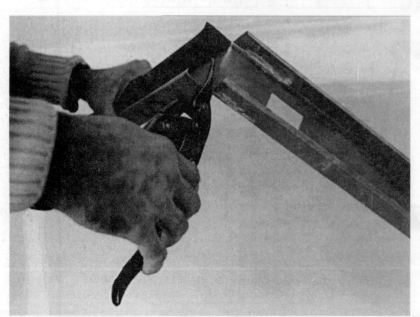

Figure 6-12.
Cutting non-load-bearing studs.

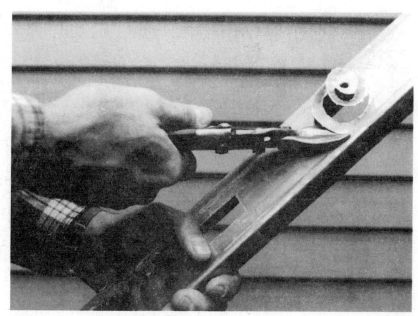

Figure 6-13.
Cutting holes in non-load-bearing studs.

marker (grease pencil), although you can't make a very fine line with one.

With load-bearing studs, if only a few cuts are required, a portable power saw can be fitted with an abrasive cut-off blade. A hacksaw or tin snips can also be used, but both can be tiring and aren't very efficient. Cutting load-bearing studs and channel is easiest with a chop saw fitted with an abrasive cut-off wheel (Figure 6-11). Many rental shops have these. They are quite noisy, so it is best to use hearing protectors when using a chop saw. Safety glasses are also necessary.

Non-load-bearing studs, being made from thinner steel, are much easier to cut. I use my chop saw if I need to cut very many of them, but they are quite easy to cut with tin snips. I first cut through the flanges, then fold back the end and cut through the web (Figure 6-12).

Light-gauge steel studs, both load-bearing and non-load-bearing, have holes prepunched in them. These are handy for feeding plumbing lines and wiring through, but the holes are not always in the right place. Cutting additional holes in the studs can be awkward, but I found an easy way to get the job done with tin snips. First, I punch a small hole

in the stud with an awl, then I use the tin snips and cut out the appropriate sized hole by working around in a spiral (Figure 6-13). For someone who works with steel studs regularly, special hole punching tools are available.

Fasteners and Screw Guns

The screws used with light-weight steel framing are self-tapping. They can be installed with an electric drill equipped with a Phillips screwdriver bit, but a screw gun is more efficient because it is designed specifically to drive screws. Screw guns have clutches to prolong motor life and an adjustable depth stop that is handy in many applications. The self-tapping screws used with load-bearing studs have a drill point (Figure 6-14). TEKS is a popular brand name for this type of point, but they are also made by other companies. Some electric drills and screw guns run at fairly high speeds that will burn up the points of these screws, making them difficult to install. In order to minimize this problem, the drill or screw gun should be rated at less than 2,500 RPM.

Because screws have limited strength, designers may specify a specific number of fasteners in

97

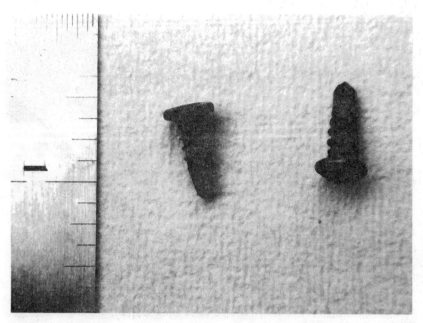

Figure 6-14.
Drill-point screws for steel framing.

critical locations. According to the Metal Lath/Steel Framing Association, when installed in 20-gauge load-bearing studs, a #8 screw will support 140 lbs. in shear and 68 lbs. in pullout. Shear loading refers to the amount of weight it will take to shear a screw in half. Enough screws are needed to support the total weight that the header must hold up. With a header over a window, shear is very important.

In some commercial jobs, all of the load-bearing connections are welded, eliminating the need for screws all together. This is perfectly acceptable, but a welder may not be available to residential contractors.

I like to use a magnetic bit in my screw gun to hold the screws in place, but this has a disadvantage. Small pieces of steel shavings can be attracted to the end of the bit, making it difficult to firmly seat the bit in the screw's head. This happens fairly often and it means that you must wipe off the bit with your finger each time you insert a screw. Using a non-magnetized bit will eliminate this.

Throughout this book, I will describe a variety of different types of screws. While some can be difficult to find at a local hardware store, most major cities have commercial or industrial suppliers listed under "Fasteners" in the yellow pages. Distributors of steel framing also stock a variety of screw types.

Assembling the Load-Bearing Walls

Sheets 8 and 9 of the Plans (in Appendix 4) show the layout of the studs, top and bottom channels, and required bracing for all of the load-bearing walls. Sheet 10 of the Plans shows the basic connection details.

For the Model Healthy House, I chose to build the two end walls first because of their odd shape. Of course, many house designs could be built with simpler rectangular walls. The trapezoidal shape that I used only resulted in a small material savings over a simpler layout, but it does demonstrate the variety of shapes that steel framing can be adapted to.

I find that the easiest way to build a wall with an irregular shape is to make a full size layout on the floor and assemble the entire wall to match the layout lines (Figure 6-15).

Upper and Lower Channels

Channels are supplied in 10' long sections, so they must be spliced together to get the required

98

Figure 6-15.
Laying out a wall on the concrete slab.

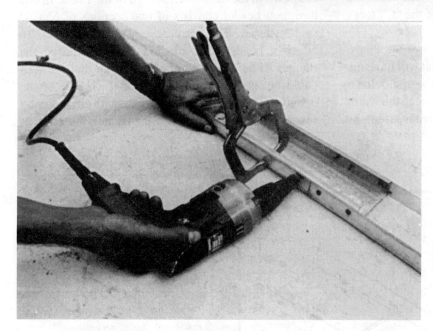

Figure 6-16.
Connecting lengths of channel.

longer lengths. Splicing is done with a short scrap of stud and a total of 8 screws. I found that quick-action clamps were handy for holding various framing members together while fastening them (Figure 6-16).

Because the lower channel is eventually bolted to the foundation, this is a good time to drill the holes in it for the anchor bolts to pass through. I drilled an ⅛" pilot hole first, then a larger ⁹⁄₁₆" hole. The anchor bolts are ½" in diameter, so the ⁹⁄₁₆" holes allow for a little misalignment. Before going further, I also cut part of the way through the bottom channel at the door openings (Figure 6-17). By leaving this short section of channel temporarily in place, the wall was easier to keep square and lift into position. Once up, the channel in the door opening was simply cut out with a pair of tin snips. Removal would have been more difficult if I didn't cut away the web before the wall was lifted into place.

Studs

Once the upper and lower channels were laid out, I cut the studs to length and slipped them in place. When the end of a stud is cut off, one of the prepunched holes may be an odd length from the end. I was careful to make sure that the studs didn't get turned end-for-end because I wanted to make sure that the prepunched holes in the studs were the same distance up from the bottom channel. This was important later for the installation of the horizontal bridging. The studs are usually placed so that the open side of the "C" faces the same direction.

Note that, according to Sheet 9 of the Plans, there are two studs on the west wall that will have the center wall header attached to them. These should be spaced apart slightly so that they will match the width of a 3⅝" stud. On the east wall there are three lengths

of blocking that the center wall will attach to. These were made up of lengths of channel in the same manner as the window sills.

Once all the pieces of one section of wall were screwed in place on one side, I turned the entire assembly over and inserted the second set of screws. Although steel framing isn't heavy, at this point, the wall is fairly flimsy, so two or three people may be required to flip it over without bending the channels out of shape. Two people were able to handle all of the walls in the Model Healthy House, but on a couple of occasions we would have been grateful to have had another pair of hands.

Door and Window Openings

Headers for doors and windows are attached as shown in the detail on Sheet 10 of the Plans. In this design, a header consists of two sections of 6" CSJ stud material. There are several different ways to attach a header. The method I used required the flanges to be cut away at each end so that the web could be attached to the studs on each side of the opening. This notching can be done with either a chop saw or a hacksaw. On top of the header, a section of

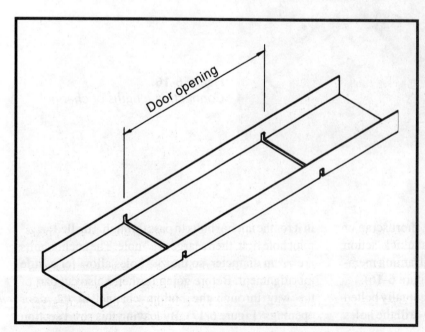

Figure 6-17.
Notching the bottom channel for a door opening.

100

Figure 6-18.
Window header.

Figure 6-19.
Window sill.

channel was attached to accept the studs over the window or door (Figure 6-18).

Before actually screwing the header to the studs, it is important to make sure that the window opening is square. This can be done with a carpenter's framing square. Once the headers are in place it can be very difficult to pull an out-of-square window opening into shape.

I made the sills for the windows from lengths of channel. By slitting the flanges two inches from each end, I was able to fold the end back 90 degrees and attach them to the studs (Figure 6-19). Before

101

Figure 6-20.
Wall plumbed in place and ready for diagonal bracing and horizontal bridging.

framing any openings, it is always a good idea to check the window and door manufacturer's literature and see if the rough opening dimensions shown on the Plans are correct. Product dimensions do change occasionally.

Standing up the Walls

Some builders will attach the diagonal wind bracing and the horizontal bridging while the wall is still lying flat on the concrete floor slab, but I decided to stand the walls up first in order to make sure they were perfectly plumb (Figure 6-20). Two or more people are usually required to get the walls up and temporarily braced so they won't fall down.

Sill Sealer

Before tilting a wall up into place, I installed a sill sealer between the bottom channel and the foundation wall (Figure 6-21). This is an energy-efficiency feature that was done to prevent the wind from penetrating the bottom of the wall cavity. It is important because wind can greatly reduce the effectiveness of insulation. I used a ¾" x ¾" adhe-

sive-backed gasket called Sure-Seal provided by **Denarco, Inc.** that was stuck to the top of the foundation wall. Sure-Seal is a high quality foam sealant tape. It has an exceptionally long life and can seal irregular gaps. When the steel stud wall was lifted into place, the gasket compressed, forming an excellent barrier to the wind. Once the wall was slipped over the anchor bolts, the ½" washers and nuts were installed and tightened down.

Diagonal Wind Bracing

With a carpenter's level, I made sure the walls were plumb and temporarily braced them to wood stakes driven in the ground. Once plumb, the 4" diagonal bracing was attached with two screws at each stud. Note the lower corner detail on Sheet 17 of the Plans to see how many screws are required. The purpose of diagonal bracing is to keep the building square when the wind is blowing against it. In a strong wind, the lower corner is subject to a considerable amount of stress so this detail is very important (Figure 6-22).

Most manufacturers supply wind bracing as a flat piece of steel. I went to my local sheet metal shop

102

Figure 6-21.
Sure-Seal gasket beneath load-bearing wall.

Figure 6-22.
Diagonal bracing meeting at a corner.

and had them put a slight crease down the center to make it stiffer. I found that the crease made it much easier to handle and get tight. Without the stiffening crease, I found a certain amount of looseness in the bracing between the studs. With the crease, the walls are as rigid and solid as possible.

Horizontal Bridging

Next, I installed the horizontal bridging. The purpose of horizontal bridging is to prevent the studs from twisting when the roof loading is applied to them (Figure 6-23). The bridging gives the studs a consid-

Figure 6-23.
Horizontal bridging.

Figure 6-24.
Load-bearing walls in place.

erable amount of strength, allowing them to support much more weight.

The bridging consisted of a U-shaped channel and a number of short angle clips. The channel was slipped through the prepunched holes in the studs at about the mid-point of the wall. This is why it was important to have all the studs oriented with the prepunched holes the same distance from the bottom. I attached the 2" x 2" steel angle clips to each stud with two screws and then to the channel with two more screws. The angle clips were predrilled, making attachment easy.

104

DATE	SOLAR ANGLE ABOVE THE HORIZON	
January 21	70° - Latitude	
February 21	78° - Latitude	
March 21	90° - Latitude	
April 21	101° - Latitude	
May 21	110° - Latitude	
June 21	113° - Latitude	
July 21	111° - Latitude	
August 21	102° - Latitude	
September 21	89° - Latitude	
October 21	79° - Latitude	
November 21	70° - Latitude	
December 21	67° - Latitude	

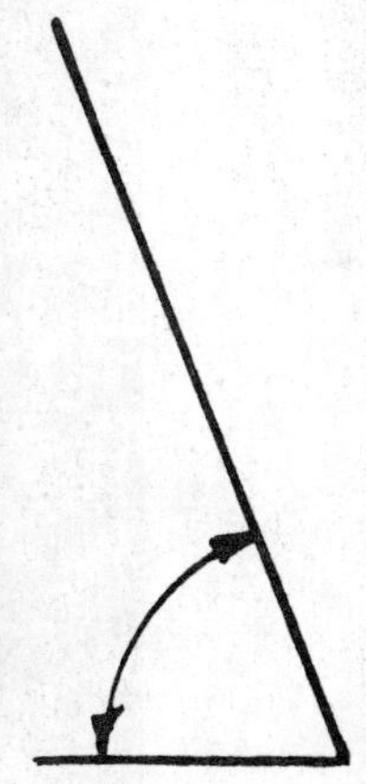

Figure 6-25.
Approximate solar angles at noon.

Once each end wall was in place, I assembled the center wall and the north and south walls in the same manner. They were fairly straightforward because of their rectangular shapes. In order to make them easier to handle, they were each assembled in two sections, then connected together once they had been raised into place. Figure 6-24 shows all of the load-bearing walls erected with temporary bracing to keep them in place until the roof was installed.

Incorporating Passive Solar Design

Most houses have a standard 8' wall height. In determining wall heights for the Model Healthy House, I first drew a wall section (Sheet 7 of the Plans) so that the south facing windows would receive full sunlight on December 21 when the sun is lowest in the sky, and no sunlight between April 21 and August 21. This is the key to passive solar heating—capture the sunlight in the winter and keep it out in the summer.

In a typical winter, in much of the U.S., triple-glazed south-facing windows will provide more solar heat during the day than they will lose at night. Because of this, a superinsulated house with too many south-facing windows can overheat in the winter. Therefore, in the Model Healthy House, I have limited the square footage of the south-facing windows to about 8% of the floor area. This percentage will vary with other designs depending on the climate and the amount of insulation.

Solar Angles

To determine the sun's angle at noon for any part of the country, you first need to know the latitude. This can be found on a map. The Model Healthy House is located about 39 degrees north of the equator. By plugging this number into the formulas in Figure 6-25, you can see that for our area the sun will be 28 degrees (67 minus 39) above the horizon at noon on December 21, 62 degrees above on April 21, and 63 degrees above on August 21.

Calculating Wall Heights and Roof Overhangs

In order for solar angles to be used to either shade or expose the windows to the sun, two critical

105

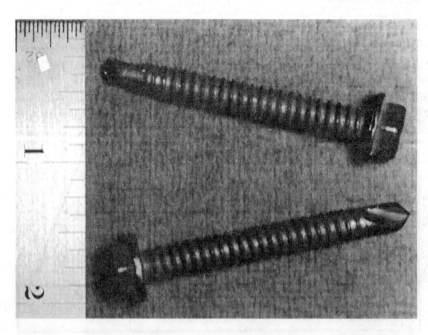

Figure 6-26.
Hex-head drill-point screws.

dimensions of the house come into play: the length of the overhang and the height of the overhang above the top of the window. By trying out various angles, wall heights, and overhang lengths on my drawing board, I arrived at the 2'-6" overhang and the 7'-10" wall height shown for the south-facing windows. These dimensions aren't critical for the north wall because it receives so little sun. However, I decided to use a matching 2'-6" overhang on the north wall so it would look the same as the south overhang.

Still working on the drawing board, I drew the south wall height and projected the roof line up at the 3 in 12 roof pitch that I selected for the roof slope, in order to calculate the center wall height. Then, taking the center wall height and projecting the roof line back down at a 3 in 12 pitch, I arrived at the north wall height. If the center wall had been exactly in the center of the house, then the north and south walls would have been the same height. The various wall heights are shown on Sheet 6 of the Plans.

Roof Framing

After all of the load-bearing steel stud walls were in place, I framed the roof. I cut out 2x12 rafters to match the full-size layout on the slab that was originally done for framing the east and west walls. The rafters were anchored to the steel walls with 2" long #14 hex head screws (Figure 6-26). These have drill points and I simply drove them up through the upper steel channel from below with a screw gun fitted with a hex-head driver bit. The 2x12s were toenailed to the 2x4 upper plate on the center wall. The reason for using a 2x4 on top of the channel in this location will become apparent when I discuss sealing the house with the Airtight Drywall Approach (ADA) in Chapter 14.

Where window and door headers made it difficult to maneuver the screw gun into place to drive the screws up into the rafters, I used a different approach to attach the rafters. This involved using the same 2" x 2" angle clips that I used with the horizontal bridging. The clips were screwed to the upper channel from above and nailed to the sides of the rafters (Figure 6-27). Figure 6-28 shows all of the rafters in place.

In order to attach wood members to steel in other locations, I found another type of screw helpful (Figure 6-29). Note that it has two wings just above the drill point. During installation, as it bores through the

106

wood, the wings create a slightly wider hole in the wood. As the screw then penetrates the metal, the wings break off and the threads cut their way into the steel. This type of screw allows wood to be pulled tightly against metal. I used them to attach the wood top plate to the center wall and the 2x4 outrigger rafters at the ends of the house (Figure 6-30).

Obtaining Extra Rafter Height

I predrilled the 2x4s that give the rafters their extra height to accept 6" long pole barn nails. Predrilling made it easier to nail them to the 2x12s. I preassembled the 2x4s and 2x12s on the ground then lifted them into place. The extra rafter height was necessary so I would have room for both 12" of insulation and a ventilation space. At least a 2" ventilation space is needed above the insulation to allow any moisture in the roof system to escape through the vented soffits.

48" Rafter Spacing

In most house designs, the rafters are placed 24" on center. By calculating the loading on the 2x12 rafters, I was able to determine that 48" on center was within their carrying capacity. If a plywood roof deck was to be used, it would have sagged between the span of 48", but in the Model Healthy House I used 2x4 purlins for the metal roofing and they easily spanned the distance.

2x4 Purlins

I nailed the 2x4 wood purlins down to the rafters at 24" on center, staggering the joints between the 2x4s so they didn't all fall on the same rafters (Figure 6-31).

In attaching the 2x4 purlins, I let the boards run long at the ends, then cut them off to match the

Figure 6-27
Angle clips attached to a rafter and an upper channel.

Figure 6-28.
House rafters in place.

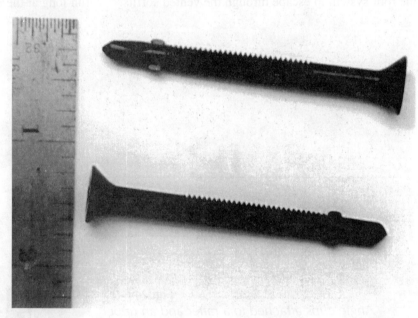

Figure 6-29.
"Winged" drill-point screws.

overhang length shown on Sheet 17 of the Plans. I found a large C-clamp helpful when I nailed the short pieces of fascia blocking to the ends of the purlins (Figure 6-32).

I assembled the short clerestory wall in sections on the ground, then hoisted it up and nailed it in

place (Figure 6-33). Then the roof structure was completed by nailing a 1x6 fascia board around the perimeter to the purlins, the blocking, and the rafter ends. Since I was planning to use large sheets of steel roofing, I took special pains to insure that the roof framing was square.

108

Figure 6-30.
2x4 outrigger rafters attached to end walls.

Figure 6-31.
2x4 roof purlins.

Metal Furring Channel

Since the ceiling drywall couldn't span the 48" spacing between the rafters, I nailed furring channels to the bottom of them at 16" on center. The drywall was later screwed to the channel. A furring channel looks like a hat in cross section, so it is often referred to as "hat channel." Available in 12' lengths, it is screwed together at splices (Figure 6-34). Extra pieces of hat channel are needed at various points for attaching interior non-load-bearing walls that run from east to west. The importance

109

of these will become apparent when the Phase 2 interior framing is done in Chapter 14. Whenever a partition wall runs parallel to the hat channel, and it falls between the 16" spacing, there must be an extra hat channel above the drywall in that area. See the wall-to-ceiling detail on Sheet 13 of the Plans.

Non-Load-Bearing Walls, Phase 1

Next, I built the secondary exterior walls just inside, and parallel to, the load-bearing walls that were built earlier. These walls don't serve to hold up the house so I was able to use the lighter-weight non-

Figure 6-32.
Attaching blocking at purlin ends.

Figure 6-33.
Short clerestory wall.

110

load-bearing studs in building them. The purpose in building this second wall was for energy efficiency— I wanted a wall system that would be 10½" in overall thickness. This entire 10½" thick cavity was later filled with insulation, yielding a superinsulated, very energy-efficient shell.

I built these secondary walls using a different sequence that made assembly somewhat easier. First, the top channel was nailed to the bottom of the rafters, or screwed to the hat channel at the east and west ends (Figure 6-35), and the lower channel was fastened to the floor with concrete expansion anchors.

Figure 6-34.
Splicing two hat channels

Figure 6-35.
Attaching upper non-load-bearing channel to the hat channel.

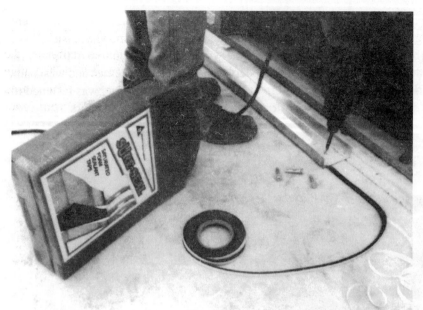

Figure 6-36.
Installing a Sure-Seal gasket under the lower non-load-bearing channel.

Sealant Gaskets

As a part of the Airtight Drywall Approach (ADA), the lower channel needed to be sealed to the concrete slab. This might have been done with caulking, but caulking could get brittle over the years and it is messy to work with. Instead, I used an adhesive-backed gasket designed specifically for this purpose by **Denarco, Inc.** This is the same Sure-Seal foam sealant tape that was used under the outer load-bearing wall as a sill sealer, but it is a little smaller (Figure 6-36). I simply adhered the gasket to the slab before the lower channel was bolted in place. When the channel was tightened down, the gasket was compressed, creating an airtight seal. This little detail may seem unimportant, but it is very critical in making an airtight house. ADA will be discussed more fully in Part 3.

Assembling Non-Load-Bearing Studs

Once the upper and lower channels were installed, I simply popped the studs in place every 24". Instead of screwing the drywall studs and channel together, I used a crimping tool because it went a little quicker (Figure 6-37). With these lightweight studs, the strength of screws isn't really necessary. Also, the thickness of the screw heads can prevent the drywall from being pulled tightly against the studs. With crimping, there are no screw heads to contend with (Figure 6-38).

Door and Window Openings

In non-load-bearing construction, door and window headers aren't necessary. Therefore, window sills and window and door headers can be handled in a similar manner. Rather than cutting through the flanges at 90 degrees as I did with the load-bearing framing, I cut through the flanges at a 45 degree angle 2" from the end, then folded back the web. This gave me an extra tab to crimp to the studs (Figure 6-39). Since the non-load-bearing studs are not very sturdy until the drywall is attached, the tab provides a little extra strength.

Blocking

In places where Phase 2 interior non-load-bearing walls will need to be attached to the Phase 1

112

insulated exterior walls (in Chapter 14), blocking should be added at this stage (behind the drywall) to give them something to attach to. This blocking consists of short lengths of non-load-bearing channel attached between studs in the same manner as the window sills (Figure 6-40).

Garage Framing

Once the house framing was complete, the garage was framed in a similar manner with 20- gauge 3⅝" load-bearing steel studs and channels. I also used the same horizontal bridging and diagonal wind brac-

Figure 6-37.
Crimping tool for non-load-bearing steel framing.

Figure 6-38.
Crimping eliminates screw heads that would interfere with the drywall.

113

Figure 6-39.
Crimping non-load-bearing window sill.

Figure 6-40.
Blocking between studs.

ing as in the house framing. Since the garage didn't particularly need a cathedral ceiling, I used standard wood roof trusses instead of rafters (Figure 6-41). The clerestory wall and rafter extensions were added to match the design of the house. The necessary 2x4s were nailed to the trusses after they were hoisted into place. Since the garage would also have a metal roof, I again used 2x4 purlins rather than a plywood deck. The garage framing, not having a superinsulated double-wall system, represents a less expensive, but less energy-efficient approach to healthy construction that would be acceptable in warmer climates.

114

Figure 6-41.
Completed garage frame.

Porches

I constructed the supporting posts and headers for the house and garage porches out of redwood (see Sheet 12 of the Plans). Being naturally resistant to insect attack, redwood doesn't require any toxic chemical treatments. Unlike most other softwoods, redwood has very little odor and I have found it is often very well tolerated even by most hypersensitive individuals.

The main drawback to using redwood is its higher cost. Many lumber yards don't stock it because of the expense. I have found that some of the outlets that do stock it price it higher than it needs to be. I often get a much better price by special ordering redwood through a lumberyard that doesn't normally handle it. The savings can be from 10-20%. Additional savings can be had by using construction-grade material rather than a knot-free grade.

In order to keep the bottoms of the redwood porch posts dry, I rested them on aluminum supports to separate them from the stone walls (Figure 6-42). For a neater installation, I added a little mortar around the lower portion of the aluminum (Figure 6-43).

Wood Deck

Since I special-ordered all my redwood at the same time, I decided to build the redwood deck now rather than wait until the exterior of the house was complete. The details are shown on Sheet 18 of the Plans.

For the wood posts supporting the deck that are embedded in the ground, I decided to use readily available CCA (Copper Chromated Arsenate) chemically treated pine lumber. I don't normally like to use this material because of it toxic arsenic ingredient, but I felt it would be risky to use redwood in this location. Soil is a very hostile environment for wood, and any wood in the ground is at risk for decay. It seemed to me that a few short posts made of treated lumber would insure that the deck would have a long life. At the same time, since most of their length is underground, they should not affect someone bothered by the odor of the pine. The CCA treatment is more of a problem with direct contact, rather than from its aroma. An alternative to using treated lumber would be to use a concrete foundation, but it is generally a higher-cost option.

115

Figure 6-42.
Redwood porch supports.

Figure 6-43.
Redwood porch supports bedded in mortar.

The joists, decking, seats, and seat supports for the deck were made of construction-grade redwood. If you are on a budget, yet still concerned with your family's health, the joists could probably be made from treated lumber, since they are not in direct contact with anyone sitting on the deck (Figure 6-44).

Children playing on such a deck will be in direct contact only with the redwood seats and deck boards, not the treated support members. However, I would not plant a vegetable garden near a deck containing treated lumber because of the possibility of the plants absorbing the heavy metals from the chemicals.

116

Figure 6-44.
Deck framing.

Figure 6-45.
Completed redwood deck.

The greatest concern in using treated lumber is for the workmen who cut and assemble the material. The manufacturers of CCA material recommend wearing a dust mask and goggles when sawing it, and gloves to avoid splinters. Also, before eating, drinking, or using tobacco products, you should wash exposed areas thoroughly. It is further recommended that clothes be laundered before reuse, and that they be washed separately from other clothing. Sawdust should be cleaned up and chemically treated lumber should never be burned. Figure 6-45 shows the completed redwood deck.

117

Update

Although still not commonplace, steel framing continues to gain a great deal of acceptance among residential builders. This is primarily because steel framing manufacturers and trade organizations have been actively promoting their product. In fact, steel framing advocates often mention the very reasons I selected it—resistance to warping, rot, termites, etc.—but they also talk about its strength in earthquakes and hurricanes, and the fact that a large percentage of steel is routinely recycled.

The only real drawback to using steel framing to come to light is the fact that an individual steel stud (or joist, or rafter) is not very energy efficient. Earlier in this chapter, I mentioned how this could lead to localized areas of high humidity and mold growth which might be seen as vertical shadows on the drywall over each stud. As a result of recent, in-depth research into the energy efficiency of steel framing, it has been determined that energy losses are more serious than was originally believed. But the solution definitely isn't to abandon steel, it is simply to use it a little differently than wood. For example, like I did in the Model Healthy House, you can space framing members apart wider than the standard 16" (I used a 24" spacing for the studs), or build a double-wall framing system. Both of these approaches help minimize heat losses in insulated walls. In addition, researchers have found that using insulated sheathing (such as the various foam boards on the market) on the outside of a wall (under the siding) can improve the energy efficiency of a steel framed wall considerably, when compared to a wall without insulated sheathing. This would be especially important when a single exterior wall system is used (as opposed to a double wall system like I used.).

When I built my first steel framed house (the Model Healthy House was actually the third steel framed house I constructed) there was very little information available about steel framing in residential construction. In fact, after a very frustrating first day of working with it, and repeatedly burning up screws, I was ready to forget the whole thing. Fortunately, a helpful factory representative from a tool company told me that I simply needed to use a slower turning screw gun. After that, everything improved tremendously. I also learned quickly the usefulness of having a chop saw and a crimping tool. As time has passed, the available literature has improved a great deal. For example, the American Iron and Steel Institute now offers a *Residential Steel Framing Manual for Architects, Engineers, and Builders* (listed in Appendix 3) that is filled with loads of useful information that I wish I had when I first started. In addition, training courses are now being offered by manufacturers, home-builders associations, and trade organizations across the country. For more information about steel framing, you can call the Steel Home Hotline at 800-79-STEEL.

Another type of framing I've often been asked about involves using specially designed foam blocks that are stacked up to make a wall, then filled with concrete. There are a number of manufacturers of these products and they each have a slightly different approach. Some look a bit like giant Lego pieces; other systems involve sheets of foam held a few inches apart by plastic spacers. The basic idea is similar. They use a foam insulation material as a form, then fill it with concrete. The concrete provides the wall's strength, and the foam remains in place to provide energy efficiency. All these systems can be easier and faster to use than the conventional way of making concrete walls because the form (the foam) remains part of the wall, so the labor to remove it isn't needed, and no form oil is necessary at all. These systems are designed so that siding can be applied to the outside, drywall to the inside, and various other details have all been worked out by the different producers. In most cases, I think these products can be used in healthy house construction, as long as the interior shell (the drywall) is made airtight. In that way, any outgassing from the foam won't be able to reach the living space. Based on my experience with sensitive people, most of the foam products currently on the market are reasonably well tolerated, especially when covered up, so the outgassing seems to be minimal. These products are never directly exposed to the living space anyway, because fire codes all require that foam products be covered up. One of the early drawbacks to foam products was that carpenter ants liked to tunnel into and nest in the foam. However, many manufacturers now use a relatively low-tox boron-based compound in their formulas to discourage this activity.

Chapter 7

ROOFING

■■■ Roofing materials generally do not contribute to indoor air pollution because roofs are well-separated from the living space. If the roofing material does release pollutants, they will likely be diluted by the outdoor air. However, roofs are exposed to the sun and can get quite hot on a midsummer day. This heat can accelerate any outgassing from the roofing material, some of which can reach the interior of the house. While most roofing does not outgas very much, I have known sensitive people who were affected by some roofing products. For example, I spoke with a woman who had had a new cedar roof put on her house only to find that the aroma of cedar indoors was too much for her. If her house had been made airtight, the odor of the roofing would not have been able to penetrate the interior. With an airtight house, you don't have to be as careful in choosing roofing materials.

Roofing Products

There are a wide variety of roofing materials available today. They vary in appearance, healthfulness, weight, life expectancy, and cost. The healthiest roofing materials are metal, slate, and concrete or clay tile, because they produce little or no outgassing.

Some types of roofing are best installed over a solid roof deck. This is called solid sheathing. Most such decks are made of plywood or oriented-strand board, both of which contain a phenol-formaldehyde glue. A solid deck can also be made from 1x8 boards in order to avoid products with formaldehyde, but this will be more expensive.

Today most wood and slate shingles, as well as concrete and clay tiles, are installed over a solid deck, but in the past they were generally attached to boards spaced several inches apart. This is called "skip sheathing." Skip sheathing enables wood shingles to last longer since they are able to dry out more easily than when they're placed over a solid deck. The faster they dry, the less prone they are to rot. Sheet metal roofs are sometimes also attached to a solid deck, but more often they are mounted to horizontal purlins of either metal or wood. Wood 2x4s spaced 24" or more apart from the eave to the peak are often used as purlins.

Composition Shingles

Composition shingles are the most common residential roofing material on the market today. In the past they were made with asphalt-saturated felt and were called "asphalt shingles." Today, most manufacturers have replaced the felt with a sturdier asphalt-saturated fiberglass mat, so composition shingles are also called "fiberglass shingles."

Composition shingles are produced in a variety of different colors, are reasonably priced, and are easy to install. They will last from 15 to 30 years. How long they actually do last depends on several factors. Fiberglass lasts longer than felt. Heavier-weight or thicker shingles will last longer than thin ones. Dark-colored shingles can get hotter since they to absorb more heat from the sun than light-colored ones; this excessive heat can shorten the shingle's life. Most composition shingles are warranted to last a certain number of years. The longest-lived shingles can cost up to twice as much as those with shorter lives.

All composition shingles contain asphalt and when heated up by the sun can emit some asphalt odors. The amount of odor released is fairly small and rarely even bothers chemically sensitive people, but it is considered a pollutant. If a roof is well-separated from the living space, then the slight smell of asphalt should not reach the occupants. However, in a house with dormers overlooking a roof, as in a Cape Cod design, the odor could easily enter an open dormer window.

Wood Shingles

Wood is also a popular choice for roofs, especially on higher-priced homes. Wood shingles are available in two different styles: smooth sawn or roughly split. Split shingles have more texture and are usually called "shakes." These products can last as long as 50 years, but if improperly installed can fail within 10 years. The best method of installing them is in conjunction with the skip sheathing I mentioned earlier. While this can entail more labor than a solid plywood deck, it is a worthwhile investment. Most roofers are familiar with these techniques. Wood shingles will cost several times more than composition shingles.

By far, most of the wood shingles on the market are made of cedar. Redwood shingles are also available and pine shingles chemically treated against mold and rot have been introduced in recent years. Since wood burns easily, a wood roof can mean higher home insurance premiums. Some wood roofs are chemically treated to render them fire resistant.

Cedar shingles can be quite odorous. Moths are believed avoid the natural aroma of cedar-lined clothes closets, however there is no evidence that cedar will actually repel moths. Because I have spoken to so many chemically sensitive people who are bothered by the cedar odor, I do not recommend them on healthy houses. I also avoid any chemical treatments because rainwater can leach the chemicals out of the wood and direct them down the gutters and downspouts into a yard or garden. Redwood shingles have a milder odor than cedar. Although not widely available, they have the same attractive look as other wood roofing products.

Slate Shingles and Clay Tiles

Slate shingles and clay or concrete roof tiles are non-toxic forms of roofing because they are subject to no outgassing, but they are quite heavy. The extra weight requires a stronger, costlier roof structure. These materials are fairly expensive, but they are also extremely long-lasting. A slate roof can last well over 100 years, so the cost over the life of a house can be fairly reasonable. Synthetic slate is made of cement and wood fibers and is about half the cost of genuine slate. Synthetic slate can last for 50 years and is just as inert. All of these materials are often recommended for healthy houses, but their high initial cost usually restricts their use to more expensive homes.

Metal Roofing

Metal roofing has received an undeserved bad name over the years. This might be because of the cheap metal roofing seen in deteriorating condition on old barns. High-quality metal roofing has been common in Europe for some time and is now starting to catch on in our country. Long-lasting, attractive metal roofing is available across the U.S. in the form of individual shingles or in large sheets.

Metal roofing is manufactured from steel, aluminum, copper, and even stainless steel. It is produced with a variety of durable baked-on finishes that are quite inert. The factory baking process hastens the curing of the paint so that the finished product produces virtually no outgassing. The life of a metal roof can be anywhere from 15 years for a bottom-of-the-line product to 100 years for a copper or stainless steel roof. Most metal roofing will last at least as long as a composition roof. Since stainless steel and copper are the longest-lasting, they are also the most expensive.

A painted metal roof can be periodically repainted to prolong its life, but repainting shouldn't be necessary until a roof is twenty or thirty years old. Since a roof is exposed to a great deal of abuse from weather and ultraviolet light, it must be painted with a long-lasting, durable paint specifically designed for the purpose.

Metal Shingles

Individual metal shingles are made to resemble clay tiles, wood shakes, as well as embossed nineteenth-century styles. The wood shake pattern is the most popular. Metal shingles must generally be ap-

plied over a plywood roof deck, but it is possible to substitute solid wood 1x8s for plywood. Most metal shingles are made of steel with a baked-on finish, so they produce little outgassing.

Sheet Metal Roofing

Besides individual shingles, metal roofing is also sold in long sheets that are up to three feet wide. These panels can be obtained in custom-cut lengths that run in one piece from the ridge to the eave, giving the roof very simple and attractive lines. Sheet metal panels can be sealed to each other for watertight installation with standing seams or with lap joints.

Standing-seam roofing is a top-of-the-line product that is attached with clips that are hidden once the roof is in place. The individual pieces fit together in vertical "standing seams" that shed water (Figure 7-1). Because of the hidden fasteners, this type of sheet metal roofing has a very uncluttered look. Many well-designed buildings are now using standing seam roofs because of their attractive appearance.

Figure 7-1. *Standing-seam roofing.*

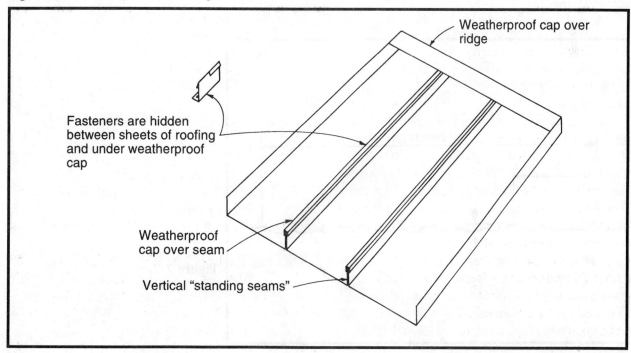

Weatherproof cap over ridge

Fasteners are hidden between sheets of roofing and under weatherproof cap

Weatherproof cap over seam

Vertical "standing seams"

Sheet metal roofing having lap joints between the sheets is a lower cost product because it is generally lighter in weight and easier to install. It is often found on commercial and agricultural buildings, but it is now finding a niche in the residential market. The edges of the long panels lap over each other, and the fasteners (screws or nails) are visible. The cost of this type of metal roofing can be competitive with composition shingles.

Roof Ventilation

Moisture generated indoors by occupants can migrate up through the ceiling into the attic. Most roofs have vents in the gables, at the ridge, or near the ridge to allow this moisture to escape into the atmosphere. This is called roof ventilation. It is necessary because moisture trapped in the attic can result in mold and rot. If a house is made airtight and vaportight, the moisture can't escape from the living space into the attic, so roof ventilation may not be required. Some recent research shows that a tightly constructed, well-insulated cathedral roof system can be safely built without any venting. However, some experts contend that the construction of such a house must be flawless and few houses are built so meticulously. I generally recommend roof ventilation in all houses as a preventive measure.

Roofing for the Model Healthy House

For the least toxic roof, I usually recommend slate, concrete or clay tiles, or metal, but redwood shingles are also quite good. However, since roofing is usually fairly well-separated from the living space, I have had cost-conscious clients opt for an inexpensive roof of composition shingles, then spend extra money on less toxic materials for the interior of the house. Personally, I prefer metal roofs because I find them both attractive and reasonably priced. I used a metal roof on the Model Healthy House.

With the cost of the various roofing materials in mind, I chose sheet metal roofing with lapped seams because it is less expensive than a standing-seam roof. However, this product can be just as attractive, and it is being used more and more on residences. The sheets of the ribbed roofing I selected are simply lapped over each other with seal-

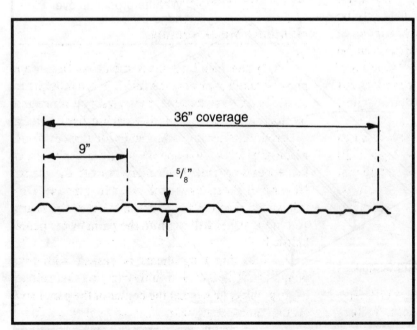

Figure 7-2.
The Pro-Panel shape.

ant tape between them to form a watertight roof. Rather than using hidden fasteners, I attached the sheets with special screws driven into the purlins. An advantage to this type of metal roofing is the fact that it doesn't need to be attached to a plywood or solid-wood deck.

The roofing for the Model Healthy House was produced by **Metal Sales Manufacturing Corporation**. I selected the steel Pro-Panel shape (Figure 7-2) in an attractive dark brown color. The ribs running the length of each sheet give this 29-gauge material its strength. Each sheet will cover an area 36" wide and can be ordered in custom-cut lengths. Having the material cut to length minimizes waste. In the factory, the roofing is manufactured from large coils of flat steel. The coils are fed through forming rollers, then cut to length. Forty feet is about the longest length that is practical. For longer slopes, sheets can be lapped over each other. The Pro-Panel roofing is protected by a four-step painting process utilizing a hot-dipped galvanized (zinc) coating, a zinc-phosphate coating, a primer, and a durable finish coat. It takes about two weeks for the roofing material to be delivered.

Cost Considerations

The actual material cost of Pro-Panel roofing is a little higher than fiberglass shingles. However, savings can be realized due to the fact that it can be fastened to 2x4 purlins rather than a more expensive plywood deck. Also, the large panel sizes can be installed very quickly, resulting in lower labor costs. For new construction, the cost of a metal roof, 2x4 purlins, and labor is similar to composition shingles, a plywood deck, and labor.

Like most manufacturers, **Metal Sales Manufacturing** warrants the paint on its roofing for 20 years, but the roofing itself should last an additional couple decades. In order to extend its life, it can be repainted by a company that specializes in cleaning and painting metal roofing and siding.

Working With Sheet Metal Roofing

Working with sheet metal roofing is different, but no more difficult than installing a roof of fiber-glass shingles. Since many residential builders are unfamiliar with this product, I will cover the techniques in some detail.

Safety and Metal Roofing

One of the main dangers in working with metal roofing is the fact that edges can be sharp and can cut your hands if you are careless. The best precaution is to be careful when handling it or to wear gloves.

Metal roofing can be especially slick when wet from rain or dew. It is safest to work on a metal roof only when it is dry. Even then, it is important for installers to wear shoes with skid-resistant soles for adequate traction.

When walking on a metal roof, it is best to walk so that your weight is supported by the purlins. The Pro-Panel roofing is capable of supporting 153 pounds per square foot of uniform loading with purlins at 24" on center. This is more than enough strength for snow loads, but an average person can exceed that when standing on one foot or walking. Once the screws are in place, it is easy to see where the purlins are located no matter what their spacing. By stepping on screw heads as you walk, you will be directly over the purlins. The screw heads will also provide added traction.

Handling Metal Roofing

When handling sheet metal roofing, care must be taken to protect the finish. Even though the coatings are very durable, they could be scratched by dragging the sheets across each other or along the ground. When unloading individual sheets from a delivery truck, two people should grasp them at the edges and pull them sideways off the stack. Never pull sheets over each other lengthwise. Doing so can result in long scratches since the sharp end of the panel will dig into the paint of the panel below it.

Carrying long sheets is easiest with two people, but I've had no trouble carrying them alone by gripping each edge in the center of the panel and curling them lengthwise.

123

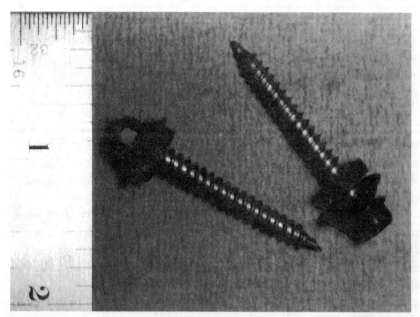

Figure 7-3.
Roofing screws.

Storage

If the roofing panels are not to be used immediately, they should be stored in a dry area. If they are allowed to get wet, moisture trapped between stacked sheets will not be able to evaporate. This could result in water staining. Once the panels are installed on a roof, staining is no longer a problem because the panels can dry uniformly if they get wet from rain or snow.

Fasteners

Special nails are sometimes used to attach metal roofing of this type, but I prefer screws because of their greater holding power (Figure 7-3). Both the nails and screws are sold in the same color as the roofing, and they have a small rubber washer under their head. When the screws or nails are tight against the roof, the washer is compressed slightly, forming an excellent seal. Even though there is a hole in the roof at each fastener, there is no danger of a leak. The screws are installed with a screw gun (Figure 7-4), but they should not be

driven so tightly that they crush the ribs. They only need be snug enough to compress the rubber washer. If you miss a purlin, be sure to remove the screw and seal the hole with 100% silicone caulking.

There should be screws through the overlapping ribs at each purlin. In addition, there should be screws in the flat portion of the roofing. See Figure 7-5 for the correct fastener locations.

Cutting

Usually the last sheet installed on a roof will need to be cut lengthwise in order to fit. Cutting can be done by hand with a pair of tin snips, but it is considerably easier and faster with a portable hand-held electric shear or a pair of power nibblers, something that can usually be rented to make any cuts needed. Shears work like electric scissors and are good for long cuts along the flat part of the sheet (Figure 7-6). Nibblers "nibble" out a small bit of metal at a time and work well either on flat areas or across the ribs. Abrasive wheels in power saws can also be used, but they leave a rough edge.

In some metal roof installations a considerable amount of cutting will be necessary at the job

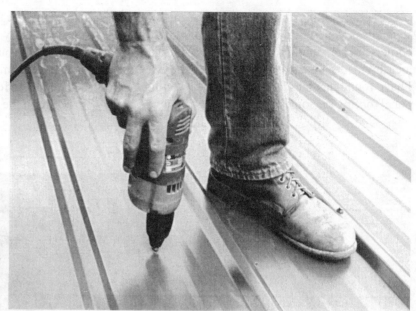

Figure 7-4.
Installing screws with a screw gun.

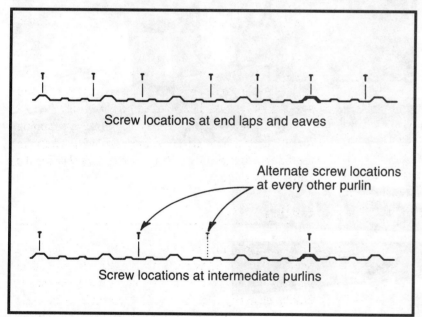

Screw locations at end laps and eaves

Alternate screw locations
at every other purlin

Screw locations at intermediate purlins

Figure 7-5.
Fastener layout.

site. For example, hips and valleys may be easier to fit on the job than by having sheets pre-cut in the factory. Complicated roof designs are best left to a contractor who specializes in metal roofing, but simple shapes like the Model Healthy House are easy for most builders.

The Actual Installation

Because of the relatively large size of the sheets of roofing, the framing for the roof structure must be square if the panels are to fit together evenly. This can be achieved by careful measuring during the construction of the framing. To check a roof for squareness, you need to measure diagonally across the corners. For a simple rectangle, when the diagonal measurements are equal, the structure will be square. I have found that laps between the sheets of the Pro-Panel roofing are somewhat forgiving. When they are lapped over each other, the top or bottom can be shifted slightly from one side to another. With a roof that is a little out of square, it is possible to shift each panel a very small amount to make up the difference. Still, every effort should be made to build a square structure in the first place.

Figure 7-6.
Cutting sheet roofing with an electric shear.

Figure 7-7.
The metal drip edge.

126

Drip Edge

The first step in the roofing installation process involved fastening a standard metal drip edge along the lower edge of the wood roof framing. This is the same product that is used under the lower edge of fiberglass or asphalt composition shingles. It is sometimes called a "starter strip" and it is manufactured in a variety of colors of either steel or aluminum (Figure 7-7). I selected a dark brown color that matched the fascia color. The drip edge is nailed to the lowest 2x4 purlin with galvanized roofing nails.

Figure 7-8.
Pulling the roofing up into place.

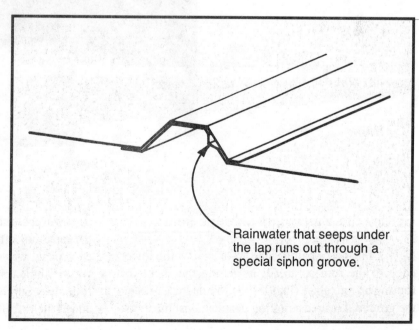

Figure 7-9.
The Pro-Panel lap design.

Rainwater that seeps under the lap runs out through a special siphon groove.

127

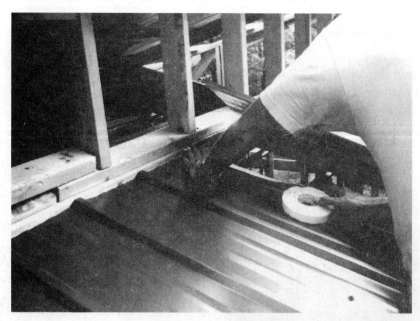

Figure 7-10.
Installing butyl tape between sheets of roofing.

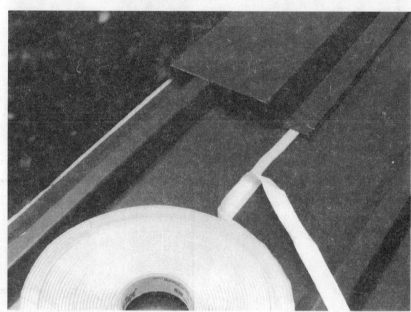

Figure 7-11.
Rake trim and butyl tape.

Getting the Material up onto the Roof

I leaned a pair of long 2x4s against the lower edge of the roof as an aid in getting the sheets of roofing up into place (Figure 7-8). While I was still on the ground, I leaned a roofing panel against the 2x4s.

Then, after climbing up on the roof, I could easily pull the panel up off the ground and into position. Once each panel was on the roof, I temporarily fastened it with a single screw at the top. After I pulled three or four sheets up onto the roof, I squared them up and added the rest of the fasteners. The sheets of roofing

128

Figure 7-12.
Optional rake treatment.

Figure 7-13.
Installing foam gaskets.

aren't heavy but they can be unwieldy, especially if the wind is blowing.

The first sheet of roofing is laid at the end of the house that is downwind of the prevailing breeze. In this way, the wind will not be able to blow under the overlapping seams.

Sealing between Sheets

The Pro-Panel roofing has a specially designed shape to the overlapping ribs so that water will not seep up under the rib by capillary action and result in a leak (Figure 7-9). This feature usually works quite

129

well but I decided to be extra safe and applied an adhesive butyl tape sealant between adjacent sheets of roofing. For a storage building or a garage, a minor leak might not be much of a concern. However, I wanted to make sure that the roof would be as water-tight as possible because even a minor leak could mean mold growth. Butyl sealant tape placed between the laps is an inexpensive way to insure that the roof won't leak. It is readily available in rolls from the roofing manufacturer and is ⅜" to ½" wide and ¹⁄₁₆" thick. It is easily applied between the overlapping ribs. (Figure 7-10).

Figure 7-14.
Peak trim in place.

Figure 7-15.
Clerestory sidewall flashing.

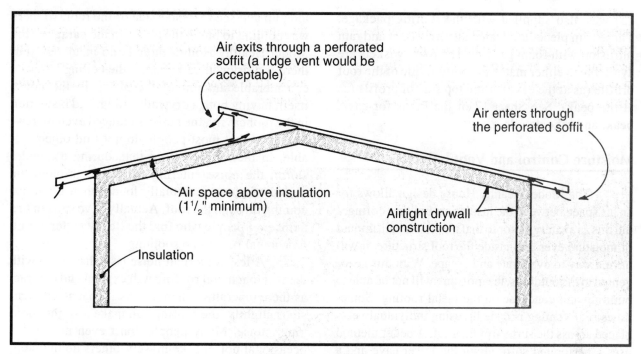

Air exits through a perforated soffit (a ridge vent would be acceptable)

Air enters through the perforated soffit

Air space above insulation (1$\frac{1}{2}$" minimum)

Airtight drywall construction

Insulation

Figure 7-16. *Roof ventilation.*

Rake Trim

To complete the roof, I trimmed the edges (rake) with special sheet metal shapes that arrived with the roofing. Sheet 17 of the Plans shows details for these areas. The trim for the rake extends over the rib in the roofing and is sealed with butyl tape (Figure 7-11). Trim pieces are fastened in place with the same self-sealing screws. **Metal Sales Manufacturing** has many standard shapes for trim and offer custom formed shapes. These can be ordered with the roofing and take about two weeks for delivery.

I used the standard method of trimming the rake in a metal roofing installation by having a cap that covers the rib and extends down the side of the fascia. Where I notched the roofing at the south edge of the garage porch, I used a different method of trimming the rake. This was because of the difficulty of sealing the upper end of a standard trim piece in this location. For this alternative method, when I attached the metal drip edge at the lower eave, I also ran an additional piece of drip edge up the rake. The roofing was then attached directly over the drip edge at the rake with the butyl tape sealant between them.

This alternative method of trimming the rake results in a very smooth appearance (Figure 7-12). It can be used at all rake edges, but it means that the rib must be trimmed off the first sheet of roofing in order to seal it to the drip edge. It also means some extra calculations are necessary prior to starting a roofing job so that the last sheet of roofing doesn't end up with a rib at the edge.

Sealing the Eaves

At the lower edge of the roofing, between the roofing panel and the drip edge, I used pre-formed foam gaskets to keep insects and rain from entering (Figure 7-13). **Metal Sales Manufacturing** stocks these to fit their various roofing profiles. They are slipped in place before the lowest row of screws is tightened down.

Peak Trim

The trim at the peak (Figure 7-14) and where the roofing meets the clerestory sidewall (Figure 7-

131

15) was also supplied with the roofing package. These trim pieces are sealed against insect and rain intrusion with foam gaskets. The foam gaskets are available to either match the bottom side of the roof profile (as at the eave) or the top side of profile (as at the peak). See Sheet 17 of the Plans for eave, peak, and rake details.

Moisture Control and Ventilation

The Model Healthy House design allows for an air space between the insulation and the roofing. I did this as a safety factor so that if even a small amount of moisture ever gets inside the roof structure, it will have a way to evaporate and escape. With this space vented to the outdoors, the moisture will not be able to build up and condense on the metal roofing. Sometimes roof venting is done by using individual vents placed across the surface of the roof. A better method uses a perforated soffit along the lower eave and a continuous vent at the peak. When the roofing is warmed by the sun, natural air currents form in the space under the roof, drawing air in through the soffit at the lower edge and escaping through the ridge vent at the top.

I could have used a standard residential ridge vent but chose a different method that resulted in a somewhat smoother roof line. With the clerestory wall, the overhang at the upper peak contains a perforated soffit that allows the air to escape (Figure 7-16). With this design, I was able to use a simple sheet-metal ridge cap which looked less cluttered than a ridge vent.

Update

The most frequent question I've gotten about metal roofing has to do with noise—particularly in the rain. Yes, the noise of rain falling on a metal roof is louder than rain falling on a roof with composition shingles. In some cases, this can be objectionable—but not always. For example, I've been in agriculture buildings in the rain that had no roof insulation, nor a ceiling, and the noise was quite loud. However, in these buildings, you could

look up and see the underside of the roof, so there was nothing to block the noise. In the garage of the Model Healthy House, there is no insulation, but there *is* a drywall ceiling, and the ceiling blocks a considerable amount of the noise. In the house itself, having both a drywall ceiling, and insulation in the roof cavity, the noise is reduced even more—to a level that most people do not find objectionable. In fact, I've noticed that, during a thunder storm, the noise entering the house through the closed windows is actually louder than the noise coming through the roof. Actually, I've spoken to a number of people who find the steady patter of rain on a metal roof to be soothing.

A less important noise issue has to do with the fact that metal roofing will expand and contract as the temperature changes. As it changes dimensions slightly, the roofing can make a slight "popping" noise. Many people don't even notice this occasional noise. Like myself, others do notice it, but don't find it objectional. However, I know of one individual who finds it very objectional—but he is hypersensitive to a wide variety of sounds that many people might not even notice. The final noise issue has to do with things falling on the roof. I actually resorted to cutting down a gum tree next to a house my wife and I lived in because it occasionally dropped small, hard berries onto the metal roof. During the daytime, we weren't bothered by the sound at all, but at night, when trying to get to sleep, the random sound of a single berry hitting near the top of the roof, followed by the sound of it rolling all the way down to the eave got to be a bit disconcerting. Acorns would have been even more so.

There's something else about metal roofing that I hadn't considered when I first started working with it, but has turned out to be quite advantageous—it can be easily removed. In the metal-roofed house my wife and I lived in, we decided to add a ceiling light in a foyer area. Because the house had a cathedral ceiling, there was no attic to crawl around in for stringing the wiring. So, I simply went up on the roof, removed a few screws, rolled back the appropriate roofing panels, slid the insulation aside, and did all the work from the top side of the ceiling. Then I replaced the insulation, the roofing,

132

the screws, and the job was complete. That wouldn't have been possible with composition shingles over plywood. By the way, removing metal roofing is somewhat easier if none of the sticky butyl tape was used between the overlapping sheets.

I've mentioned that, in many cases, using sheet metal roofing over wood purlins can be in the same cost range as composition shingles over plywood. However, in recent years, more complex roof designs have become quite popular—designs that are characterized by many ridges and valleys.

Using sheet metal roofing on these roofs can be somewhat more expensive because of all the cutting and fitting that is necessary—and the fact that there will be a considerable amount of waste. So, if you're considering metal roofing on a complex roof, it's a good idea to get a cost estimate from someone with adequate experience, and compare the cost with that of a more conventional roof. But keep in mind the fact that if a metal roof is going to last longer than a less costly composition roof, the life-cycle cost can still be reasonable.

Chapter 8

WALL SHEATHING AND WIND BARRIERS

■■■ The exterior walls of a house are usually covered with sheathing, which is then covered with siding. It isn't unusual to find older houses with solid boards for sheathing or no sheathing at all. Today, there are a wide variety of materials used for sheathing, all of which may have a tendency to outgas minor odors. However, since sheathings are always covered with an exterior siding material, they are separated from direct contact with the occupants. Sheathing will generally only be bothersome when the side of a house is warmed by the sun and the sheathing outgasses through gaps in the siding. I consider sheathing to be a fairly minor source of pollution.

Sheathing

One of the most common kinds of sheathing is asphalt-impregnated fiberboard. It is black or dark brown in color and is very fibrous. Gypsum sheathing, a product that resembles drywall, is also brown in color because asphalt is added to the paper to make it water-resistant. Both fiberboard and gypsum sheathings can release small amounts of asphalt odors.

There are several different foam boards that are used for sheathing. Extruded polystyrene (like I used to insulate the foundation of the Model Healthy House), expanded polystyrene (beadboard), and polyisocyanurate are the most common. Even though they are made from synthetic materials and can theoretically outgas small amounts of synthetic chemicals, I have found that many chemically sensitive people tolerate them reasonably well.

Some foam sheathings have a foil facing that tends to minimize outgassing. Foil-faced cardboard is also available for use as sheathing. These products do not outgas very much because the foil acts as a diffusion retarder to the core material. However, it can be risky to use foil-faced sheathings in cold climates because any moisture that migrates through a wall from the interior can condense on the cold foil surface, resulting in mold growth or rot within the wall cavity. Foil-faced sheathing can be used in a cold climate if it is thick enough, but precisely how thick depends on the climate. With a thick material, the surface closest to the interior of the house remains fairly warm—too warm for moisture to condense on it. Foil-faced cardboard is only about ⅛" thick, so it should only be used as sheathing in warmer parts of the U.S.

Plywood and oriented-strand board are also commonly used as sheathing. They contain a phenol-formaldehyde glue that releases formaldehyde.

Sheathing for Structural Purposes

From a structural standpoint, sheathing can be used to provide bracing for a house. I have seen old houses without any sheathing that lean slightly to one side because, over the years, the wind simply pushed them out of square. This is why plywood is often used at the corners of a building. It provides the strength necessary to resist the forces of the wind. In the Model Healthy House, the steel frame is made rigid with diagonal wind bracing, which performs the same function as structural sheathing, so an additional structural sheathing isn't necessary.

Insulative Sheathing

When foam panels are used as sheathing, they add to the insulating ability of the wall. Some builders use plywood at the corners of a house for strength and then fill in between with foam. Foam panels can be used for all of the sheathing on a house if diagonal wind bracing is used at the corners prior to attaching the foam panels. The Model Healthy House has walls that are filled with 10½" of insulation, so it doesn't need the addition of insulative sheathing.

Sheathing as a Stiffener behind Siding

Some siding materials, such as vinyl and aluminum, are not especially stiff. Without sheathing they can be pushed in and out with your hand. With a rigid sheathing behind them, the siding will be much stiffer. In the Model Healthy House I used a heavy-gauge aluminum siding that is sufficiently stiff by itself.

Sheathing as a Wind Barrier

The fourth function of sheathing is to act as a wind barrier. Without some kind of wind barrier, any wind that penetrates the siding will tend to reduce the effectiveness of the insulation. Old houses without any sheathing at all can be especially drafty because the wind blows right through them.

The "house wrap" that is used around many of today's houses, just before the siding is installed,

is a wind barrier. Most of these houses are both sheathed and wrapped. House wrap isn't really necessary if the seams between the panels of sheathing are caulked or taped. After all, the seams are the only places where air can get through a sheathed wall. In the Model Healthy House, I used a separate house wrap, but no sheathing.

Is Sheathing Necessary?

Since sheathing is always covered with siding, any outgassing reaching the occupants will be minimal. With an airtight house (see Part 3), the outgassing can't reach the living space. The only way people can be exposed is when they are outdoors and the siding is warmed by the sun. Once this siding gets warm, the sheathing would also be warmed and it could then outgas through a loose-fitting siding material. While this is a fairly minor consideration, in constructing the Model Healthy House I chose not to use any sheathing. Since sheathing has a number of functions, I simply used different methods to perform the same tasks. I performed all four functions of sheathing with other materials. Diagonal bracing provides strength, extra insulation isn't necessary, heavy gauge siding provides stiffness, and a separate barrier blocks the wind.

Wind Barriers

In the past, when solid boards were used for sheathing, builders often wrapped 36" wide rolls of building paper around the house as a wind barrier. It did a reasonable job of keeping the wind from blowing between the siding boards and into the house. Today, a number of different manufacturers have plastic house wraps that work well as wind barriers. Tyvek is one of several popular brands. Even though the outgassing from such products is minimal, I used an even more inert product—aluminum builders foil.

Builders Foil

The builders foil I used was manufactured by **Reynolds Metals Co.** and is sold in 36" rolls.

136

This material is a kraft paper/aluminum foil sandwich with small pin pricks every ⅛". It is an effective wind barrier, but the pin pricks allow moisture to migrate through it. It is especially important in most climates in the U.S. to allow any moisture from the interior of the house that gets into the wall cavity to escape to the outdoors. With airtight construction, such moisture migration should be minimal, but it is a good idea to allow for it anyway. In very hot climates, where high outdoor humidity can drive moisture into a wall from the exterior, a foil wind barrier should probably not be perforated. It is important that moisture not be allowed to accumulate within a wall cavity because it could easily lead to mold growth or rot.

Builders foil is often sold as a "reflective insulation" because it reflects radiant energy. This helps to insulate a house. The benefit comes primarily in hot climates where the foil will reflect away the radiant energy from the sun, reducing air conditioning requirements. Radiant barriers are much less effective in heating climates. The concept of radiant barriers is rather controversial and there are many exaggerated claims about their effectiveness. A radiant barrier must remain shiny to work, so if the foil ever gets a layer of dust on it, it will no longer function very well. These questions do not apply in our case because we are using it solely as a wind barrier.

Disadvantages of Using Builders Foil without Sheathing

A big disadvantage to using builders foil without sheathing is the fact that it is so easily damaged. It is quite easy for a workman to accidentally poke holes in it or a child to throw rocks through it. It is difficult to police a building site 24 hours a day to prevent such occurrences. Any holes need to be sealed with foil tape before the builders foil is covered with siding. Once it is covered up, the foil is less prone to damage.

If the siding is going to be brick veneer, builders foil is probably not a good idea. With brick veneer, there should be an air space between the brick and the wall framing. If builders foil is used instead of a rigid sheathing material, the foil will billow in and out slightly within this space whenever the wind blows. This will eventually weaken the foil, causing it to deteriorate. If the foil billows out enough to touch the brick veneer, then any moisture on the back of the brick will be transferred to the foil, then to the framing. This defeats the purpose of the airspace. Therefore, a rigid sheathing of some type is generally recommended with brick veneer siding.

Installing the Wind Barrier on the Model Healthy House

Sheet 12 of the Plans shows the detail I used for installing the wind barrier. Basically what is involved is wrapping the exterior of the house with the builders foil and taping all the seams.

Aluminum Foil Tape

In order to prevent the wind from blowing between the 36" wide pieces of builders foil, all of the seams should be sealed with aluminum-foil tape. The barrier is also taped to the inside of door openings and the outside of window openings. The tape was supplied by **Polyken Technologies**. Their aluminum foil tape has often been recommended as being well-tolerated by sensitive people. I used their #339 tape because it has an excellent, long-lasting adhesive. They also have a #337 tape that is a little thinner and uses a different adhesive. These tapes are primarily used by heating and air conditioning contractors for sealing the seams in ductwork, but I use them in a number of places in healthy house construction.

Working with Builders Foil

When I stretched the first row of builders foil across a wall, I held it to the metal studs with small pieces of aluminum foil tape (Figure 8-1), then I added the remaining rows of builders foil in the same manner. Once I had a wall covered with foil, the seams were taped shut. Aluminum foil tape is very sharp

Figure 8-1.
Installing the wind barrier.

Figure 8-2.
Taping seams of the wind barrier.

along its edges and can easily cut your fingers. Rather than smoothing it down with a bare hand, I recommend using a piece of cloth (Figure 8-2). Cotton gloves can also be used as hand protection.

If there is very much wind blowing, I will usually only cover one wall at a time with builders foil.

In a strong wind, it is a good idea to install the siding to that wall before applying the foil to the next wall. Otherwise, a strong wind could rip the foil off and destroy your work.

At the very top of the wall, rather than trying to tape the foil to the wood, I stapled the foil barrier

Figure 8-3.
Stapling the wind barrier to the rafter ends.

Figure 8-4.
Completed wind barrier.

to the ends of the 2x12 rafters to secure it in place. Adhering a piece of foil tape to the barrier, and then stapling through the tape makes for a much stronger attachment that won't tear in the wind nearly as easily (Figure 8-3). Once the wind barrier was in place, the house, looking like it was gift-wrapped, was ready for windows, doors, and siding (Figure 8-4). Personally, I find it fairly difficult and time consuming to install a foil wind barrier, and I don't feel it is really that advantageous. In the future, I will probably use one of the commercially available plastic wind barriers on the market.

139

Update

In this chapter, I've tried to analyze the reasons why sheathing is used, and show why it isn't always necessary. While it didn't come to mind as I was working on this project, I soon realized that there is a reason I missed. It's nice to have rigid sheathing on a multiple-story house to lean a ladder against. With the Model Healthy House being a single story, I mainly worked off a step ladder, but with a taller house, where you need to lean an extension ladder against the wall regularly, the ladder will undoubtedly poke unwanted holes in a wind barrier—unless there is rigid sheathing behind it.

As I stated earlier, it's a lot of work to install a foil wind barrier. And, based on additional experience, I really don't think there is a significant advantage to it. In fact, my wife, Lynn, and I built ourselves a new house recently (see Chapter 28), and we didn't use it. Instead, we used more conventional materials. We installed standard construction-grade plywood at the corners for wind bracing, and filled in between with asphalt-impregnated fiberboard. Lynn, who is chemically sensitive to the outgassing from a wide variety of materials, is bothered by both of these materials when she is directly exposed to them. However, after they have aired out for a short while and are then covered with siding, she is no longer bothered by them—not even when the house is warmed by the sun. I'm certainly aware of situations where individuals are bothered by sheathing but, based on my experiences in working with many hypersensitive people, such cases aren't common.

140

Chapter 9

WINDOWS AND DOORS

■ ■ ■ Windows and doors are not major sources of pollution in houses, but they sometimes contain materials that can contribute to poor indoor air quality. Your choice of windows and doors will also affect the energy efficiency of the house.

Window Frames

Window frames are made from a number of different materials, but vinyl, wood, and aluminum are the most common. They vary in cost, insulating ability, required maintenance, and healthfulness.

Vinyl-Framed Windows

Since they are manufactured from synthetic materials, vinyl window frames are subject to a small amount of outgassing. However, they do have the advantage of being maintenance-free; therefore, they will never need to be painted. Vinyl window frames do not conduct heat very well so they are an energy-efficient choice. In order to minimize outgassing, choose lighter-colored window frames. Darker colors tend to get warmer in the sun, leading to increased outgassing.

Wood-Framed Windows

Wood window frames can be quite attractive, but most are chemically treated with preservatives to make them resistant to mold and mildew. These chemicals can be sealed into the wood fairly well once the windows are painted or varnished, but paints and varnishes have their own outgassing characteristics (see Chapter 21).

Aluminum-Framed Windows

Aluminum window frames are usually either coated with a baked-on finish or anodized. Anodizing is an electrolytic process similar to plating. Both methods result in an inert frame. Aluminum is also durable, attractive, and long-lasting.

Aluminum windows received a bad name when they were originally introduced because they were subject to sweating in the winter. The reason metal window frames "sweat" is that metal is an excellent conductor of heat. In the winter, the frames can get quite cold and moisture from the indoor air will condense on them in the same way it condenses on a glass of iced tea in the summer. Today's high-tech aluminum windows have thermal breaks in the frames.

In effect, they actually consist of two frames separated by an insulating barrier. With a thermal break, the interior of an aluminum window stays warm and dry. This is not only an energy-saving feature but also a health feature as well, since sweating window frames could eventually lead to a mold problem. In climates where sweating is possible, aluminum windows with thermal breaks are far superior to the aluminum windows without them.

Windows and Energy Efficiency

The overall energy efficiency of a window depends on the energy efficiency of the frame and the energy efficiency of the glass. There probably isn't a great deal of difference between wood, vinyl, and aluminum frames with thermal breaks, but aluminum frames without thermal breaks are very inefficient. The energy efficiency of the glass can be improved in several ways. First of all, multiple layers of glass (or sometimes plastic) will create air spaces that increase energy efficiency. This is why storm windows reduce heat loss in the winter—there is an air space between the main window and the storm window. The more air spaces there are, the more efficient the window is, so three panes of glass are better than two.

Energy efficiency can also be increased by coating the glass with a metallic "low E" coating. E stands for emissivity and refers to a window's ability to absorb or reflect radiant energy. Another way to increase the efficiency of the glass is to fill the space between the panes with a gas other than air. Argon and krypton gas are sometimes used and both are inert.

Multiple panes of glass are often separated by metal spacers. Since heat passes through the spacers fairly quickly, some manufacturers are looking at more efficient spacers. Heat loss through spacers can be minimized by choosing windows with two or three large panes rather than a number of smaller panes (as in a Colonial style).

Windows as Fire Escapes

It is a very important safety measure to be able to use windows as fire escapes. As a result, most building codes have requirements that specify a minimum size for windows in bedrooms. Building codes

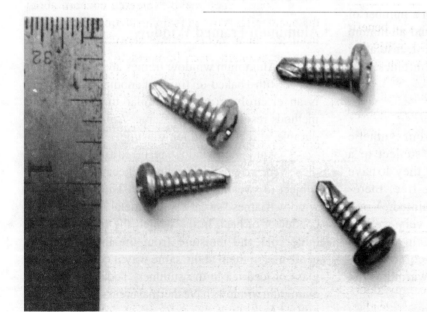

Figure 9-1.
Cadmium-plated screws for siding and windows.

Figure 9-2.
Installing windows.

also often require that the window sill be below a certain height. The code varies in different locales, so be sure to check on the requirements in your area before ordering any windows.

Solar Considerations

Houses in most parts of the U.S. can benefit from solar heating. In the Model Healthy House, the south-facing windows will result in a considerable amount of free heat in the winter. Although solar heating is not an issue directly affecting human health, there are indirect benefits. For example, if more houses had solar heating, outdoor pollution levels would improve because power generating plants could be smaller and less polluting.

Exterior Doors

Like wood-framed windows, most exterior wood doors are chemically treated to render them resistant to mold and mildew, and some wood doors contain a large amount of phenol-formaldehyde glue.

In general, wood doors do not seal as well as metal doors, so they are not as energy-efficient. Since doors are exposed to considerable physical abuse from being opened and closed and from the temperature extremes of the weather, they can require frequent repainting, thus exposing the occupants to volatile chemicals from the finishing materials.

Some people have expressed concern about the health effects of the foam insulations used inside insulated metal doors. While sensitive individuals have occasionally been bothered by such products when directly exposed to them, it should be remembered that a steel skin separates the insulation in a door from occupants. Therefore, any outgassing reaching the occupants should be negligible. Metal doors often have very tight-sealing magnetic weather-stripping, like refrigerator doors—for energy efficiency and to keep out pollutants when they are shut.

Windows and Doors in the Model Healthy House

In the Model Healthy House I used triple-glazed aluminum windows from **Norandex**. The

Figure 9-3.
Entry door with leaded glass window.

Plans called for the windows to be sliders, but single-hung windows that are triple-glazed are readily available. In the garage, I used a **Norandex** #950 Series double-glazed casement window. Since the garage isn't heated, the window located there doesn't need to be as energy-efficient as the windows in the house, but this type of casement window can be fitted with an optional interior-mounted storm window to increase its efficiency. With multiple glazing, all these windows are very energy efficient, making them good environmental choices. The thermally-broken aluminum frames are also the healthiest choices for sensitive individuals.

I ordered all of the windows for the Model Healthy House in a dark brown color, without the optional muntins, but with screens. Some fiberglass window screens have a very strong odor because they are chemically treated with insecticides, but **Norandex** uses healthier, untreated screens.

With the #1100 Series sliding windows, you can remove the screens and all but one panel from the interior of the house for cleaning. The panels are easy to open and close because they slide on adjustable brass rollers. The sliders are available from **Norandex** in sizes ranging from 22" x 22" up to 105" x 58". For the south facing windows I selected the 93" x 46" units. The bedroom windows are 46" x 38" and the casement window in the garage is 24" x 60".

The windows were supplied with a standard nailing flange. To attach them to the steel studs of the Model Healthy House, I simply used screws instead of nails. The screws were cadmium-plated to protect them from corrosion (Figure 9-1). They were easily driven through the flanges into the studs (Figure 9-2). On the wide south-facing windows, I found it necessary to install some thin wood shims under the interior of the frame to prevent the sill of the interior storm panel from sagging.

I selected the high-quality entry doors made by **Stanley Door Systems**. They are energy-efficient, and with their magnetic weather-stripping, are virtually airtight when closed. Both the doors themselves and the aluminum sills have thermal breaks like the windows, so they are energy-efficient and won't sweat. I chose a front door with an attractive leaded-glass window (**Stanley #K20**, Figure 9-3), and a kitchen door with a large clear window (**Stanley #D20**) to allow for maximum visibility outdoors. The entry door for the garage has a smaller window (**Stanley #K10**). All the windows in the doors contain insulated glass. The two doors for the house were ordered with standard jambs and sills suitable for 2x6 wall framing.

Window Installation

There are several rules to follow when installing windows. First, apply a bead of 100% silicone caulk around the perimeter of the frame to seal it to the structure for a weathertight installation. If an aluminum window is being installed in a masonry wall or a steel frame, it must be blocked up slightly off the sill. This will prevent the masonry or steel of the structure from short-circuiting the thermal break in the window frame.

When placing the window in the opening, be sure all of the movable sashes are locked shut. This will help to keep it square. As you fasten it in place, use a level to make sure the unit is plumb and take care not to twist the frame. When installing screws or nails around the perimeter of the window, remember not to use any at the top of the frame because the header above the window could sag over the years and pinch the window frame. This is of more concern with a wood header than a steel header, since wood is more prone to sagging.

Painting the Doors

Because they are more solidly built than most wood doors, metal doors should not need to be painted nearly as often. **Stanley Door Systems** supply their doors with a quality baked-on primer. When I first received the doors, I applied a finish coat immediately so the paint would have a chance to outgas before the house was completed. While there are a number of healthier alternative paints on the market today, I chose an off-the-counter commercial paint. This is

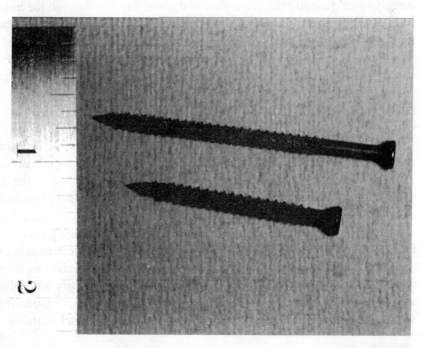

Figure 9-4.
Trim-head screws.

Figure 9-5.
Wide door threshold.

because I don't feel the alternatives are up to handling the weather extremes that a door is subjected to. A sensitive person should test some different brands to see which is the least offensive. In the Model Healthy House, I used a semi-gloss exterior latex paint that was available locally, which seemed to outgas rather quickly. As a general rule, semi-gloss and gloss finishes usually outgas faster than flat finishes. I prefer to spray the paint on the doors for a better-looking finish. As a precaution, I always wear a cartridge-type respirator when applying any paint.

Door Installation

Installing doors in a 10½" thick double-wall system is a little more involved than in a conventional 2x4 wall. Since the doors swing in, they must be flush with the inside finished wall. This results in the outer edges of the jambs being several inches from the exterior of the house. This could be remedied by using jambs that are 11" thick (10½" wall plus ½" drywall). Such wide jambs are not readily available, so I used some of the aluminum siding to fill in. The result is attractive and an easy way to handle most walls that are wider than normal.

The actual door installation in the rough opening of the Model Healthy House is no different from installing a door in any other house except that screws are used instead of nails. When the door frame was plumb and shimmed in the opening, I predrilled pilot holes through the wood, then drove trim-head screws through the holes into the steel studs. Predrilling the wood makes the installation much smoother. Trim screws are the screw counterparts to finish nails. They have a small Phillips head that can be slightly recessed, puttied over, and touched up with a bit of paint (Figure 9-4). I used a screw gun with an adjustable depth collar to drive the screws in so their heads were just below the surface.

The door frame should first be attached to the steel studs at the hinge side. When that side is plumb and solid, the lock side of the door is adjusted for proper clearance and squareness, then it is anchored to the studs. I found that the light-weight non-load-bearing studs were not very rigid when anchoring the door frame because they had no exterior sheathing attached to them. These studs stiffened up tremendously when the drywall was attached (Chapter 13).

Door frames are generally supplied with a "brick molding" trim around the outer perimeter. For

146

the 10½" thick wall installation, I first had to remove the brick molding, then I hung the doors so that they projected ½" into the interior. This way, once the ½" drywall was in place, the interior of the frame was flush with the finished wall. I ordered jambs for the house that were 6⁹⁄₁₆" thick, the standard width for a 2x6 wood wall. With this size jamb, I found that trimming the exterior with pieces of siding was quite easy. See Sheet 11 of the Plans for a detail.

Special Door Threshold

I added an auxiliary aluminum threshold under the standard door threshold to make up for the wide wall at the sill. I had this custom-made at my local sheet metal shop. It was set in two beads of 100% silicone caulk to adhere it to the foundation wall (Figure 9-5). See Sheet 11 of the Plans for dimensions of the special threshold.

Update

At the time I ordered the windows for the Model Healthy House, some of the energy efficiency features that are common today weren't available from many manufacturers. In fact, the manufacturer (**Norandex**) who supplied the windows didn't offer low-E coatings or gas-filled glazing units at that time. Also, a few they soon stopped making aluminum-framed windows altogether. So, to help readers locate windows similar to those I used in the Model Healthy House, I have listed two other window companies in Appendix 2. They both offer windows with low-E coatings and argon-fill—energy savings features I have used successfully on other houses. One thing I should point out is that I have spoken to one hypersensitive person who was bothered by low-E coatings on windows. We were not able to determine precisely why, but she was sensitive to a number of things besides outgassing (electromagnetic fields, for example). Fortunately, this is not a common problem.

Regarding the painting of exterior doors, it was recently suggested to me that metal doors could be coated with automotive paints. These are very durable finishes and are designed to withstand extremes of weather. Some of these paints can be quite toxic to the painter who applies them, so high-quality respiratory protection is mandatory. However, once the finish has been applied, and has cured (curing times vary), it can be quite inert. For the most inert finish, try to locate an automotive body shop that has the facilities to bake on the finish.

Chapter 10

SIDING

■■■ Simply because it is outdoors, the siding on a house will have much less effect on indoor air quality than interior finishing products. However, some siding materials, as well as exterior paints or stains, can outgas bothersome pollutants. While most of this outgassing will dissipate into the atmosphere, the occupants can be exposed when they are outdoors near the siding, or when odors drift indoors through open windows or through a ventilation system. Outgassing from siding will be more noticeable when the siding is warmed by the sun.

Siding Materials

There are a wide variety of sidings available today. They vary in initial cost, the amount of maintenance they require, and healthfulness. Siding materials include vinyl, metal, wood, masonry, stucco, and cement fiber.

Vinyl Siding

Vinyl siding is one of the most popular residential siding materials in use today. Vinyl siding is available in several horizontal and vertical patterns and in a wide variety of colors. Vinyl, especially when it is warmed by the sun, can outgas synthetic odors. This is not a major problem because it is outside the house, but it can be bothersome to some sensitive people. Of course, it is never really a good idea for anyone to breathe synthetic odors anywhere if it can be helped.

Like many plastic materials, when vinyl burns in a house fire, it can release extremely toxic gases. These gases can be of serious concern to firefighters. If given a choice, I will generally recommend something other than vinyl siding. However, I have worked with clients on a budget who elected to use it because of its low cost. Then they spent their limited funds on non-toxic interior products. I agree with their thinking—when compromises must be made, you should spend your money indoors where it will do the most good.

Metal Siding

Both aluminum and steel are popular non-toxic siding materials. Metal siding is durable and available in a variety of long-lasting baked-on colors that have very little outgassing characteristics. It requires little maintenance and is only moderately more expensive than vinyl. Both horizontal and vertical styles are readily available.

I have heard people express their concern that a metal-sided house might expose its occupants to excessive electromagnetic fields from the house's electrical wiring. Some even speculate that a metal-sided house will prevent its occupants from being exposed to the earth's natural background radiation that controls biological rhythms like our sleep/wake cycle. On the other hand, some people feel that a metal-sided house will protect its occupants from being bombarded by radio and television waves.

There may be some truth in all of this, but I have seen no real evidence of a problem with most of my clients. My own house has both metal siding and roofing. Although we do not receive very good radio reception indoors, I haven't been able to measure any unusual electromagnetic fields, and my wife and I have normal sleep patterns. A metal-sided house could definitely be a problem for someone with metal sensitivities. Such sensitivities are not common, but affected people report unusual sensations in their teeth or body when around very much metal. Individuals with metal sensitivities should choose a non-metallic siding.

Wood Siding

Manufactured wood products such as plywood are a popular and reasonably priced siding material. Available in four-foot wide sheets, plywood siding can be smooth or have a textured finish. It may have vertical grooves cut in it, or it may have 1x2 wood battens attached. Plywood siding contains the phenol-formaldehyde glue I discussed in Chapter 4.

Solid wood siding is also popular. Pine, cedar, and redwood are the primary species used for solid wood siding, although other locally grown woods are sometimes available. Solid wood siding contains no formaldehyde-based glue.

There are drawbacks to all types of wood siding, with or without formaldehyde glue. Wood is an absorbent material. It can become quite wet in the rain and, depending on the climate, may dry very slowly. The longer wood siding remains wet, the more susceptible it is to mold and rot. When two pieces of

siding overlap (as with clapboards), the area between the two pieces can trap moisture. In arid climates, wood siding can dry out quickly, but in most cases, it is a good idea to coat wood siding with a finish to prevent damage from moisture absorption. In fact, many experts recommend priming clapboard siding on the back side prior to installation.

A variety of paints and stains can be found on the market today suitable for wood siding. Unfortunately, these materials will expose occupants to volatile organic chemicals (VOCs) each time the siding is recoated. With paints, this may be every 7-8 years, but with stains it could be as often as every 2-3 years. Clear finishes may need recoating every year because of their susceptibility to degradation from the sun's ultraviolet rays.

For an existing house with wood siding, I usually recommend using a high-quality water-based paint. Because exterior finishes are subject to a considerable amount of abuse from the weather and ultraviolet rays, they must be very durable. I feel that the major paint manufacturers have formulas that are better able to protect wood siding for longer periods of time than the alternative "environmental" finishes currently on the market, which are not as durable. It may be necessary for people sensitive to paint odors to leave the house when it is being repainted. Depending on the person's degree of sensitivity, this could take anywhere from a few days to a couple months. Extremely sensitive people will probably want to re-do the siding with a healthy material rather than go into "paint exile."

Masonry Siding

Masonry products like brick and stone are generally very inert and require virtually no maintenance. Most houses built today with masonry exteriors are actually framed out of wood (or steel). The masonry is then added as a facing. This is called masonry veneer.

Brick is vulnerable to moisture penetration. Leakage can occur around improperly flashed windows and doors, or through cracks in the masonry itself. Also, brick and mortar are porous, so a certain amount of moisture can pass directly through the wall. Because of this, brick veneer walls should be built with an air space between the brick and the frame wall. This air space is typically 1" deep. If this space were completely empty, 1" would be sufficient, but the cavity often becomes partially filled with mortar droppings during construction. A 2" space between brick veneer and a steel-stud wall is now being recommended by some researchers because of the fact that steel can be permanently damaged by moisture penetration.

A brick wall should also have "weep holes" at the bottom. Weep holes are simply small ¼" to ⅜" holes in the mortar. They are occasionally lined with short pieces of plastic or copper tubing. Water that penetrates the masonry wall will run down the back side and drain back to the outdoors through these holes. Weep holes can easily become clogged during construction with mortar droppings, or later with debris or insect nests. They should be checked periodically and cleaned with a length of stiff wire when necessary.

If these precautions are not taken, the wall framing behind masonry veneer can be damaged by moisture. A wood-framed wall can be somewhat forgiving, because it can dry out after getting wet, and

only with persistent moisture is it at risk for mold or rot. A steel-framed wall, however, is less forgiving; once steel starts to rust through the galvanized coating, it can be permanently weakened.

Stucco

Stucco can be a non-toxic siding choice. A traditional stucco installation involves mixing cement, lime, sand, and water, and applying two or three coats to make a 1" thick layer on the outside of a building. This can yield a very inert wall. Modern stucco mixes may be based on the traditional formula, but with added synthetic admixtures to improve workability or durability. These admixtures may only comprise a few percent of a stucco mixture, so they generally have few outgassing characteristics. However, very sensitive people should test a stucco mix containing admixtures for personal tolerance.

There are also stucco-type products on the market that contain no lime or cement whatsoever. They are composed of synthetic plastic resins mixed with sand or gravel. These resins are often two-part mixtures that, by means of a chemical reaction, cure into a relatively inert product. They can, however, still

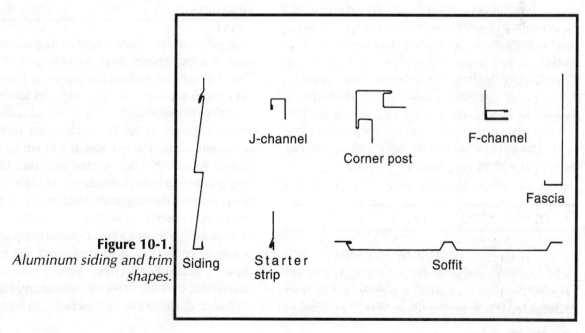

Figure 10-1.
Aluminum siding and trim shapes.

J-channel

Corner post

F-channel

Fascia

Siding

Starter strip

Soffit

Figure 10-2.
Installing the starter strip.

be subject to some outgassing, so they should be used with care. My first choice would be to use a traditional stucco mix without admixtures, but sometimes the synthetic mixtures can be acceptable.

Cement Fiber Siding

Cement fiber siding is virtually the same thing as the artificial slate roofing I mentioned in Chapter 7. It is a cement product, somewhat like concrete, that is reinforced with wood fibers. It is quite inert, and although it used to be more commonly sold as roofing, it is now also available as siding. It can be purchased as individual wall shingles or as clapboards. This material does not require painting, but it comes in a limited range of colors, so you might want to consider painting it with conventional exterior paints.

Siding the Model Healthy House

For the Model Healthy House, I selected a horizontal double 4" American Classic aluminum siding in a light brown Sandlewood color produced by **Reynolds Metals Co.** The baked-on color finish is generally quite

well-tolerated even by sensitive individuals. Since I didn't use any exterior sheathing on the house, I ordered a heavier 0.024" thick siding for additional strength. The standard product is 0.019" thick. Since my walls were quite well insulated, I ordered the siding without the addition of foam insulation on the back side.

Fasteners

When aluminum siding is attached to steel studs, there is some concern about possible galvanic action. This is a corrosion process that can occur between two different metals—in this case steel and aluminum. It should be remembered that the galvanized coating helps protect the steel in the same way paint protects the aluminum siding. The two metals will not be in direct contact with each other because the wind barrier of builders foil will be between them. But fasteners form a bridge between the aluminum siding and the steel frame. In coastal climates, this connection could result in localized rusting. By using cadmium-plated screws, the possibility of corrosion can be minimized, but in severe climates, steel siding may be a better choice. For most parts of the country, however, aluminum siding over steel studs should not be a problem.

Figure 10-3.
Capping the end of a corner post.

Figure 10-4.
A finished window installation.

My own house has aluminum siding over a steel frame. I was curious as to how the screws were holding up, so after about five years, I removed some of the siding to see how the fasteners were doing. I found no signs of corrosion or rusting on the siding, the studs, or the screws.

Installing Aluminum Siding

Figure 10-1 shows the various siding and trim shapes that I used on the Model Healthy House. An aluminum siding installation begins at the bottom with the corner posts being attached first then the starter strip (Figure 10-2). On a new house this is fairly straightforward, but on an older house with uneven wall heights, you must establish a straight reference line around the perimeter of the house before attaching the starter strip. I trimmed the ends of the corner pieces so I could fold over two tabs to prevent insects from nesting inside them. This also strengthens the corners (Figure 10-3).

J-channels are used around windows and doors for a finished appearance (Figure 10-4). They can be mitered at the corners. I used 100% silicone caulking behind the J-channel in these locations to prevent water intrusion. A sometimes-overlooked detail at windows is the addition of a small piece of aluminum flashing under the J-channel at the bottom of the window. The flashing should be long enough to lap over the first complete row of siding below it. This will direct out from behind the siding any rain penetration at the channel (Figure 10-5). This piece of flashing can usually be cut from a scrap of siding.

At the top of the north and south walls, I ran the siding up as far as I could, then covered the top edge with an F-channel. The F-channel, the soffit, the fascia, and the guttering all are the same dark Federal Brown color from **Reynolds Metals Co.** On the east and west walls, I used J-channel under the F-channel to trim the gables (Figure 10-6). These areas are shown in more detail on Sheet 17 of the Plans.

Once all the trim was in place, I attached the siding itself to the studs, starting at the rear corner of the house so the laps between the sheets would be away from the front, making them less visible.

Since aluminum is known to expand and contract with temperature changes, an allowance must be made for this when it is installed. A ten-foot length of siding will be about 1/8" shorter at ten degrees below zero than it will be at 100 degrees. This may not seem like much, but if the siding is rigidly anchored to the wall, unsightly buckles can form at different times of the year. To prevent this, siding is manufactured with

Figure 10-5. *Flashing at windows.*

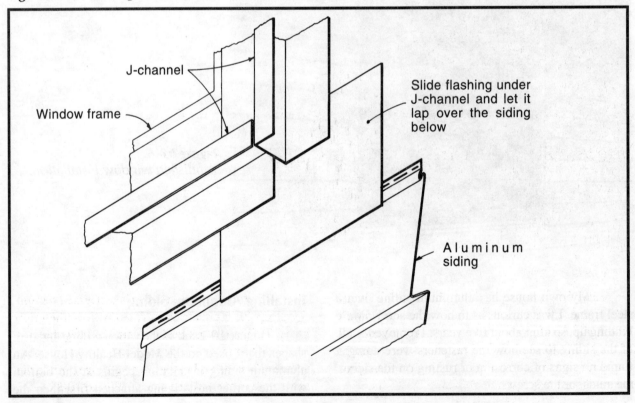

154

Figure 10-6.
Installing J-channel and F-channel at the gables.

Figure 10-7.
Installing the siding.

horizontal mounting slots along the top edge. In attaching the siding to the framing members, I didn't tighten the self-tapping cadmium-plated screws all the way down (Figure 10-7). This allows for the slight seasonal movement of the siding. This standard procedure should be known to all siding installers.

Cutting aluminum siding is performed with tin snips or with a circular saw fitted with a fine-tooth blade. Tin snips work best for small or irregular cuts and a saw works well for long cuts, or where more accuracy is needed. I made a wooden jig to guide the saw so the cuts would be square (Figure 10-8).

155

Soffits and Fascia

Once I had all the siding in place, I installed the aluminum soffit and fascia. An F-channel was run around the perimeter and attached to the framing. Then the soffit was slipped into the channel and nailed to the 1x6 fascia board (Figure 10-9). I used aluminum nails to minimize the chances of any corrosion. The aluminum fascia was slipped over the 1x6, and tacked in place from below with brown aluminum trim nails. Figure 10-10 shows how the upper edge of the fascia fits under the steel roofing's drip edge. I used soffit

Figure 10-8.
Cutting the siding.

Figure 10-9.
Installing the soffit.

156

material that is perforated so air could enter and leave the roof structure easily. This is important so that any moisture that migrates into the roof system from the interior of the house can escape. With an airtight house, such moisture intrusion should be minimal, but I feel that ventilating a roof is still a good idea.

I installed the porch lights for the garage and main entry at the same time as the soffits (Figure 10-11) because it was convenient to do so then. I used recessed lighting fixtures so that there would be nothing protruding downward that could be struck by someone carrying a package.

Figure 10-10.
Fascia in place.

Figure 10-11.
A recessed porch light.

Figure 10-12.
Installing gutters.

Caulking

Because I used 100% silicone caulking underneath all of the J-channel at all of the window and door openings, additional caulking in those areas was unnecessary. I did caulk around the door thresholds and the wide door jambs to insure that rain wouldn't penetrate those areas. No other caulking was needed on the exterior of the house.

Gutters

Adding gutters to the house completed the exterior (Figure 10-12). They were nailed to the rafter ends. There are downspouts located at each of the four corners of the house. In order to help direct rainwater exiting the downspouts away from the house foundation, I used a precast concrete splash block at the base of each downspout. The gutters and downspouts are the same Federal Brown color as the soffit and fascia trim and they were also supplied by **Reynolds Metals Co.** This completed the exterior of the house. I then completed the exterior of the garage with aluminum siding and gutters in a similar manner.

Update

I mentioned in this chapter that I removed some of the siding on my own house after about five years to see if there was any corrosion around the fasteners. Being able to remove the siding in this way has proved to be quite handy—just as I found that being able to remove the roofing was handy (see the "Update" in Chapter 7). For example, a situation arose where I needed to run an electric wire from the main electrical power panel in the center of my house to another building. What I did was remove some metal roofing, snake a wire down to the power panel, then run the wire under the roofing. When I got to the end wall, I simply unscrewed and removed some of the siding, ran the wire down to the ground inside the wall, then into a trench toward the other building. To do this in a house where the siding is nailed in place would end up damaging or destroying the siding, as the nails aren't as easy to remove as screws. While this certainly isn't a health feature, it is one of the advantages to assembling a house with screws and steel framing.

Regarding stucco, there is a synthetic stucco product on the market called EIFS, which stands for

158

"exterior insulation finish system," and is pronounced *eefs*. The installation of EIFS involves attaching foam insulation board to the exterior of a house then applying a layer of synthetic stucco. While this sounds simple enough, it has evolved into a serious problem—so much so that it has caused serious rotting in hundreds of houses—primarily in rainy climates. North Carolina has been hit particularly hard with EIFS failures. As it turns out, the difficulty is all in the details because EIFS is extremely susceptible to having water get behind it wherever it meets another material. In other words, if the details aren't correct, moisture can get behind the EIFS wherever it meets a door or window frame. Once the water gets behind it, it can't always easily get out, with the result being mold and rot. After millions of dollars in damage, claims, blame, denials, lawsuits, and repairs, manufacturers have made some serious changes in their installation recommendations. They now claim that EIFS can be installed successfully. I remain skeptical—I'd still be leery of it in a rainy climate, but it seems to work well in dry areas, like the southwestern U.S.

PART 3: AIRTIGHT CONSTRUCTION

Chapter 11

THE AIRTIGHT HOUSE

■■■ Airtight house construction has evolved over a number of decades. When sheet goods like drywall, plywood, and foam panels came into use, houses could be built with fewer gaps and cracks than were common in houses 100 years ago. During the energy crisis of the 1970s, houses were "tightened" even further. As the cost of energy skyrocketed, caulking, insulation, and storm windows were added to millions of homes. The new tight houses saved fuel, but people living in them began to get sick. It was suggested that houses had become "too tight" and that they should be built a little "looser." This was a simplistic response to a more complicated situation. The real problem was that houses were being built with polluting materials and without provisions to supply the occupants with fresh air. When one examines how the laws of physics apply to houses, it becomes apparent that a tighter structure is actually a very good idea.

An Unhealthy Airtight House

If an airtight house has no ventilation system, indoor humidity can be quite high because the moisture has no way of escaping. The moisture generated from showering, laundry, and washing dishes just keeps building up. In extreme cases, high indoor humidity levels have caused drywall nailheads to rust away and the drywall to fall off the walls and ceilings. High humidity can lead to mold growth on window frames and other surfaces, including furnishings. Carpet laid on a concrete floor slab can be especially susceptible to mold when indoor humidities are high. If unchecked, mold growth can result in rotting wood.

Moisture problems are not an inevitable side effect of an airtight house. The cause of moisture problems is not tight construction but lack of ventilation. Unhealthy airtight houses are filled with bad air because there is no ventilation system to remove the pollutants that are released by noxious building materials.

Simplified Example of Healthy House Construction

Imagine a hermetically sealed box made of polluting materials. If you lived in that box, you would quickly run out of fresh air as you breathed polluted air. This is how the early airtight houses were constructed. If you build the box out of inert materials, the

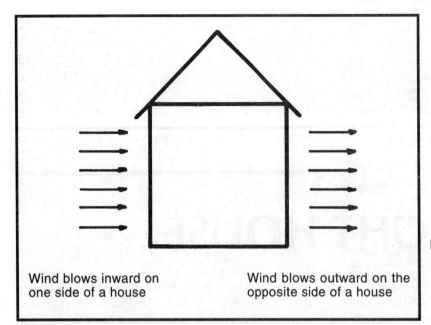

Wind blows inward on
one side of a house

Wind blows outward on the
opposite side of a house

Figure 11-1.
Wind pressures on a building.

situation improves, but you would still eventually run out of fresh air. Now add two holes in the box. One hole has a fan blowing fresh air into the box; the other has a fan blowing stale air out of the box. That is the basic principle of healthy house construction: build an inert, airtight house and use fans to provide the fresh air. Even with the expense of electricity to run the fans, this is usually more cost-effective from an energy standpoint than building a leaky house and relying on infiltration for fresh air.

Energy Efficiency

In most climates a well-insulated house is a very good idea. An energy-efficient house will reduce your utility bills during the heating season in places as far north as Canada and during the air-conditioning season in the summer as far south as Florida. However, there are negative health effects associated with most insulating materials. Even though insulation is located within the wall cavities, air passing through the wall of a loosely built house can pick up bits of insulation or odors from inside the wall and bring them into the occupied space. In an airtight house,

insulation levels can be as high as you want and it will not migrate into the living space because there are no gaps or cracks for it to travel through. Of course, even in an airtight house, it would be foolish to tempt fate by using an extremely noxious insulation.

Water Vapor Control

Airtight houses are desirable for a number of technical reasons. One of the most important is that they allow for better control of water vapor. All houses have moisture generated in them. The sources include human respiration and perspiration, bathing, washing dishes, and doing the laundry. In a loosely built house, this moisture leaks through the random gaps in the structure and eventually reaches the outdoors. In cold weather, the temperature of the moisture-laden air indoors is about 70 degrees, while the outdoor air is much colder. As the humid air passes through a wall, it gets cooler as it nears the outdoors. When it reaches the outer sheathing it can be so cold that the water vapor will start to condense into a liquid. Since this occurs hidden inside the wall cavity, it won't be noticed until some damage has been done.

164

A similar problem can occur in a hot climate when the outdoor air is very humid. This is because air can pass into a loosely built house as easily as it can leak out. If a house in a hot climate is air-conditioned, the humid outdoor air can pass through the wall and condense on the back of the cool drywall. The end result is the same as in the winter in a cold climate—water inside the wall cavity.

How Air Moves Naturally

In order for air to move naturally in and out of a house, two things must be available: an air-pressure difference and holes of some kind. In a loosely built house, there are plenty of holes, even though they may not be visible. They are located around windows, doors, electrical outlets, and plumbing lines. There are only two naturally occurring phenomena that cause air-pressure differences: wind and stack effect.

Wind

Most obviously, an air-pressure difference can be caused by the wind. When the wind blows, it will force air through the holes on one side of the house. On the opposite side, the air will escape through another set of holes. Air entering the house is called infiltration, while air exiting is called exfiltration. Infiltration and exfiltration always occur together (Figure 11-1).

Stack Effect

The other naturally occurring phenomena that can cause an air-pressure difference, and can force air into or out of a house, is called "stack effect." Most people know that warm air rises because it is lighter (less dense) than cold air. In the winter, the warm air in a house rises and escapes (exfiltrates) through holes in the upper half of the house. This causes denser, cold outdoor air to infiltrate at the bottom of the house. The whole house acts like a giant chimney, with air moving in at the bottom and escaping at the top (Figure 11-2).

Stack effect works only if there is a temperature difference between the outdoors and the indoors. There is no air-pressure difference due to stack effect in the spring or fall when indoor-outdoor temperatures are similar.

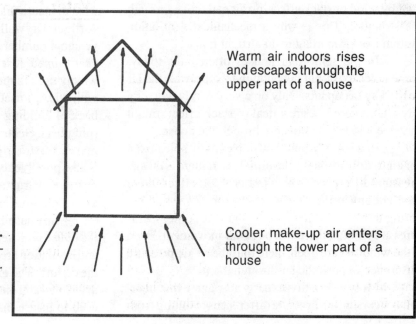

Figure 11-2. *Stack effect pressures on a building.*

Warm air indoors rises and escapes through the upper part of a house

Cooler make-up air enters through the lower part of a house

A good analogy that helps explain stack effect is to think of a house as a hot air balloon. If it is filled with warm air, the warm air will push up on the roof, trying to lift the house off the ground. In a loosely built house, the warm air will seep out (exfiltrate) through holes in the upper half of the house. A balloon is flexible so, if it had holes, it would deflate, but in a rigid structure like a house, when air exfiltrates at the top, an equal amount of air must infiltrate through the bottom of the house.

In an air-conditioned house in the summer, stack effect actually works in reverse because it is cool indoors and warm outdoors. The heavy cool indoor air falls to the floor and exfiltrates at the bottom of the house while the lighter warm outdoor air infiltrates at the top. Stack effect isn't as dramatic in the summer because the temperature difference between indoors and outdoors usually isn't as great as it is in the winter in cold northern climates. The greater the temperature difference, the greater the air-pressure difference generated by stack effect.

Why You Shouldn't Rely on Natural Phenomena to Supply Fresh Air

In an airtight house, there are no holes. No matter how strong the air-pressure differences generated by wind or stack effect, no air can move through the structure. This is why a mechanical ventilation system is so important in an airtight house.

In the semi-tight houses often built today, some holes exist, but not enough to supply all the air needed by occupants. Only on a very windy day, or a day when there is a great deal of stack effect, might there be enough air flowing through the house.

In a loosely built house plenty of holes exist for air to flow through. Nevertheless, if there is no air-pressure difference from wind or stack effect, there won't be any infiltration or exfiltration. On a windless spring or fall day when indoor and outdoor temperatures are similar, there will be no air movement. Even if the windows are open, there must be an air-pressure difference to push the air through them.

Most ventilation experts now agree that naturally occurring air-pressure differences resulting from wind and stack effect are too unreliable to supply a house with fresh air. There are either too many times when the air-pressure differences are too weak to do any good, or there are not enough holes in the house to supply the occupants with sufficient fresh air, no matter how strong the air-pressure differences are.

Control of Indoor Air

Control of indoor air is an important health consideration. In an airtight house, infiltration and exfiltration are minimized. A mechanical ventilation system then becomes very important because it is the only source of fresh air. A mechanical ventilation system can be turned off and on by the occupants as needed, just like the ventilation systems in our automobiles. In the Model Healthy House, mechanical ventilation is coupled with a state-of-the-art air filtration system so that the outdoor air will be cleaned of any pollutants before it enters the house. The homeowner will have maximum control over the indoor air.

Airtight Construction Using the Two-Phase Technique

In the Model Healthy House, the technique I used to insure that the house was airtight is called the Airtight Drywall Approach (ADA). ADA was invented a number of years ago in Canada by an engineer named Joseph Lstiburek, and it is now being widely used in the U.S. In order to show how to build with ADA, I used a two-phase technique. The drawback of building in two phases is that some workers (plumbers, electricians, drywall workers) will need to make an extra trip to the job. A single-phase process is also possible, but I felt that using two phases would be more instructive for someone who has never built an airtight house before.

In Phase 1, the load-bearing walls are built and the house is closed in. The wiring, plumbing, ducting, and insulation are installed in all the exterior walls and the ceiling. The exterior walls and the ceiling are then drywalled and the seams taped. Special techniques are used to insure that the gaps around windows, doors,

Figure 11-3.
Ventilation ducts.

electrical outlets, and other penetrations are adequately sealed. At this point, the house might look like one giant room. It will be possible to walk around the interior and make sure that there are no holes in the structure. In Phase 2, the interior walls are framed, wired, plumbed, and finished in the normal sequence. The end result doesn't look any different than conventional construction, but the two-phase process makes ADA easy to understand. I'll discuss ADA more fully in later chapters.

Alternative ADA Techniques

There are a number of different ways ADA can be used to seal up a house. The method I chose is by far the easiest to visualize. However, it can be inconvenient because it requires various subcontractors such as plumbers and electricians to make an extra trip to the job site. It also requires them to schedule their work so that Phases 1 and 2 can dovetail efficiently.

It is possible to build an airtight house with ADA using more conventional scheduling. This can make the job of the subcontractors somewhat easier, but more care is necessary to make sure that all potential holes are sealed. The easiest way to use conventional scheduling it is to assign the job of airtightness to one person. He can then review the books on the subject listed in Appendix 3 (*The Airtight House* or the various *Field Guides* or *Builder's Field Guides*) and plan out how they apply to the project. For crawl space or basement construction, it will involve placing **Denarco, Inc.** Sure-Seal gaskets at various points between framing members as the floor system is built. This is not difficult for framing crews to accomplish as long as they are told what to do. If the electricians use the airtight electrical boxes on the insulated walls and ceilings that were made by **Nu-Tek Plastics, Inc.**, those areas will need no further attention. Other openings can be sealed with caulking.

If a house is framed in a conventional manner, with all the interior partition walls in place prior to any drywall installation, a gasketing technique can be used to seal the drywall throughout the house. Just before the drywall is hung, a single workman can apply the Sure-Seal gaskets to all the necessary surfaces. At this time, he should also seal wiring or plumbing penetrations that will be hidden

167

Figure 11-4.
Terminus of ventilation ducts.

once the drywall is in place. Drywall installation can then be performed in the usual manner. These techniques are covered in more detail in the two books mentioned above.

As long as the worker in charge of air sealing understands the concepts and carries them out correctly, ADA can be used in a variety of ways to seal up a house. Which methods are used are not as important as carrying them out conscientiously.

Phase 1 Rough-In in the Model Healthy House

Once the house was closed in, I roughed in the portions of the ventilation, plumbing, electrical, and other systems that penetrated the exterior insulated shell. I refer to this as the Phase 1 rough-in and it is covered in this chapter. For a discussion of the health aspects associated with these systems, see Chapters 15-19. After the Phase 1 rough-in was complete, the insulation was installed (Chapter 12). Then the insulated walls and ceilings were covered with drywall and all the penetrations were properly sealed (Chapter 13). The result was a single large

airtight room. This completed Phase 1. During Phase 2, the interior partition walls were built, the remaining rough-in work for all the systems was finished, and the house was completed.

Ventilation Rough-In

I stubbed the various ventilation ducts through the siding and terminated them about 2" inside where the drywall would be hung (Figure 11-3). There were two 6" round ducts for the heat recovery ventilator, two 3¼" x 10" ducts (for the range hood and one of the bathroom fans), and a 4" round duct for the other bathroom fan. All ducts were galvanized steel and all seams were sealed with the same #339 aluminum foil tape by **Polyken Technologies** that I used on the wind barrier. This was done to insure that pollutants couldn't leak into the ductwork. Because these sections of ducting were eventually hidden within the structure of the house, this was the only time it was possible to tape them.

The various ducts all terminate at the outdoors in the clerestory wall (Figure 11-4). They are more weathertight in this location than they would be if they penetrated the roof. The fresh air intake for the heat

168

recovery ventilator (HRV) is at the western end of the house, well-separated from all the exhaust ducts, so there is no danger of cross-contamination.

Sheet 5 of the Plans shows where the ductwork penetrates the drywall. In most cases, the dimensions aren't critical. The locations can vary by a few inches without causing any difficulty because the equipment itself can be moved slightly. The range hood outlet, however, should be located where shown so it will align properly with the hood itself.

The two 6" weather hoods were supplied by **Nutech Energy Systems, Inc.**, the manufacturer of our HRV. They have protective insect screening, but do not have backdraft dampers. The other weather hoods are all standard, readily available items, and do have backdraft dampers.

Plumbing Supply Rough-In

The only plumbing supply line that penetrated the exterior walls was the ½" copper water line that served the outdoor faucet. Located near the redwood deck, it was stubbed through the drywall in such a place that it would later be hidden inside the wall between the kitchen and dining room (Figure 11-5).

Solar Water Heater Rough-In

The Copper Cricket solar water heater made by **Sage Advance Corp.** has a roof-mounted collector that I installed at this time (Figure 11-6) and a solar pad that was installed later when the water heater was hooked up. (See Chapter 25 for details) These components are interconnected by using two insulated ¾" copper lines. One line carries a cold coolant up to the collector and the other returns the heated coolant back down to the solar pad. During operation, the coolant continually circulates back and forth.

At this time I extended the two ¾" copper lines down from the collector through the roof so they would reach just past the drywall. I used two lengths of flexible copper which were provided by **Sage Advance Corp.** with the solar water heater installation kit and soldered them in place. These two lines were then insulated with the thick pipe insulation also provided.

Sage Advance Corp. includes a very complete installation manual that describes how to mount the collector on a variety of different roofs. This particular installation involved driving 4 lag

Figure 11-5.
Outdoor faucet rough-in.

screws through the collector's legs, through the metal roofing and into the 2x4 purlins. I used 100% silicone caulking to insure there would be no roof leaks. In the installation kit, the manufacturer even provides a rubber boot and mastic to seal the opening where the two ¾" lines pass through the roofing.

Plumbing Drain/Vent Rough-In

Next, I ran the 3" PVC plumbing vent through the roof. The roofing supplier, **Metal Sales Manufacturing**, provided a special rubber roof jack to seal the pipe to the metal roof. The roof jack is

Figure 11-6.
Solar collector on roof.

Figure 11-7.
Plumbing vent with roof jack. (Radon removal tube in clerestory wall.)

designed so it can be formed over the ribs in the roofing no matter where the vent penetrates it. To be extra safe, I applied a bead of 100% silicone caulk around the perimeter to prevent any leakage (Figure 11-7). As with the ventilation ducts, the plumbing vent pipe was terminated just inside where the ceiling drywall would be hung. I didn't connect it to the 3" pipe coming through the floor slab until later, after the ceiling drywall was in place. Even though this vent pipe will later be connected to the 3" pipe in the floor slab, it is not aligned directly above it. The reason is discussed in Chapter 16.

Figure 11-8.
Plumbing vent and radon removal tube rough-in.

Figure 11-9.
Electrical rough-in through the upper channel of the center wall.

171

Figure 11-10.
Electrical rough-in where wires penetrate a Phase 2 wall.

Figure 11-11.
Airtight electrical box.

Radon Removal Fan Rough-In

The 4" PVC line for a possible future radon fan was stubbed through the same way as the plumbing vent. It terminated outdoors at the clerestory wall where it was caulked to the siding. It was placed under the overhang of the roof, where it will be protected from the weather if a fan is ever attached to it. Figure 11-8 shows both the plumbing vent and radon fan pipes in place. The 4" radon line through the ceiling is offset from the 4" line in the floor slab (see also Chapter 16).

172

Figure 11-12.
Airtight ceiling electrical box.

Central Vacuum Rough-In

The only portion of the central vacuum installed during Phase 1 was the 2" PVC exhaust tube. Supplied by **Beam Industries** it terminates in the clerestory wall near the other exhaust equipment. It should be noted that this PVC tubing, the elbows, and the other fittings are a different size than the material used for plumbing lines. It is made specifically for central vacuum systems.

Electrical Rough-In

In Phase 1, the only electrical wiring that was installed was what was in the insulated walls and ceiling. Where it was later necessary to connect a wire to an electrical box on another wall, the wire was routed along the ceiling and through the upper channel of the center wall. I was careful to mark each such wire as to its final destination. Once all of the wires were in place, I used 100% silicone caulking to seal them to the metal track for an airtight seal (Figure 11-9). The caulking also protects the wire from being cut by the sharp edges of the steel. In a few places, wires were aligned with

blocking so they could run into one of the Phase 2 walls (Figure 11-10).

All of the television outlets contain both a 75-ohm coax cable and a 4-wire antenna cable. This gives the occupants the flexibility of locating the antenna rotor control near any television set in the house.

I installed the base for the electric meter and the main disconnect switch on the outside of the house, then stubbed the main service entrance power cable through the upper center wall channel. At this time, I also ran the necessary electric and telephone lines underground to the garage. The garage has its own electrical sub-panel and was wired in a conventional manner.

The outdoor receptacle box near the wood deck was also installed at this time, as was a junction box with a blank cover near the outlet of the radon-removal tube on the clerestory wall. This will be used to power a radon-removal fan if it is ever necessary to install one. I also located a junction box on the east exterior wall for the television hook-up. In this case, it will be later connected to an antenna. It could also be connected to a cable system or a satellite dish.

173

Airtight Electrical Boxes

All of the electrical boxes that were installed in the insulated walls or ceiling were designed especially for airtight construction. Supplied by **Nu-Tek Plastics, Inc.** they have a foam gasket where the wires are inserted. The gasket is slit with a knife, the wires are pushed through, then a small bead of caulk is used to seal any gaps between the wire and the gasket. There is also a gasketed flange around the face of the box (Figure 11-11). When the drywall is installed tightly against the flange, an airtight seal is formed between the electrical box and the drywall. These unique electrical boxes are available in single- and double-gang sizes, as well as round ceiling boxes. While they may seem like a small item, these airtight electrical boxes are quite important. Without them, it is very difficult to prevent infiltration and exfiltration around conventional metal or plastic electrical boxes.

In order to locate the round ceiling boxes in between rafters, I mounted them to short lengths of metal studs that I nailed between the 2x12 rafters (Figure 11-12).

Clothes Dryer Rough-In

The 4" metal duct for the clothes dryer was stubbed through the north exterior wall. It has a damper flapper on the outside to prevent unwanted air from entering when the dryer isn't operating. Once the Phase 2 walls were erected, the dryer vent was extended inside a 6" wall that contained various plumbing lines.

Air Conditioning and Telephone Rough-In

The last bit of rough-in I did in Phase 1 was to install two short lengths of PVC pipe through the north wall in the vicinity of the electric meter. The 3" pipe will be used for the air conditioner refrigerant lines and the other (a 1" pipe) will be used for the incoming telephone lines. They extended just inside the drywall and were caulked to the aluminum siding to prevent rain from entering. Figure 11-13 shows these two stubs, along with the 4" metal dryer vent.

Once all the preparatory work was done, it was time for the insulation to be installed. But first, I applied a low-tox insecticide.

Figure 11-13.
Dryer, air conditioner, and telephone rough-in.

Figure 11-14.
Boric acid insect control.

Boric Acid

Boric acid is an excellent insecticide for ants and cockroaches and is less toxic than many conventional insecticides. There are several manufacturers who package boric acid powder for this purpose. It is usually sold through hardware stores. I like to poke a few nail holes in the lid and sprinkle it inside the exterior walls before the insulation is installed (Figure 11-14). In this location it will be totally isolated from homeowners and pets, but it will kill any insects that find their way into the wall from the outdoors. Many synthetic pesticides lose their potency over time and need to be reapplied, but boric acid will be effective as long as it is in the wall.

Rough-In Summary

The following list contains everything that was installed as a part of the Phase 1 rough-in.

Qty.	Item
12	Receptacles, indoors
1	Receptacle, outdoors
1	Electrical box for radon fan, outdoors
1	Double switch box, indoors
1	Single switch box, indoors

Qty.	Item
8	Ceiling lights, indoors
1	Front porch light, outdoors
1	Deck light, outdoors
4	TV outlets, indoors
1	TV junction box, outdoors
1	Doorbell button, outdoors
1	Elect. disconnect for air conditioner, outdoors
1	200-amp electric meter base, outdoors
1	200-amp main disconnect, outdoors
1	Main electrical panel, indoors
1	Entrance cable from disconnect to electrical panel
1	Feed cable from electrical panel to garage and all wiring in garage
1	Freezeproof faucet, outdoors
1	Solar collector on roof
2	¾" insulated collector pipes through ceiling
1	3" PVC plumbing vent through ceiling
1	4" PVC radon-removal tube through ceiling
1	3" PVC for air-conditioner lines at north wall
1	2" PVC central vacuum exhaust at clerestory wall
1	1" PVC for telephone lines through north wall
2	6" ducts for HRV at clerestory wall
1	4" duct for bath fan at clerestory wall
1	4" dryer vent through north wall
1	3¼" x 10" duct for bath fan at clerestory wall
1	3¼" x 10" duct for range hood at clerestory wall

175

Update

Airtight construction continues to gain in popularity among builders throughout North America, yet it is still not commonplace. Thus, I still routinely hear people say that houses are too tight, that they should be built looser. So, here's another way of stating my case. Picture a house with an attached garage on one side, a crawl space under it, and an attic on top. If this is a loosely built house, a good percentage of the air you will be breathing in the living space will have traveled from the outdoors, then through the garage, the crawl space, and the attic on its way to you inside the living space. Now, think about all the noxious items in a typical garage: gasoline, lawn chemicals, paints, solvents, etc. Then think about all the mold in the crawl space and the dust, insects, and loose insulation in the attic. You really don't want to be breathing this kind of stuff on a regular basis. Well, with tight construction and a mechanical ventilation system, you don't have to.

I mentioned in this chapter how I sealed the ventilation ducts with aluminum-foil tape. Sealing ducts is a very important thing to do, but there is a growing body of evidence that duct tape (either the fabric variety, or the aluminum-foil type) is not the best product to use. The

reason has to do with the fact that tape often deteriorates and falls off after a while. I have seen situations where it has come off after less than a year. In the Model Healthy House, I've checked the tape and, fortunately, it has remained in place. I attribute the fact that it's still functioning correctly to the high quality tape used, and that the ducts were brand new and very clean. On older ducts, where the galvanized surface has started to oxidize, there is an excellent chance that no tape will last. So, to insure that ducts will remain sealed, and I won't have to worry about redoing them sometime in the future, I've switched from using aluminum-foil tape to using a water-based duct-sealing mastic (Figure 11-15). These mastics are available from heating/cooling equipment outlets.

Unfortunately, **Sage Advance Corp.**, the manufacturer of the Copper Cricket solar water heater I used, has gone out of business, so the Copper Cricket is no longer on the market. However, while this was a definite energy saving feature of the Model Healthy House, it was not a health feature. So, building a house without this feature will not compromise the indoor air quality.

The airtight electrical boxes that I used are no longer available through **Nu-Tek Plastics, Inc.** However, they are still readily available and are distributed by a different company that I've listed with an address and phone number in Appendix 2.

Figure 11-15.
Applying duct sealing mastic.

176

Chapter 12

INSULATION

■■■ Insulations are made from dozens of different materials, and there are negative health effects associated with most of them. In most cases insulation stays inside walls or ceilings where it was placed. However, there have been instances in which insulation has migrated into the living space during installation or remodeling, and cases where insulation moves through the gaps and cracks in the walls or into ductwork, causing health problems for occupants. On the whole however, insulation installers are at greater risk than occupants of insulated houses.

Insulating materials

Even though insulation is not usually a problem, many people are concerned about the negative health effects which can potentially be very serious. Therefore, I will cover the most common residential insulations on the market today (foam products, cellulose, and fiberglass) as well as alternative products.

Foam Insulation

Expanded polystyrene (beadboard), extruded polystyrene, and polyisocyanurate are the usual rigid foam insulating boards that are available today. I discussed some of these materials in Chapter 6 in conjunction with the foundation and in Chapter 9 as sheathing. They all outgas small amounts of chemicals that, in theory, can cause reactions in sensitive individuals. Surprisingly, I have found that when sensitive people are exposed to these products, they are often not affected. Apparently, the rate of outgassing is so slow that the concentration of airborne chemicals is too low to be a problem.

Polyisocyanurate foam is currently manufactured with a CFC chemical that damages the ozone layer. Until recently, all manufacturers of extruded polystyrene used similar chemicals, but they have begun switching to HCFC chemicals that have 94% less potential for ozone depletion. They still aren't perfect, but there has been considerable improvement. Expanded polystyrene uses pentane, a hydrocarbon gas, instead of CFCs or HCFCs. The pentane can contribute to localized smog but has almost no effect on the ozone layer because of its short lifetime in the atmosphere.

Foam insulation is also available in a form that can be injected into walls, ceilings, or floors by trained installers. It typically has the consistency of shaving cream when installed, then hardens to a rigid or semi-rigid product. The most notorious of these foam insulations was urea-formaldehyde foam insulation (UFFI). This material was popular during the energy crisis of the 1970s. Unfortunately, when improperly installed, it released large amounts of formaldehyde into the indoor air. I once spoke with a very conscientious installer of this material who felt that, in his opinion, it was impossible to install it correctly. He said it was so tricky to work with that you either got a great deal of shrinkage, which meant that it didn't insulate very well, or it gave off formaldehyde gas. Because of these drawbacks, UFFI has virtually disappeared from use.

Air-Krete is a relatively new foam insulation available in some parts of the country. Like UFFI, it is injected into wall cavities where it hardens. Unlike UFFI, it is quite benign. Air-Krete releases no formaldehyde and is well tolerated by most sensitive people. Air-Krete is a very lightweight cement-like product, so it outgasses very little, but it is quite expensive, costing up to six times more than fiberglass insulation.

Cellulose Insulation

Cellulose insulation is made from recycled newspapers that often contain toxic inks. It is chemically treated (usually with boron compounds) to make it fire-resistant and to discourage insects from nesting in it. There are actually very few regulations dealing with cellulose insulation, so it could become contaminated with virtually anything.

Cellulose insulation can be installed in two different ways—wet or dry. The dry method, used most often in existing houses, involves "blowing" the insulation through hoses into small holes drilled in the side of a house. The holes are then plugged. Since dry cellulose is a very finely ground material, during installation it can filter its way through gaps in the structure into the living space where it will be breathed by the occupants. This can be minimized by requiring the installer to have an assistant indoors at all times to watch for any insulation that is getting into the house. If any material enters the occupied space, work should stop immediately until any leakage points are sealed. Special care should be taken when insulating walls to

which cabinets or indoor soffits are attached, near false ceilings, and around ducts.

Wet cellulose is more suited to new construction. The insulation, moistened with water and/or a small amount of glue, is sprayed into wall cavities before they are enclosed. It must be allowed to dry thoroughly before being covered up or the excess moisture will encourage mold growth.

There are a number of cases of people becoming ill after their house was insulated with cellulose insulation. In the cases I am aware of, dry cellulose was the culprit. It became a problem because it did not remain within the wall or roof cavity. During installation it filtered into the living space where it was breathed by the occupants. In one case, the furnace ductwork was accidentally filled. When the furnace was turned on, the fan blew cellulose throughout the house.

Fiberglass Insulation

One of the most publicized concerns about the health effects of insulation has to do with fiberglass. There is scientific evidence that suggests that fiberglass can cause lung cancer in much the same way as asbestos. This is based on the proposition that asbestos causes cancer not because of what it is, but because of its small fiber size (Very small fibers can be inhaled deeply into the lungs, where they become lodged and damage tissue). Some people now believe fiberglass can also cause lung cancer when the glass fibers are small enough.

Two types of fiberglass insulation are commonly used in houses: fiberglass batts and a chopped fiberglass product. The batts are usually placed between the framing members of a house before the walls are enclosed. Chopped fiberglass can be poured out in an attic or blown into the wall cavities of existing houses through small holes drilled in the walls, in the same way dry cellulose insulation is installed. Most of the health concerns are linked to chopped fiberglass insulation because of its small fiber size. Because of the way it can be blown into the walls of existing houses, it is more likely to enter the living space. For chopped fiberglass, I suggest the same precautions as those used with dry cellulose.

178

Figure 12-1.
Safety equipment required when working with fiberglass.

Fiberglass batt insulation is held together with a formaldehyde-based resin that can release small amounts of formaldehyde gas. This has been a concern to many sensitive individuals. I have heard it said that yellow fiberglass is less noxious than pink insulation, but after researching the various products, I found no significant difference.

Alternative Insulations

There are many kinds of materials that can be used to insulate houses, such as feathers, sawdust, or straw. Most turn out not to be very suitable because they are prone to insect attack. Natural cork is insect-resistant, but it is relatively scarce and fairly expensive. Air-Krete is considered an alternative product.

One of the newest alternative insulations on the market is made from cotton. Cotton batt insulation is actually made of a cotton/polyester blend. It usually has a bluish color from recycled jeans. Since cotton is flammable, it must be chemically treated to render it flame-resistant. The chemicals are similar to those used on cellulose insulation. Although they don't seem to outgas in the conventional sense, if cotton insulation is sniffed, the flame-retardant chemicals will leave a biting sensation in your nose. Cotton batt insulation is equivalent in price to fiberglass, but it is not widely available, so additional shipping costs are involved.

Working with Insulation

Even if fiberglass doesn't cause lung cancer, it is definitely an irritant and certain precautions are necessary when working with it. The following are recommended by fiberglass manufacturers. You should use a tightly fitting respirator because the fibers can irritate the respiratory tract (Small fibers can easily get around a loose fitting respirator). You should wear eye protection because fiberglass can irritate the eyes. Wear long-sleeved, loose-fitting clothing and gloves because fiberglass can irritate the skin. Wash with soap and warm water after handling to remove particles from the skin. Launder work clothes separately and wipe out the washer to avoid contaminating other clothes. Very few workers follow these simple safety precautions.

Figure 12-1 shows how I protect myself when dealing with fiberglass insulation. I would recommend these same precautions when working with any kind of insulation capable of being dusty—fiberglass, cotton, or cellulose.

Most packages of batt insulation (cotton or fiberglass) are compressed for shipping. When the package is opened, the batts must be fluffed up to their full thickness by slapping the sides of the batts or shaking them. For example, twelve-inch thick batts are slightly over 6" thick directly out of the package, but they easily fluff up to 12". Unless at the proper thickness, they will not have full insulating value.

Insulating the Model Healthy House

After analyzing all of the options, I decided to use fiberglass batt insulation in the Model Healthy House. The decision was not based solely on the healthfulness of the material, because there are healthier alternatives. Air-Krete is less noxious but its high cost and limited availability discouraged me from using it. Cotton insulation is another option, but it too is not widely available.

With an airtight house having a good diffusion retarder (see Chapter 13), I have found that it really doesn't matter what kind of insulation you use inside the walls because it simply cannot migrate into the living space. If it can't reach the interior of the house, it can't affect the occupants. Of course, I wouldn't recommend an extremely hazardous product like UFFI.

From building other healthy houses for sensitive individuals, I have found that if you use airtight construction techniques, it is possible to use a less-than-healthy insulation and not worry about it contaminating the living space. Therefore, I based my selection of fiberglass on its insulating ability, cost, ease of installation, availability, and my personal past experience—always keeping in mind its potential health effects.

Superinsulation

An airtight house is more energy-efficient than a loosely built house because it can be designed to have the proper amount of ventilation—neither too much, nor too little. For the Model Healthy House, I decided to go the extra mile and use enough added insulation—enough to be called superinsulation—so that the future homeowners would have a very low

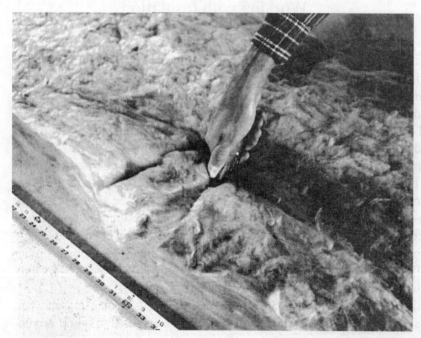

Figure 12-2.
Cutting fiberglass.

heating bill. Superinsulation is healthy for the homeowner's pocketbook and it places less demand on the supply of electricity. And if all houses were superinsulated, electric utilities would have less need to build new, polluting generating plants or to increase the capacity of existing plants.

Considering the way I constructed the 10½" thick superinsulated double exterior wall system (Chapter 6), I was able to use approximately three times as much insulation as is typically found in a 2x4 wall. The roof is also insulated considerably better than average.

Figure 12-3.
Fiberglass and steel framing.

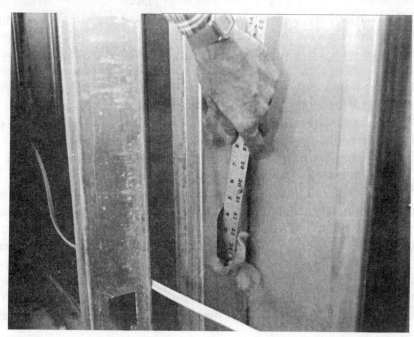

Figure 12-4.
Stuffing fiberglass inside a pair of steel studs.

181

Figure 12-5.
Insulation complete.

Ordering the Correct Size

Most builders use fiberglass batts that are 14½" or 22½" wide. This is to allow for the thickness of a 2x4 (1½") in wood framing that is spaced 16" or 24" on center. I used steel wall studs placed 24" on center. Steel studs are quite thin, so I ordered batts that were a full 24" wide by 3½" thick. They are rated at R-11, and because the walls contain three layers of these batts, the total R-value is 33. By using the recently developed, and more expensive, R-15 batts (also 3½" thick), the same wall thickness could have had an R-45 insulating value. I considered the new batts, but decided that R-33 was sufficient for the Indiana climate.

Since my 2x12 rafters were spaced 48" on center, I used 24" wide batts there also and compressed the edges slightly to make them fit. The batts used in the roof structure were 12" thick and rated at R-38.

Many fiberglass batts are sold with a kraft paper or aluminum foil facing. Because I used drywall with a foil diffusion retarder laminated to the back side of it (more on that in the next chapter),

there was no need for a second diffusion retarder inside the wall. Therefore, I ordered all the fiberglass batt insulation unfaced.

Cutting Fiberglass

When cutting the fiberglass insulation to size, I found that a utility knife worked well cutting directly on the concrete slab (Figure 12-2). The concrete wore down the point somewhat, but it still cut easily. Wherever there were electrical outlets, I was careful to fit the insulation closely in order to eliminate any gaps. Air spaces do not insulate nearly as well as fiberglass.

Ceiling Batts

I installed the 12" fiberglass batts in the ceiling prior to insulating the walls. The batts were simply laid in place on top of the hat channel. I found that when working overhead, it was especially important to wear eye protection. My goggles quickly became coated with fine glass fibers. I normally wear glasses, but they weren't sufficient to keep the fibers out of my eyes. Goggles are a must.

182

Wall Batts

For the walls, I first placed batts vertically in the outer wall of load-bearing studs. Then I added a second layer horizontally between the two exterior walls. The third layer was placed vertically between the studs of the inner wall (Figure 12-3). This method seemed to work easily and resulted in a full 10½" of insulation in the walls.

Where two steel studs were located next to each other, I stuffed scraps of fiberglass inside them with a metal yardstick (Figure 12-4).

The Smell of Formaldehyde

Once the entire house was insulated (Figure 12-5), a noticeable odor of formaldehyde pervaded the indoors. Workers are advised to have plenty of ventilation when working with fiberglass batts, and a cartridge-style face mask is an excellent precaution. I have seen no research on how long it takes for the formaldehyde odor of insulation to dissipate, but once the drywall was hung and sealed, the insulation was isolated from the living space and the smell of formaldehyde disappeared.

Update

Insulation continues to be a topic of interest among many people concerned about their health. While it isn't often a health problem in houses, I attribute the interest to the massive negative publicity in the 1970s that was heaped on one particular type of insulation—urea-formaldehyde foam insulation (UFFI). Although UFFI has long been off the market, a fear of insulation seems to lives on. One of the results has been the introduction of various less-toxic products. Unfortunately, one of these newer insulations—cotton—is no longer available.

Apparently there wasn't enough demand to justify producing it. However, the fiberglass insulation industry has responded to the negative publicity surrounding their product, and begun offering a less hazardous fiberglass batt insulation. While it isn't yet produced in a wide variety of sizes, it can be used in many situations. To minimize contact with the fiberglass itself, it is packaged in a finely perforated plastic sleeve. (The perforations minimize moisture problems.) It is also made by a different process, so it doesn't require any type of formaldehyde-based resin binder. Instead it is made from longer, springier strands of fiberglass that are less likely to become airborne and enter deeply into an exposed person's lungs.

Even with the healthier products currently on the market, it is still important to build a house in an airtight manner. This is for several reasons, but primarily to minimize moisture problems hidden inside wall cavities. And put quite simply, airtight houses (with mechanical ventilation systems) give you the most control of the air indoors, so they are the healthiest houses that can be built.

As I mentioned in the "Update" at the end of Chapter 6, the most recent research into steel framing shows that the heat loss through each stud is somewhat greater than it is with wood framing. So, in order to minimize heat losses, if I were building this same house today, I believe I would consider using fiberglass batts with a higher R-value. (I used three layers of R-11 batts in the walls, and today I would consider switching to R-15 batts.) However, I believe that more benefit would be obtained by using an insulating sheathing. As I mentioned in the "Update" at the end of Chapter 8, I can't really justify the extra labor involved with installing a foil air barrier on the outside of a house, so I believe—if I were doing it today—I'd use a foam board sheathing instead of the foil wind barrier, and seal the seams with caulking.

Chapter 13

DIFFUSION RETARDERS AND DRYWALL

■■■ I've already discussed how airtight houses minimize problems from moisture migrating from the living space into wall cavities, and how they help prevent pollutants from migrating into the living space. This chapter discusses diffusion retarders. A diffusion retarder prevents gases or vapors from passing through a solid surface. A diffusion retarder is different from an air barrier, although the same material sometimes can perform both functions.

Difference Between Air Barriers and Diffusion Retarders

A great deal of confusion exists among homeowners, as well as many builders and designers, about what constitutes a barrier (or retarder) and how they function. I still see incorrect information on this subject in national magazines, although the incidence of such misinformation has begun to decrease the past few years.

An air barrier is anything that stops air movement. It can be made of drywall, metal, glass, paper, or virtually any other solid material. In an airtight house, several different materials usually make up the air barrier. The key to their effective use lies in combining or joining the various pieces together so there are no gaps between them. Since a variety of solid materials can be used, the process of putting pieces together to create an air barrier is more important than what the pieces are actually made of.

Gases and vapors can actually move (diffuse) through solid materials, but the speed with which they do so varies. For example, water vapor or formaldehyde gas will diffuse through a piece of paper much faster than through a piece of plastic or metal. If you are only interested in stopping the diffusion of gases and vapors, the diffusion retarder doesn't need to be airtight. Two pieces of plastic lapped over one another make an excellent diffusion retarder even if they aren't taped or caulked. With a diffusion retarder, the type of material used is more important than how the material is assembled.

Which Is More Important, Air Barriers or Diffusion Retarders?

As it turns out, air barriers are far more effective in stopping pollutants and moisture than diffusion retarders. This is because many more gas and vapor molecules can pass through the gaps and cracks in a house than will diffuse through solid surfaces. That is not to say that diffusion retarders aren't important, because they are. Air barriers just happen to play a more critically important role than diffusion retarders in safeguarding your house—in fact, a role a hundred times more critical.

To understand why an air barrier is so much more critical than a diffusion retarder, consider an inflated balloon. If you untie the stem, the air escapes very quickly—even if you pinch it partially shut. If the stem is tightly knotted, the air will still escape slowly by diffusing through the surface of the balloon. This may take several days because diffusion is a such a slow process. A balloon with a metallic surface will lose air slower than an ordinary latex balloon because metal is a better diffusion retarder than latex. However, making the balloon airtight by tying a tight knot is still the most important thing to do to keep air in the balloon.

Most builders have been using diffusion retarders in homes for years, but they have been calling them "moisture barriers" or "moisture retarders." Sometimes they use insulation with an asphalt-impregnated paper facing for this purpose. Other times they use large pieces of plastic sheeting (visqueen is popular). Although they are called moisture barriers (or retarders), they also prevent gases such as formaldehyde from diffusing through a wall.

While it is commendable that diffusion retarders are so widely used, many builders are not addressing the more important issue—air barriers. Diffusion retarders are easy to install, but it takes a little more thought and care to create an air barrier—and often there is a lot of confusion about the difference.

Diffusion Retarders

As I've stated, gases and vapors travel through different materials at different rates. With diffusion, the direction they travel depends on their concentration. They always move from an area of high concentration to one of low concentration. If there is a great deal of formaldehyde inside a house, but none outdoors, the formaldehyde will move from the indoors through the wall toward the outdoors. If it is humid outdoors and dry indoors, water vapor will travel from the outdoors toward the indoors. With diffusion, there

can be some gases moving in one direction, and other gases moving in the opposite direction simultaneously, depending on their concentrations.

Diffusion retarders prevent gases and vapors from passing through solid surfaces. They are often rated in "perms" (short for permeance). Poor diffusion retarders have high perm ratings. For example, with a rating of 20 perms, standard drywall isn't a very good diffusion retarder. Polyethylene has a fairly low perm rating of 0.08. Glass and metals have perm ratings of zero, meaning that they are perfect diffusion retarders. A perm is defined specifically in relation to water vapor, but similar ratings could be obtained for formaldehyde and other gases.

Polyethylene plastic sheets installed behind drywall work quite well as diffusion retarders. However, one drawback to using polyethylene is the fact that it can deteriorate inside the wall. (For example, polyethylene can degrade if exposed to heat from a nearby baseboard heater or electric range.) Fortunately, a polyethylene sheet that is damaged will generally still be a good diffusion retarder. To be effective, a diffusion retarder need not be perfect.

Diffusion Retarders in Different Climates

The primary reason a diffusion retarder is installed is to prevent moisture from getting into a wall or ceiling and causing damage. This is more important than controlling pollutant movement because considerably more moisture is usually present in the air than pollutants, even in a house with poor indoor air quality.

The location for a diffusion retarder for moisture control is on the warmest side of the wall. In cold climates, it should be installed close to the interior. In hot humid climates, when a house is air conditioned, the inside of the house is cooler than the outside, so the diffusion retarder should go toward the exterior, under the siding. In mixed climates, most experts recommend that the diffusion retarder be placed toward the interior of the house. As a rule, two diffusion retarders in the same wall are not recommended because moisture can get trapped between them. In-depth information about the locations of diffusion retarders in different climates can be found in the *Moisture Control Handbook* listed in Appendix 3.

In a hot, humid climate, a diffusion retarder on the exterior of a house for moisture control will not offer occupants total diffusion protection from small amounts of formaldehyde gas released by fiberglass insulation. However, because diffusion is so slow and because even drywall itself will stop some diffusion, an interior diffusion retarder probably isn't necessary. To be extra cautious, you may wish to choose a more benign insulation in hot, humid climates, but I personally doubt whether it is necessary.

Air Barriers

A house is made airtight because it has an air barrier. However, because an air barrier is usually made up of several different materials combined in an airtight manner, an air barrier is often more difficult to visualize than a diffusion retarder made of one material like polyethylene. Basically, an air barrier will consist of a series of surfaces joined together in such a way that there are no gaps between them.

Gases, vapors, *and* particulate pollutants can ride piggyback on the air currents that move through holes in the structure of a house—around electrical outlets, poorly sealed window and door frames, plumbing penetrations, etc. Blocking the pathways of the air currents will prevent far more pollution and water vapor from getting through a wall than installing a diffusion retarder. As I explained in Chapter 11, wind and stack effect are the two natural phenomena that cause this air movement to take place. Mechanical ventilation systems that pressurize or depressurize houses also contribute to air currents through the holes in a house. And leaking furnace ductwork can also cause pressure imbalances in a house.

Any solid material will block the air currents and act as an air barrier: drywall, glass, metal, wood, etc. The trick is to connect all the different solid surfaces in such a way that there are no pathways for air to move between them.

There are two somewhat different ways of building an airtight house, both of which have several variations. Some builders have taken special precautions to seal up all openings in the polyethylene sheets that they were already using. This must be done around electrical outlets, plumbing penetrations, windows, doors, etc. With this method, a good diffusion retarder is made to also function as an air barrier. The second method uses a good air barrier (drywall) and couples it with an imperfect diffusion barrier. This has come to be known as the Airtight Drywall Approach (ADA).

The Airtight Drywall Approach (ADA)

The basic purpose of ADA is to stop air movement through the wall. Since drywall is a solid material, it is a very good air barrier. The key to ADA is to assemble the drywall sheets with the other components of a wall (electrical outlets, windows, doors, etc.) so that the entire wall system acts as a unified air barrier. (One of the largest, though often unnoticed air gaps is between the drywall and the floor, but I will discuss all the ways of sealing these cracks and gaps a little later.) Once you have plugged all the holes, you have stopped most moisture and pollution transport because, to reiterate, air movement is far more significant than diffusion.

A sheet of drywall without any holes in it is an excellent air barrier. Two sheets next to each other also prove to be an excellent air barrier—if the seam between then is taped. The paper tape commonly used in drywall finishing works fine. This is how most of the drywall in a conventional house is installed anyway. However, a number of holes are often made in the drywall to accommodate windows, doors, and electrical outlets. Using a few special techniques, these holes can be sealed up to create an airtight house.

With ADA, diffusion can be handled in several ways. A loose, imperfectly installed polyethylene sheet can be used inside the wall, just as is routinely being done by many builders already. The asphalt-impregnated kraft paper on some fiberglass batt insulation is also a diffusion retarder, as are some paints. All these products will stop moisture and pollutant transport from diffusing through a wall (but not necessarily air movement). However, each has its own peculiar outgassing characteristics so that each releases pollutants itself.

I prefer to use aluminum foil as a diffusion retarder because it is more inert. Metal foil is a better diffusion retarder than polyethylene sheeting because it has a perm rating of zero. In fact, it is one of the best diffusion retarders available. Aluminum foil also has the advantage of not deteriorating like polyethylene can.

Aluminum foil can be used as a diffusion retarder in a wall in three different ways. First, some fiberglass batt insulation is foil-faced. When using unfaced insulation, rolls of builders foil can be applied over the insulation. In both cases, the foil is then covered with drywall and the drywall is sealed in an airtight manner. The foil stops diffusion and the drywall (sealed per ADA) stops air movement. The third alternative is to purchase drywall that has a foil backing sheet already applied. Available from all major drywall manufacturers, foil-backed drywall is not stocked by every building supply store, but it can usually be special ordered. It resembles standard drywall except that there is a thin facing of aluminum foil glued to the back surface. While the retarder isn't continuous in any of these methods (there are seams between the sheets of drywall or the rolls of builders foil, for example), its important to remember that foil doesn't actually have to be perfect to be effective against diffusion.

Aerosol-Foam Insulation

In several areas of the Model Healthy House I used a "single-component polyurethane" aerosol-foam insulation to get an airtight seal (Figure 13-1). Unlike some foam insulations, this material contains no chemicals that can damage the ozone layer. It comes out of the can's nozzle like shaving cream and is extremely sticky until it cures. Once it is hard, it loses its tackiness. Care should be taken to keep it from getting on your hands during application because it can be difficult to remove. If it gets on the window or door frame, it can be hard to get off, so I use masking tape to protect the finished surfaces. Once the excess foam is trimmed away with a sharp knife, the masking tape can be removed, leaving a clean surface.

Figure 13-1.
Foam sealant at window frames.

I have used several different brands of this material and haven't found one that seems healthier than another. In fact, it is surprisingly benign after it has aired out a couple days. However, I don't use a lot of it and I always cover it with aluminum-foil tape (**Polyken Technologies**) where it is exposed to the living space.

Caulking

I have tried acrylic, latex, and several other kinds of caulking but in most cases prefer to use 100% silicone. It is somewhat odorous when wet,

Figure 13-2.
Drywall lift.

Figure 13-3.
Drywall lift in operation.

189

but once it has outgassed for several days, is quite inert. One-hundred-percent silicone caulking is also a very long-lasting product. The only place I use a different kind of caulking is around bathtubs, where mold growth is common. For that application I prefer the "tub and tile" caulk sold in most building supply stores.

Barriers and Retarders and Sealing the Model Healthy House

As I mentioned in Chapter 11, there are a number of ways of using ADA to construct an airtight house. The method I used is fairly simple to follow, but it requires that the house be built in two phases. To summarize Phase 1, the following four steps are involved:

1. Construct the exterior shell (Chapters 5-10).

2. Install the portions of the plumbing, wiring, ventilation, central vacuum, heating, and air conditioning systems that go in the exterior shell (Chapter 11).

3. Install the insulation (Chapter 12).

4. Cover the insulation with a diffusion retarder and drywall, then seal all penetrations in an airtight manner (this chapter).

In Phase 2, the interior partition walls are built (Chapter 14), then the plumbing, wiring, ductwork, and the rest of the house is completed using conventional sequencing.

Hanging the Drywall

In the Model Healthy House, I decided not to use a polyethylene diffusion retarder to avoid any minor outgassing from the plastic material. Instead I used foil-backed drywall. I covered all of the insulated exterior walls and ceiling in the usual manner, attaching it with screws. For a more complete discussion of drywall, see Chapter 20.

The method of attaching drywall that will yield the most rigid installation is to hang it with its long length at right angles to the framing members. For the ceiling, with the hat channels running the length of the building, that meant that the sheets would

Figure 13-4.
Sure-Seal airtight gasket tape.

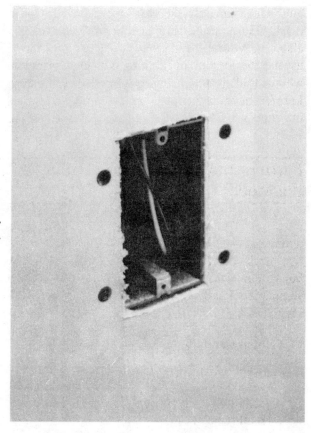

Figure 13-5.
Airtight electrical box.

run up and down the slope. By using 14'-long sheets cut to exact length, I was able to run single sheets the full length of the ceiling.

Normally it would take three people and some scaffolding to attach long sheets to a sloped ceiling, but with a little ingenuity, I was able to do it by myself. I made a lifting device out of some 2x4s and a pair of hinges (Figure 13-2). It was attached high on the center wall with two quick-action clamps. After cutting a piece of drywall to the correct length, I placed it onto the lift. A thin sheet metal bracket at the bottom kept it from sliding down. With the hinges at the top, I pivoted the drywall up to the ceiling and held the lower end in place with the single support leg (Figure 13-3). Once up, the sheet of drywall was screwed to the hat channel, then the lift was moved down 4' for the next sheet.

On the exterior walls, I hung all the sheets horizontally. But before I attached the sheets to the

walls, I adhered the ⅜" x ⅜" Sure-Seal foam gasketing by **Denarco, Inc.** to the face of the lower channel to seal the drywall in an airtight manner (Figure 13-4). In order to compress the gasket tightly, I drove extra screws into the channel at the base of the drywall. A gasket in this location, combined with the gasket installed between the channel and the slab in Chapter 6, resulted in an extremely airtight floor-to-wall joint.

At the airtight electrical boxes, I drove extra screws into the flanges in order to pull the drywall tightly against the gasketed boxes (**Nu-Tek Plastics, Inc.**) for an airtight fit (Figure 13-5).

ADA Sealing at Windows

Sheet 12 of the Plans shows the detailing I used to seal the windows. Once the windows were securely in place, the first step was to use cans of the

Figure 13-6.
Airtight window installation.

single-component polyurethane aerosol-foam insulation to fill the space between the aluminum window frames and the steel wall framing. The foam expands to fill the space quite well. By the next day the foam is cured enough to trim away the excess with a knife and cover with aluminum-foil tape. Next, I applied a Sure-Seal foam gasket (**Denarco, Inc.**) around both sides and the top of the steel wall framing next to the window frame. When I then attached the drywall to the sides of the window opening, it compressed the gasket, resulting in a perfectly airtight seal.

I covered the window sills with an ⅛"-thick foil-faced cardboard and taped it with foil tape around the perimeter for an airtight seal. This cardboard material is usually sold as an exterior wall sheathing, but it is not available in all parts of the country. Either a non-perforated builders foil or heavy-duty household aluminum foil could be substituted. The only drawback to them is the fact that they are not as sturdy

as the foil-faced cardboard. Therefore, they could be damaged during the construction process. To reinforce them somewhat, they could be applied over a layer of regular cardboard. From a technical point of view, foil-backed drywall would do the job on the sill as well as the sides and top of the opening. However, its ½" thickness would cause the wood sill to be higher than the window track, making removal of the window panes for cleaning difficult. The thinner foil-faced cardboard is a better choice. Figure 13-6 shows a sealed window.

ADA Sealing at Doors

At the doors, I used the aerosol foam to fill the space between the wood door frame and the steel wall frame. When it had hardened the next day, I trimmed away the excess foam with a knife and covered the foam with aluminum foil tape

(Figure 13-7). The tape would later be covered with wood interior trim.

ADA Sealing at the Center Partition Wall

Where the sheets of ceiling drywall met the center partition wall, I used paper drywall tape and non-toxic joint compound (**Murco Wall Products, Inc.**) to tape the drywall to the upper steel channel to achieve an airtight seal. The 2x4 wood plate used on top of the center partition wall (Chapter 6) resulted in the metal channel extending low enough to tape to. If no 2x4 had been used, the channel would have been up inside the ceiling, making sealing difficult. Later, the Phase 2 drywall (Chapter 20) was taped to the ceiling drywall. While this means a double taping, it doesn't take much extra time and is an easy way to obtain an airtight seal.

I injected aerosol foam inside the header that intersects the west exterior wall above the entry door in order to seal it from the inside. Once the foam was hard and trimmed away, I taped the drywall to the outside of the steel header (Figure 13-8).

ADA Sealing, Miscellaneous

Where the ductwork and plumbing pipes penetrated the drywall, I used a variety of methods to seal the gaps. The small plumbing lines are easy to seal with caulking. On the north wall, there was a 1" plastic pipe for telephone lines, a 4" dryer vent, and a 3" plastic pipe for air conditioning refrigerant lines. They were caulked around their outer perimeter to the drywall. Later (in Chapter 23), when the telephone and refrigerant lines were run through them, I filled them with either aerosol-foam insulation or caulking.

The 2" central vacuum exhaust tubing, two solar water heater lines, and the ½" plumbing line to the outdoor faucet were caulked to the drywall. I found it

Figure 13-7.
Airtight door installation.

easy to seal the larger metal ductwork to the drywall with paper tape and drywall joint compound. Figure 13-9 shows the ventilation ducts, central vacuum exhaust, and solar water heater lines sealed to the drywall ceiling.

Because the 3" PVC plumbing vent and the 4" PVC radon vent will tend to expand and contract with seasonal temperature changes, I felt that a more flexible seal than caulking was necessary. For these two penetrations I slipped a standard roof flashing over the pipes from the bottom, and sealed the flashing to the drywall with a bead of silicone caulking (Figure 13-10). With this method, the

Figure 13-8.
Airtight seal at entry header.

Figure 13-9.
Ductwork sealed to drywall.

194

pipes are sealed, yet are free to move up and down slightly as they expand and contract. Because these pipes are hidden within the space above the hallway's dropped ceiling, the appearance of the flashing is not a problem. This detail is shown on Sheet 12 of the Plans.

At this time I also caulked the electrical wires that penetrated the drywall. Most were the wires that were stubbed in place for the baseboard heaters, but some were miscellaneous wires (Figure 13-11). I also made sure all wires passing through the upper channel of the center partition wall were caulked.

Figure 13-10.
Piping sealed to drywall with roof flashing.

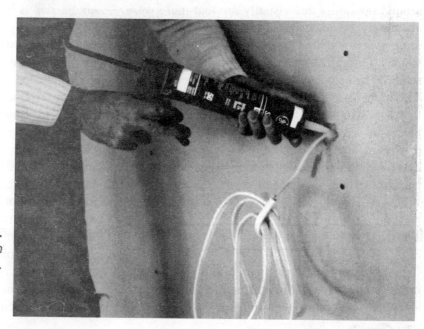

Figure 13-11.
Wiring sealed to drywall with caulking.

195

Figure 13-12.
Phase 1 complete.

Airtight at Last

Once I had completed sealing all of the penetrations in the drywall, I used a non-toxic joint compound (**Murco Wall Products, Inc.**) and paper drywall tape to seal all the joints between the sheets of drywall. Once this was done, it was easy to walk around the house and visually see that there were absolutely no undesirable air gaps. The drywall joints were sealed, as were the window and door frames. The gap between the floor and drywall was sealed. The electrical boxes and wires were sealed. The ductwork and the plumbing lines were sealed to the drywall and ready to hook up to the various pieces of ventilation and plumbing equipment. At this point, Phase 1 was complete (Figure 13-12). The remainder of the construction sequencing proceeded in the usual manner.

Update

Not too many years ago, I (along with many other people) used slightly different terminology in reference to moisture control. In the past, the words

"diffusion barrier" were popular, while in this chapter I have used the words "diffusion retarder" because, technically, most of the materials used to block the diffusion of gases and vapors are not true 100% "barriers," so the word "retarder" is technically a more accurate and correct term when applied to diffusion. While blocking air flow with an air barrier is also not 100% effective, the word "retarder" might be more appropriate there also but, among building scientists, "air barrier" remains the more conventional choice. Over the years, there has been a great deal of discussion about using correct terminology and, as a result, the most important message often gets lost. That message is that *airtightness is far more important than diffusion tightness*. In other words, it is much more important to build a house as tight as possible than it is to worry about the diffusion retarder. Don't get me wrong—both are important, it is just that one is more important than the other.

I should note that aerosol foam will expand considerably once it leaves the can. When it is injected into an enclosed area it can, as it expands, sometimes generate enough pressure to warp the sides of the enclosed area. For example, when injected between a wall stud and a window jamb, it might cause the window frame to warp. This didn't happen in the Model Healthy House because, apparently, the aluminum window frames were stiff enough to resist the expansion pressure. However, I have seen it happen in other houses. It is particularly problematic with vinyl window frames because they aren't nearly as stiff as metal or wood frames. As a result of this, some window manufacturers recommend that aerosol foam *not* be used. To avoid the problem, you might use one of the foams with the words "minimally expanding" on the label.

You might also secure the window frame to the wall studs in more places (if the fasteners are 8" apart, warping is less likely than when fasteners are 24" apart). Thirdly, you can simply use less foam because, in reality, the cavity doesn't need to be filled completely. Let's say there is a ½" gap between the window frame and the wall stud. The amount of energy efficiency you gain from filling that ½" completely full, as opposed to only slightly filling it, is not significant. The goal is to seal the area to make it air tight. The fact that it is airtight is more important than filling the cavity completely.

197

Chapter 14

INTERIOR FRAMING

■ ■ ■ In this Chapter I cover the non-load-bearing partition walls that break up the large room created in Phase 1 into the smaller individual rooms shown on the floor plan. Once these walls were erected, the rest of the scheduling for the project (Phase 2) proceeded in a conventional construction sequence.

Light-Weight Steel Framing

The studs and channels used in this Phase 2 framing are the same non-load-bearing material from **Dietrich Industries, Inc.**, that was used for part of the Phase 1 framing (Chapter 6), so the same assembly techniques were employed. With this light-weight material (25-gauge), I was able to use tin snips for most of the cutting. I used my crimping tool to attach the studs to the channels, except in a few locations where I couldn't maneuver it to fit. In those spots I used a screw with a very thin pan head (Figure 14-1). The shallow heads later allowed the drywall to be pulled tightly against the studs. I also used screws where there would be drywall attached on only one side of a stud. The thin metal studs gain a great deal of rigidity from the drywall, but in these places the screws provide a little more strength than crimping.

Interior Framing Variations

I used steel studs for all of the wall framing (load-bearing and non-load-bearing) in the house to avoid toxic termite treatments, and to eliminate the smell of pine that can bother some sensitive individuals. In a cold climate where termites are not a problem, wood framing is a viable option as long as the occupants are not sensitive to pine.

Wood can be used within the insulated walls with pine sensitive occupants if airtight construction techniques are employed, because the wood will be well-separated from the living space. Steel framing can then be used for the non-insulated non-airtight interior partition walls.

Interior Framing in the Model Healthy House

One of the advantages to using non-load-bearing steel framing is that it is available in a variety of sizes. I decided to frame most of the interior walls in the Model Healthy House out of 2½" material. When covered with ½" drywall on both sides, this yielded a total wall thickness of 3½", the same width as a 1x4. This wall thickness allowed me to make my own door jambs out of 1x4 poplar lumber that I purchased at a local mill. Most 2x4 wood-framed walls are a full inch thicker, taking up slightly more floor space. The narrower walls will mean a small amount of extra square footage will be part of the living space.

One disadvantage to building walls that are thinner than normal is that the electrical boxes can't be as deep as with thicker walls. I used 2½"-deep boxes throughout the interior of the house. Although these

Figure 14-1.
Shallow pan-head screws.

Figure 14-2.
Six-inch wall at plumbing and radon vents.

were adequate, with 2x4 wood framing they could have been a full inch deeper if necessary.

The wall between the kitchen and living room is 9 ¾" thick. I framed it by building two thin (1⅝") walls spaced apart for a wide overall wall width. I needed the extra thickness for the built-in pantry,

bookcase, and the pocket door. A double wall of this type is often called a "chase wall." This construction is frequently used when extra room is needed inside a wall for running utility lines.

I framed the wall between the bathrooms, as well as the wall containing the plumbing vent and the

Figure 14-3.
Attaching the floor channel to the concrete slab.

Figure 14-4.
Room layout can be visualized once all the floor channel is in place.

Figure 14-5.
Wall stud in place.

Figure 14-6.
Ceiling channel in place.

radon removal tube, out of 6" studs (Figure 14-2). Because these walls contained a variety of plumbing, ventilation, and electrical lines, they needed to be somewhat roomier. As it turned out, I found it a little cramped trying to fit everything into the 6" wall. There would have been more room to run these lines if I had built a thicker chase wall out of 1⅝" studs, something I will probably do in the future.

I built all of the interior non-load-bearing walls by first attaching a channel to the floor and another to the ceiling, cutting the studs to length and inserting them in place between the two channels, then crimping or screwing the studs to the channels. This is the same procedure I used to build the 3⅝" non-load-bearing insulated walls earlier in Phase 1 (Chapter 6).

202

Figure 14-7.
Door studs and header in place.

Figure 14-8.
Completed non-load-bearing wall.

203

Figure 14-9.
Horizontal Z-furring.

Figure 14-10.
*Z-furring along the bedroom and
closet walls.*

204

Figure 14-11.
Framing for hall ceiling.

Figure 14-12.
Framing for built-in pantry and bookcase.

205

Figure 14-13.
Opening for the pocket door.

Figure 14-14.
Plumbing line for the outdoor faucet.

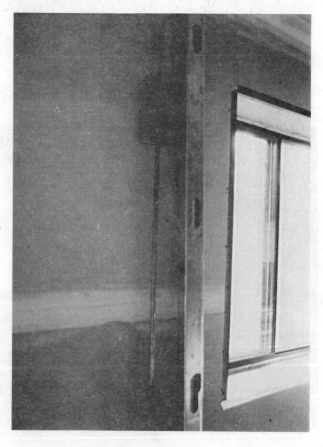

Figure 14-15.
Completed double wall in kitchen.

Figure 14-16.
Framing for the built-in display case.

Installing the Channel on the Floor

I first used a chalk line to locate all of the interior walls on the concrete slab per the dimensions shown on the floor plan (see Sheet 13 of the Plans). Once I knew where all of the walls went, I started attaching the correct size channel to the floor (Figure 14-3). I used ¼" concrete expansion anchors every 3 or 4 feet and on each side of doorways. The lower channels are shown installed in Figure 14-4. Once all the lower channels are in place, it is easy to visualize the layout of the various rooms.

207

Figure 14-17.
"Blocking" at Z-furring for an electrical box.

Installing the Channel on the Ceiling

There are several ways to position the channel on the ceiling so that it is directly over the floor channel. The simplest way is to start at a channel that butts up to a Phase 1 wall at each end. I placed a stud of the correct length at each end of the floor channel, plumbed it, and anchored it in place (Figure 14-5). I then snapped a chalk line between the tops of the two studs and used the line as a guide to position the channel on the ceiling (Figure 14-6). To anchor the channel to the ceiling, I drove screws through it, through the ceiling drywall, and into the hat channel.

Where the upper channel ran parallel to the slope of the ceiling, I couldn't use a standard U-shaped channel. Instead I had my local sheet metal shop fold 2½" x 2½" angles out of 20-gauge galvanized steel (see Sheet 13 of the Plans). During Phase 1, when the hat channel was being installed (Chapter 7), I had located some additional lengths where they would be above these particular walls. Now, all I had to do was use a chalk line to position the angles on the ceiling and screw them through the drywall into the hat channel.

Installing the Studs

I popped the first studs into the channels at the doorways (Figure 14-7), then added the remainder of the studs to the wall (Figure 14-8). Where there was a standard U-shaped channel at the ceiling, I crimped the studs and channels together just as I did with the Phase 1 non-load-bearing framing. Where there was an angle bracket at the ceiling, and it would only be possible to crimp one side of the studs, I had to use screws for additional strength. Even though I could only anchor one side of the stud, this provided a wall that was as strong as it needed to be. The drywall gives the wall a considerable amount of strength. For non-load-bearing applications, an angle bracket is usually all that is necessary at the top.

Z-Furring

In places that required thicker walls in order to run horizontal ventilation ducts, I attached Z-furring to the studs (Figure 14-9). Z-furring is readily available from steel framing manufacturers, but only in thicknesses up to 2½". Since the smallest rectangular ducts are 3¼" wide, I had a sheet metal shop custom-make some Z-furring 3½" thick. In the past, rather than using Z-furring, I have fastened 3½" studs horizontally to accomplish the same thing. It costs a little more to have material custom-made, but it is easier to work with in this particular application. The Z-furring ran along the north side of the center load-bearing wall, then turned to allow the ducts to reach the

bedroom closets (Figure 14-10). The location of the Z-furring is shown on Sheet 13 of the Plans.

Hall Ceiling

For the dropped ceiling in the hall and in two closets (see Sheet 13 of the Plans), I attached a channel around the perimeter at the correct height, then ran short lengths of studs between them (Figure 14-11). I used the pan head screws on the connections to provide a little more strength than crimping. It is important to keep in mind that this material in not load-bearing, so the dropped ceiling is not meant to support very much weight.

Double Wall in Kitchen

I built the wall between the living room and the kitchen extra-thick (9¾") in order to install some

Figure 14-18.
"Blocking" for an electrical box.

209

Figure 14-19.
Interior framing complete.

built-in cabinets. In the living room there is a book-case that will have a glass door, and in the kitchen there is a pantry with paneled doors (Figure 14-12). I also framed an opening for a 30" wide by 30" high kitchen wall cabinet. This metal cabinet is 12" deep and will be recessed into the wall about 6" so it won't protrude very far into the room.

The end of the thick kitchen wall has an opening that accepts a pocket door (Figure 14-13). Above the pocket door will be a glass panel to make the area seem more open and airy. As I framed this area, I installed the aluminum track for the pocket door. The door has a 3/16" safety glass panel, so it is fairly heavy. To support the weight, I used heavy-duty track and hardware and attached it to a length of load-bearing framing material. See Sheet 14 of the Plans for the built-in cabinetry and pocket door details.

For the stud along the south wall that supports the end of the pocket door track, I also used a load-bearing stud to support the extra weight. The 1/2" plumbing line that runs to the outdoor faucet is hidden within this stud and within the support for the aluminum pocket door track, so I had to extend the plumbing line up and over the door opening, and into the

thick kitchen wall, at this time (Figure 14-14). In order to eliminate any corrosion between the copper water line and the steel, I slipped a length of garden hose over the copper. Figure 14-15 shows the completed thick wall.

Built-Ins

The rough openings for the built-ins were framed slightly larger than the cabinet sizes to insure that the cabinets would fit. Once the cabinets were installed, they were trimmed with molding (see Chapter 27).

The rough opening for the display case at the entry is in a wall that is strapped with Z-furring. I used a hammer to pound flat one of the legs of the Z-furring to use around the perimeter of the opening. The finished opening is 6" deep (2½" stud plus 3½" Z-furring) (Figure 14-16).

Blocking

There were a number of places where I used short scraps of steel framing as "blocking." Pieces of Z-furring were used vertically where I knew they would be needed for attaching electrical boxes. (Figure 14-17) In other locations, where I wanted to mount an electrical box on the open side of a steel stud and there was no web to which I could attach the box, I screwed a short length of track to the stud. (Figure 14-18) A builder who is not accustomed to working with steel framing will soon pick up small tricks like this. Once the miscellaneous blocking was finished, the house was ready for the Phase 2 rough-in work (Figure 14-19).

Update

While steel framing hasn't yet caught on with many contractors, I feel that it is going to be used more and more. For builders who are leery about jumping right in and framing an entire house out of steel, or who are apprehensive about selecting sizes and gauges for load-bearing applications, I'd suggest first doing a project or two with non-load-bearing steel studs. In other words, frame the load-bearing portion of a house conventionally with wood—then frame the partition walls with non-load-bearing steel studs. That is basically what I did when my wife and I built our own healthy house recently (see Chapter 28). Non-load-bearing steel studs can be very straightforward and easy-to-use, and they are generally less costly than wood. Once the framing crew, and the subcontractors are comfortable with them, they will probably be ready to frame an entire house with both load-bearing and non-load-bearing steel studs. There is no reason a house has to be framed out of all the same material, and I predict that more and more houses will opt for a hybrid approach—using wood in some places and steel in others.

211

PART 4: SYSTEMS

Chapter 15

VENTILATION AND FILTRATION

■■■ Ventilation is a mechanical process whereby a house is supplied with fresh air and stale air is expelled. Filtration involves cleaning pollutants out of the air. They are not the same thing, although they sometimes can be combined into a single system.

As discussed in Chapter 11, most houses rely primarily on the natural phenomena of wind and stack effect to obtain fresh air. The Model Healthy House is built as tightly as possible to minimize this naturally occurring infiltration. In a house constructed in an airtight manner, a mechanical ventilation system becomes very important. Unfortunately, well-designed mechanical ventilation is not a common feature in houses being built today and the concept is often poorly understood. Filtration is probably even less well understood.

Ventilation Strategies

Houses can be ventilated mechanically in several ways. When properly designed, these methods will provide the *correct* amount of fresh air—neither too much nor too little. A system that is too large for a house will result in high heating and cooling bills. One too small will not move enough

air to be effective. Some ventilation strategies can be controlled more easily than others; some have a high initial cost yet are more economic to operate. Some lend themselves to being easily connected to a central filtration unit. Simple or complex, all mechanical ventilation strategies have the capacity to provide the occupants with fresh air.

There are literally hundreds of different designs for mechanical ventilation systems, depending on the house layout, occupants' needs, climate, and budget. My book *Understanding Ventilation: How to design, select, and install residential ventilation systems* (see Appendix 3) is an excellent in-depth source of further information. The various ventilation equipment manufacturers can also provide general literature and installation manuals that are becoming increasingly sophisticated. Following are four basic approaches that be used to move air into, and out of, houses. They will all be more effective and easier to control if they are used in conjunction with airtight construction.

Exhaust Systems

Exhaust systems already exist in many houses in one form or another. A bathroom exhaust fan or a kitchen range hood are typical examples. Their purpose is to expel stale, polluted, or moisture-laden air from the house. Clothes dryers and central vacuums can be exhaust devices, if they are exhausted to the outdoors like they should be, so they also fall into this category, although we don't usually think of them as contributing to ventilation. Furnaces, fireplaces, and water heaters can also be thought of as exhaust devices if they cause air to move from inside the living space to the outdoors by way of a chimney or flue.

When air is blown from a house, "make-up air" must enter somewhere else. (It is called "make-up air" because it makes up for what was exhausted.) A house only contains a certain volume of air, and when some is blown outdoors by an exhaust device, the house becomes slightly depressurized. As soon as a house starts getting depressurized, outdoor air tries to enter wherever it can in order to rebalance the indoor/outdoor pressures. For an analogy, place a pop bottle up to your lips and try to suck the air out of it. You are depressurizing the inside of the bottle. If there were small holes or gaps in the bottle, air would rush in to relieve the depressurization. An airtight house is like an airtight pop bottle.

A loosely built house will have plenty of make-up air randomly entering through gaps and cracks in the structure, but as I discussed earlier, this can sometimes contribute to indoor pollution, hence one of the reasons for building an airtight structure.

If you simply blow air out of an airtight house, you will tend to depressurize the whole building (Figure 15-1, This is like the pop bottle without any holes in it.). If this happens, the exhaust device won't work very well—a bathroom fan won't blow very much air out of the house or the chimney won't function correctly. If there are several exhaust devices operating simultaneously, they can compete with one another. For example, when a clothes dryer is blowing air out of the house, make-up air could be entering the house by coming down the flue of a nearby gas water heater.

An easy way to prevent depressurization and competition between exhaust devices is to purposefully place some holes in the exterior walls. At first, this may seem silly: building a tight house, then poking holes in it. But it does make sense when your goal is to create a system that provides for ventilation and air distribution around the house without causing problems.

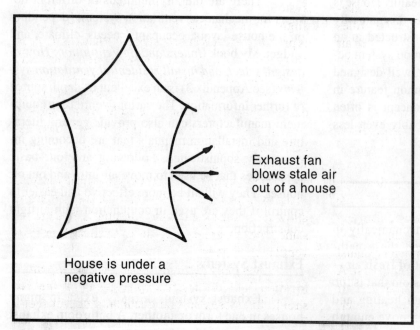

Exhaust fan blows stale air out of a house

House is under a negative pressure

Figure 15-1.
Exhaust ventilation depressurizing a house.

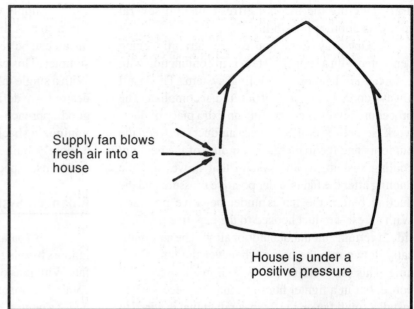

Supply fan blows
fresh air into a
house

House is under a
positive pressure

Figure 15-2.
Supply ventilation pressurizing a house.

Several manufacturers produce small grilles that can be placed in the exterior walls to provide specific pathways for air to enter. They are relatively small, so a limited amount of air can enter through any one grille. This reduces the chance of feeling a draft. The grilles are often placed in closets or other out-of-the-way locations. Whenever an exhaust device is operating, whether a range hood or a fireplace, make-up air will enter the living space through the grilles automatically. The designer must know how much air can be expelled from the house by all of the exhaust devices, then can select the locations, quantity, and sizes for the grilles.

A designer may choose to use central exhaust ventilation equipment that will expel air from a central point in the middle of the house on a 24-hour basis. Another approach is to provide a central fan with a certain amount of ductwork so that air is pulled from several rooms (usually rooms with excess moisture such as the kitchen, baths, and laundry), then exhausted to the outdoors through a single duct.

The primary advantage of using an exhaust strategy to ventilate a house is its low initial cost. A big disadvantage is the fact that the incoming air will be cold in the winter or hot in the summer.

Filtering and distributing the incoming air can also be difficult because you would need a separate filter on each of the intake grilles.

Supply Systems

Like the name implies, a supply ventilation system blows air into a building. This results in slight pressurization (Figure 15-2). When a house is pressurized, radon is kept out and backdrafting of chimneys isn't a problem. However, if a house isn't constructed in an airtight manner, pressurization can force moisture from the living space into wall cavities, resulting in possible mold growth and rot. In some cases, moist air in a pressurized house has been forced through exterior door locks, causing them to freeze up.

In an airtight house, small grilles can be placed in the exterior walls to relieve any pressurization and allow air to escape from the building. These are the same types of grilles that can be used with exhaust ventilation systems.

A supply fan can blow air into a central location, but the specific placement of the fan should be chosen so that occupants do not feel a

217

draft. Ducting the incoming fresh air into several rooms is another possibility.

One way some houses are currently being ventilated with a supply system is in conjunction with a forced-air heating or cooling system. This isn't always done, but it isn't difficult to accomplish. The procedure involves connecting an extra piece of duct-work (sometimes called a fresh-air duct) between the outdoors and the main return-air duct of the heating/cooling system. In any system that moves air, the ducting after the fan is under positive pressure and the ducting before the fan is under negative pressure. With a fresh-air duct hooked to the negative pressure side, a certain amount of outdoor air will be automatically drawn into the house whenever the fan is running. This can work relatively well in a loosely built house, but in a tighter house, it may be necessary to install a small fan on the fresh-air duct that is wired to run whenever the main furnace fan is operating.

A disadvantage to coupling the ventilation system to a heating/cooling system is that it will only supply fresh air when the furnace fan is running. Some furnace fans can be set to run continuously, but because they have fairly large motors, this can mean a high operating cost.

Supply ventilation has a relatively low installation cost. A disadvantage is the fact that the incoming air can be very cold in the winter or very hot in the summer. This can contribute to a high operating cost. With a single inlet port, incoming air can be filtered if desired—a definite advantage. Pressurization is a good approach to keeping radon out of a house and minimizing backdrafting of chimneys and flues, but in a loosely built house it can cause hidden moisture problems, especially in cold climates.

Balanced Systems

In a balanced ventilation system, air is brought indoors by one fan and exhausted outdoors by another fan. With fans of the same capacity, the amount of air coming in matches the air leaving, so the house is under a neutral pressure (Figure 15-3). Ductwork can be used to distribute air throughout the house.

A balanced system requires only two holes in the structure: an inlet port and an exhaust port. In contrast, the first two strategies require several openings in various locations throughout the house. With fewer holes, less unwanted air will enter the house when a balanced system is shut off.

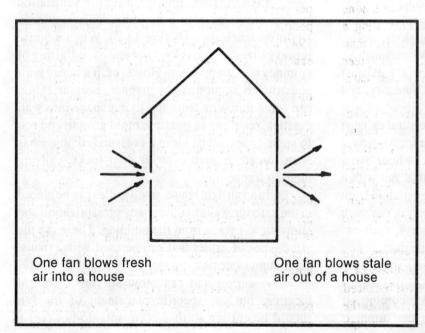

One fan blows fresh air into a house   One fan blows stale air out of a house

Figure 15-3.
Neutral pressure with balanced ventilation.

218

Balanced ventilation systems that operate independently of the furnace system have a definite advantage. They can be turned on and off no matter what the heating or cooling requirement. For example, a furnace is more likely to run at night in the winter, but the outdoor air may be more polluted at night because of a neighbor's wood smoke. In that case, it may be desirable for the ventilation system to only run during the daytime.

This strategy is more costly to install than the previous two, but it does offer more occupant control. The single inlet can be fitted with a filter, if desired, to clean the incoming air. A big advantage to a balanced ventilation system is that, when it is shut off, the house is more tightly sealed than with supply or exhaust strategies having multiple openings in the exterior walls. This is desirable when outdoor pollution levels are high and the homeowner wishes to temporarily shut the system down.

Heat Recovery Ventilation

With all of the above approaches, cold air will be brought indoors in the winter and warm air expelled. In the summer, if the house is air-conditioned, cool air will be exhausted and warm humid air brought in. While there is definitely an amount of control, and much needed air is being supplied to the house, none offer a very energy-efficient way of ventilating a house. In fact, they are no more energy-efficient than installing a fan in an open window. If it is ten degrees below zero outdoors, you will be bringing in air that is quite cold.

To provide ventilation in a controlled manner, that is both comfortable and energy-efficient, devices known as heat recovery ventilators (HRVs) have been developed. Sometimes they are called air-to-air heat exchangers or energy recovery ventilators (ERVs). HRVs first appeared in cold Scandinavian and Canadian climates, but now they are readily available in the U.S.

Basically an HRV is a balanced system, like those described above, but it has the addition of a specially constructed core. (Actually, most balanced systems currently on the market are HRVs.) Both the incoming and the outgoing airstreams pass through the core. While they don't mix and contaminate each other, the design of the core allows them to exchange heat. In the winter, 70% or more of the heat in the warm exhaust air is transferred to the cold incoming air. "Cool" is similarly transferred in air conditioning climates. If it is 10 degrees outdoors, 70 degrees indoors, and an HRV is 75% efficient, 45 degrees will be transferred [(70-10) x 75%]. Therefore the 10-degree air will be warmed up to 55 degrees once it passes through the core. Granted, this still needs to be warmed up to a comfortable 70 degrees, but it takes considerably less energy than if the 10-degree air were brought directly into the living space.

HRVs have a higher initial cost compared to the other systems, but, because of the energy savings feature, the total operating cost can be somewhat less. In very cold climates, they can pay for themselves in just a few years, but in moderate or in air-conditioned climates, where there is less energy to recover, the payback period can be quite long. While ventilation, of some type, is considered mandatory, heat recovery can be viewed as an option, depending on the climate.

How Much Ventilation Is Enough

A figure of 15 cubic feet per minute (cfm) per person seems to work well to provide air for people. This ventilation rate was established in 1989 by the American Society of Heating, Refrigeration, and Air Conditioning Engineers (ASHRAE). As an alternative, ASHRAE suggests that 0.35 air changes per hour will also provide sufficient ventilation air. (Actually ASHRAE recommends that the larger of the two figures be used as a *minimum* ventilation rate. Many houses require more.) These rates are enough to remove occupant-generated pollutants, including moisture, body odor, bad breath, etc. A family of four, requiring 15 cfm per person, would need 60 cfm whenever everyone is in the house. It is also possible to provide a greater volume of air for fewer hours per day—as long as the average daily rate is sufficient.

It should be remembered that while 15 cfm per person is the rate necessary for people only, it is not enough to remove the larger quantities of pollutants

219

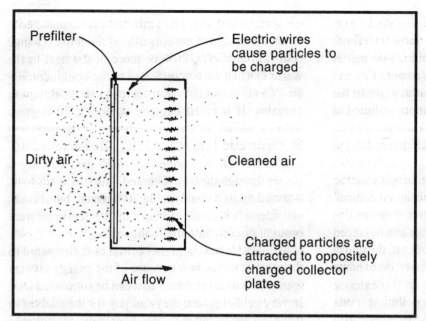

Prefilter

Electric wires cause particles to be charged

Dirty air

Cleaned air

Charged particles are attracted to oppositely charged collector plates

Air flow

Figure 15-4.
Electrostatic precipitator.

generated by such activities as cooking, laundering, or certain hobbies. The amount required for these activities varies widely. As an example, a kitchen may only require minimal ventilation when warming up some soup, but much more if toast is burned. Similarly, a hobby like oil painting will require more fresh air than wood carving.

If central ventilation is relied on to handle activity-generated pollutants, it will need to have a fairly large capacity, much larger than is needed most of the day.

A moderately sized central ventilation system can certainly be used to remove many activity-generated pollutants, but in practice those types of pollutants are often handled best by what is called "local ventilation." This involves exhaust equipment located near the pollution source: a range hood in the kitchen, an exhaust fan over the laundry. These could have air-inlet grilles located near them for make-up air, or you could simply open a window when they are operating. While it is permissible to move a certain amount of air from the kitchen through an HRV, it is not a good idea for this to be the only ventilation equipment removing air from the kitchen. This is because kitchen air often contains minute particles of

grease that can create a fire hazard within the HRV's core. A range hood is better designed to handle kitchen air contaminated with grease.

Filtration Strategies

All filters can definitely improve the air quality in your house, but the big questions are "How much?" and "Is it enough?" If the air is relatively clean to begin with, a small portable air filter may be all you need to remove the few pollutants. With very contaminated air and sensitive occupants, a huge, complicated, expensive system may be required. Different types of filters are designed to remove different types of pollutants, so it is important that you know what is in the air before selecting a filter. Most indoor air quality experts agree that it is best to clean the air by other means first (for example, eliminating or separating pollutants from the living space, and ventilating), then use filtration if necessary.

Filtration can be an attractive option for a couple of reasons. First of all, the outdoor air that is being brought indoors may not be very pure and clean. It could be laden with exhaust gases, pesticides, pollen, or mold spores. Second, if the indoor air is filtered, less ventilation air is needed to flush out the pollutants that are generated indoors. It should be kept in mind that filtration is not a substitute for ventilation because filtration can only clean contaminants out of the air; it cannot provide the oxygen that is depleted as we breathe.

The full range of air pollutants can be placed into two broad categories: particles (more correctly called particulates) and gases. Particulates include mold spores, pollen, asbestos, house dust, dead insect parts, etc. Gases include combustion gases, formaldehyde, and the hundreds of other VOCs floating in the air. Tobacco and wood smoke are composed of both gases and particulates. The type of filter that works well with particulates does nothing to remove gases, and vice versa. To remove both categories of pollutants, you need two different types of filters.

Particulate Filters

The standard 1"-thick furnace filter falls into this category. It is designed to remove particulates from the air. Unfortunately, it doesn't do a very good job of it. Actually, its primary purpose is not to clean the air for occupants, but rather to help protect the fan motor in the furnace. It is a *furnace* filter, not a *people* filter. A motor doesn't need a very efficient filter. People require more, and fortunately there are two kinds of filters available that do a much better job: electrostatic precipitators and extended-surface filters.

Electrostatic Precipitators

Most people have heard of an electronic air cleaner. Its proper name is an electrostatic precipitator. These devices fit into the furnace ductwork and operate by placing an electrical charge on any particles of dust that pass through. They also contain metal plates that have an electrical charge that is opposite that of the dust. Since opposite charges are drawn toward each other, the charged particulates are attracted to, and cling to, the metal plates (Figure 15-4). Once the plates are full of dust and can hold no more, they must be removed and cleaned. This is usually done in a dishwasher or a tub of water. Depending on how dirty the air is, cleaning may be necessary as often as each week.

Electrostatic precipitators work fairly well, although they lose their efficiency as the plates fill

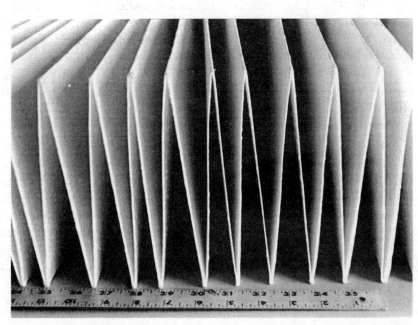

Figure 15-5.
Extended-surface filter.

221

with dust. While they are considerably better at handling particulates than a standard furnace filter, they have one primary disadvantage. Because of the electrical charges, small amounts of ozone are produced when they are operating, and ozone is a well recognized air pollutant. Manufacturers are quick to point out that the levels of ozone generated are quite low, yet some people react negatively even to small amounts of ozone. During a smog alert in a large city when ozone levels are high, people experience eye and respiratory irritation. This is because ozone reacts with soft tissues of the body.

I know of many people who use electrostatic precipitators with good results. At the same time, there are others who are bothered by the ozone.

Extended-Surface Filters

With their very fine pores, extended-surface filters can have more resistance to the flow of air than a standard furnace filter. In order to compensate, they are often manufactured in a pleated accordion shape (Figure 15-5). This configuration results in much more surface area and less overall air resistance. When such a filter starts to get dirty, it actually becomes more efficient because the pores get smaller as they become clogged. But clogged pores also mean increased resistance to air movement. If a filter has too much resistance, the fan won't be able to blow air through it as easily, so it won't operate as effectively.

An extended-surface filter is usually made of fiberglass or polyester fibers held together with some type of resin. While it is doubtful if any fibers could be released into the air stream, some sensitive individuals are bothered by the slight odor of the resin. This odor can often be eliminated by removing the filter from the cabinet and heating it in a 200 degree oven for a couple hours. When doing this, be sure to have the range hood turned on at high speed and have a kitchen window open. If you are very chemically sensitive, you should not be in the house when this is done, and the oven and kitchen should be aired out thoroughly when the process is complete.

An extended-surface filter will generally have a lower initial cost than an electrostatic precipitator and will require less regular maintenance. There is no electrical expense, but there is a cost associated with the periodic replacement of the filter when it gets clogged. The service life of an extended surface filter is often in the range of a year or more.

Figure 15-6.
HEPA filter.

222

Figure 15-7.
Adsorption material. (Activated carbon, left. Activated alumina, right.)

HEPA Filters

HEPA filters are a special type of extended-surface filter. HEPA stands for high-efficiency particulate accumulator. They are sometimes called "absolute filters" because they are typically 95-99% efficient. Developed originally for use in nuclear and biological laboratories, they are now available in both portable and central residential equipment.

HEPA filters are more costly than other particulate filters, but they represent the state-of-the-art as far as clean air is concerned. Since their pores are so small, they have considerably more resistance to air flow than other extended-surface filters (Figure 15-6). As a result, they often require a more powerful fan motor to drive the air through them. Like all of the filters discussed so far, they will do nothing to remove gases from the air.

Gaseous Filtration

Particulate filters work much like a coffee strainer—they simply trap the pollutants that are larger than their pore size. Gaseous filtration re-quires a totally different approach: adsorption. Adsorption is a process by which gas molecules adhere to a solid surface. A crude analogy would be to compare an adsorption filter to flypaper. Once the adsorption filter has captured all the gases it can hold, it must be replaced.

Activated carbon (sometimes called activated charcoal) is one of the most common adsorption materials on the market. It can be made from coal, coconut husks, or a variety of other materials. Activated carbon does an excellent job of removing most gaseous pollutants from the air. Unfortunately, it is less effective at capturing gases with low molecular weights. Formaldehyde, a very common indoor pollutant, is one of the gases that activated carbon doesn't adsorb particularly well.

In order to remove formaldehyde from the air, specially treated carbons are readily available. Activated alumina impregnated with potassium permanganate is another type of adsorption material that works well against formaldehyde (Figure 15-7).

Like extended-surface filters, adsorption filters can have a considerable amount of resistance to air flow. For very polluted air, a lot of adsorption material is necessary; therefore, a great deal of surface

223

area is required for a fan to function properly. In commercial applications, trays filled with the adsorption material are arranged in an accordion shape to provide plenty of surface area. This approach is generally too costly for residential applications, although it can be done.

A more cost-effective approach for using an adsorption filter in a residence is to use less carbon (less air resistance) and replace it more often. As a rule, adsorption filters are quite expensive because of their size and special fan requirements. However, those with less carbon, while not as efficient, are much lower in cost, and within the budgets of many homeowners. Of course, there are some activated carbon filters on the market that have so little carbon in them that they probably are not worth the effort.

In a house with very contaminated air, an adsorption filter of small to moderate size may not be big enough to provide any noticeable improvement in air quality. In a relatively unpolluted house, such a filter can be used to "polish" the air.

Miscellaneous Air-Cleaning Devices

There are several other miscellaneous approaches to cleaning the air. None are as effective as electrostatic precipitators, extended-surface filters, or adsorption filters, but they do have applications, primarily because they are usually lower in cost.

Occasionally, air fresheners are sold as air cleaners. In reality, they do absolutely nothing to clean the air. Instead, they add fragrance to cover up the odor of pollutants. The pollutants are still there, but aren't as immediately noticeable. The fragrance actually adds to the pollutant load.

Electrostatic Air Filters

Electrostatic filters operate similarly to electrostatic precipitators but require no electricity. Instead, they are made of plastic and rely on static electricity to capture particles of pollution. Some electrostatic filters are permanently charged with "electrets." The plastic may bother someone sensitive to synthetic materials. While they aren't very effective at

capturing very small-sized particles, they do a reasonable job with mold spores and pollen.

Negative-Ion Generators

Negative-ion generators can also be used to clean the air. Some models simply spew out negatively charged ions into the air. These charged ions attach themselves to dust particles, then cling to oppositely charged surfaces like walls and ceilings. The result can be dirty walls and ceilings. After awhile, some of the particles will lose their charge and re-enter the air. Some negative-ion generators contain a collection filter of some type to capture the charged particles.

Ozone Generators

Ozone is a widely studied air pollutant that has the capacity to react with some gases in the air and neutralize them. Sometimes ozone reacts with air pollutants and creates new and different gases. Unfortunately, ozone can easily react with a person's eyes or mucous membranes and damage them. Ozone generators are currently being marketed for use in homes to purify the air. Many experts point out that while these devices sometimes reduce pollution levels, they are potentially a very dangerous way to clean the air because the ozone itself can harm occupants.

House Plants

The National Aeronautics and Space Administration (NASA) has done research on the use of house plants as air-cleaning devices. Spider plants in particular have been shown to remove formaldehyde from the air. NASA's original studies were done in a controlled laboratory setting. More recent research has attempted to determine if the same holds true in residential applications. Unfortunately, it has been found that, while spider plants indeed can reduce formaldehyde levels in a house, the amount of reduction is not nearly as significant as NASA's original research implied. In fact, it is believed that the reduction may be due, not to the plants metabolizing the formaldehyde, but to soil bacteria consuming it.

224

Having plants in a house raises indoor humidities, resulting in increased populations of mold or dust mites which thrive at higher moisture levels. Cacti or succulents need less water, so generally don't contribute to higher humidities.

Ductwork

Many houses have ducts that run between the central heating or air-conditioning system and various rooms. The purpose of this system of ductwork is to distribute heated or cooled air throughout the house. The Model Healthy House does not have a heating or air-conditioning system that uses ducts. However, the ventilation/filtration system does require ductwork, so I will cover it in this chapter. If you have a furnace or central air-conditioner that uses ducts, all of the points discussed below will apply.

Duct Material

In the past, nearly all ducts, round and rectangular, were made of rigid galvanized steel. This is a very inert product, although when new, it is sometimes coated with a thin layer of oil, from the manufacturing process, that can be bothersome to some sensitive people. The oil can be easily removed by washing the ductwork prior to assembly with a tri-sodium-phosphate (TSP) solution. (TSP, a heavy-duty cleaner that rinses off very well, is sold in paint and hardware stores.) Galvanized steel ducting is readily available, and aluminum ducting is also sold in some sizes.

Today, much of the round ductwork being installed is flexible. Although some is uninsulated, most of it is in the form of a multi-layer insulated sleeve with the interior of the sleeve (the part exposed to the air stream) having a plastic liner. This liner is not subject to very much outgassing, but a similar product is available that has a metal foil liner. The foil should not outgas at all. Since all the air you will be breathing passes through these ducts, they should probably be as inert as possible.

Ductboard is a semi-rigid fiberglass product with aluminum foil on one side. It can be easily cut to size and taped together to form rectangular ducts of any dimension. Ductboard is assembled with the raw fiberglass facing the air stream. Not only will the fiberglass release small glass fibers and formaldehyde into the air you will be breathing but, because of its porosity, the ductboard can also become a home to millions of microorganisms. There are numerous installations where the ductboard has become black with mold. I never recommend it.

I prefer using rigid metal ducts or flexible metal-lined ducts because they are the most inert. Plastic-lined flexible ducts would be my second choice, but I suggest that sensitive people test them for tolerability prior to use. I can't see any use whatsoever for ductboard because the potential to contaminate the air passing through it is too great.

Duct Locations

It is my considered opinion that all ductwork be kept within the conditioned (heated or cooled) space as much as possible. In many houses, the ducts are located in an unconditioned attic or crawl space. At each floor, ceiling, or wall register, and each time a duct passes from a conditioned space into an unconditioned space, the air barrier is penetrated. This results in a house that is far from being airtight. In order to tighten up such a house, each penetration must be sealed to prevent leakage into, or out of, the occupied space. Generally this involves taping and/or using a mastic sealant compound around the perimeter of registers and grilles. In the average house being built today, this is rarely done because it can be time-consuming. And in many cases, it is difficult to achieve a very good seal. By locating the ductwork within the conditioned space, it is much easier to build a house in an airtight manner because you don't have to penetrate the air barrier with the ducts. With a little preplanning, ducts can be run in conditioned spaces within walls, above dropped ceilings, between floors, or in conditioned basements.

Leaky Ducts

A ductwork system is composed of a number of different-shaped pieces: elbows, straight lengths, tees, register boots, adapters, etc. Such a system will have many leaky connections. They should all be sealed to prevent air from leaking out or pollutants from getting in. I prefer aluminum-foil tape, but there are water-based mastics designed specifically for duct sealing that are fairly benign. (They should still be tested by sensitive individuals.) It is advantageous to do this sealing in existing houses as well as in new construction.

When air seeps into or out of leaky ductwork, it can have a major effect on the pressures in a house. For example, return-air ducts are under a negative pressure, so if they are leaky, air will tend to be pulled into them. If leaky return air ducts are located in a basement, they will depressurize the basement. That will result in the main floor being pressurized. In this situation, radon could be pulled into the basement, and humidity in the air on the main floor of the house could be blown into the exterior wall cavities where it could condense during cold weather. Since a furnace or central air-conditioner fan is so powerful, leaky ducts often result in more pressure-related problems than either wind, stack effect, or ventilation fans.

Duct Insulation

When ducts are located in unconditioned attics or crawl spaces they generally must be insulated. This is important in all houses for energy efficiency. For example, without insulation, in the winter the ducts will radiate heat into the unconditioned space. It makes little sense from an energy-conservation standpoint to heat your attic or crawl space when you don't live there. Sometimes ducts in a crawl space are left uninsulated to warm the crawl space and prevent water pipes from freezing. A more energy efficient way of reducing the chance of pipe freezing is to insulate the pipes themselves.

Ducts should also be insulated to prevent loss of energy in the summer when cool air is circulating within them. Since a cool duct in a humid, warm attic can have water condense on it, the insulation should also have an exterior moisture barrier (plastic or foil) to prevent moisture damage and mold growth.

Insulating ductwork is not always important. For example, ducts that exhaust air from a house are generally not insulated because the air is going outdoors anyway, so there is no reason to prevent heat loss in them. Ductwork needs to be insulated to preserve the temperature of the air within it and to prevent condensation. Most of the time, this is necessary for ducts that move air between conditioned and unconditioned spaces. If the ductwork is located entirely within the heated or cooled space, it needs no insulation.

Insulated flexible ducting has a built-in moisture barrier. To add insulation and a moisture barrier to the outside of a rigid or flexible metal duct, there are two products available. First, you can use insulation blankets with a plastic facing and cut them to fit around the ducts, taping securely all seams. This product works for round or rectangular ducts. Round flexible sleeves, consisting of an inner layer of fiberglass and an exterior moisture barrier, can be slid over round ducts. Before using either product, be sure to seal all the seams in the rigid ductwork prior to wrapping the insulation so that the insulation can't migrate into the airstream.

Ventilation/Filtration Rough-in for the Model Healthy House

The ventilation and filtration equipment is generally installed prior to the plumbing, central vacuum, and wiring systems because the ductwork is relatively large and more difficult to locate. By comparison, the electrical wiring is flexible and can be snaked around the other systems fairly easily. It's always easier to install the big items first.

Ventilation and filtration systems can be simple or complex. In the Model Healthy House, I assembled a package that is probably more complicated than most. At the same time, I have incorporated a fairly simple control system to make it easy for occupants to use.

The Design Criteria

There are literally hundreds of different ways of ventilating houses, or of filtering the air in them. In designing the ventilation-filtration system for the

Figure 15-8.
Installed CRSI 600H filter unit.

Model Healthy House, I wanted to include the following requirements:

- For maximum flexibility, the system should operate independently of the heating and air-conditioning systems.
- The capacity should be large enough to provide at least 15 cfm of outdoor air per person without running continuously.
- The layout of the ductwork should provide for air circulation throughout the house, including closets.
- There should be a filtration system capable of removing pollen and mold spores, and occasional wood smoke from the incoming air.
- The filtration system should also contain a moderate amount of adsorption media.
- The filtration system should have a recirculation mode whereby the indoor air can be cleaned, even if the outdoor air supply is turned off.
- The entire system, including ductwork, should be within the conditioned space.
- The system should be energy-efficient.
- There should be local ventilation in the form of bathroom fans and a kitchen range hood.

Filtration Equipment

The filtration package in the Model Healthy House consists of a CRSI #600H filter provided by **Pure Air Systems.** It can be either coupled to a standard forced-air furnace, or it can stand alone. It consists of a metal cabinet, a fan, a HEPA filter, an adsorption filter, and a prefilter. I selected the optional two-speed fan for maximum flexibility. On high speed, the fan capacity of 600 cfm can process all of the air in the house every 20 minutes.

As air enters the CRSI #600H filter unit, it is first pulled through the prefilter, then the activated carbon filter, and finally the HEPA filter. Pulling air through filters makes better use of all of the filter material than if the air is pushed through.

The HEPA filter supplied with the CRSI #600H has a 99.97% efficiency rating in capturing particles as small as 0.3 microns (that translates into 0.000012 inches). Most mold spores are larger than 1 micron, and pollen is usually larger than 10 microns. The HEPA filter should last 3-5 years before it needs to be replaced.

The adsorption filter contains approximately 2½ pounds of activated carbon in a polyester mesh,

227

enough to capture about 1¼ pounds of gas. It should have a life of 3-6 months.

The prefilter is made of a coarse, non-woven polyester material and should be changed about every three months. Its function is to remove the large dust particles from the air so the HEPA filter doesn't need to work as hard.

Filter life can vary considerably. It depends on how long the fan runs each day, the quality of the air, temperature, humidity, particle size, number of occupants, etc. The figures given above can be considered average. In the Model Healthy House, there will be few pollution sources, so a longer life may well be possible. The annual filter media replacement cost should be in the $100-150 range. **Pure Air Systems** mails out postcards to their customers to remind them when to change their filters.

Filtration Layout

I hung the filter cabinet horizontally in the space above the dropped hallway ceiling (Figure 15-8). A 16" x 16" galvanized steel plenum about 12" long was attached to the inlet. To the plenum I connected a series of ducts (5" diameter and 3¼" x 12"

rectangular) that run from various rooms and closets in the house (Figure 15-9). The outlet from the filter cabinet is 8" diameter, but rather than use 8" ductwork, I used an 8" x 12" adapter and ran 12" duct from the cabinet to the living room. The larger diameter is for noise control, something I will discuss later. The filtered air enters the living room above the entrance to the hallway (Figure 15-10).

Sheet 21 of the Plans shows a schematic layout for the ductwork. When in operation, the filter unit will recirculate the air throughout the house by pulling air from all the closets, master bath, and kitchen, then filtering it, and blowing the cleaned air into the living room. The process repeats when the filtered air then flows back through each room, into the closets and back through the filter. When I later installed the interior doors, I left a 1" gap at the bottom so that air could flow under them even when they are closed. With filtered air entering all the closets, they will always be fresh smelling.

Where the 3¼" x 12" ducts pull air from the closets, I fitted either a 5" round collar on the side of the duct, or a rectangular collar on the end. These function as the pick-up points for pulling air from the closets (Figure 15-11).

Figure 15-9.
Filtration system ductwork (seen from kitchen).

Ductwork

When I originally planned the room layout for the Model Healthy House, one of my criteria was to be able to keep the ducts within the conditioned space. In that way very little duct insulation was needed and it was much easier to preserve the integrity of the air barrier.

I designed the layout of the ducts to pull stale air from all the closets and supply fresh air to the living room. This meant I had to figure out a way of running ducts from the filtration and ventilation equipment,

Figure 15-10.
Supply duct to the living room.

Figure 15-11.
Return duct in closets.

229

which was in a central location, to all the closets and living room. This all had to be done within the conditioned space, because there was no crawl space or conventional unheated attic.

With cathedral ceilings throughout the house, I created a small, conditioned mechanical space above the hallway, with a dropped ceiling. With typical 8' high flat ceilings, it would have been impossible to get this same volume of space without sacrificing floor space. I also dropped the ceiling in the laundry and hall closets. This gave me a central location with plenty of overhead room for the ventilation and filtration equipment. There is easy access to the equipment by standing on a stepladder in the central hallway. When ventilation equipment is located in an unconditioned attic or crawl space, it can be difficult to get to and maintain.

The airflows within the ducts can be varied by either using adjustable grilles or adjustable dampers. Dampers fit inside ducts, and grilles are mounted to the wall where the ducts terminate. I used both in various locations so I could balance the airflows to the different rooms. Dampers are also used to balance the fresh air entering the house with the stale air being exhausted outdoors.

The Model Healthy House is heated and air conditioned without ductwork. (I will cover those systems in Chapter 19.) The only ducts required were for the ventilation/filtration system. Since they circulate less air than the average furnace, the ducts were smaller and easier to hide within the walls.

Duct Locations

I was able to run ducts to the master bath, laundry closet, hall closet, kitchen, and living room easily within the mechanical space above the hall. I also used this space for central vacuum lines, plumbing vent and supply lines, and exhaust ducts from the kitchen and bath fans.

In order to run ducts from the mechanical space to the three bedroom closets and the entry closet by the front door, I had to make room for horizontal duct runs inside some of the walls. This involved building thicker-than-normal walls with Z-furring in a few locations (See sheet 13 of the Plans). An alter-native approach would have been to design the floor plan so all the closets were clustered around the central hallway. With closets adjacent to the mechanical space, duct runs can be short and easy to locate. This would, no doubt, have pushed the bedrooms further apart and resulted in a much longer hallway. My decision was to build some thicker walls instead of a longer hall. I figured that the extra material and extra work involved in building the walls would only need to be done once. With a longer hall, extra steps would be necessary every day.

Sealing the Ducts

To avoid any synthetic odors associated with plastic ducting, all the ducts in the house are metal. All of the seams were sealed with the same #339 aluminum-foil tape (**Polyken Technologies**) which I used to seal the exterior wind barrier in Chapter 8. While galvanized metal ducting is quite inert, I washed it with TSP, then rinsed it thoroughly prior to installation to remove any traces of oil left over from the manufacturing process.

Heat Recovery Ventilator

The central filtration system does not provide any fresh air; rather it simply recirculates and filters the air in the house. For fresh air, I decided to use a heat recovery ventilator (HRV). Dozens of manufacturers of HRVs can be found in the U.S. and Canada. These units come in a variety of types, shapes, and sizes. The LIFEBREATH models by **Nutech Energy Systems, Inc.,** sport several features that are important in healthy house construction. The LIFEBREATH units have all-aluminum cores that are removable for cleaning. Some companies use plastic cores that could conceivably bother individuals sensitive to the minor outgassing from synthetics. Cores that aren't removable can be difficult, sometimes even impossible, to clean.

A cabinet for an HRV needs to be insulated for energy efficiency and to prevent it from sweating. The insulation in the LIFEBREATH models consists of fiberglass covered with an aluminum-foil facing to prevent fibers from getting into the

Figure 15-12.
Installed LIFEBREATH heat-recovery ventilator.

airstream. Some synthetic foam seals are used to make the cabinet airtight, but in my experience, they do not seem to have a negative effect on the air passing by them. However, I have had a couple clients who covered the foam seals with aluminum-foil tape as a precautionary measure.

Nutech Energy Systems' LIFEBREATH Model 195DCS is one of the most advanced on the market (Figure 15-12). It uses a single motor coupled to two fans, one for incoming air and one for outgoing air. The motor itself is located in the outgoing airstream. This can be an important design consideration for sensitive individuals who react negatively to minor odors given off by an operating electric motor. This particular model holds the record as far as energy efficiency is concerned. Having dual cores, it is capable of recovering 77% of what would otherwise be wasted heat when the outdoor temperature is -25° C (-13° F). At higher temperatures, it is even more efficient. Manufacturers of other models claim equally high efficiency, but when tested by an independent testing facility, their products generally don't compare favorably. The record 77% figure attributable to the LIFEBREATH model was established by the Canadian Standards Association.

HRV Layout

HRVs typically have 4 connections: fresh air from outdoors, stale air to outdoors, fresh air to indoors, and stale air from indoors. The first two contain cold air in the winter, while the other two contain warm air. Any duct within the conditioned living space that contains cold air must be insulated, like the HRV cabinet itself, to prevent sweating. I used galvanized steel ducts for all connections, taping the joints just as I had done with the filter ducting. On the two cold ducts, I insulated them on the outside with a readily available fiberglass duct insulation. It consists of a plastic sleeve around a 1" thick sleeve of fiberglass. Since the seams in the metal duct are taped, the fiberglass cannot possibly enter the air stream. This product is slipped over the metal duct and taped at each end. When properly installed, the fiberglass is trapped between the metal duct and the plastic sleeve so it is well-separated from the occupants. I used two different brands of duct insulation and found almost no difference between them. The two cold ducts were connected to the two ducts that were stubbed through the ceiling during the Phase 1 construction (Figure 15-13).

231

The HRV cabinet is located above the dropped hallway ceiling near the CRSI #600H filter. The duct that removes stale air from the house is connected directly to the kitchen and the master bath. The duct supplying fresh air into the house is hooked to the plenum on the filter.

In cold climates, it is possible for the cold incoming air to cause the core of an HRV to freeze up. The LIFEBREATH Model 195DCS has a special defrost system in case the core freezes in the winter. This can happen in very cold climates because of the low temperature of the incoming air. The defrost

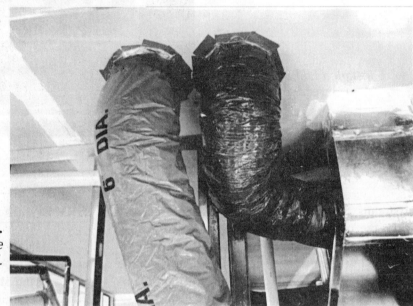

Figure 15-13.
Insulated ducts through the ceiling to the HRV.

Figure 15-14.
Defrost duct connection on the bottom of the HRV.

232

Figure 15-15.
Ventilation/filtration system in place.

system has a fifth duct connection, located on the bottom of the HRV cabinet, that can be run anywhere in the living space. I hooked a rectangular metal boot to it that would later be covered with a grille on the ceiling of the hall closet (Figure 15-14). LIFEBREATH HRVs also have a pair of coarse aluminum prefilters that are easily cleaned in a dishwasher or kitchen sink. Figure 15-15 shows the filter and HRV in place above the hallway.

Operating the HRV & Filtration System

The recirculating filtration system can be operated alone without the HRV bringing in fresh air. It is activated by a 12 hr. crank timer (Model #71 by **Broan Mfg. Co., Inc.**) located in the hallway. The occupants can turn the timer on for as many hours as they like, day or night, and the filter unit will shut off automatically at the end of that time.

In the Model Healthy House, the HRV cannot be operated alone. It can only be run in conjunction with the filtration system. By turning on the "Fresh Air" switch in the hallway, the HRV will come on whenever the filter is turned on by the crank timer. Both will then shut off together.

The filter unit recirculates about 600 cfm of air through the house when operating alone (300 cfm at low speed). When the HRV is also turned on, it blows about 200 cfm of outdoor air into the plenum of the filter. The amount of air passing through the filter is still 600 cfm, but now consists of 400 cfm of recirculated air from the house and 200 cfm of fresh air. This mixture passes into the living room, then travels through the other rooms, through closets and back to the filter, where it is mixed with more fresh air, then the process repeats itself. The 200 cfm provided by the HRV is enough to completely change the air in the house approximately once an hour. With a family of four requiring 60 cfm (15 cfm per person), the HRV would only need to be operated for about 8 hours a day to provide enough fresh air. Fewer people in the family would require less fresh air and if everyone is out of the house, say at work or school, for part of the day, the requirements would be even less. While a smaller HRV could have been selected, I have found from my experience that a system capable of changing the air in the house every hour offers the most flexibility.

While this HRV and filter layout is somewhat more complicated than most setups, it has all the

233

requirements I set down during the design process: It is totally controllable by the occupants, it can be operated independently of the heating or air-conditioning system, it provides plenty of fresh air, air can be circulated throughout the house, both recirculated and incoming fresh air can be filtered, the equipment is easy to access above the hallway, and the HRV is the most energy-efficient available.

While the filtration system is capable of removing a wide variety of pollutants, it is not a good idea to overtax it by trying to filter very dirty air. In the winter, wood smoke often hovers near the ground at night. Therefore, it might be best to only bring in fresh air during the day. On the other hand, in the summer, if neighbors should happen to burn trash, apply chemicals to their lawn, mow it, or otherwise pollute the air during the day, it might be best to bring in fresh air only at night. After living in a specific locale for awhile, a homeowner will usually get to know the peculiarities of the outdoor air and operate the system accordingly.

While the entire ventilation/filtration system may seem complex, the controls are actually quite simple. One switch controls whether the air will be recirculated or will contain fresh outdoor air. The crank timer controls how long the system will run. In the winter, the homeowner may get up in the morning and open the front door to see if there is any lingering wood smoke in the air. If the air is clear, he or she might set the controls on fresh air for 6 hours (or whatever time period seems appropriate). It will soon become routine.

The third control that the homeowners may elect to use is the speed control. It changes the speed of the fan in the filter between 300 cfm and 600 cfm. In most cases the low speed should be sufficient, but the high speed might be useful if a strong odor is generated by a hobby or some other activity. No matter what the setting is for the filter fan, the HRV will still bring in 200 cfm.

Noise Control

Noise control is very important in any mechanical system of this type because, if there is too much noise coming from it, the occupants simply won't turn it on. There are two areas of concern: vibrational noise and air noise.

Vibrational Noise

I used lengths of chain to hang the filter cabinet from the ceiling. This prevents sound vibrations from being transferred from the filter motor to the structure of the building. The HRV was supplied with reinforced rubber straps to be used in hanging it from the ceiling.

Rather than connecting it rigidly, I used a flexible collar between the filter cabinet and the plenum. Collars of this type can be fabricated by most heating and air-conditioning contractors. They are made from a synthetic plastic material that may bother some sensitive people. However, since they are only about 2" long, they shouldn't have much effect on air quality. Their purpose it to cut down on sound vibrations between the filter and the ductwork. I also used similar round collars on the two warm round ducts leaving the HRV.

Air Noise

Whenever air moves through a duct, it makes a sound. The faster the air moves, the louder it will be. This air noise can be reduced by slowing down the air by using a larger duct size. As I mentioned earlier, the filter has an 8" outlet, yet I used an adapter and ran 12" duct to the living room. This is an effective way to reduce the sound of the air. Air noise can also be reduced by running a fan at a slower speed. This can be done with the two-speed filter control.

Local Ventilation Equipment

Besides the central equipment just described, I used three other exhaust fans in the house that can be operated occasionally to remove occupant-generated pollutants and moisture. In addition, there is an exhaust fan in the garage to help rid it of pollutants. All were supplied by **Broan Mfg. Co., Inc.** I selected their products because they offer a wide variety of high-quality exhaust fans that can be used in many different situations.

Figure 15-16.
3¼" x 10" duct for range hood.

Kitchen Range Hood

While the range hood itself wasn't installed at this time, the ductwork needs to be in place before the drywall. In Phase 1, a 3¼" x 10" rectangular duct was stubbed through the ceiling. At this point I extended the duct down inside the wall and terminated it at the correct height for the range hood with a 90 degree elbow (Figure 15-16). All seams were sealed with aluminum-foil tape. The range hood itself (**Broan Mfg. Co., Inc.** Model #76000), is rated at 200 cfm, enough to clear out the kitchen fairly quickly. It was installed later with the kitchen cabinets in Chapter 23.

In general, I don't like gas ranges because of their potential to pollute the indoor air with combustion gases, but I also realize that many people prefer to cook over an open flame. For them, I recommend a more powerful range hood. **Broan** has models as large as 500 cfm.

Master Bath Fan

This fan is mounted on the wall above the bathtub and is connected to the 4" round duct that was stubbed through the ceiling earlier (Figure 15-17). Again, the seams in the ductwork were taped with aluminum-foil tape.

Most bathroom exhaust fans are rated at 50 cfm, a size dictated by many building codes. Inexpensive models rarely move as much air as their rating implies. This is because the airflow is sometimes tested without the fan being hooked up to ductwork. Any ductwork at all causes air resistance and results in reduced capacity. For the Model Healthy House, I selected a larger than normal 110-cfm unit (**Broan Mfg. Co., Inc.** Model #676).

The bath fan is controlled by a unique wall switch (**Broan Mfg. Co., Inc.** Model #64) located near the door that has a special delayed-off feature.

235

Figure 15-17.
Master bath exhaust fan.

Figure 15-18.
Bath-laundry exhaust fan.

The fan can be turned on and off just like a conventional on-off switch, but this switch also has a third position that has a built-in timer. When set in this position, the fan will turn itself off after a certain amount of time has passed. By removing the cover plate, the homeowner can adjust the time period manually from 5 to 60 minutes. Once it is adjusted, the switch can simply be switched to the delayed-off position when you leave the bathroom, and the fan will continue to run for the predetermined time. This is a very handy feature that aids in ridding the bathroom of moisture or odors. With a simple on-off

236

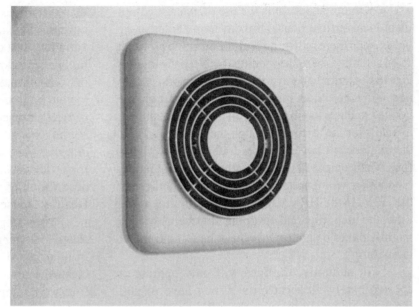

Figure 15-19.
Garage exhaust fan.

switch, the occupant might forget to shut the fan off and waste energy.

Bath-Laundry Fan

I located the bath-laundry fan in the dropped ceiling of the laundry closet and, taping the seams, connected it to the 3¼" x 10" duct stubbed through the ceiling in Phase 1 (Figure 15-18). When running, this fan will pull air through the bathroom, through the closet and exhaust it outdoors, so it is a bathroom fan as well as a laundry fan.

For this application I selected one of **Broan Mfg. Co., Inc.'s** LoSone Ventilators. These are much quieter than most fans. A quiet model is a good idea for a fan that may be left running for several hours at a time, as in a laundry area. I used a **Broan Mfg. Co., Inc.** Model #360 rated at 110 cfm. For someone particularly sensitive to laundry odors (either detergent or soiled clothes), a larger capacity might be in order. LoSone Ventilators are available as large as 1,000 cfm.

This fan is controlled by the same **Broan Mfg. Co., Inc.** Model #64 on/off/delayed off control switch that was used in the master bath.

Garage Fan

Even if a garage isn't filled with the typical variety of offensive materials such as gasoline cans, paint cans, solvents, cleaning products, pesticides, etc., it is a good idea to install an exhaust fan. This is because a hot automobile can have a number of odors associated with it: the rubber smell from the tires, grease and oil from the engine, and gasoline. For the garage, I used a **Broan Mfg. Co., Inc.** Model #508, 270 cfm wall mounted exhaust fan (Figure 15-19). It is controlled with a **Broan Mfg. Co., Inc.** Model #71, 12-hour crank timer. When the car is pulled into the garage, the overhead door can be closed and the timer activated for 2 or 3 hours to clear out any odors given off as the car cools down.

Operating Local Ventilation Equipment

When any of the above local exhaust equipment is used, the building will tend to be depressurized and the fans won't operate as efficiently. Depressurization in a garage won't be of concern if the overhead door isn't weather-stripped, because it will be leaky enough for plenty of make-up air to enter.

Of more concern is the use of exhaust equipment in an airtight house. If there are no holes in the house, then there will be no way for make-up air to get in. In actuality, there are openings between the interior and the exterior wherever there is ductwork is connected to the outdoors. All of the exhaust fans are hooked to ducts having backdraft dampers, making it difficult for air to enter through them, but the HRV ducting doesn't have any backdraft dampers. Therefore, when a piece of exhaust equipment is operating, outdoor air will tend to find its way indoors through the HRV. If the HRV happens to be running at the time, the incoming and outgoing airstreams will be slightly out of balance while the exhaust equipment is operating.

In actuality, the fans will only operate at approximately 50% capacity if they have to pull make-up air solely through the HRV because it is too much work for them. To remove small amounts of pollutants, like the moisture generated from taking a shower, the fans will probably work just fine. To remove larger amounts of pollutants, such as odors from laundry detergent or cooking odors in the kitchen, the fans will work at full capacity only if a window is cracked open. This is an important concept for homeowners to grasp, but once they understand it, it will become routine.

An open window doesn't need to be in the same room in which the exhaust fan is running. For example, with the kitchen range hood running and a bedroom window is open, make-up air will flow in the window, through the bedroom, into the kitchen, and then outdoors. By opening different windows, this can be an easy way to air out different rooms quickly with the range hood.

It is important to keep in mind that the clothes dryer and the central vacuum both exhaust air to the outdoors. They too will operate much more effectively if a window is cracked open whenever they are used.

Update

As I said earlier, the ventilation/filtration system in the Model Healthy house is more complicated than systems used in other houses. There are certainly dozens—perhaps hundreds—of other approaches and variations that can be used for filtering and exchanging the air indoors. You just need to consider all the options and make up a list of criteria that are important to your particular situation, and then design a system to meet your needs. For a complete discussion, please see my book, *Understanding Ventilation: How to design, select, and install residential ventilation systems*. The last few pages of this book contain a description of it and other books published by The Healthy House Institute.

It is important to realize that filters are often asked to do far more than they are capable of doing. In other words, they are called upon to magically clean the air in a very polluted house. While all filters will improve air quality to a degree, many installations are simply not powerful enough to work miracles. Ideally, you should insure clean air by first implementing the three Healthy House Design Principles discussed in Chapter 2: 1) Eliminate pollutant sources, 2) Separate pollutants from the living space by building a tight structure, and 3) Ventilate to supply fresh air and to remove stale air. If you have done that, less filtration will be necessary, and it will be much more effective.

Many people are drawn to simple solutions to air quality problems. I like simple solutions also—but only if they actually work. Using ozone or house plants to clean the air in a house fall into this category and, unfortunately, they just aren't viable approaches. I know of no technically oriented indoor air quality researcher anywhere who advocates them. So, I don't recommend them. At the same time, sometimes high-efficiency filtration is being sold where it isn't really needed. For example, mold spores and pollen, even though they are microscopic in size, are actually relatively large particulates. Thus, they are relatively easy to filter out of the air. So if your allergies are such that you are only interested in removing mold and pollen from your air, a HEPA filter may be overkill, and a medium-efficiency extended-surface filter may work just fine for you.

I should note that, for extremely sensitive people, filters can often be a problem. That is because they might react to the minor outgassing from the resin holding a filter together or the material making up a filter's housing, or to minor odors given off by a warm fan motor, or to any ozone generated by the filter. Thus, people who stand to benefit the most from a filter, may be bothered by the filter itself. If you suspect that you are that sensitive, you should state your concerns before purchasing a filter, and see if it can be returned if you cannot tolerate it.

Filters are often used in conjunction with forced-air heating/cooling systems. This is certainly a viable approach, but it will be most effective only if the fan is allowed to run continuously. Many forced-air heating/cooling systems have a switch that will allow for continuous fan-only operation but over the course of a year this can be costly in terms of electricity used—unless the fan motor is an energy efficient one. Currently, the most efficient fans have "ECM motors" but they are only used in a handful of forced-air heating/cooling systems.

Finally, as I discussed in the "Update" to Chapter 11, in general, I now prefer using water-based duct sealing mastics instead of aluminum-foil tape for sealing ductwork. I feel that the mastics are easier to use, more durable, and longer lasting.

239

Chapter 16

PLUMBING

■ ■ ■ There are a couple of ways that a plumbing system can affect the health of the occupants. The first is by contaminating the water. Pollutants can be released into the water from the water mains in the street, from the house plumbing lines, or from the solder or glue used to connect the pipes and fittings together. A less important problem is the fact that plastic piping materials themselves can outgas small amounts of pollutants into the air.

Plumbing Lines and Pipes

Throughout history, a wide variety of different materials have been used for water pipes. Although it is no longer being installed, asbestos-cement pipe has been used for underground water mains. Historical museums sometimes display pieces of old wooden water mains. Cast iron, lead, and galvanized steel pipes can be found in many older houses. Today, most residential plumbers use copper or a variety of different types of plastic. The copper pipes can be connected together with either mechanical brass fittings (compression or flared), or they can be soldered together. Plastic pipe is usually glued together but sometimes compression fittings are used.

If your drinking water is contaminated with lead, it could be that your house has lead piping, or that the pipes were soldered with a product containing lead. Both of these components can release lead into the water. If you suspect this is the case, have a plumber check out your piping to determine the source of the lead.

Although there have been problems reported with all the different pipe materials, cast iron, copper, and galvanized steel are generally the most inert.

There are three classifications of plumbing lines. Supply lines carry water into a house and to all of the faucets and fixtures. Drain lines carry the water away after you are finished with it and are often called "waste lines." Large-diameter drain lines are called sewers. Vents are pipes that usually don't have any liquid in them. They are connected to drain lines to enable the waste water to flow easier. If you look up on your roof, you will see a plumbing vent pipe that is open to the atmosphere.

Water Supply Lines

For the water supply lines, I prefer to use copper. It is easy to install and usually less expensive than galvanized steel. Many builders use plastic for supply lines because it is the lowest cost option. I don't like to use it because of the possibility that the plastic, or especially the glues, used will contaminate the water. Supply lines (½" and ¾") are considerably smaller than drain lines (1½" to 4"), so the additional cost of copper over plastic for supply lines is fairly small.

Most municipal water systems have many plastic water mains under the street. This is something that can't often be avoided. However, most water mains aren't glued together like residential plastic lines, so they won't pollute the water nearly as much. In any case, I like to use a water filter that will remove any contaminants from the water before it is used by occupants.

Solder

There have been numerous cases of household water being contaminated with lead from the solder used to connect copper pipes together. For this reason, some people have recommended the use of fittings that don't require solder as a healthier way of joining copper pipe. I generally prefer solder because the mechanical fittings sometimes have more leak potential.

Lead-free solder was at one time somewhat difficult to find, but in 1986 the EPA banned the use of solder containing lead in residential plumbing systems. As a result, lead-free solder is now commonplace. It works just as well as the older types and is far healthier, for both homeowners and plumbers.

The actual process of soldering together copper pipe and fittings is no different in healthy house construction than in any other house. The copper is cleaned with a wire brush, flux is applied, the fittings are assembled, the joint is heated with a propane torch, and the assembly is soldered together. It is important to keep in mind that the torch releases combustion gases that can be absorbed by drywall and inhaled by the plumber, so ventilation is important when soldering. The flux helps clean the copper and allows the solder to flow smoothly. Small amounts of flux can remain inside the piping after it has been soldered, but any residual flux will usually be flushed out of the lines after the water is turned on.

Drain Lines

I use PVC plastic drain lines under a concrete floor slab without hesitation because, isolated from the living space, there is no way that they can affect the health of occupants.

For the above-ground drain lines, there are three choices: cast iron, copper, or plastic. Copper and cast iron are both very inert, but plastic is by far the least expensive. For occupants, the main concern with plastic drains is that they could outgas small amounts of pollutants into the air. Also, the glues and cleaners used to install plastic piping are especially noxious. This is particularly detrimental to plumbers.

Based on personal experience in building houses for sensitive individuals, I don't feel that there are any major drawbacks to using plastic for all the drain lines. The piping is hidden within wall cavities once the drywall is in place, so it isn't directly exposed to the living space. Even if walls are not built in an airtight manner, plastic plumbing lines within walls do not seem to pose a problem, even for sensitive occupants. In some cases, as a safety measure, I have wrapped all of the plastic drain lines with household aluminum foil before installing the drywall. I use whatever brand of foil is the cheapest at the grocery store. This is fairly easy to do and can give a sensitive occupant a certain amount of peace of mind. It may not really be necessary, but it could be considered cheap insurance.

Something else that can be done to reduce the amount of outgassing from plastic piping is to purchase the pipe and fittings early in the construction process. By doing so, the plastic can be airing out while the early phases of construction are being carried out. The material can be stored in a garage until it is ready to use.

The glues and cleaners used with plastic piping seem to outgas very quickly, in a matter of hours, so they do not seem to have a lasting effect to bother homeowners once the house is occupied. However, it is still a good idea to air out the building when such products are being used. This will prevent absorbent materials such as drywall from becoming contaminated with the odor, and more importantly, will protect the health of the plumbers who are in close proximity to the glues. I usually wear a cartridge-type respirator when I work with these products.

Vents

Vents are an important part of a plumbing system. They allow water to flow down drains smoothly without gurgling. This is important because it prevents sewer gases from entering the living space. Without proper vents, odors from a sewer in the street or from a septic tank could gurgle through the traps under sinks or bathtubs and enter the living space. Vents are required by building codes and are well understood by plumbers.

Since vent lines are actually a part of the drain system, the same three choices are available: plastic, copper, and cast iron. Again, my choice is plastic because of its low cost, and the fact that it isn't a material that outgasses a great deal. Plastic piping for vents can be purchased early to air out and can be wrapped with aluminum foil after installation, just like the drain lines.

Bathtubs

Bathtubs are either made of plastic (usually fiberglass or acrylic) or metal (cast iron or steel). Metal tubs are inert from an outgassing standpoint. However, because they have no seams, one-piece plastic tub/shower units may be a better choice for someone allergic to mold. By not having any corners or crevices for water to penetrate, they are less likely to harbor mold or mildew.

Water Filters

Water can become contaminated in a variety of ways. Pollutants can be released from piping, solder, or glue. Pollutants such as chlorine are routinely added to drinking water by most water utility companies. Water may contain pesticides because the source (an underground aquifer, or a lake) has been contaminated. You can ingest these pollutants by drinking the contaminated water; volatile compounds may be absorbed through your skin while bathing; and some pollutants can be released into the air from the water and then inhaled.

Nearly every public water system in the country uses chlorine as a disinfectant. It does an excellent job of killing pathogenic bacteria and, as a result, has saved tens of thousands of lives over the years. But at the same time, chlorine is considered a contaminant. Chlorine can react with common organic pollutants in water to produce chloroform, a carcinogen. Several studies have found an increase in cancer among people who drink chlorinated water. Many sensitive people cannot tolerate even small amounts of chlorine in water.

The easiest way to remove chlorine and other volatile chemicals from water is to use an activated carbon filter. These filters use the same activated carbon found in air filters. There has been some concern expressed that bacteria can grow inside an activated carbon filter. This is certainly possible, but if the water was originally chlorinated, the bacteria are generally not disease-causing. To alleviate a potential problem, many people let the water run for a few seconds before drinking from the tap. This helps to flush out some of the bacteria. A bacteria problem can also be minimized by changing the filter cartridge on a regular basis. In most situations, the advantages of an activated carbon filter seem to outweigh the risks. However, if your water comes from a private well and it has not been chlorinated, it could contain a wider variety of bacteria, some of which are disease-causing. If your water comes from a private well you should have your water tested to insure that an activated carbon filter is really called for.

There are several other kinds of water filters on the market that are capable of removing nearly every contaminate from the water, but they can be expensive to buy or operate. For example, a reverse osmosis unit will flush several gallons of water down the drain for each gallon of water that is purified. Distillation units can remove a number of pollutants from water, but they also remove desirable minerals. For a complete discussion of water filters, see *The Healthy Household* listed in Appendix 1.

Fortunately, most people do not require extremely pure water. For those who do, they generally

Figure 16-1.
Copper plumbing lines isolated from steel to prevent corrosion.

only need it for cooking or drinking, so a small under-the-counter model in the kitchen is often sufficient.

Water Heating

Healthy houses frequently have electric water heaters to avoid polluting the indoor air with combustion products from a gas water heater. But heating water electrically can be expensive. If feasible to install, solar water heating can reduce this cost significantly.

I chose **Sage Advance Corporation's** Copper Cricket solar water heater for the Model Healthy House because its unique design has no moving parts, no pumps, no electronics. It requires almost no maintenance and doesn't freeze in the winter. Most solar water heaters on the market have one or more of these disadvantages. The Copper Cricket moves the heated solar liquid by a process called "geyser pumping" that is similar to a coffee percolator. It has been getting good reviews among solar designers and is backed with a 10-year guarantee.

The Copper Cricket works by transferring heat from the rooftop collector down to a standard electric water heater only when the sun is shining. On a cloudy day, the electric water heater works just as it would if there were no solar heater. Thus, there is never any danger of running out of hot water. Actually, the solar heater functions like a pre-heater.

As to electric water heaters themselves, I prefer those with glass-lined tanks over those with a plastic lining since they're less likely to contaminate the water. I also have some concern about outgassing from the insulation surrounding the tank. Most of the outgassing should dissipate relatively quickly, but I like to help the process along by temporarily removing the covers over the water heater thermostats and setting the temperature as high as it will go for a few days. This will hasten the outgassing, then the thermostats can be lowered to an energy-conserving 120 degrees and the covers replaced. It is a good idea to provide extra ventilation during this "baking" period.

Plumbing Rough-in for the Model Healthy House

I installed some of the plumbing lines earlier in the construction process: the drain lines

244

under the concrete floor slab, the vent through the roof, the main water supply line entering the house, and the outdoor faucet near the redwood deck. In this chapter, I will cover the remainder of the plumbing items that need to be roughed in before the interior walls are closed up.

Water Supply Lines

The copper supply piping was assembled with lead-free solder per the schematic drawing shown on Sheet 20 of the Plans. Copper pipes must not be allowed to touch the steel studs because the two dissimilar metals can corrode if placed in contact with each other. A leak resulting from corrosion can develop quickly if moisture is present on the outside of the pipes—something that can easily occur if the plumbing lines sweat.

I obtained some plastic clips from an electrical supply house that snapped into the prepunched holes in the studs. They worked like a charm to protect the copper pipe (Figure 16-1). I also found that where I needed to clamp the copper piping to the side of a stud, a short length of garden hose made a perfect insulator (Figure 16-2).

Anti-Scald Valves

The bath/shower valves are installed at this stage. I chose the Model #1548 valves from the **Delta Faucet Co.** They are designed to protect bathers from sudden temperature changes in the water. With a standard valve, if a person is showering and someone else flushes a toilet, most of the cold water goes to the toilet and the water in the shower suddenly becomes much hotter. **Delta** uses pressure-balance valves to eliminate the possibility of being scalded in such a situation. The valves also have an internal adjustment for the maximum-desired temperature. This is an important feature if there are children in the household who might accidentally turn the faucet to a high temperature. It is also a good feature for a disabled person with limited dexterity. Once the internal control is adjusted, the water at the tap will never be any hotter than the internal setting. A third feature these valves offer is that they cycle from off to cold to hot to prevent burns when they are first turned on. That is, when they are initially turned on, the water is cold, then you adjust it up to the desired temperature. These valves are supplied with shower heads that operate at a water-saver volume of 2.5 gallons per minute.

Figure 16-2.
Isolating copper plumbing lines from steel framing.

245

The brass used in most faucet valves contains minute amounts of lead.

The brass used in most faucet valves contains minute amounts of lead. Delta Faucet Co. uses machined brass bodies for their valves because it contains significantly less lead than the sand-cast valves used by other companies. All their single-handle faucets also conform to the requirements set by the American National Standards Institute for the disabled.

Leak Testing

Once all the supply lines were in place, I turned on the main shut-off valve at the water meter and checked all the soldered connections for leaks. Leak testing is required by many building codes. It is important to prevent water damage and wasteful leaks. From a health standpoint, even a tiny leak inside a wall could eventually result in mold growth.

Water Filter

Since the Model Healthy House is hooked up to a municipal water supply, my main concern had to do with chlorine contamination, so I wanted to use an activated-carbon filter to remove it. Until recently, whole house activated-carbon water filters designed to process all the water entering the house were prohibitively expensive. Today there is an affordable option. The Model WH-400S filter by **Ametek** contains both a large activated-carbon filter and a large sediment prefilter. It is said to have a life of up to 75,000 gallons. This translates to between 6 and 12 months for a family of four. Of course, the actual filter life will depend on local water conditions and the occupant's usage.

The **Ametek** filter should remove not only chlorine, but also any contaminants from the plastic water mains under the street that might contaminate the water before it enters the house. This filter can be considered a generic approach. By removing any chlorine or other volatile compounds, there will be no danger of absorbing them through the skin or inhaling them while bathing.

To provide a solid mounting surface for the filter, I attached a scrap piece of the load-bearing steel framing material I used for window headers to the 6"

non-load-bearing wall. The filter itself wasn't installed at this stage, only the steel framing for mounting it, and the two roughed-in ¾" copper lines.

Drain and Vent Lines

A schematic of the plumbing drain and vent layout is shown on Sheet 20 of the Plans. The system consists of 1½" to 3" PVC piping, various elbows, and other fittings. It was all glued together using the standard cleaners and adhesives. I highly recommend open windows, fans, and the use of a cartridge respirator to reduce exposure to glue odors.

When I installed the plumbing lines in the foundation, they were carefully located so the drains and vents would later be hidden inside the walls. As I mentioned in Chapter 11, the 3" vent through the roof that was installed during the Phase 2 sealing process was purposefully not aligned directly over the 3" pipe in the concrete slab. If it were directly above it, the flashing I used to seal the vent to the drywall would have stuck beyond the wall and been visible on the finished ceiling. By having the ceiling pipe offset, it is hidden in the mechanical space above the hall's dropped ceiling. With a pair of elbows, it was easily connected to the pipe rising up from the floor so that the entire plumbing system could be vented to the atmosphere.

In the kitchen, I stubbed a 1½" PVC vent pipe through the wall in the vicinity of the kitchen sink cabinet (Figure 16-3). It was later hooked up to the drain line in the floor after the cabinets were installed.

Bathtubs

In the Model Healthy House I opted for standard steel bathtubs to avoid any outgassing from plastic units. Cast iron would have been an equally healthy choice, albeit somewhat more expensive. For shower walls, I chose stainless steel. They will be discussed in Chapter 24.

Bathtub Drains

Before I set the bathtubs in place, I used a utility knife to cut the tops out of the plastic forms that

Figure 16-3.
Vent for kitchen sink.

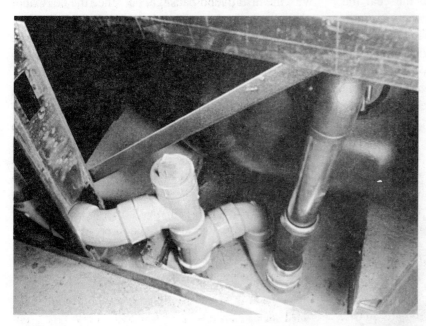

Figure 16-4.
Bathtub drain.

were placed around the bathtub drain lines in the concrete floor slab (see Chapter 5). Then I sealed the sides of the plastic forms to the concrete with 100% silicone caulking. This resulted in an airtight pocket beneath the bathtub that could accommodate the tub's trap and drain. If this area had been left open, it could be an easy path for radon to get into the living space. The drain itself was a standard brass model. While not required by the building code, I also installed a clean-out in the drain. It was easy to do and it might come in handy someday if the drain ever gets clogged (Figure 16-4).

247

Washing Machine Drain

The 1½" PVC drain for the washing machine was attached to a plastic wall box that also contains the two faucets for the washer hoses. Based on experience, these plastic boxes do not seem to outgas very much after installation. Actually, the washing machine itself is more likely to pollute the air because of odors from its internal pumps, hoses, motor, and belts.

I attached a 1½" PVC drain for the HRV and the air conditioner to the side of the 1½" PVC washer drain pipe. The HRV has a small ½" drain line for draining away the water that can sometimes condense inside its cores. The air conditioner, because it removes moisture from the air when running, also requires a small drain line. I didn't connect the standpipe for these drains to their own trap because during some periods of the year the trap would dry out. A trap must always contain water to prevent sewer gas from entering the house. Because the washer drain will be used regularly, its trap should always contain water. By attaching the AC/HRV drain to its side, I was confident it was hooked to a trap that would always contain water.

Solar Water Heater Connection

During Phase 1, the two ¾" copper lines from the rooftop-mounted Copper Cricket water heater (**Sage Advance Corp.**) were stubbed through the ceiling. At this time I extended them across the dropped ceiling and down inside a wall to a point near where the water heater would be located. The joints were soldered in the same way as the plumbing lines. It is important that the solar lines slope at least ¼" per foot toward the electric water heater for the solar heater to function correctly. The lines also need to be insulated with standard foam rubber pipe insulation having a ¾"-thick wall (Figure 16-5). It is important that the two lines not get mixed up, so I labeled them "Blue" and "Red" just like they had been marked on the rooftop collector.

Some of the insulation material is supplied with the installation package, but since the company can't predict how much insulation your particular set-up will require, I needed to buy a little extra locally. Like the plastic plumbing drains, the insulation might bother sensitive individuals if they are exposed to it directly, but once covered with drywall, it is doubtful if this will become a problem. Some homeowners may

Figure 16-5.
"Red" and "blue" solar liquid lines.

Figure 16-6.
Pressurizing the solar liquid lines.

wish to specify that it be wrapped with household aluminum foil as an added precaution.

Sage Advance Corp. stresses the importance of flawless solder connections for proper operation. Since the company realizes that many of their solar water heaters will be installed by do-it-yourselfers, they even include a soldering instruction sheet in their manual.

Once the two solar lines were in place, I soldered caps temporarily on the ends and fitted one with a snifter valve (Figure 16-6). A snifter valve is similar to a tire valve, and it enabled me to use a bicycle pump to pressurize the system and check for leaks. I pumped the pressure up to 50 pounds per square inch and it held steady for several days—meaning there were no leaks.

Radon Removal System

Like I did with the main 3" plumbing vent, I offset the 4" PVC radon removal tube in the ceiling from the one in the concrete slab (see Chapter 11). With a pair of elbows, they were easy to connect together. If high indoor radon levels are ever measured, it will be a simple matter of con-

necting a suction fan to the terminus outside the house. A simple radon test will be performed once the house is complete to see if a fan is necessary.

Update

Unfortunately, as I mentioned in the "Update" in Chapter 11, **Sage Advance Corp.**, the manufacturer of the Copper Cricket solar water heater, is no longer in business. While a solar water heater is a definite energy saving feature, it is not a health feature so, without it, the indoor air quality will not be compromised.

I continue to have slightly mixed feelings about what type of bathtub to use with sensitive people. I like the fact that steel and cast-iron tubs are made of inert materials—but some do have a soundproofing material on the back side that might be bothersome if a sensitive individual were exposed to it directly. On the other hand, I like the one-piece plastic tub/shower units because they have no seams in which mold can grow. Since the Model Healthy House was built, my wife and I built ourselves a new house (see Chapter 28), and we

249

used a one-piece fiberglass model and it has worked out quite well. Based on my experiences with various sensitive people, it seems that fiberglass out-gases less that acrylic, but we still bought the fiberglass unit early in the construction process and allowed it to air out before installing it.

250

Chapter 17

CENTRAL VACUUM

■ ■ ■ All houses have a certain amount of dust in them. But a dust mop does more to move dust around than pick it up, and most portable vacuum cleaners have such inefficient filters that the fine particles of dust are blown through the filter bag and back into the room. A central vacuum is a much cleaner and healthier choice, but it should have an outdoor exhaust so that any dust particles that do happen to get past the filter are blown outdoors.

While there are portable vacuums on the market with high-efficiency HEPA filters or special water filters, I usually recommend central vacuums because they are much more convenient. Central units are comparable in cost to the high-efficiency portables, and most homeowners prefer them.

The central vacuum unit itself can be located in a basement, laundry area, closet, or attached garage. It is then connected to several wall inlets in different rooms of the house with 2" plastic tubing and small electric wires. To use the vacuum, you simply plug the hose into one of the inlets and the machine automatically turns on.

I chose a Model #189S central vacuum made by **Beam Industries** for the Model Healthy House. It came with an installation kit pre-packaged with the average number of elbows and fittings required.

(You can also order individual fittings.) **Beam** also supplies the required straight tubing.

Central Vacuum Rough-in for the Model Healthy House

The **Beam Industries** Model #189 central vacuum unit has a 2-horsepower motor (try and beat that with a portable model), mounted in a steel housing. **Beam** uses a special system that does not need a paper filter bag. You just empty the 5-gallon dirt receptacle a couple times a year. The standard accessory kit contains the various wands and tools for most applications. Although it isn't necessary in the Model Healthy House, a power head with rotating brushes for more efficient carpet cleaning is also available from **Beam**.

Rough-in for a central vacuum consists of assembling the 2" PVC plastic tubing, elbows, and other fittings inside the walls. I installed three inlets (in the kitchen, master bedroom, and living room), connected them together, and extended the suction tubing into the laundry closet in the bathroom where I planned to mount the vacuum unit itself. I used the same type of glue that plumbers use with

Figure 17-1.
Installing plaster guard over vacuum inlet.

plastic drain lines, so similar ventilation precautions are necessary when using it. The tubing for the vacuum's exhaust, that was stubbed through the ceiling in Phase 1 (Chapter 11), was also extended into the laundry closet.

A pair of wires (also supplied by **Beam**) needs to be run from each wall inlet to the central unit. These will later be used to activate the motor. To complete the rough-in, I temporarily installed plastic plaster guards over the three inlets (Figure 17-1). **Beam** supplies these so that the inlets are not inadvertently drywalled over. I made sure that there was a stud located where the vacuum unit's mounting bracket would later be located inside the laundry closet. In fact, I used a heavier load-bearing stud for added support strength.

Update

Beam Industries has recently introduced a very handy gadget that I have found to be very useful. It's called a Vac-Pan because it is a vacuum-assisted dust pan. Here's how it works. There is a short hinged door mounted along the floor that is connected to one of the 2" PVC suction lines. To use it, you push the door open with the toe of your shoe. This turns the vacuum's motor on. Then you can use a broom to sweep any debris on the floor into the Vac-Pan. When finished, you simply tap the door closed, and the vacuum shuts off. No more stooping down with a conventional dust pan. A Vac-Pan is handy to have in a kitchen, and I've heard of them being mounted on top of a workbench.

Chapter 18

ELECTRICAL

■■■ The electrical systems of a house can affect your health in several ways. Most importantly, improperly wired receptacles can result in electrocution. Plastic components can outgas small amounts of pollutants into the air. The invisible electromagnetic fields surrounding electrical equipment can also have health effects.

Electrical Components

Many components of a house's electrical system are made of plastic. This is because plastic is a good insulator and it helps to protect occupants from being shocked. However, some of these components can outgas to a certain degree. Other electrical components are designed to protect people from hazards: ground-fault interrupters insulate us in shock-prone situations, smoke detectors warn us if there is a fire.

Electrical Wire

The electrical wiring typically used in residential work is called "romex." It has a plastic jacketing that is bothersome to some sensitive people. For this reason, it is sometimes recom-mended that wiring be encased in metal conduit. This is often done in commercial applications, but it can be somewhat more expensive because of the increased material and labor costs. I have found that if the romex is purchased early in the construction process and allowed to air out prior to being installed, it loses much of its odor. It has also been my experience that once the drywall is installed, the wiring (like the plastic plumbing drains) is no longer a problem. However, there are many different manufacturers of romex, and some brands can have a stronger odor than others. In the past, I have wrapped any odorous plastic jacketed wiring with household aluminum foil, an inexpensive measure that seems to reduce any residual outgassing to a minimum.

When stringing romex through metal studs, the plastic jacketing must be protected or the sharp edges of the studs will cut through it. This can result in a short circuit and possibly an electrical fire. Special plastic clips are sold through electrical supply houses for this purpose (these are the same clips I used with the plumbing lines in Chapter 16). The clips come in several different shapes (Figure 18-1). Round inserts that require a special hole punching tool may be specified by some electrical codes because they totally surround the wire.

Electrical Boxes

From an outgassing standpoint, most plastic electrical boxes are relatively inert, but some can have a very slight odor. I used plastic airtight electrical boxes in Phase 1 (**Nu-Tek Plastics, Inc.**) because their advantage of being airtight seemed to far outweigh the fact that they were made of plastic. For the remainder of the house, I decided to use conventional metal electrical boxes because they don't outgas anything. Since the walls between conditioned rooms don't need to be airtight, the metal boxes will work fine, and they don't add very much to the overall cost of the house.

Ground Fault Interrupters

Most building codes require the use of ground fault interrupters (GFIs) in locations where electrical shocks could be especially dangerous. This includes bathrooms, kitchens, garages, and outdoor receptacles. GFIs offer increased protection from electrical shock because they sense a dangerous situation quickly and shut off the circuit. You can buy special GFI receptacles that look a little different than conventional receptacles, or you can install special GFI circuit breakers in the main power panel. According to the electrical code, convenience outlets within 6' of the sink must be protected with GFIs. For added electrical safety, I wired all of the convenience outlets in the kitchen through GFI circuit breakers.

Smoke Detectors

Smoke detectors are now required by most building codes. Even if they weren't, I would highly recommend them because they do save lives. There are two basic types on the market: ionizing and photoelectric. The ionizing type are much more common because of their lower cost. Unfortunately, ionizing smoke detectors require small amounts of radioactive material in order to operate.

While the amount of radioactive material found in smoke detectors is considered, by both manufacturers and government regulators, to be insignificant (less than 5 microcuries), I don't like the idea of bringing any radioactive material indoors if it can be helped. These types of smoke detectors are supposed to be shielded so that there is no release of radiation, but if they are damaged, occupants could be exposed.

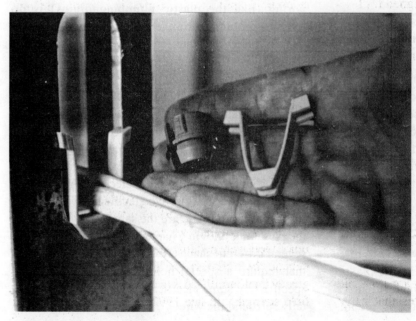

Figure 18-1.
Protecting plastic-jacketed wiring from being cut by steel studs.

Figure 18-2.
Metal electrical box.

Eventually, when these detectors are worn out, they will end up in landfills that are not designed for low-level nuclear waste.

It can be argued that the amount of radiation in ionizing smoke detectors is so small that we shouldn't be concerned about it. However, a safer, more-effective alternative is readily available, so why not use it? While they cost a little more than the ionizing type, "photoelectric" smoke detectors contain absolutely no radioactive material. And, according to *Consumer Reports* they are also more efficient at detecting early combustion and are subject to fewer false alarms.

Electromagnetic Fields

Electromagnetic fields (EMFs) are invisible areas of energy that surround all wires that carry electric current. EMFs also surround electric motors, household appliances, baseboard heaters, and any other kind of equipment that is operated electrically. While they are called electromagnetic because they are part electrical and part magnetic, most of the health concerns over EMFs have focused on the magnetic component. In our modern electrically operated society, it is virtually impossible to avoid EMFs completely.

The negative health effects associated with electromagnetic fields have nothing to do with getting shocked or electrocuted. This subject first received widespread attention in 1979 when a report in the *American Journal of Epidemiology* revealed that some children were at increased risk of developing leukemia if there were certain types of electrical power lines outside their homes. The EMFs in this study were greater than 3 milliGauss (a measurement of magnetic field strength). In late 1992 a major Swedish study

Figure 18-3.
Kitchen wiring rough-in.

found that children exposed over long periods to 3 milliGauss (mG.) fields had almost four times the expected rate of leukemia as children in the general population.

There are two things that are very important to keep in mind when considering the possible negative health effects of EMFs: the strength of the field and the length of exposure. Most experts are of the opinion that the greatest danger is to someone who spends a considerable amount of time around fairly strong EMFs. For example, various studies have reported that workers in electrical occupations, such as cable splicers, electricians, linemen, and TV repairers, have increased risks of leukemia, brain cancer, or breast cancer. There are also reports of individuals who are hypersensitive to very low levels of EMFs.

In his book, *Cross Currents*, Robert O. Becker suggests a policy of prudence avoidance. He recommends avoiding field strengths greater that 1 mG. for continuous exposure. Others have suggested that anything below 3 mG. is probably a relatively safe level. Becker also notes that higher field strengths can probably be tolerated for short periods.

I have taken a gaussmeter and measured the field strength in an average residence. In many cases,

it is difficult to measure any EMFs resulting from the 110-volt electrical wiring that feeds the majority of the circuits in a house. I have measured a field strength of 30 mG. right next to an electric baseboard heater, but since the field strength diminishes rapidly the further you move away from the source, the reading was only 1 mG. about a foot away from the heater. I have seen readings as high as 50 mG. at the main power panel, but 18" away the field strength drops off to the safe range. Moderately high readings can also be found close to dimmer switches (50 mG.) and doorbell transformers (100 mG.), but the field strength diminishes a short distance away from them as well.

As a general rule, the greatest field strengths that an average person will be exposed to in a typical residence are from household appliances. Electric shavers, hand held hair dryers, and electric ranges, all have fairly high field strengths near them. However, it is important to keep in mind that in most cases we do not use these things for extended periods of time, so they should not be of major concern.

Personally, I feel items like electric blankets and the clock radio next to your bed are of more concern because you can be exposed to their high field strength for 8 hours each night. The concept of prudent avoidance would dictate that you minimize the amount of time spent near high-strength fields. The solution can be as simple as avoiding the use of electric blankets or moving the clock radio further away from your bed.

I know of a number of people who have extreme sensitivities to EMFs. However, I know of many more instances where individuals are bothered by synthetic materials and outgassing. Both are definite concerns, but it is my opinion that chemical pollution is a bigger problem than electrical pollution simply because of the

Figure 18-4.
Kitchen cabinet fluorescent light rough-in.

Figure 18-5.
Recessed hall ceiling light.

Figure 18-6.
Main electrical panel.

numbers of people experiencing hypersensitivity reactions. Therefore, I don't feel overly threatened by most residential exposures. For example, I don't get concerned when I walk past the electrical panel in my home, but at the same time, I wouldn't live close to a high-voltage power line. I have also moved the clock radio by my bed a little further away from my head, and I won't use an electric blanket.

There is a great deal of research currently underway to determine the precise health effects of EMFs. But unfortunately, at this time no one knows precisely what EMFs do to the body at low (or high) field strengths, or what field strengths are totally without risk. The subject is quite complicated, but in my mind it makes sense to avoid long-term exposure to high-strength fields whenever possible.

In order to determine the strength of the electromagnetic fields in your home, you must have a gaussmeter to measure them. Since there is an in-

creased public awareness about this subject, many local electric utilities have purchased the appropriate test equipment. If you live near a high-voltage power line, you may be able to get them to measure the field strength inside your house. Some mail order catalogs, such as **Baubiologie Hardware**, offer gaussmeters for sale. Prices start at about $150.

Electrical Rough-In for the Model Healthy House

The electrical rough-in consisted of attaching the metal electrical boxes directly to the steel studs with self-tapping screws (Figure 18-2), and stringing all the wiring. Be sure to install the plastic clips in the holes of the metal studs to prevent the plastic jacketed wiring from getting cut or otherwise damaged.

At this stage I installed boxes and wiring for everything that wasn't done during Phase 1: receptacles, switches, lights, telephone, television, and doorbell. In the kitchen, I stubbed the wiring in place for the dishwasher, the two receptacles to be built into the cabinetry to the left of the sink (Figure 18-3), and the fluorescent light under the wall cabinet between the stove and refrigerator. (Figure 18-4) The only other lights that needed to be roughed in at this stage were the lights over the bathroom sinks, the hall light (Figure 18-5), the pull-chain light in the mechanical space above the hall, and the three walk-in closet lights. The electrical panel (Figure 18-6) was located in the hallway for easy access.

As I did in Phase 1, all the television outlets contain a 75-ohm coax cable and a 4-wire antenna rotor cable. I mounted the small transformer for the doorbell to an electrical box above the hall. The telephone wires from the phone boxes (See Sheet 19 of the Plans for locations) were pushed through the 1" PVC pipe in the north exterior wall, then that pipe was sealed shut with 100% silicon caulking for an airtight seal. The telephone company later installed a junction box on the outside of the house and hooked the house wires up to their system.

I used two special GFI circuit breakers in the power panel and wired all the appropriate receptacles to them. Most of the actual wiring in the Model Healthy House is no different than that in a conventional house. Sheet 19 of the Plans shows the locations of the various electrical components and which receptacles are GFI-protected.

Update

I continue to get a lot of questions about EMFs, such as "How far away from a high-voltage power line is a safe distance?" Unfortunately, that is an impossible question to answer. I believe that if power lines result in a reading at your house of less than 3 mG., you are reasonably safe—but no one knows for sure how safe. In order to determine what the reading is in your particular situation, you simply can't guess—you must take a measurement with a gaussmeter.

If you are concerned about nearby power lines, or with an electrical substation, you might contact the power company that supplies you with electricity. Because so many people have concerns about EMFs, many electric companies now have gaussmeters, and they will often measure the electromagnetic fields near your home for you. However, no matter what the measurement, they will probably tell you that it isn't high enough to worry about, that you will most certainly have higher readings inside your house due to things like appliances. They are correct in that there will likely be higher isolated readings indoors—I call them EMF hotspots. But most of the time the field strength drops off from a hotspot within 1-3 feet, so you are only occasionally exposed—when you walk by the hotspot. However, if there are high strength EMFs from nearby high-voltage electrical power lines, you will be bathed in them continuously. Keep in mind the fact that electrical companies will probably not take measurements *inside* your home. To do that you must purchase or rent a gaussmeter and do so yourself.

Recently **Baubiologie Hardware** has gone out of business. However, there are a number of other mail-order sources for gaussmeters (devices used to measure electromagnetic fields). I've listed one company in Appendix 2.

Chapter 19

HEATING AND AIR CONDITIONING

■■■ Most of the houses being built today are heated and air conditioned with forced-air systems that circulate warm or cool air to and from the different rooms through a series of ducts. There are also forced hot water systems that pump hot water to radiators or into radiant tubing embedded in the floor of each room. These are generally referred to as central systems because they are designed to service the entire house.

Electric baseboard heaters and individual space heaters are not considered central systems because each heater only supplies heat to the room in which it is located. Similarly, a window air conditioner will generally only cool the room in which it is located.

Forced-Air Systems

A forced-air system consists of an air handler (with heating and/or cooling capacity), a filter (usually an inexpensive one), supply ducts (that supply heated or cooled air to the various rooms), and return ducts (that return the air to the air handler so it can be heated or cooled again). The air handler is basically a metal box with a blower. Its purpose is to move air. The box is usually lined with fiberglass as an insula-

ting and soundproofing material. If the system is designed to heat the air, it is called a furnace; if it cools the air, it is called a central air conditioner. Many forced air systems today have both heating and cooling capability.

Central air conditioners have a cooling coil mounted just above the blower. The cooling coil is connected to a compressor which is located outside the house. The compressor pumps a refrigerant through copper tubing from the outdoor unit to the cooling coil and back. In doing so, heat from the house air is pulled into the refrigerant within the cooling coil and transferred through the tubing to the outdoors. Refrigerants have been implicated in damaging the ozone layer of the atmosphere and are not good for people to breathe, but manufacturers are now using less-damaging refrigerants. However, in any case, this is a closed system and as long as it is not damaged and is in good working order, the refrigerant should remain sealed within the system.

The heat for a forced-air furnace can come from a combustion process—the burning of wood, oil, coal, natural gas, bottled gas, etc. All such furnaces should be connected to a flue or chimney so that the burned combustion gases can escape to the outdoors rather than pollute the living space. The heat for a forced-air furnace can also come from electricity. Electric furnaces have coils in them, much like toasters, that warm the air passing over them. Heat pumps work like air conditioners, except in reverse. They extract heat from the outdoor air and transfer it, by way of the refrigerant, to a heating coil in the furnace. Most heat pumps are actually capable of providing either heat or "cool" depending on the season. However, many heat pumps cannot supply all of the heat needed during the coldest months. Therefore, they have what are called back-up resistance heaters. These are the same types of electrical heating elements used in electric furnaces (and toasters).

One of the reasons that forced-air systems are popular is the fact that they circulate air in the house. Because they circulate air, many people believe that they automatically provide the house with fresh air from the outdoors. After all, they are often called HVAC (heating, ventilation, and air conditioning) systems. Unfortunately, most residential HVAC systems are not designed to supply a house with fresh air. In fact, sometimes running a furnace will cause the indoor air to become more polluted than when the furnace is idle.

Problems with Forced-Air Systems

There are several ways in which forced air systems can affect health. First of all, the fiberglass insulation that lines the metal air handler cabinet is directly exposed to the airstream. That means any odors or fibers released from the insulation will be blown into the living space. Fiberglass insulation can also become contaminated with mold and release mold spores into the airstream. The insulation can sometimes be removed from the cabinet, but I don't recommend doing so unless you first contact the manufacturer to determine whether or not it will result in any damage to the system.

The blower that moves the air is also located within the airstream, and there can be odors released from a warm electric motor that can be bothersome to some people. There is not much that can be done about this problem, but fortunately it usually isn't a major consideration except for very sensitive people. I have heard of resourceful con-

tractors who have remounted the motor outside the air-handler cabinet, but this can be difficult to do.

Natural gas piping and fuel oil lines can be subject to leakage, and they can release gas or oil into the living space. A bad leak will be detected quickly with your sense of smell, but many houses have small leaks that aren't readily noticeable. Your gas company has the proper equipment to test for leaks, and they are generally happy to do so, because a leak can not only affect health, it can also result in a serious explosion.

Backdrafting and Spillage

In most of the furnaces that rely on a combustion process for heat, the hot combustion gases rise up into a flue or chimney simply because they are warm. The fact that warm air rises is a naturally occurring phenomenon, and it is possible to measure how much force is exerted by warm air rising in a chimney. Problems occur when a house gets depressurized. This happens when air is blown out of a house by an exhaust device (ventilation fan, clothes dryer, central vacuum, etc.). If the force generated by the exhaust device is stronger than the natural force in the chimney, then the combustion gases can't go up the chimney fast enough, and some of them spill into the air of the room around the furnace. This is called spillage. If an exhaust device is especially powerful, then none of the combustion gases can make it up the chimney. This is called backdrafting.

Various studies in Canada have found that backdrafting and spillage can be a problem in about half of the houses examined. Gary Nelson of The Energy Conservatory in Minneapolis manufactures testing devices called "blower doors," and has measured air pressures in hundreds of houses. He has found that 50-80% of the houses with conventional combustion appliances are susceptible to backdrafting or spillage. If this is a chronic problem, or if a particularly serious episode occurs, the result could be asphyxiation of the occupants due to carbon monoxide poisoning.

To determine if your house is prone to backdrafting or spillage, you should locate someone familiar with analyzing the air pressures in a house. Most

262

heating and air-conditioning contractors aren't, but some home inspectors are. Often this requires the use of a blower door that can artificially depressurize a house to determine if and when a problem might occur. Even though backdrafting and spillage won't occur in the Model Healthy House because it contains no combustion sources, I had the house tested with a blower door to determine precisely how airtight it was. It is a fairly simple procedure (see Chapter 27).

You can often cure a backdrafting and spillage problem in an existing house by constructing an airtight furnace room that draws its combustion air from the outdoors. This can be done in the basement, or in some cases a furnace can be mounted in a small storage building outside the house to keep the pollutants out of the living space. A remote furnace like this would be connected to the house with well-insulated ductwork. The goal is to create an area for the furnace to operate that is not subject to pressure changes in the rest of the house.

Very high-efficiency gas furnaces are now available on the market that have totally sealed combustion chambers. These furnaces are connected to the outdoors by means of two small diameter plastic pipes: an air inlet and an exhaust outlet. Since the combustion process is in a sealed chamber, it is totally separated from the living space. In effect, these furnaces are ventilated separately from the house. They are so efficient that they require no conventional chimney. The combustion gases have had so much heat extracted that the gases can be blown outdoors though one of the plastic pipes. These "new generation" furnaces are immune from backdrafting problems unless they are damaged. You can obtain them from most major furnace manufacturers and they are often easier to install than trying to construct an airtight room around an existing furnace.

Solar systems and electric furnaces are also immune from backdrafting and spillage because there is no combustion process. Actually, there can be a tiny amount of combustion going on in an electric furnace. This occurs because electrical resistance heaters get quite hot. In fact, they can get so hot that any dust that falls on them can get burned, and this "fried dust" can release pollutants into the airstream. If you are using a high-efficiency filter, less dust gets into the system,

and "fried dust" will be less of a problem. Unfortunately, most furnaces aren't designed to accept the extremely efficient HEPA filters that will eliminate the problem. In general, "fried dust" is not considered a major issue; it is much less important than backdrafting and spillage. Electric furnaces are not as popular as other types of furnaces because of their higher operating costs.

Duct Problems

Ductwork was discussed in Chapter 15. In general, duct problems are more pronounced in forced-air heating and air-conditioning systems than in ventilation systems, because of the higher air pressures and greater volumes of air being moved. When air leaks out of or into ducts, there can be major pressure changes in houses that can result is excessive heating or cooling bills or backdrafting and spillage.

Problems with ductwork can be minimized by thoroughly sealing all joints and seams. In many houses, wall cavities are used for return-air ducts. These can be difficult to seal and can get particularly dirty. All-metal ducts are preferable. Also, many houses have only one or two return air-grilles. Fewer problems with uneven pressures will occur in a house having a return air-grille in every room that has a supply register.

Ductwork can easily become contaminated with dust, mold, bacteria, and a variety of other microorganisms. Commercial duct cleaning services use high powered vacuums that can help considerably in reducing the problems of dust contamination in metal ducts. Fiberglass ducts, because they are so porous, are impossible to clean effectively once they become contaminated.

After a thorough vacuuming, some duct-cleaning companies recommend misting or fogging a biocide inside the ducts to seal in, or kill, any remaining microorganisms. I feel this is a very risky procedure because all of the air in the house will pass through the ducts and the chance of it becoming contaminated with the biocide is too great. In fact, some experts claim that biocides are ineffective anyway, because the mist doesn't always reach into tiny crevices where the microorganisms can hide.

Forced-Hot-Water Systems

Forced-hot-water systems consist of a heating chamber (a boiler), a pump, piping, and radiators. The pump circulates heated water from the boiler through the piping to the radiators where it releases heat into the rooms. The cooled water then is pumped back to the boiler to be reheated.

Forced-hot-water systems have several health-related advantages. They do not have insulation or a blower exposed to the airstream, because there is no airstream. They operate at lower temperatures than electrical resistance coils, so there is no problem with "fried dust." And since boiler systems require no ductwork, the difficulty of sealing ducts is eliminated.

Problems with Forced-Hot-Water Systems

A boiler that heats water with a combustion process can be subject to backdrafting and spillage just like a forced-air system if a house gets depressurized. One solution is to place the boiler outdoors in a small storage building. The piping can be insulated to prevent heat loss, then run inside to the radiators. A boiler with a sealed combustion chamber will be immune from backdrafting and spillage, as will an electric boiler.

Leaks in the fuel oil or natural gas pipes that feed a boiler will pose a health problem. Also, if the hot water piping ever springs a leak, water damage or mold growth are possibilities. Leaks in radiant floor pipes cast into a concrete floor slab were a major problem in the past, but manufacturers of today's radiant floor systems have developed more leak-resistant tubing.

There are "combo" systems available that combine a boiler with a forced air system. The boiler can be a sealed combustion unit, perhaps one mounted outdoors. It feeds hot water to a coil in the forced air furnace where the coil heats the air. These systems have some of the advantages and some of the disadvantages of both systems they are derived from. "Combo" systems are becoming more popular, especially where heating requirements are low, as in apartments. With a low heating requirement, a water heater can take the place of the boiler.

Electric Baseboard Heaters

Electric baseboard heaters are much lower in initial cost than forced-air or boiler systems. However, because they operate on electricity rather than natural gas or fuel oil, they can have a higher operating cost. Most electric baseboard heaters have a high-temperature electrical element, like a toaster, that will burn any dust that falls on it. Some also have a strong paint odor when they heat up due to the paint used on the metal case. Baseboard heaters that are classified as "radiant" heaters have sometimes been recommended for sensitive people, but some of them have an odor when they are warm.

Advantages to electric baseboard heaters include the fact that there is no ductwork, no blower, no backdrafting or spillage, and there will be no gas or oil leaks. Since a baseboard heater is located in each room, it is quite easy to control the temperatures in different rooms independently. A bedroom could be kept cooler than a living room, for example.

I have used electric baseboard heaters in the Model Healthy House in spite of the fact that they are not a very energy-efficient way to provide heat. Ducted systems with heat pumps or high-efficiency gas furnaces will generally use less energy. However, in a superinsulated house, the heating requirements are very low. For example, the heating bill in the Model Healthy House (with electric baseboard heaters) may be as low as $200 for an entire year.

I could have cut the $200 heating bill in half by installing a more efficient heating system, but a more efficient system would have cost several times as much money, and it would have necessitated an annual maintenance budget probably equal to the savings. I simply couldn't justify the extra cost of a more efficient heating system because the house is so well-insulated. It made more sense to install simple, maintenance-free baseboard heaters rather than a complex, costly heat pump.

I like to use the Intertherm brand hydronic electric baseboard heaters made by **Nordyne** be-

264

cause they seem to be the least-polluting units on the market. Most baseboard heaters operate at a temperature hot enough to burn any dust that falls on them, but **Nordyne's** heaters don't get that hot. They have a self-contained heating element surrounded by a liquid in a sealed copper tube and operate at temperatures low enough so that there is no possibility of "fried dust."

Nordyne manufacturers two model types of Intertherm hydronic heaters, the NBH Series and the EBH Series (which I used), in sizes ranging from 300 to 2,000 watts. (The NBH and EBH heaters look a little different, but both are equally healthy.) The sizes shown on Sheet 19 of the Plans were selected for southern Indiana's climate. Houses located in colder climates would need to use proportionally larger units, while in warmer climates they could have less capacity.

Built-in baseboard heaters are made to be permanently wired to the house, but for temporary situations (like renters) **Nordyne** has Intertherm portable heaters that can be plugged into 110 volt receptacles.

Ductless Air Conditioners

Until fairly recently, the only alternative to a ducted forced-air central air conditioning system was a noisy window unit. Now there is something else. A ductless split system consists of an indoor unit and an outdoor compressor. They are connected with refrigerant lines just as are central systems, but they do not require any ductwork. Actually, there are a number of differences between these ductless split systems and either central or window units. They are usually more efficient, are very versatile, and are extremely quiet. While the indoor units vaguely resemble window air conditioners, they are much less bulky and don't need to be mounted in a window or even on an exterior wall.

In a superinsulated house, the air-conditioning requirements are quite low, so most central systems are usually much too large. Window units are noisy and unsightly. A ductless split system is the perfect answer. They range in sizes from 8,700 BTU to 29,000 BTU. Some are heat pumps, so they

can supply the heat needed in milder weather more efficiently than baseboard heaters. Most manufacturers have models with a single outdoor compressor and multiple indoor units that can be placed in different rooms.

Heating Rough-in for the Model Healthy House

The only thing needing to be done during rough-in for the **Nordyne** Intertherm baseboard heaters was to run electric wires from the main power panel to the heater locations. Because the heaters are all located on insulated exterior walls, this was actually done earlier in Phase 1 of the construction process (see Chapter 11).

Air-Conditioning Rough-in for the Model Healthy House

The Hitachi split system air conditioner for the Model Healthy House was supplied by the U.S. distributor, **Burnham Corp.** It is a 12,000-BTU Model #RAS3128H. It has a single outdoor compressor, as in most central systems, and an indoor unit that hangs high on the wall of the living room. This particular model is a heat pump. It has enough air-conditioning capacity for the Model Healthy House, but not quite enough heating capacity for the coldest months of the year. Like all heat pumps, it relies on electric resistance heaters to supply heat when it gets very cold. The heat pump can be used by occupants to save energy in the spring and fall, then they can rely on the Intertherm baseboard heaters at colder times of the year.

The indoor and outdoor units are connected with two insulated refrigerant lines and six 12-gauge electrical wires. These inter-unit lines and wires were roughed in at this stage. I extended a couple of feet of each to the outdoors through the 3" PVC pipe in the north exterior wall that was roughed in during Phase 1. Indoors, the lines and wires ran through the 6" wall between the bathrooms and over the laundry closet to a point near where the

Figure 19-1.
Rough-in complete.

back of the indoor unit would later hang on the living room wall.

Once the refrigerant lines and wires were in place, I used the single-component urethane aerosol-foam insulation to seal up the inside of the 3" PVC pipe. This is one of the last things I did as a part of the ADA sealing process. Figure 19-1 shows all the rough-in work complete.

Update

If you are to avoid air-pressure imbalance problems in houses (such as backdrafting and excessive energy losses), sealing the ducts is particularly important for forced-air heating/cooling systems. In the "Update" to Chapter 11, I mentioned my current preference for using a water-based duct-sealing mastic rather than aluminum-foil tape for sealing the ducts. Should you decide on a forced-air system, I can't recommend strongly enough that it have a sealed duct system. In the "Update" to Chapter 3, I discussed how to locate a heating/cooling contractor familiar with both backdrafting and sealed ducts.

As far as what kind of material the ducts should be made of, my first preference is for galvanized steel. If the ducts require insulation, it can be applied on the exterior after they have been sealed. Regarding fiberglass-lined ducts where the fiberglass is directly exposed to the airstream (often called ductboard), I can't think of a more unsuitable material. I never recommend fiberglass-lined ducts.

The good news is that many major forced-air heating/cooling system manufacturers now offer air handlers which no longer have exposed fiberglass. Today, they are tending to use an aluminum-foil-faced fiberglass, so the foil is exposed to the airstream—not the fiberglass. Some new higher-efficiency furnaces have a sealed plastic exhaust pipe, but they draw their intake air from the living space. This is a significant improvement over older models that were connected to a chimney because it minimizes the chance of backdrafting. However, I still prefer furnaces with totally sealed combustion chambers—those that have a sealed intake pipe as well as a sealed exhaust pipe. Most major manufacturers offer them.

Since the Model Healthy House was completed, **Burnham Corp.** no longer offers ductless, split-system air conditioners. However, there are

266

other companies who do offer them (see Appendix 2) and, over the years, I have used three different brands and found them to be very similar. However, I have noticed a problem with periodic mold growth—a problem that can occur with conventional ducted air conditioners as well. When an air conditioner is running, moisture will condense on the cooling coil, and some of this moisture can remain on the coil during the off cycle. If the moisture doesn't dry off quickly, mold growth can result. Cleaning can be difficult for both central, ducted models, as well as ductless air conditioners.

A simple way to minimize this mold growth is to set the fan to run continuously during the cooling season. With the fan running all the time, it will dry out the coil as the cooling compressor itself cycles on and off. At the end of the season, run the unit on fan-only (without cooling) to dry the coil before shutting it off for the winter.

The Intertherm baseboard heaters I used in the Model Healthy House are no longer made by **Nordyne**. However, they are still readily available. They are now called by the name Softheat, and are distributed by Cadet Manufacturing Co., as listed in Appendix 2.

PART 5:
INTERIOR FINISHING

Chapter 20

WALLS AND CEILINGS

■■■ Walls and ceilings are often finished in a similar manner, so I will discuss them together in this chapter. Since they literally surround all the living space, they have more capacity to pollute that space than many other components of a building. Therefore, in healthy house construction, wall and ceiling materials must be chosen with care.

Plaster was once the most common wall and ceiling material, but today less expensive drywall (sometimes called "sheetrock") is more often used. Both are generally painted. Wood paneling is also popular, and ceramic tile is frequently found in kitchens and baths.

Plaster

Plaster is a mineral product made primarily of gypsum. It is purchased in powder form and, when mixed with water, hardens into a fairly inert rock-like material. The age-old traditional method of application involves troweling a ½" thickness of the plaster over metal or wood lath. Today, most builders opt for a less expensive veneer plaster which is troweled in thin ⅛" coats over plasterboard. Plasterboard (often called blueboard because of its color) is a sheet prod-uct that consists of a gypsum core with a paper facing on both sides. Although it looks similar to drywall, the paper is specially treated so that the thin coat of wet plaster will adhere properly.

Both gypsum board and plaster can contain small amounts of synthetic additives. In spite of this, a completed plastered wall, whether the traditional or the veneer method, is usually very inert. In fact, it is one of the least polluting wall and ceiling finishes available. This is because the cured plaster surface is so hard and dense that it is subject to almost no outgassing.

Plaster is such a durable material that it is possible to leave it unpainted. This can be an advantage for someone sensitive to paint odors. However, leaving a plastered wall unpainted may be easier said than done. If there are any outside corners in a room, they will need metal corner beads imbedded in the plaster for strength. When the plastering job is completed, there will be about ⅛" of these gray corners visible against the white plaster wall. Some people view this as unsightly, but if done neatly, it can be an attractive design element. Since most house layouts have some outside corners, an alternative solution can be to use wood trim to cover up the metal corner bead.

Figure 20-1.
Installing drywall screws.

Plaster has three basic disadvantages. First of all, because the application requires a certain amount of skill, it can be difficult to locate an experienced plaster contractor in some parts of the country. Second, plaster is expensive, adding several thousand dollars in cost even to a very small house. Third, plaster is more difficult than drywall to seal in an airtight manner. When the joints of a plaster wall are finished, they are taped with a fiber-mesh tape, rather than the paper tape used with drywall. The mesh reinforces the plaster to make the joint stronger. This is necessary because plaster is very brittle. Since all houses flex and move around slightly over time, the brittle finish can crack. This will result in an air leak, one that can be difficult to repair. Drywall with paper tape can tolerate more flexing, so it will be more likely to remain airtight for the life of the house.

Drywall

Drywall, like the plasterboard used in veneered plaster construction, is a board product having a gypsum core and paper facing on both sides. The paper facing on drywall is made from recycled newspaper and the residual smell of printing ink can be bothersome to some people.

Drywall is available in a standard 4' width and in lengths of 8', 10', 12', 14', or 16'. The sheets are tapered along their long edges for easier finishing. The ends are not tapered and require more care to tape and finish in order to make the joint invisible. It is advantageous to minimize what are called "butt joints" at the ends of sheets to facilitate finishing; hence, the reason for using sheets as long as practical. The difficulty with the very long sheets is the fact that they are heavy and unwieldy. A 4' x 14' x ½"-thick sheet of drywall weighs about 100 pounds. Where special fire protection or soundproofing are required, thicker and heavier, material may be needed. If the drywall is to be attached to ceiling framing that is 24" on center, ⅝"-thick material is generally used to prevent sagging between the framing members. With ceiling framing on 16" centers, ½" drywall is usually sufficient.

Drywall is easily attached to wood framing with nails and to metal framing with self-tapping screws. Many drywall installers use screws in wood studs because they result in a more securely fastened job. Also, with the screw gun's depth guide properly adjusted, there is less of a dimple to fill with joint

272

compound. A screw gun can be adjusted so it will drive the screws just slightly below the surface for ease of finishing (Figure 20-1).

I have not noticed any difference, as far as tolerability, between the major manufacturers of drywall. One brand can sometimes have a different odor than another, but the difference isn't consistent. There are a couple of reasons for this. The manufacturing plants of competing products are often located very close to each other because they extract gypsum from the same geologic deposits. I was told by a drywall manufacturer's representative that sometimes, when their plant runs out of the facing paper, they borrow some from the competition down the road. Therefore, the finished product leaving the factory one day could have slightly different characteristics than a product shipped out the next day. Drywall is also very absorbent, so it can pick up odors easily. For example, drywall delivered on a diesel-powered delivery truck could smell like diesel exhaust. Usually this will only be a significant concern for the sheet on top of the stack because it will tend to protect the sheets beneath it.

Because of drywall's advantages over plaster—lower cost and better sealing capability—I recommend it much more often than plaster. The primary difficulty that I see with using drywall is the fact that, if you are chemically sensitive, you must select a paint that is both tolerable and will seal in any minor odors from the paper facing on the drywall. Once a tolerable paint is found, drywall can be just as inert as plaster.

Drywall Joint Compound

Finishing drywall involves applying paper tape and two or more coats of joint compound to all the seams, using wide finishing tools. In many situations, two coats over the tape are standard, but for a higher quality job, I often opt for an extra coat on the flat areas of the walls and ceiling. With flat wall paints, minor imperfections in the drywall won't be noticeable, but gloss or semi-gloss finishes demand a more perfect surface.

Once the joint compound has dried, it is lightly sanded to remove any ridges or imperfections. Some drywall finishers use a damp sponge rather than sandpaper to smooth out the joints. A sponge will leave no sanding dust, so clean-up before painting can be easier. However, sponging can result in a messy

Figure 20-2.
*Mixing **Murco's** non-toxic joint compound.*

273

floor—something that must be cleaned up before ceramic tile can be applied. If sanding is done, the ventilation system should be shut off until the dust settles and is cleaned up; otherwise, the ductwork could become filled with drywall dust.

Commercial drywall joint compounds are much more offensive than the drywall itself. They contain a variety of ingredients such as antifreeze, adhesive, fungicide, preservatives, etc. Fortunately, there are non-toxic compounds available.

I like to use a non-toxic joint compound called M-100 Hipo Compound made by **Murco Wall Products, Inc.** It contains none of the above bothersome ingredients. This product is shipped in powdered form and is mixed on the job with water (Figure 20-2). The manufacturer recommends that not more be mixed than can be used in a single day because, without preservatives, it will not keep very long if allowed to sit at room temperature. However, I have had no problems with storing small quantities in a refrigerator for a few days. The only drawback to this product is that it must be ordered directly from the manufacturer in Texas. I have used it several times and have found shipping charges to run in the $100 range for enough material to do an entire house. Yet, this isn't that much money in relation to the total cost of the house. The M-100 Hipo Compound itself is comparable in price to conventional joint compounds, and it is applied in a similar manner.

Wood Paneling

Wall paneling is manufactured in 4' x 8' sheets with glues that release formaldehyde into the indoor air. Solid wood paneling is an alternative, but it can be expensive. To add the warmth of wood to a house, I often suggest solid wood wainscoting. It is less costly than an entire wall of solid wood and can be equally attractive.

Solid wood paneling and wainscoting are difficult to seal in an airtight manner because there are so many seams between the individual boards. However, they can be used in airtight construction if they are applied over the top of a well-sealed air barrier, such as taped drywall.

Ceramic Tile

Ceramic tile is one of the most inert materials commonly used on walls. Its main drawback is expense, so it is usually only found in bathrooms and kitchens, and then only for smaller areas like shower surrounds or backsplashes. However, with the variety of tile styles and textures available today, it may be worth considering for other applications. Ceramic tile has the definite advantages of never needing painting, is easy to clean, durable, and has long life.

Ceramic tiles with glazed surfaces do not require the use of potentially offensive sealers, but some glazes can contain lead. This is more of a concern for tiles imported into the U.S. from other countries. While they don't outgas anything, tiles with glazes containing lead used on a kitchen countertop could leech out lead into the food. This shouldn't be a problem with tiles used on walls.

Most ceramic tile today is adhered with mastic adhesives or cement-based thinset mortars. Thinset mortars are more inert, and although they can contain some chemical additives, I haven't found them to be major pollution sources. Once covered with tile, they are well-separated from the living space. The grout used in the spaces between the tiles is more problematic than the mortar because it is exposed to the living space. A non-toxic grout can be made from scratch using cement, sand, and water, or cement and water only. Commercially made grouts that require damp curing have fewer additives than other grouts. See Chapter 22 for additional comments on ceramic tile.

Walls and Ceilings in the Model Healthy House

I used drywall for all walls and ceilings in the Model Healthy House because of its advantage over plaster in yielding a more airtight structure. I have had good luck in sealing any odors released by the paper surface of drywall with **Pace Chem Industries, Inc.'s** Crystal Shield paint. While the ability to make drywall airtight was the primary determining factor, it's lower cost was also important to keep the house affordable.

274

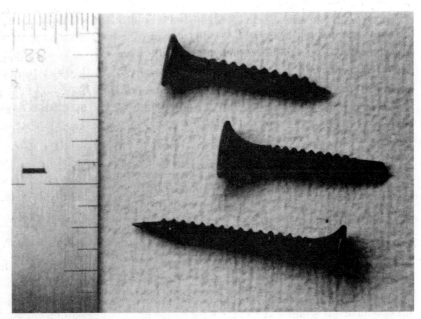

Figure 20-3.
Drywall screws.

Foil-Backed Drywall

I used foil-backed drywall in the Phase 1 construction (Chapter 13) as a diffusion retarder to block both moisture and pollutants. Moisture migration only results in a problem when it moves from a warm area to a cooler area, so it generally isn't a concern between the rooms of a house because they are at similar temperatures. (It can be a factor when there is a major indoor moisture source in one room, such as a swimming pool.) The foil on the exterior walls blocks the diffusion of pollutants released by the insulation, wiring, and plumbing lines, but the insulation is by far the biggest pollution source found inside walls.

The interior partition walls, which are not insulated, do contain plastic jacketed electrical wiring and plastic plumbing drain lines. As I mentioned earlier, I have, on occasion, wrapped those materials with aluminum foil prior to installing the drywall. While I believe that the outgassing of pollutants from plastic wiring and plumbing is minimal, in the final analysis I decided to use foil-backed drywall throughout the house. The additional cost was relatively minor, and it saved a considerable amount of time compared to wrapping aluminum foil around all the plastic wiring and plumbing lines.

Although I haven't found it to be much of a problem, using foil-backed drywall on the uninsulated interior walls also eliminates another possible minor source of emissions—the back surface of the drywall. Like the front, this surface is covered with paper made from recycled newspaper and the foil backing provides an effective seal.

My primary reason for using foil-backed drywall for all of the interior walls is not so much that I am convinced that it is necessary, but for peace of mind. When you consider the expense of building a house, the small added cost is negligible.

Attaching the Drywall

I used mainly 10' and 14' lengths of ½"-thick sheets of drywall for the walls. The only ceilings that needed to be done at this stage were the central hall and a couple of closets. The rest of the ceilings were done in Chapter 13.

All the drywall was attached in the usual manner using screws. These are available with drill points for heavy-gauge studs, but the standard needlepoint screws work fine for light-weight studs (Figure 20-3). They pierced the 25-gauge non-load-bearing studs with ease, and using a little extra pressure with my screw gun, needle point screws also worked well in the 20-gauge load-bearing center partition wall. However, in the 18-gauge headers over the window and door openings, I had to use drill-point screws in order to penetrate the heavier steel.

I didn't plan to use a wooden back panel on the three built-in cabinets as a cost-saving measure. Instead, I used a painted drywall back. Rather than attach the drywall to the wood cabinet frames, I

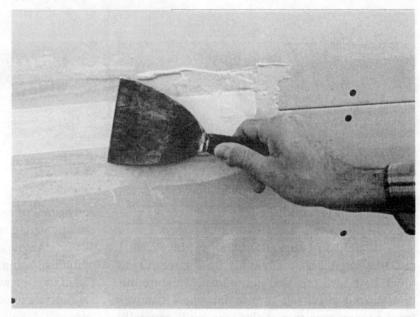

Figure 20-4.
Taping drywall joints.

Figure 20-5.
Drywall in place and taped.

276

installed it in the rough openings at this time. With a few spots of construction adhesive, I fitted a piece of drywall into the rough opening and adhered it to the back side of the drywall that had been attached to the opposite side of the wall. This yielded a cabinet back consisting of two layers of drywall for a total thickness of 1". The amount of construction adhesive used was quite small, and I have found that it outgasses very quickly, so isn't bothersome once the house is complete. I would be leery about using a large quantity of construction adhesive in a healthy house, but a few small dabs don't seem to be

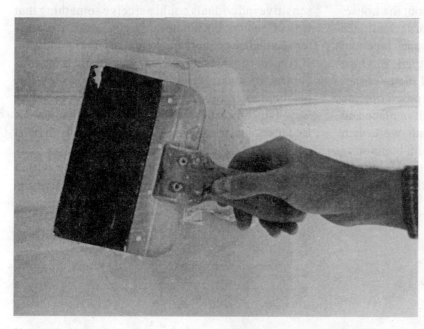

Figure 20-6.
Finishing drywall joints.

Figure 20-7.
Sanding the joint compound.

277

a big deal. In this application there isn't much strength required, so white or yellow carpenter's glue could probably be substituted.

Taping and Finishing

Because of the potentially bothersome ingredients in commercial joint compounds, I used the non-toxic M-100 Hipo Compound made by **Murco Wall Products, Inc.** throughout the house. Once all the drywall was hung, standard techniques were used to tape the joints, using paper tape and M-100 Hipo joint compound (Figure 20-4). Once all the seams were taped, I attached metal corner beads wherever there would be an exposed outside corner. Figure 20-5 shows the drywall in place and taped. All the seams and screw heads were then finished with two or three coats of joint compound (Figure 20-6). Once dry, the joint compound was lightly sanded (Figure 20-7) and the walls and ceilings were ready for paint.

Update

Since completing the Model Healthy House, I have spoken with a number of hypersensitive people who, for a variety of reasons, have opted for plaster walls instead of drywall. In several of these cases, the plaster has been bothersome for a few weeks. While it hasn't had a synthetic odor, the sensitive individuals could perceive something that was offensive. Fortunately, after a while, the plaster seemed quite inert and no longer bothered them. If you are considering plaster, you should have your contractor make up a sample for you to test for personal tolerability. This can be done in the same way I recommend testing paints in Chapter 21. Because plaster and painted drywall will both need an airing out period, hypersensitive people may wish to prepare some paint samples along with a plaster sample and test them as well to determine which airs out the quickest.

PAINTS, STAINS, AND FINISHES

■■■ There are a variety of ways that paints, stains, and finishes can affect your health, but over the past several years, a number of less toxic coatings have been developed and made available to health-conscious individuals. I'll refer to them as alternative finishes.

Before I start, I feel that it is important to state that I don't consider any coating to be truly non-toxic, even the healthier alternatives, because none can actually be ingested. Also, *all* coatings have an odor when wet that can be bothersome. The effects of these odors can be minimized by having plenty of ventilation or wearing a cartridge respiratory mask while painting.

Environmental Concerns

When discarded, all paints, stains, and finishes should be considered household hazardous waste materials. As such, they should be disposed of carefully. They should not be put out with the regular trash because conventional landfills are not designed to accept them. And they should not be poured down the drain because they will contaminate your septic system or the sewage treatment plant. If you have old cans of paint that you want to get rid of, give them away to someone who can use them or contact your sewage department, trash hauling service, health department, or mayor's office to get the location of an organization that accepts household hazardous waste. Many municipalities offer such services. Some mix similar colors of paint together into larger batches and use it.

Health Concerns

Several components of paints and other coatings can negatively affect health. Solvent-based products can contain up to 60% volatile organic compounds (VOCs). Because water-based finishes have less than 10% VOCs, they are clearly better choices if you are interested in reducing your exposure to VOCs. Painters, routinely exposed to VOCs, have a higher incidence of cancer than other tradesmen. VOCs have also been linked to loss of balance and nervous system dysfunction in painters.

Though lower in VOCs, water-based paints are subject to spoilage due to mold or bacterial contamination. To minimize this possibility, manufacturers add biocides—chemicals that make the paint poisonous to microbes. Most paints, if exposed to continuously high humidity, can be attacked by mold even after they are dry, but the primary purpose of a biocide is to extend a paint's shelf life while it is still in liquid form inside the can. Unfortunately, biocides can affect people as well as mold and bacteria. The most widely reported incident involved a young child who contracted a rare form of mercury poisoning after his family painted the interior of their house. The paint contained toxic mercury as a fungicide and the child absorbed it into his system.

Mercury is a poisonous heavy metal, but the most notorious heavy metal that has been used in paint is lead. It can be found in paint on the walls of millions of existing houses where it can slowly deteriorate and be taken up by the bodies of the occupants. To determine if the paint in your house contains lead, contact your local health department to locate an inexpensive test kit. For a more thorough evaluation, contact a lead paint removal contractor. Removing lead paint must be done with extreme care; it is not a job for untrained do-it-yourselfers.

Mercury is now banned from interior paints, and lead has virtually disappeared from newly manufactured paint. Some companies, however, still use cadmium, another heavy metal, as a colorant in some of their formulations.

Hundreds of other ingredients are found in off-the-shelf paints, many of which have not been studied for their precise health effects. Still, water-based paints used today are considerably healthier than products containing lead or a high percentage of VOCs. However, in recent years, a number of alternative paints and finishes have been introduced that are even more benign.

Healthier Alternatives

Most of the healthier alternative finishes are made by small companies. These manufacturers all seem to have different ideas as to what constitutes a healthy finish, so it is difficult to compare one product with another. Comparisons are also complicated by the fact that the exact formulas generally aren't made available, and the companies sometimes change their formulas slightly to make "new and improved" products. Besides producing alternative paints, stains, clear finishes, oils, and waxes, some of these companies also distribute healthier cleaning products.

Basically, the healthier finishes can be divided into two broad categories: low-outgassing and natural.

Low-Outgassing Finishes

The low-outgassing finishes contain mainly synthetic ingredients, but are formulated to have little odor. Originally developed for chemically sensitive individuals, they are now being used by many environmentally conscious people who have no particular health problems. Some of these products are manufactured from scratch by using ingredients deemed to be the safest available. One company produces a low-biocide paint that is basically a conventional paint with 90-95% less biocide than usual, and one conventional paint manufacturer is now promoting a zero-VOC interior paint.

Although all these products are low outgassing, it is important to note that all have an odor during application and for some time afterward until they cure. Most of the curing of water-based finishes takes place within two weeks, but some sensitive people find they can detect an odor as long as several months later. I have used most of these products at one time or another and haven't found one that is universally tolerable for all sensitive people. This is because we are all biologically different, and once sensitized, tend to tolerate different materials.

Natural Finishes

The natural paints, varnishes, and stains on the market are made from natural ingredients like plant oils, natural resins, citrus solvents, mineral pigments, etc. There are currently three popular brands being imported from Germany. They are very good environmental choices because they are derived from renewable resources like trees and other plant materials, rather than non-renewables like petroleum. Some natural finishes contain solvents derived from citrus products, so they might be bothersome to individuals allergic to oranges, lemons, or grapefruit. Other natural finishes contain terpenes, the same chemical compounds found in turpentine, which is derived from softwood trees. The smell of terpenes is often offensive to sensitive people.

Milk paint is a finish that is also made from natural materials. It is composed primarily of lime, earth pigments, and casein which is derived from milk. Milk paint is sold in powdered form, and when mixed with water, can be applied with a roller or brush like any other paint. It contains no VOCs or biocides, so it is one of the most inert paints on the market. Yet someone allergic to milk may be bothered by its odor. Milk paint does have a few drawbacks, however. It can be susceptible to mold growth if used in a damp area, such as a bathroom, it doesn't cover as well as a conventional paint, and it is relatively expensive.

Interior Stains

Many people like to stain wood floors or cabinetry to change the color or enhance the grain pattern. Like other coatings, stains are either solvent- or water-based. I prefer using water-based stains, and some of the alternative manufacturers have stains in their product lines.

Stains are generally used as a first coat on wood. They are then covered with a clear protective finish (standard water-based or alternative), which tends to seal in any residual odor from the stain. The selection of a stain isn't as critical as the selection of a clear finish, because the stain will be covered up, but water-based stains are preferred. If you are very sensitive and opt for a solvent-based stain, be sure to make up a test sample first (with the stain covered with the clear finish) and see how you tolerate it.

Finishing Wood Floors

The big difficulty in using wood floors is selecting a non-toxic clear finish. As with paints, there are a number of alternative finishes on the market, some natural, some low outgassing. I have found that with sensitive individuals, the synthetic

low-outgassing finishes are generally better tolerated and longer lasting. Actually, some conventional water-based clear floor finishes are quite benign once cured. The natural finishes, being made from renewable resources, are perhaps better environmental choices, so someone without severe sensitivities may wish to choose them.

Using Coatings as Barriers or Sealants

Paints and clear finishes are often used to block the smell of an outgassing building material. For example, drywall or bare wood may emit a slightly bothersome odor, but once covered with a finish may be odor free. This is because the finish is acting like a diffusion retarder and it is blocking the outgassing of molecules from the surface of the wood or drywall.

The Crystal Aire (**Pace Chem Industries, Inc.**) I used for a clear finish in the Model Healthy House was originally designed as a sealant to reduce formaldehyde emissions, so it usually seals in any natural wood odors fairly well. In a test of its effectiveness, formaldehyde emissions from a piece of particleboard were reduced from 240 parts per million (ppm) to 11 ppm when the sample was sealed with 4 coats of Crystal Aire. While these results are impressive, if you don't use materials like particleboard in the first place, there will be zero formaldehyde. Some sensitive individuals can only tolerate formaldehyde when levels are below 0.03 ppm.

In general, the synthetic low-outgassing finishes seem to make better sealants than the natural finishes. However, some people have had good luck using an alcohol-based shellac primer that is sold in paint stores as a sealant for drywall. This product is extremely odorous during application, but it outgasses most of its odor within a few days. It is considered a natural finish because shellac is a resin derived from the lac insect, and alcohol can be derived from plant materials. Alcohol-based products have the disadvantage of being incompatible with the **Murco Wall Products, Inc.'s** M-100 Hipo non-toxic drywall compound that I used in the Model Healthy House. The alcohol can cause the joint compound to deteriorate. Personally, I prefer using the M-100 Hipo compound and a different sealant.

Outdoor Paints

Paints and finishes used outdoors are subject to a great deal of abuse from temperature extremes, moisture, and ultraviolet light from the sun. They must be very durable to withstand the ravages of Mother Nature. I feel that conventional off-the-shelf exterior paints are better able to handle this kind of assault than the alternative finishes, most of which are designed for interior use anyway. Finishes used outdoors will outgas, but the odors tend to dissipate into the atmosphere simply because they are outdoors. However, the odor can enter open windows during application, so you should do whatever you can to minimize your exposure. This may mean closing windows, using window fans, or leaving the house temporarily.

If exterior painting is necessary, I generally recommend high-quality 100% acrylic or acrylic-latex paints because they are water-based and fairly durable. Exterior stains and clear finishes are not nearly as long lasting. Depending on the climate, stains can need recoating after only a few years, and clear finishes may only last a year.

Selecting a Paint

While they certainly aren't perfect, the conventional water-based coatings on the market today are healthier choices than solvent-based finishes, or the older products containing lead. If you are interested in using a paint that is even less noxious, any one of the alternative low-outgassing or natural finishes would be a good choice.

If you are chemically sensitive, I cannot recommend one particular product over another. You must test them for personal tolerability. I have clients who praise one particular brand of paint as being extremely benign for them, while other clients report they can't be near that very same product. Even

though the alternative finishes are generally better than off-the-counter finishes, they should still be tested for tolerability by sensitive people.

The main drawback to the alternative finishes is the fact that they must be ordered through the mail, but since most suppliers accept credit card orders over the telephone, you can usually receive your order within a few days. These products are advertised in environmental health magazines. My book, *The Healthy House*, contains phone numbers and addresses of a large number of suppliers of healthy materials as do several other sources listed in Appendix 3.

Testing Finishes for Chemically Sensitive People

For chemically sensitive people, I recommend testing at least two or three different coatings for personal tolerance, perhaps a natural finish and a couple of low-outgassing finishes. Some of the manufacturers have small samples available for just this purpose. Testing should generally be done under the supervision of a physician, but the following procedure often works well. Coat both sides of a piece of drywall (about 2' x 4') with a paint sample, label and date it, then set it aside to dry until it seems to have lost its odor. This may take a couple of weeks. Once the sample appears to be odor-free, place the drywall next to your bed and see how you sleep with it. A good night's sleep usually indicates a tolerable paint. Nightmares, restlessness, an extremely deep sleep, or some other symptom, indicate that you are probably reacting to the sample. If none of your samples are tolerable, wait another week or two and test again. I have had some sensitive people who could only tolerate a paint after several months of curing, while others tested OK after a week.

Wallpaper

I don't know of any wallpaper on the market today that is just plain paper. Some is 100% vinyl, some has a plastic coating, and some is chemically

Figure 21-1.
Crystal Shield paint.

treated with fungicides. These products are all subject to outgassing. The glues used to adhere them to the wall also contain synthetic ingredients and fungicides. Fungicides are necessary to deter mold growth. This wasn't done until recent decades—something obvious to anyone who has removed old wallpaper only to find the wall beneath black with mold. In addition, the inks used to print wall coverings have their own outgassing characteristics.

I don't feel that wall coverings are a very good choice for healthy houses. However, there are some things that you can do to reduce your risk. You can roll out a wall covering in an uncontaminated garage until the outgassing period is over, then install it indoors. Use thumbtacks to hang it up so you don't accidentally step on it on the floor. It may take a few days to become odor-free, or as long as several months, depending on the product. A metal foil wall covering could be a good choice, or you might consider using some 100% cotton fabric instead of a conventional wall covering. The main drawback would be that cloth would be susceptible to stretching and more difficult to hang. It would also be hard to clean. Some of the manufacturers of low-outgassing paint also have low-odor wallpaper paste.

As an alternative to wallpaper, you might consider using an alternative paint and stenciling a pattern on the wall. It could be equally attractive. Hobby stores often have stenciling patterns and kits.

Painting the Model Healthy House

As I mentioned in Chapter 9, I painted the entry doors early in the construction process so they could be airing out while the remainder of the house was being completed. I used a conventional off-the-counter water-based paint for durability. This was the only paint I had to apply anywhere on the outside of the house, so the exterior is quite maintenance-free.

Pace Chem Industries, Inc. was one of the first manufacturers to produce finishes specifically for hypersensitive people. I used their Crystal Shield paint and Crystal Aire clear finish for the interior of the Model Healthy House. They are highly durable, washable, and long lasting. While they both have a fairly strong odor when wet, once cured they are quite inert. Some other low-outgassing paints have less odor when wet, but seem to have a long-term low-level odor that can be detected by some sensitive individuals as long as a year after application. For the Model Healthy House, I wanted a paint that was as inert as possible over the long haul. Since Crystal Shield is so durable, it will not need repainting nearly as frequently as other paints, so the occupants won't be exposed to paint odors as often in the future.

Painting the Walls and Ceilings

Pace Chem Industries, Inc. recommends that Crystal Shield paint (Figure 21-1) be applied over a primer rather than directly to bare drywall. Since Crystal Shield is such a good sealer, I was able to use a conventional off-the-counter latex paint for the primer. With the alternative finishes being higher-priced, the use of a conventional paint as a primer can help keep costs down. It is a good idea to let the prime coat dry for several days before applying the finish coat to minimize the chance of an unwanted reaction

between the two different paints. This is especially important for people sensitive to paints in general.

After the primer was dry, I lightly sanded any areas on the walls and ceiling that looked a little rough. This may be necessary if the joint compound is sanded during the finishing stage because the paper facing of the drywall can get slightly roughed up. While this is rarely noticeable with a flat paint, it can show up with a gloss or semi-gloss top coat. Crystal Shield is a semi-gloss paint and it is sold in two colors, Antique White (my choice) and Snow White. It can be tinted at your local paint store to obtain other shades.

On some projects, I have used two coats of Crystal Shield paint over bare drywall. This is more costly, but it avoids the chance of two different paints reacting with each other. If you choose to do this, **Pace Chem Industries, Inc.** suggests that there be at least a 24-hour drying period between coats to allow each coat to cure properly.

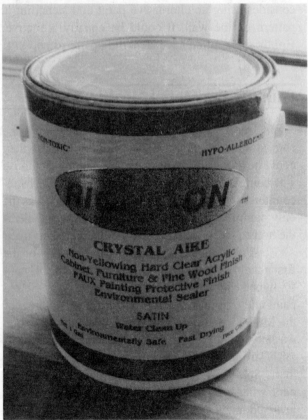

Figure 21-2.
Crystal Aire clear finish.

Figure 21-3.
Prefinished woodwork stored in the garage.

The painting itself was fairly straightforward. I used a brush to cut in near windows and in corners, and a roller for the majority of painting. Since Crystal Shield is a semi-gloss, I recommend a roller cover made specifically for gloss or semi-gloss paints. It will result in a smoother job.

I chose Crystal Shield because it yields a very inert and durable wall and it forms an excellent barrier; however, it does have a strong odor when wet and it can take a certain amount of time to cure. In new construction, it will generally be aired out by the time the house is complete. I always wear a cartridge mask as a safety precaution whenever I am painting, even with the alternative healthier paints. This is because a painter can be more easily affected by the strong odor of wet paint than a homeowner exposed to the dried finish. Eye protection is also a good idea when painting a ceiling.

Finishing the Woodwork

In selecting a finish for the woodwork, I could have used the same Crystal Shield paint that I used on the walls, but I decided that the natural appearance of the wood would be enhanced with a clear finish. It would make the house feel warmer and would look more attractive. Many people like to stain wood, but I feel that the poplar wood I used is quite attractive in its natural state, without a stain.

Pace Chem Industries, Inc. produces two clear finishes: Crystal Shield clear and Crystal Aire clear. The Crystal Shield clear is harder and designed for the abuse to which wood floors are subjected. I chose the Crystal Aire in a satin finish for all of the woodwork (Figure 21-2).

I finished both sides of all the woodwork in the house with two coats of Crystal Aire. Some people are sensitive to the natural aroma of various woods, and coating both sides reduces any such odors to a minimum. The woodwork was finished early in the construction process so that the finish would have plenty of time to cure. I stored all the prefinished woodwork in the garage until it was time to install it (Figure 21-3). I have found that once completely cured, Crystal Aire seems to be more inert than some of the other alternative finishes I have tried, but it is still important for sensitive individuals to test several products prior to selecting a particular brand.

I generally spray the clear finish on woodwork because it is faster than using a brush. When

285

spraying any kind of finish, respiratory protection is mandatory, because the fine mist produced by a spray gun can float in the air and be inhaled deeply into the lungs. It is probably not a good idea to spray a finish inside a healthy house because of the possibility of overspray getting on the walls and floors. Woodwork can be sprayed in a shop or garage having adequate ventilation.

Update

Since the completion of the Model Healthy House, several additional manufacturers have come out with healthier paints. So, there are now more choices than ever before. For example, a number of major paint manufacturers now offer zero-VOC paints, and additional smaller companies now offer paints specifically formulated for sensitive people. I've used several of them and, overall, have been very pleased. Some are priced very competitively, seal reasonably well, and are quite tolerable. With the lower-priced products, I often use two coats of the paint, rather than one coat of primer and one coat of paint. This minimizes the chance of a reaction between a paint and a primer.

For clear finishes, most major manufacturers now offer water-based polyurethane finishes. While sensitive people rarely tolerate oil-based polyurethanes, they tend to do quite well with the water-based versions—often tolerating them barely a week after application.

In spite of the fact that more and more companies are offering healthier finishes, I still recommend that hypersensitive people test these products for personal tolerance. I have heard people ask too many times "I'm chemically sensitive, and my painter is coming in the morning, what should I tell him to use?" I simply can't answer a question like that because sensitive people react differently to different products, so for them, personal testing is imperative. And testing takes a certain amount of time. For example, it takes time to order paint samples through the mail, to prepare the samples, to air the samples, then to finally test them.

If you are planning to use either a clear finish or a paint as a sealer over an offensive product, you should remember that all sealers are imperfect. When trying to seal in minor odors—like the paper facing on drywall—paints often work well. However, when trying to seal a very strong outgassing source—like new plywood wall paneling—you may not be as successful. For example, I've spoken with a number of sensitive people who put four coats of a clear finish on new kitchen cabinets to seal in the formaldehyde, and they have almost always said the same thing: "It was a lot of work, and it helped, but it didn't help enough."

Finally, I should mention a problem with using 100% cotton for a wall covering. Cotton is flammable, and in the event of a fire it can burn rapidly. Thus, using cotton on the walls isn't a good idea. However, there is a new type of painting system in the do-it-yourself market that can give you an attractive wall finish that often looks as good as wallpaper. It uses textured rollers, which are available with different patterns embossed on them. There are several ways to use the system, such as dipping two rollers in two different colors of paint and rolling them on top of each other. You can also roll a contrasting color on an already painted wall for a border effect.

Chapter 22

FLOORS

■ ■ ■ Wall-to-wall carpeting is today's most popular floor covering. Although there are negative health effects associated with many components of a house, carpeting is one of the worst offenders. It can affect people's health one way when new— because of its characteristic new carpet smell—or when old, as it becomes a reservoir of dirt, mold, and dust mites. Carpeting is also a poor environmental choice because it is usually made from non-renewable resources. I will generally recommend anything for flooring other than carpeting.

Carpeting

Beginning in October 1987, over 20,000 square yards of new carpeting were installed in an EPA office building in Washington, DC. Soon, many employees began getting ill. Eventually some became permanently disabled with Multiple Chemical Sensitivities (see Chapter 1). After much discussion between employees and administrators, some of it not very friendly, all the carpeting was removed. The problem was believed (but not proven) to be related to a chemical called 4-PC (short for 4-phenylcyclo-hexene) that was released as a gas from the carpet.

In April 1991, partially as a result of the EPA's carpet problems, the New York State Attorney General petitioned the U.S. Consumer Product Safety Commission (CPSC) to require a warning label on new carpeting, as well as on carpet pads and installation materials like glues. He cited the fact that, besides 4-PC, there are over a hundred other gases released by new carpet, some of which are toxic or carcinogenic. The petition pointed out that small children and pregnant women are at increased risk. Despite the fact that half of the state attorneys general in the country also signed the petition, and the CPSC had received hundreds of complaints about new carpeting, the petition was denied.

In October 1992 "CBS Evening News" with Dan Rather and "Street Stories" with Ed Bradley both reported on recent carpet testing being done by the Anderson laboratory in New England, in which mice actually died after breathing air blown across carpeting. Not believing the test to be valid, the carpet industry sponsored Carpet and Rug Institute had their own tests performed, and the results were the same—dead mice. In early 1993 the EPA obtained similar results in preliminary testing, yet consumers are still able to purchase new carpeting with no warning label whatsoever.

Microorganisms

Mold spores, dust mites, bacteria, and other microorganisms make their home in carpeting. Various studies have measured tens of millions of living creatures in every square foot of carpeting. While some of these tiny beasts are quite benign, others are highly allergenic. Adult noses are generally about five feet off the floor, but children crawling and playing on a carpeted floor are directly exposed to these allergens.

The reason microorganisms thrive in carpeting is because there is so much food there. Dust mites thrive on the flakes of dead skin that we all shed daily. Mold can eat virtually everything, and will be especially prolific in higher relative humidities, as when carpeting is attached to a cold or damp concrete slab. I don't think that wall-to-wall carpeting in bathrooms is a good idea because of the amount of moisture that is usually present. Carpet in a kitchen can easily become contaminated with food spills and grease—great food for microbes. Some microorganisms may be more prevalent in natural-fiber carpets because they can consume the fibers themselves.

Carpet Pads

Carpet padding is also subject to outgassing. I have had people ask me if natural fiber pads are better than synthetic pads. In my opinion, they are probably a little better but not much, because they are usually held together with some type of adhesive, and they may be chemically treated.

Fibrous carpet pads do have an advantage over foam rubber pads when it comes to cleaning. Vacuuming a carpet that is installed on top of a fibrous pad will be more effective than vacuuming a carpet that is on top of a foam pad. This is because the vacuum can move air more easily through the fibers. The less resistance there is to the movement of air, the more thorough the cleaning.

Carpet Installation

The adhesives and glues used to install carpet can be even worse sources of outgassing than the carpet itself. In June 1990, a chemical gas detection alarm went off in the Seattle Children's Hospital and Medical Center. The sensor was in the hospital's poison center where tanks of chemicals were stored, but there were no chemical leaks. After a brief investigation, it was determined that the alarm was triggered by the glue used by workers laying carpet nearby. I can't imagine that an adhesive so noxious that it can set off alarms would be routinely used by carpet installers, especially in a children's hospital. Would you want it used in your home? Water-based adhesives are definitely preferred.

Cleaning Carpet

The millions of microorganisms in carpeting represent only the tip of the iceberg as far as debris in carpeting is concerned. If the outside of a house was painted with lead paint, the surrounding soil will contain lead dust which will be brought indoors on your shoes. Similarly, you will track in pesticides or fertilizers applied to lawns, animal waste accidentally stepped in, and who knows what else. All of this will eventually build up in the carpet, and none of it is good for children to be exposed to as they play on carpet.

Most portable vacuum cleaners have very inefficient filters that aren't able to capture the fine particles of dust that are sucked up. They simply blow a considerable amount of dust and debris back into the room. This fine dust can float around in the air for up to a half hour after you have finished vacuuming. Once airborne, the fine dust is easily inhaled into your lungs.

There have been several reports of Kawasaki Syndrome occurring after carpeting has been shampooed. Experts aren't sure of the reason, but they believe that it might be because the moist carpet allows some particular bacteria (along with mold and dust mites) to thrive, resulting in illness. Kawasaki Syndrome strikes mainly children under age five. Its symptoms include fever; bloodshot eyes; red and sore lips, mouth, and throat; rash; swollen glands; and swollen hands and feet with peeling skin. Kawasaki Syndrome can be cured, but if it is not treated it can sometimes lead to coronary damage.

Carpet and the Environment

Most carpet is made from synthetic fibers that are derived from non-renewable resources. When it is worn out, carpeting is almost never recycled because the fibers (one kind of plastic) would need to be separated from the backing (another kind of plastic). Instead, carpet usually finds its way to overflowing landfills.

Since the average life span of carpeting is only eight years or so, it is not a very long-lasting or cost-effective floor covering. In a new house, you will have replaced and thrown away the carpet long before you have paid off the mortgage. In other words, you will be paying for carpet many years after it has been discarded.

Do You Still Want Carpeting?

I do my best to discourage people from having carpet in their homes, but I have had clients who still want it. If you are one of those people, I have some suggestions that can reduce (but not eliminate) your risk.

You can roll carpeting out in a uncontaminated warehouse or garage and let it outgas there before you have it installed in your home. It is difficult to predict how long this will take because some carpets are worse than others. It could take as long as several months, but I have heard reports of carpeting much older than that being bothersome. Some of the samples that killed mice in the Anderson laboratory tests were as much as 12 years old. I'd suggest purchasing the least odorous product in the hope that it will outgas quickly. There is a sealant on the market that is supposed to reduce carpet emissions. I have tried it on a couple of occasions and have not found it to be very effective.

Cotton, wool, and other natural fibers are made from renewable resources, they are usually longer-lasting than synthetic fibers, and sometimes they have less odor. However, I have seen some 100% cotton carpet samples that had a very strong and irritating synthetic smell. Natural fiber carpet can also be more expensive than synthetic fibers.

To reduce microorganisms in carpet, I strongly recommend a central vacuum cleaner. They are more powerful than most portable models, and if they have an outdoor exhaust they won't blow dust back into your face. Since mold, dust mites, and other microbes thrive at high humidities, I would discourage the use of any cleaning method that uses water or steam. If you get in the habit of removing your shoes at the front door, Japanese or Swedish style, you will have much cleaner carpet because you will not be tracking pollutants indoors on your shoes.

To install carpet, water-based adhesives are less toxic choices than solvent-based adhesives, but I recommend no adhesives at all. You should select a carpet that can be installed with tack strips. Tack strips are fastened around the perimeter of a room and the carpet is stretched in place and anchored to the strips. The tack strips are made of thin pieces of plywood, which releases some formaldehyde, but I believe that they would be less offensive than the carpet glue.

A carpet pad can be aired out in an uncontaminated garage just like the carpet to minimize your exposure to synthetic odors, or you can install carpet without padding. Carpet without a pad won't be as comfortable to walk on, and it won't last as long, but it will mean that there is one less thing indoors that is capable of affecting your health. The use of a fibrous pad can mean more efficient vacuuming.

Natural fiber area rugs are vastly superior to wall-to-wall carpeting because they can be easily removed for cleaning. While wool rugs are often sent out to a commercial cleaner, cotton rugs can be laundered in a washing machine. Oriental rugs, and native American rugs are often as attractive and comfortable as wall-to-wall carpeting, and they usually last much longer, sometimes for generations.

Composition Flooring

Composition flooring can be made of asphalt, cork, rubber, or linoleum, but vinyl is the most popular. These products are either sold in rolls (up to 12' wide), or individual squares (12" squares are common). In the past, some vinyl and asphalt floor tiles contained asbestos, but manufacturers voluntarily quit using it in the early 1980s. Composition flooring can

289

also contain a variety of fillers, colorants, additives, plasticizers, and gums that contribute to outgassing when the material is new.

I rarely recommend composition flooring to my clients as a first choice because of its outgassing potential. Many people find these materials intolerable, however there is much less outgassing than with carpeting. And these products do have the major advantage of being much easier to clean than carpeting, so they don't tend to become a reservoir for dirt and microbes. They can also be less expensive than alternatives such as hardwood and ceramic tile. So here are some suggestions for reducing your risk from composition flooring.

To minimize your exposure to outgassing, you can air out composition flooring in an uncontaminated garage or warehouse for a while before bringing it indoors for installation. This shouldn't take as long as carpeting, but it could still take several weeks. I have found that harder, stiffer vinyl flooring is less noxious than softer, more flexible, or cushioned flooring. This is because toxic chemicals called plasticizers are added to make cushioned vinyl flooring more flexible.

Composition flooring made from natural materials such as rubber and cork all have a distinctive odor that some people find offensive; sometimes they also contain synthetic resins. Linoleum is another natural material. It is made from flaxseed oil, wood powder, and jute, all renewable resources, so it is good environmental choice. However, linoleum also has a distinctive odor, and it must be coated with a potentially bothersome sealer as part of a routine maintenance program. Linoleum is also susceptible to water damage.

Most composition floors must be glued down. I recommend less toxic water-based adhesives rather than solvent-based formulations. If you are using large sheet material (rather than individual squares), it is sometimes possible to install it without adhesive. Once cut to fit, the baseboard molding around the perimeter of the room can be used to hold it in place.

Wood Floors

Wood can make a excellent floor that is both attractive and healthy. You can use hardwoods like oak, maple, or beech; or softwoods like pine or fir. Once finished, the odor of the wood is often sufficiently sealed to render the wood tolerable. I recommend floors that are nailed down rather than those needing to be glued down, although some of the water-based adhesives are less noxious than those produced just a few short years ago. To further reduce your exposure to adhesives, I also recommend solid wood floors, rather than products laminated of several layers of wood.

Oak is probably the most common wood flooring material, but I have had a number of sensitive clients who have found its natural aroma to be offensive. This may be due to natural compounds in the oak called tannins that can be used to tan leather. Softwoods release natural terpene compounds that can also bother some people. Maple and beech are two of the more inert hardwood choices.

Although wood floors can be expensive to install, they are usually cost-effective over their life. This is because they will probably not need to be replaced within your lifetime. Most wall-to-wall carpeting only lasts 8-10 years, sometimes less, so when you add up the cost of periodically replacing carpeting, the wood floor ends up cheaper in the long run. To reduce the cost of a wood floor, I often recommend a #3 grade of wood rather than a blemish-free grade. I find that such a floor is not only less expensive, but many people feel that the more pronounced color variations give it character.

Whatever type of wood you choose, it is imperative that you select a healthy finish. The finish protects the wood, and it acts as a diffusion retarder to seal in any odors released from the wood itself. See Chapter 21 for a discussion of floor finishes.

Ceramic Tile

Ceramic tile is my personal favorite floor covering. While some people may find it unusual to have a house with ceramic tile on all the floors, even bedrooms and closets, I find it quite attractive. My own home has such floors, as does the Model Healthy House. If properly installed, ceramic tile can result in a long lasting, beautiful, durable floor.

Occasionally a ceramic-tile floor will have some mold growing on it, but the mold is usually related to a moisture problem or a cold uninsulated concrete slab.

Types of Ceramic Tile

Ceramic tile is made from various combinations of clay, shale, gypsum, talc, vermiculite, and sand. It is fired in kilns at temperatures between 900 and 2200 degrees F., yielding a very inert product. Longer and hotter firing makes the tile harder and more impervious to water. The hardest and densest tile is called vitreous, meaning that it is glass-like throughout. Vitreous tile is suitable for outdoor applications where freezing could occur. Ceramic tile is manufactured in hundreds of colors, patterns, sizes, and styles.

Generally, ceramic tile is classified as either glazed or unglazed. The glaze is a glass-like coating that is applied to the surface of tile to provide color, decoration, texture, or resistance to abuse. There is no difference between the two from a health standpoint, but unglazed tile usually needs to be sealed to protect the surface from staining. Most of the sealers are water-based, but the most inert sealer is simply a mixture of sodium silicate (sometimes called "water glass") and water. Personally, I prefer glazed ceramic tile because it does not require a sealer.

Mortar

Some of the earliest examples of ceramic tile are found in 6,000-year-old Egyptian temples. During the Roman Empire, it was often used in homes and businesses. The centuries-old method of attaching ceramic tile involved using a pure cement paste on top of a 1¼"-thick mortar bed. For the cement paste to stick to the mortar bed, the bed must still be "plastic," that is, not cured. (A cement paste will not adhere properly to a cured mortar bed or over cured concrete.) Though still practiced, this method takes a certain amount of skill, and as a result, can be expensive.

After World War II, ceramic tile began to be used a great deal in average homes. This boom was the result new tile-mounting adhesives. The new adhesives required less skill because they didn't need a thick mortar bed. They came to be known as thinset (or dry-set) mortars. If they are asphalt or vinyl mastics, epoxies, or furans, they can be somewhat odorous, but cement-based thinset mortars are quite benign. Despite the fact that cement-based thinsets contain some minor chemical additives, I have had very good luck with them, particularly a product called Multi-Cure (**C-Cure**). It is what I used in the Model Healthy House.

Grout

In general, the commercially produced grouts that require "damp curing" have the least number of potentially bothersome ingredients. The advantage to using commercially made grouts is that they are premixed and are available in a wide range of colors.

I often mix my own grout from scratch to avoid as many chemical additives as possible. I feel this is important for sensitive people because, unlike the mortar, the grout is exposed to the living space. For people who have no sensitivities or only minor ones, commercially-made cement-based grouts are often acceptable.

According to the Tile Council of America's *Handbook for Ceramic Tile Installation* (listed in Appendix 3), grout can be made on-the-job with 1 part Portland cement to 1 part fine graded clean sand for joints up to ⅛" wide. For joints up to ½" wide, use 2 parts sand, and for joints over ½", use 3 parts sand. Sometimes up to ⅕ part lime is added for workability. To add color, you can use mason's pigments that are made from ground minerals. These are available in several different colors at most places that sell brick or concrete block.

I buy bags of white sand at my local lumberyard to use in making grout. Brown play sand, for sandboxes, is usually too coarse and dirty to use. I purchase sand in bags rather than in bulk because it is clean and dry. Bulk sand is usually stored outdoors, so it is often wet. Using bagged sand allows me to mix a large batch of the ingredients dry, then add water to smaller amounts as I need it. By preparing one or two large batches, rather than several small batches, I am assured of a more uniform grout color. When

Figure 22-1.
Mixing grout from scratch.

making grout from scratch, it is important to mix the ingredients thoroughly. I use a plastic tub (Figure 22-1), but a child's small plastic swimming pool also works quite well.

Grout made without additives needs to be damp cured for three days. In other words, it needs to be kept moist for 72 hours. This helps the grout develop its full strength. Grouts that do not need to be damp-cured contain chemical additives to aid in curing. The easiest way to damp-cure grout is to simply cover the floor with sheets of plastic. The plastic prevents evaporation and the grout retains moisture as long as it remains covered. As an alternative, you can use a garden sprayer (be sure it is a clean one) to mist water on the surface every few hours as the grout starts to dry out.

Other Floor Coverings

Marble is a healthy flooring material. It can be installed in a manner very similar to ceramic tile, with thinset mortar and grout. Terrazzo is another option. It consists of a mixture of cement and marble chips. When water is added, it is troweled

smooth and allowed to harden. Then the surface is polished with powerful grinding machines. Though marble and terrazzo are quite attractive and non-toxic, they can be costly.

For a low-cost healthy floor, bare concrete is a viable option. If mineral colorants are used when the concrete is originally poured, the floor will have a more attractive appearance than the standard gray color. Metal forms are available that can be used to texture the surface of wet concrete so it will resemble bricks, pavers, or cobblestones. When accented with area rugs, the result can be quite attractive.

Floors in the Model Healthy House

As I stated earlier, my decision to use ceramic tile on all the floors of the Model Healthy House was one of the earliest decisions I made. I actually picked tile as the floor covering before I chose the foundation type. To many people, this may seem backwards, but it does make sense knowing that it is easier to attach ceramic tile to a concrete slab than to a wood subfloor. If I had decided to go with an oak or maple floor, I might have opted for a basement, pier, or crawl space foundation.

The Tile

In selecting the ceramic tile for the Model Healthy House, I went with **American Olean Tile Co.**, one of the largest manufacturers in the country. Since the tile was to be used throughout the entire house, I wanted a quality product that would be long lasting. I chose their glazed Creekstones pattern in a 9" x 9" size and Sand color. It has attractive rounded corners and the gentle slope of the edges gives it a nice pillow effect. This finished floor has a softly textured appearance.

While I only used it on the floor, Creekstones tiles can also be attached to walls and countertops. A 4" x 4" tile is available, as are a variety of different shapes of trim pieces. Colors include Chalk, Rose, Gray Slate, and Azure Blue. All are 5/16" thick.

In the Model Healthy House, I decided to use the same color of tile in all the rooms of the house in order to tie them together visually. This was based purely on personal taste. I could easily have chosen a different color for each room or had borders or patterns of complementary colors. For anyone planning a ceramic tile floor, I highly recommend getting a copy of the **American Olean Tile Co.** catalog. It is filled with color photos containing many ideas to fit every taste. There are tiles in a wide variety of patterns, colors, and styles.

No matter what kind of tile installation you plan, there will invariably be some tiles that will need to be cut down to a smaller size. Straight cuts are easy with a tile cutter (Figure 22-2). It works by scoring the surface with a small wheel similar to that found in a glass cutter, then the tile is broken evenly along the scored line. For irregular cuts, nippers can be used to chip away a small chunk at a time. Many ceramic tile installers have a power saw with a diamond tipped blade for cutting irregular shapes.

Laying Out the Job

When tiling a single room, it is best to start in the center of the floor. To lay out the guide lines, I use a chalk line and a carpenter's square to locate two crossing lines in the center of the room. I then lay some tiles loosely in place along the guide lines to see how much I will need to cut off the last tile next to the wall. If that piece of tile is going to be very narrow I adjust my lines a little. This is because a ceramic tile job looks nicer without a thin row of tile along a wall.

Figure 22-2.
Cutting ceramic tile.

Figure 22-3.
Rough tile layout.

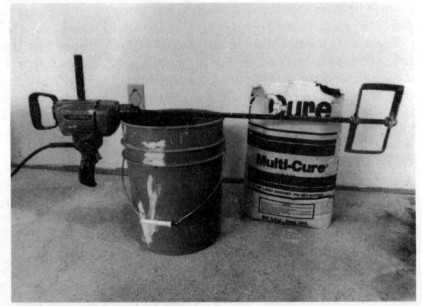

Figure 22-4.
Thin-set ceramic tile mortar.

In this particular project, I planned to tile the entire house—considerably more than a single room—so I had to compare the layouts in different rooms to see how they would all come together without having to cut tiles anywhere but at edges. I arrived at a layout by first laying a loose row of tile down the center of the hallway, then branching loose tiles off at right angles into different rooms (Figure 22-3). The leg running into the living room turned and extended into the kitchen. With so many rooms to coordinate, I decided not to worry about closets. If some narrow strips of tile fell along the walls in closets, I figured that that wouldn't be a major problem.

Figure 22-5.
Spreading the thin-set mortar.

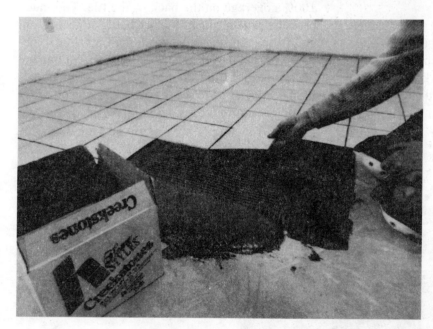

Figure 22-6.
Setting tile in the thin-set mortar.

As an alternative to coordinating the tile layouts in the various rooms as I have done, I have seen people tile each room separately and not worry about how the joints related to adjoining rooms. By using tile of a contrasting color for a threshold at the doorways between rooms, the room tiles can abut the threshold tiles on both sides. This can be attractive in itself and be an easy way to separate rooms if you want to use several different colors or styles of ceramic tile in a house.

Once I arrived at a satisfactory layout, I snapped chalk lines in the center of the master

295

bedroom to correspond with the tiles that were loosely laid on the floor. My plan was to do the master bedroom, closet, and bath first. Then I tiled the hall, the hall closet, and the second bathroom. This was followed by the second bedroom and its closet, then the living room. Finally, I tiled the kitchen and the den/office. I placed chalk lines in each room only when the tile was laid up to the edge of that area. That way, if my rough layout was off slightly, I could adjust the chalk lines accordingly.

Setting the Tile

I adhered the ceramic tile to the concrete slab with a thinset mortar called Multi-Cure that is manufactured by **C-Cure** It is a cement/sand mixture that does contain some minor chemical additives, but they aren't a serious consideration. Importantly, there is no odor once the tile job is finished.

I mixed the Multi-Cure with water using a paddle on a heavy-duty electric drill (Figure 22-4). It is important to mix at a low speed to avoid entrapping air in the mortar. It takes about 1½ gallons of clean water for a 50-pound bag of Multi-Cure. After mixing until smooth, I let the thinset set for 15 minutes before remixing and using it. This is called "slaking" and it is necessary with many cement-based products for proper curing.

The thinset is applied directly to the concrete slab with a trowel having ⅜" x ⅜" notches (Figure 22-5). Starting in the center of a room, along the chalk layout lines, the mortar is spread first with the flat side of the trowel to make good contact with the slab, then additional mortar is added and spread out using the notched side of the trowel. I covered an area about 5-6 sq. ft. at a time, then filled that area with tile before proceeding further (Figure 22-6).

The tiles should be set in the thinset with a slight twisting motion. Don't slide them in place. Some tilesetters place a block of wood on top of the tile and by hitting the wood with a mallet "beat in" the tile to get good contact with the mortar. The goal is to compress the ridges of mortar enough to have 100% coverage on the back of the tile. Too much pressure will result in mortar being squeezed out and filling the spaces between the tiles. For someone who has never set tile before, I recommend occasionally lifting up a tile immediately after it has been installed to see if your technique provides sufficient mortar coverage.

Figure 22-7.
Applying grout with a rubber squeegee.

Figure 22-8.
Removing excess grout with a damp sponge.

I spaced the tiles about ¼" apart, but a little more or a little less is usually fine. The important thing is to get the spaces uniform. Don't have some wide spaces, then some narrow ones. I have good luck eyeballing the layout, but some people use a straight piece of wood or plastic spacers to make sure the tiles are in perfect alignment. The tiles can be adjusted slightly while the mortar is still tacky, but they should be left alone once the mortar starts to set.

After I have tiled a room, I usually grout it the next day before going on to the next room. In this installation I tiled the master bedroom, closet, and bath together, then grouted that whole area before moving down the hall.

Grouting

To have grout that was as inert as possible, I mixed my own from scratch. One hundred pounds of Portland cement (Type 1), two hundred pounds of sand, and one pound of brown mason's mineral pigment yielded enough dry grout mixture for the entire house. I only combined enough grout with water for about 100 square feet of tile at a time so I was not rushed during the grouting process. I used a plastic bucket and mixed in enough water to give the grout a medium heavy slurry consistency. It was allowed to slake for 15 minutes, then remixed.

With the edge of a rubber squeegee, and working about 10 square feet at a time, I forced the grout between the tiles, then used diagonal strokes to drag the excess grout off the surface of the tile (Figure 22-7). Next, I used a damp sponge to make the joints smooth and uniform (Figure 22-8). With a bucket of clean water and a sponge, I wrung as much water as possible out of the sponge and used it to go over the 10 square foot area to clean the surface of the tile. Then I flipped the sponge over and went over the area again. After going over the floor once with both sides of the sponge, I rinsed the sponge out and repeated the process until the tile was clean. It can take three or four rinsings to remove all the excess grout from the surface of the tile. It seems more important to wring the sponge out as much as possible than to use clean water. By starting with a bucket of clean water, I was able to clean about 150 square feet of tile before changing the water. I finished up the grouting process by buffing any remaining haze off the tile with a clean terry cloth towel. It is easier to remove the haze at this stage than waiting until after it has cured for very long.

Once the tile I had just grouted was clean, I proceeded on to grouting the next 10 square foot area until the entire room was finished.

To damp-cure the grout, I let it sit overnight. In the morning I misted the surface of the tile with a little water (using a clean garden sprayer), then covered the floor with sheets of plastic for 72 hours.

After the entire house is tiled, if some small spots of haze appear anywhere on the surface, they can usually be cleaned off with a non-abrasive cleanser like Bon-Ami and a little elbow grease. As an alternative, some tilesetters use a mild muriatic acid solution. This works quickly, but it can etch the surface of some tiles, weaken the grout, or damage metal or porcelain fixtures. If acid is used to clean the grout, it should be rinsed off thoroughly.

Update

Soon after the initial experiments with mice and carpet, various other laboratories—including the EPA—claimed that they couldn't duplicate Anderson's results. But in most cases they changed the experiment by altering the humidity in the test chamber. At much higher humidities, no one (including Anderson) came up with dead mice. Unfortunately, this valuable clue—that humidity changed the results—was ignored, as the carpet industry struggled to counter the negative publicity. At the same time, no other lab wanted to get involved in the controversy that Anderson Laboratories found itself in, so virtually no independent laboratory is following up on this type of testing.

I'm often asked if carpeting is still a problem—if it is still capable of killing mice in a laboratory experiment. After asking this question of Anderson Laboratories recently, I was told that they still receive samples from concerned homeowners, and that some of those samples do, indeed, kill mice. Someone else told me about a high-school science-fair project in which a student got results similar to Anderson. I would like to think that the carpet industry is working behind closed doors to solve the problem, but if they are, they are keeping very quiet about it.

Since the Model Healthy House was completed, I've learned about a possible problem with commercially made thinset mortars and grouts. It seems that many of the larger manufacturers (including **C-Cure**) have several manufacturing plants around the country, and they purchase their raw materials from different suppliers. Thus, while the basic formula is similar at different plants, it may not be 100% identical. I had one hypersensitive client who purchased a very strong smelling thinset mortar in one part of the country that was usually quite benign when purchased elsewhere. What I have come to realize is that some additives can have a very strong chemical odor, sometimes even when dry. The solution has been simple. Get a small sample of mortar or grout, mix it with water, and see if it has a chemical odor. Most of these materials have a somewhat "earthy" odor when wet, and they are benign when dry. But if it has a strong chemical odor—and it will be quite noticeable—you should get a different brand, because the odor can linger after the job has been completed.

Chapter 23

KITCHEN

■ ■ ■ With its cabinets, plumbing, electrical, ventilation, and appliance requirements, the kitchen is the most complicated room in any house. It can also be the most polluted, although that certainly doesn't have to be the case. While many cabinets, appliances, and other kitchen components seem like they were designed to contaminate the indoor air, the Model Healthy House is a perfect example that there are beautiful, durable, high-quality products already available that will minimize indoor pollution.

Kitchen Cabinets

Most of the kitchen cabinets on the market today are constructed with manufactured wood products like plywood, particleboard, or medium-density fiberboard, all of which contain a potent urea-formaldehyde (UF) glue. These products are often veneered with a thin layer of an attractive wood like oak, maple, or cherry. The veneer does very little to seal in formaldehyde emissions. Therefore, the gas will be released for several years after the cabinets have been manufactured. There can be as much as a 50% decline in formaldehyde emissions after cabinets are 6 months old due to the release of unreacted formaldehyde.

After that the emissions will continue to decline over time, but at a much slower rate. Because UF glues are somewhat unstable, formaldehyde expert Thad Godish, Ph.D., has said that the "release of free formaldehyde from UF products can be expected to continue for an indefinite period."

In addition, the clear finish on the vast majority of commercially made kitchen cabinets is a very volatile acid-catalyzed UF finish that outgasses much more formaldehyde than manufactured wood products. In *Indoor Air Pollution and Control*, Godish has written that "such finishing materials apparently represent the most potent sources of formaldehyde on the market today." The outgassing from these finishes will be very high initially, but there can be a 90% decline after 4-6 months.

Most wood cabinets do have some solid wood components, usually the doors and the framework the doors are attached to. A few manufacturers advertise that their cabinets are made entirely of solid wood, because they don't contain particleboard or medium-density fiberboard. These cabinets are still made with plywood, which the manufacturers claim is solid wood. It isn't. It is a manufactured wood product that contains a UF glue, and it is no doubt finished with the potent formaldehyde-based clear finish.

Healthy Cabinet Options

There are three basic options for people interested in healthy kitchen cabinets. First, because formaldehyde emissions decrease with time, you could use older cabinets that have had some time to air out. Second, you could have cabinets custom-made out of solid wood and coated with a low-tox finish. Third, you could opt for steel cabinets which typically have a baked-on finish.

Older Cabinets

Predicting how long it will take kitchen cabinets to become safe is difficult because the emission rate varies depending on the temperature, humidity, exact formula of the formaldehyde resin, thickness of the finish, type of manufactured wood product, etc. Formaldehyde is a suspected human carcinogen and many scientists believe that no level of a carcinogen is completely without risk. Formaldehyde is also a known sensitizer, meaning that it can cause someone to begin reacting to very low levels of it. I know of people who, after being exposed to a relatively high level of formaldehyde, can no longer be around very low levels—levels that they were previously able to tolerate.

It is possible to store new cabinets in an uncontaminated garage to air out for awhile, then bring them indoors and install them after the emission levels have decreased. Be sure to remove them from their cardboard cartons and leave the cabinet doors open for maximum exposure to the air. I would say that cabinets 6-12 months old would be a vast improvement over new cabinets. However I would never say that 6-12 month old cabinets were safe. I certainly wouldn't put them in my home.

Cabinets salvaged out of an older home would be a better option than waiting on new cabinets to air out. But again, the question "How old is safe?" is difficult to answer. Five years old would be pretty good, but 10 years old would be better. For someone who is very chemically sensitive, I would be hesitant in recommending salvaged cabinets because of the possibility of long-term residual formaldehyde emissions, or the possibility that the cabinets have become saturated with pesticides, or cleaning products, over the years. Older cabinets could also have become contaminated with mold.

Custom-Built Wood Cabinets

Any cabinet shop can construct cabinets out of solid wood. This can be a way to have the beauty of wood without the danger of formaldehyde, but it can be both time-consuming and expensive. Some cabinetmakers have been using manufactured wood products so long that they do not understand the nuances of how solid wood expands and contracts with the seasons. Such knowledge is essential in order to build long-lasting and durable wood cabinets. There are certainly cabinetmakers who are familiar with solid-wood construction, but it may take a few phone calls to locate one in your area.

In order to reduce the cost of custom-made wood cabinets, I often recommend that the shelves and interior partitions be made of a less expensive wood such as poplar or basswood. Drawer bottoms and cabinet backs can easily be made of galvanized sheet steel.

Steel Cabinets

The best choice for healthy kitchen cabinets is steel. Unfortunately, whenever I mention steel cabinets, most people visualize the low-cost white steel cabinets of the 1950s. Steel cabinets have come a long way since then. They are now sturdy, colorful, attractive, and long-lasting.

Most steel cabinets on the market today are used in laboratories where they are exposed to a great deal of rough treatment. Most wood cabinets wouldn't stand up to that kind of abuse. These same steel cabinets are also available for residential applications. They typically have an inert baked-on finish and are available in a wide variety of colors. They are also available in stainless steel.

I had seen the slick colorful manufacturer's literature, but the first time I actually saw steel cabinets in a healthy kitchen, I was pleasantly surprised at how nice they looked—very European. Steel was my choice for the Model Healthy House.

300

Countertops

The most popular countertops are plastic laminate. The thin sheets of plastic are actually fairly inert, but they are generally glued to a particleboard or plywood base that emits formaldehyde. Such a countertop can be made safer by using a water-based adhesive. Also, if you cover all of the edges, the top, and the bottom of the base material with laminate, you will tend to seal in most of the formaldehyde emissions. It is also possible to cover the underneath exposed surfaces of the base material with aluminum foil. Using construction-grade plywood (which contains a less noxious glue) rather than particleboard, will also help reduce formaldehyde emissions. Even when all these precautions are taken, plastic laminate isn't my first choice. I'm often asked if plastic laminate can be glued over solid wood. Unfortunately, it can't because solid wood expands and contracts with the seasons too much. This can cause the countertop to warp and the laminate to come unglued.

Most people believe solid wood chopping block countertops should be avoided for work surfaces because they can be difficult to clean and sanitize. Yet, a few years ago, research conducted at the University of Wisconsin found wood cutting boards to be more sanitary than plastic ones. This received a great deal of press coverage, but more recent research by NSF International in Ann Arbor, Michigan found that there was little difference between wood and plastic cutting boards.

The most inert countertops, from an outgassing standpoint, are made of ceramic tile, stainless steel, or solid-surfacing products like "Corian." However, ceramic tile counters can be susceptible to mold growth in the grout. The solid-surfacing materials have surprisingly little odor, but they do contain synthetic resins, and they are quite expensive..

My personal favorite countertop material is stainless steel, and I have yet to meet anyone who has worked on a stainless counter who doesn't love it. All stainless steel countertops need to be custom-made. To find a local fabricator, look in the Yellow Pages under "Commercial Kitchens" or "Restaurant Equipment." Most major cities will have at least one supplier. Some fabricators use a thin-gauge material and attach it to a plywood base for stiffness. I prefer to specify a heavier 14-gauge stainless sheet material that requires no extra base. Series 300 stainless steel is considered a food-grade material.

Appliances

With appliances, there are two concerns—the health of the occupants and energy efficiency. As a rule, electric appliances are the healthiest for the occupants; however, there aren't clear-cut answers when it comes to appliance selection. They all pollute the air to a certain degree. For example, ranges, refrigerators, and dishwashers all contain insulation that bothers some people. The electric motors in appliances can emit small amounts of ozone and are surrounded by electromagnetic fields. Pumps and motors can give off bothersome odors when they get hot. For these reasons, kitchens must be equipped with adequate ventilation.

Most modern appliances are far more energy-efficient than those produced in the past. However, some appliances are definitely more efficient than others. To compare the efficiency of similar products from different manufacturers, see the *Consumer Guide to Home Energy Savings* listed in Appendix 3.

Range

I have talked to too many people who were severely bothered by the emissions from gas ranges to consider them a viable alternative for a healthy house. The newer models having electronic ignition are less polluting because they do not have a constantly burning pilot light, and burners that are properly adjusted give off fewer combustion by-products, but I still prefer electric. They are not perfect choices, but in my mind they are better than gas.

There are three types of electric ovens on the market today: standard, continuous-cleaning, and self-cleaning. Standard ovens are typically cleaned with elbow grease and/or toxic chemicals. Continuous-cleaning ovens have a special porous porcelain coating on the walls that prevents grease from clumping or beading together. The resulting tiny particles of grease get burned off wherever the oven is turned on. This may be odorous, although it is most noticeable when the oven is heated to over 400 degrees. I prefer self-cleaning ovens because they have a separate cleaning cycle that is only in operation when you specifically activate it. Cleaning is accomplished by a very high temperature that breaks down any food particles in the oven. I recommend only using the cleaning cycle when you can be out of the kitchen (or even out of the house). When the cleaning cycle is engaged, it is important to have the range hood turned on high and a window open to clear the kitchen quickly. All ovens give off an odor the first few times they are turned on. I recommend operating a new oven on the highest temperature setting for several hours with plenty of ventilation, before cooking in it.

Electric burner elements, when new, give off an odor, apparently due to a coating on the element itself. It can take as long as several months of regular use before it is totally burned off. While not a serious concern, the odor can be bothersome to sensitive individuals. The solution for some sensitive people has been to obtain used burners and put them on their new range. Radiant burners mounted under a glass cooking surface seem to be less polluting than conventional burners. These cooktops have a smooth black glass surface, and when the burners heat up, they glow through the glass. The radiant burners heat up quickly and the tops are easy to keep clean; however, the glass surface can get scratched and they are somewhat expensive.

Microwave Oven

In spite of the fact that the vast majority of American households have a microwave oven, I don't recommend them in healthy houses. They certainly offer conveniences not found with conventional ovens, but in my mind there are too many unanswered questions about their safety.

While most people believe microwave ovens to be safe, there are many injuries reported (and probably many more unreported) each year related to their use. The incidence of burns from microwaved food is on the increase because foods can be heated to

very high temperatures quickly, often much higher that the user realizes. While there are no "documented" cases of injury due to a malfunctioning oven, there are physicians who believe that some of the injuries they have seen are the direct result of ovens failing to shut off when the door was opened. In *The Smart Kitchen*, healthy cooking guru David Goldbeck lists 38 warnings that he feels should be attached to all microwave ovens.

Manufacturers repeatedly talk about the safety of microwaves, that any energy releases from ovens are below that allowed by current U.S. standards. It is interesting to note that the Russian standard is one thousand times stricter than ours. Their standard was set that low to reduce exposure to levels of microwaves that they believe can alter brain-wave activity.

One of my big concerns with microwave ovens is the fact that they are regularly used by children who are often unsupervised. Children may not always use the appliance correctly. In *Healthy Homes, Healthy Kids*, the authors suggest that children not stand next to an operating microwave oven. *Consumer Reports* extends this warning to adults as well. Since the strength of the microwave energy decreases with distance, this is an excellent suggestion for someone who wishes to own a microwave oven. An adult's arm length is probably a minimum distance to maintain. With children as young as 4 years old regularly using these appliances, basic safety like this must be taught early.

Refrigerator

Sometimes bothersome odors can be given off by the coils on the back or bottom of a refrigerator. This happens because the coils are painted and when they get hot the paint can outgas slightly. Although I have heard of this affecting people, I haven't found it to be a widespread problem. Plastic interiors can also outgas synthetic odors, but because outgassing rates are lower at lower temperatures, this isn't a major consideration inside a cold refrigerator.

Mold growth is a more prevalent problem with refrigerators, both inside due to spilled or spoiled food, and outside in the drip pan that is under a self-defrosting refrigerator. Few homeowners realize that such a pan even exists. When a refrigerator goes through its automatic defrost cycle, the melting frost from the freezer drains down through plastic tubing into an open drip pan near the floor. The water in the drip pan eventually evaporates into the air. Until the water has completely evaporated, it can be the perfect place for mold to grow. Usually there is a small fan in the vicinity that helps to hasten the water's evaporation. The fan will blow mold spores throughout the kitchen. I strongly recommend that homeowners get down on their hands and knees, pull off the narrow cover plate near the bottom of the refrigerator, and check the drip pan regularly for mold growth. Periodic cleaning will greatly reduce the chance of mold becoming a problem. A manual defrost refrigerator has no drip pan, so it is a healthier choice.

Manual defrost refrigerators are also more energy-efficient than self-defrosting models. However, very few people today are willing to put up with manually defrosting their refrigerator. Because this is one of the most used appliances in the house, you should select features that you'll use every day. It makes little sense to save $10 per year on your electric bill if you curse your freezer every time you open it.

Dishwasher

All dishwashers contain pumps, motors, and some plastic and rubber components. Therefore, they all have the potential to outgas bothersome odors. These odors will diminish with time and regular use. Activating a range hood during operation will improve the kitchen ventilation and minimize occupant exposure. Most dishwashers have plastic interiors, but stainless steel or porcelain is much more inert.

As far as efficiency is concerned, there are two issues pertinent to dishwashers: electricity consumption and water consumption. There are models on the market that use less than half as much water as others. This is important for an appliance that will be operated every day. Another concern with dishwashers is noise. When running, most dishwashers are relatively loud. It is sometimes difficult to carry on a conversation when one is operating. A quiet model will be less irritating to be around.

Range Hood

Many kitchens today are fitted with a "recirculating" range hood. These have a thin (¼") filter that they pull air through, then they blow the air back into the room. Recirculating range hoods do almost nothing to clean the air in the kitchen. A range hood should be ducted to the outdoors in order to remove pollutants from the kitchen. It should have a capacity of at least 200 cfm. If you have a gas range (I don't recommend them), the capacity should be larger. A range hood will operate much more efficiently if a kitchen window is partially open during use. This is especially true in an airtight house. A downdraft kitchen ventilation system, like those built into some ranges, is generally not as efficient as an exhaust hood located above the range. Downdraft fans need to be more powerful in order to counteract the tendency of warm cooking odors to rise.

Even if a house is equipped with a general whole-house ventilation system, a range hood is still necessary to remove cooking odors and moisture quickly.

The Kitchen in the Model Healthy House

Kitchens and Baths by Don Johnson was the supplier of our low-tox version of St. Charles steel cabinets. They are called Series CRE for "chemically reduced environment." Don Johnson and his son Dale, both Certified Kitchen Designers, have been pioneers in several areas of kitchen design. They have been involved for decades in applying the needs of the physically disabled to kitchens and bathrooms. More recently, they have been active in developing and promoting the concept of a chemically uncontaminated environment in both magazine articles and seminars. In a recent article in *Kitchen and Bath Design News,* Don pointed out that "A growing number of people are becoming concerned about the hazards in their own homes," and that kitchen and bath cabinets are often a significant source of indoor air pollution.

In the St. Charles Series CRE cabinets, some of the sheet metal details are designed differently from conventional steel cabinets. This is so that all surfaces can be adequately cleaned and painted. It also means that there are fewer places for debris to collect and mold to grow.

For individuals who prefer the look of wood, **Kitchens and Baths by Don Johnson** can supply the Series CRE cabinets with wood doors and drawer fronts. Currently, they are the only St. Charles dealer offering this option. Any species of wood can be chosen, and it can be sealed with whatever clear finish the customer specifies. The wood doors are available in a variety of attractive styles. I chose this option for the two bathroom vanities (see Chapter 24).

Figure 23-1.
36"-tall base cabinets provide extra storage in the Model Healthy House.

Figure 23-2.
Sub-bases shimmed to be level.

While many steel cabinets contain sound-proofing and/or mastic within the door panels, these kitchen cabinets are made of furniture-grade steel welded and mechanically fastened together without glues. Prior to painting, the steel is thoroughly cleaned of all oils, lubricants, and dirt. The enamel paint finish is oven-baked to reduce emissions, and "sterilize" the cabinets. The result is probably the most inert cabinet commercially produced in the U.S. today.

On special request for extremely sensitive individuals, the rollers and hinges can be degreased in the factory. If this is done, the homeowner must

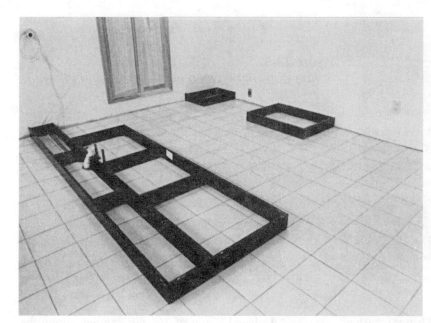

Figure 23-3.
All sub-bases in place.

Figure 23-4.
Assembling base cabinets.

305

Figure 23-5.
Scribe strips fit between end cabinets and the wall.

periodically lubricate the rollers and hinges with a tolerated product. Some sensitive people have used vegetable oil, but it can become rancid over time. Vaseline brand petroleum jelly is another often-tolerated alternative. I feel that the amount of factory applied lubricant is so small that it shouldn't be a concern for most people. It is a longer-lasting product than the alternatives and is specifically designed for the purpose.

Like the finish on many refrigerators, these low-tox cabinets have an attractive textured steel surface that will not show fingerprints. Of the 18 colors available, I chose a Beige Camel that coordinated well with the woodwork and ceramic tile floors. For door and drawer handles, I selected a standard ash wood pull with a medium finish that is similar in color to the poplar woodwork I used in the rest of the house. The complete kitchen layout is shown on sheet 22 of the Plans.

I placed a row of 36"-tall cabinets along the bank of cabinets containing the sink (Figure 23-1). This provides a tremendous amount of storage in what is a relatively compact kitchen. The upper cabinet to the right of the sink was recessed into the wall so that it wouldn't appear to stick out into the room. It is a handy place for glasses and plates.

Kitchens and Baths by Don Johnson was very helpful in planning the kitchen layout. They offered a number of suggestions that I probably never would have thought of on my own. For example, a 36"-wide range hood over a 30"-wide range will capture rising pollutants more efficiently than a 30" hood.

Installing Steel Cabinets

I had never personally installed steel cabinets before this project, so I was a little apprehensive. I shouldn't have been, because **Kitchens and Baths by Don Johnson** provided me with a 35-page manual that described everything I needed to know. In some ways they are installed similar to wood units, but in other ways the techniques are a little different. All in all, the installation went very smoothly.

It is usually recommended that the wall cabinets be hung first, then the base cabinets. Because I used one-piece stainless steel countertops with integral backsplashes, I decided to reverse the normal procedure. By having the base cabinets and stainless tops in place first, I was able to hang the wall cabinets so that they fitted tightly on top of the backsplash.

Cabinet Base Units

The first step was to anchor the 4"-high sub-bases to the floor. These must be shimmed to be perfectly level if the base units are to sit on them properly (Figure 23-2). In most installations the floor isn't perfectly level and there will be a small gap in some places between the floor and the sub-base. I filled the small gap with 100% silicone caulk once the installation was complete. After the sub-bases were in place, I extended the two ½" copper water lines through them to the vicinity of the sink. These lines were later hooked up to the faucet and dishwasher. Figure 23-3 shows the sub-bases in place and ready to accept the base units.

The base cabinets themselves were attached to the sub-bases, to each other, and to the wall (Figure 23-4). Scribe strips were supplied that fit between the end cabinets and the wall. These strips can be trimmed to fit a wall that is not plumb. In our case, I took extra pains to build a perfectly plumb wall and ordered the scribe strips, which are normally 4" wide, precut to a uniform 1½" (Figure 23-5). I wouldn't use scribe strips much narrower or the doors and drawers on the

Figure 23-6.
Wooden frame and scribe strip adjacent to the dishwasher space.

307

end cabinets will be too close to the wall. At the right side of the dishwasher space, I anchored a wooden frame to the wall to which I attached one of the 1½" scribe strips. The frame will also support the stainless countertop (Figure 23-6). The base cabinets contain handy rollouts that make it easy to retrieve items stored in them (Figure 23-7).

Stainless Countertops

Sheet 23 of the Plans contains the fabrication details for the stainless-steel countertops in the Model Healthy House. Because welded seams can be polished and made invisible, stainless countertops can be made in virtually any shape imaginable. I like to have the countertops and backsplashes formed in one piece to minimize any seams where mold could grow. Although it probably wasn't really necessary, I decided to play it safe and had the panel behind the range made as a separate piece in case there were any minor irregularities in fabrication.

I find it easier to install the kitchen sink and the faucet before the countertops are attached to the cabinets. By turning the countertop upside down on a pair of sawhorses, I was able to fasten everything in place while standing up. It is much easier than lying on your back inside a cabinet. I selected a Model #400 single-handle faucet with a convenient spray nozzle manufactured by the **Delta Faucet Co.** In order to seal the joint between the sink and the countertop, I used plumber's putty. This has a slight odor, but I haven't found it to be a big problem. This is because the putty ends up being completely covered by the sink on the top side and only minimally exposed on the bottom. Just to be safe, I like to cover the putty on the bottom side with aluminum-foil tape as a precaution against outgassing. Many top-of-the-line stainless steel sinks have an undercoating that outgasses slightly. In order to obtain one without such a coating, you can select a lower-priced sink.

The countertops were fastened to the base cabinets with self-tapping screws driven up through the cabinets from below. The tops can also be held in place with 100% silicone caulking.

Cutting holes in the stainless for the sink and electrical receptacles can be done with a saber saw with a heavy-duty blade, but stainless is difficult to cut, and you can end up wearing out several blades. I decided to have all the holes cut by the fabricator, so I waited until the base cabinets were in place before taking the final measurements and finishing the draw-

Figure 23-7.
Convenient rollouts in base cabinets.

Figure 23-8.
Adjustable shelves in upper cabinets.

Figure 23-9.
Completed kitchen.

ings. This meant about a three-week delay before the kitchen could be completed, but it was worth the wait because if a dimension had been incorrect, stainless tops can't be easily trimmed to fit like other materials. They can be recut, rewelded and repolished, but it can be costly.

Upper Cabinets

Once the countertops were in place, the upper cabinets were attached to the wall so that they rested on the top of the backsplash. I used #14 sheet metal screws and washers through the cabinet backs

309

Figure 23-10.
Completed kitchen.

into the steel studs. Because this was a load-bearing wall, the studs were 20-gauge material, not the light 25-gauge steel used in the non-load-bearing framing. This provided plenty of support for the cabinets. Predrilling pilot holes in the studs made it easy to drive the screws in. The wall cabinet to the right of the sink was set into the rough wall opening, squared up and screwed to the wall.

Once all the cabinets were in place, I attached the wood pulls and hung the adjustable steel shelves in their respective locations (Figure 23-8). Figures 23-9 and 23-10 show the completed kitchen cabinets.

Appliances

Once the cabinet installation was complete, I installed the range hood (**Broan Manufacturing Co.** Model #76000). I selected a stainless steel hood to match the stainless countertops. It has a built-in light

and a variable-speed control for the fan. The 200 cfm capacity should be sufficient to clear the kitchen of cooking odors quickly (Figure 23-11). The ductwork and wiring for the hood were roughed in earlier, so all that needed to be done at this stage was to mount the hood to the cabinet over the range and hook up the electrical wire. I sealed the back of the hood to the ductwork with aluminum-foil tape.

I choose a fairly standard self-defrosting refrigerator for the project, and after weighing the alternatives, picked an electric range with a self-cleaning oven. The glass cooking surface with radiant heating elements seems more inert than conventional electric burners.

The only major appliance manufacturer I approached to be a sponsor of the Model Healthy House was **Asko, Inc.** This company imports and distributes a line of Scandinavian dishwashers that I feel are vastly superior to any models produced in this coun-

310

try. With stainless steel interiors, they are hygienic, inert, and extremely durable. They contain a hidden child-proof lock, and are roomy enough for 14 place settings. I selected the Model #1402B (Figure 23-12). **Asko, Inc.** dishwashers operate on considerably less electricity (an average of $42 per year) and have shorter running times than comparable brands. Because they operate at half the noise level of other models, they are extremely quiet. When you add in the fact that they use only about half as much water (4.7 gal. per regular cycle) as most dishwashers, it is easy to see that **Asko Inc**. dishwashers are a clear environ-

Figure 23-11.
Broan range hood.

Figure 23-12.
Asko dishwasher.

311

mental choice. They are capable of surprising efficiency through the use of a specially designed "super cleaning system." With triple filtration, dishes come out cleaner than with some other dishwashers.

While I haven't included a washing machine and clothes dryer in the Model Healthy House, **Asko, Inc.** also imports equally energy-efficient appliances for the laundry.

Update

In discussing custom-made wood cabinets, I mentioned that drawer bottoms and cabinet backs could be made of sheets of galvanized steel. This can be an easy way to avoid some manufactured wood products. I recently made some wood cabinets and went a step further, and substituted galvanized steel for the shelves in the lower cabinets (See Chapter 28). The lower shelves are nearly 24" deep and are almost always made of a manufactured wood product. To make them out of solid wool, you must be very careful to allow for seasonal expansion and contraction. But with galvanized steel, you just have them fabricated at a local sheet-metal shop, then screw them to the solid wood frame. In a cabinet with solid-wood doors, you only notice the shelves when the doors are open. I've found this to be a very good option. As an alternative for narrower upper shelves, I sometimes recommend ¼"-thick glass.

Kitchens and Baths by Don Johnson provided the St. Charles brand cabinets for the Model Healthy House. The St. Charles company has since been sold and split into two separate companies, one specializing in commercial cabinets, and the other dealing in residential cabinets. All-steel cabinets are not available through the residential cabinet company, but can still be had from the commercial cabinet company. In the meantime, **Kitchens and Baths by Don Johnson** has begun producing their own line of less-toxic steel cabinets.

I continue to have mixed feelings about microwave ovens, yet my wife and I recently bought on for our own home. In order to minimize our risk, we located it in the corner of the kitchen, away from the main work area. That way we tend to be at least a few feet away from it when it is operating.

In discussing range hoods, I mentioned using a more-powerful model in some situations. If this is done, the house will become depressurized, and the stronger the fan, the greater the depressurization. If a house is depressurized too much, backdrafting of chimneys serving furnaces, water heaters, and fire places is a serious health concern. Fortunately, any depressurization can be reduced by cracking open a window when operating the range hood, but homeowners don't often do this religiously. So, many experts feel that an air intake vent should be installed along with a powerful range hood. This would consist of a duct between the outdoors and the kitchen. It is a good idea for the duct to have a motorized damper to keep it closed most of the time. The damper should be wired so it opens automatically whenever the hood is turned on. This is what I did in my own new house (see Chapter 28). Of course, depressurization doesn't always cause problems like backdrafting. For example, in an electrically heated house without chimneys bakdrafting won't be a concern.

Chapter 24

BATHROOMS

■ ■ ■ Because of water spills and high humidity, the primary health consideration in bathrooms is mold growth. Exhaust fans (see Chapter 15) are mandatory to lower humidity levels, but fixtures should also be selected that do not have crevices where mold can hide and proliferate. Because higher humidity levels can cause formaldehyde to outgas faster, materials containing manufactured wood products should be avoided.

Bathtub Surrounds

The bathtubs and anti-scald shower valves (Model #1548 by **Delta Faucet Co.**) were discussed in Chapter 16 because they were installed during the plumbing rough-in. For shower surrounds, there are several possibilities—plastic, ceramic tile, porcelainized steel, or stainless steel.

Plastic shower surrounds can be made integral with a plastic bathtub. Having no seams, they are the easiest to keep clean and dry, so they are the best choice to minimize mold growth. If caulked carefully, plastic surrounds made of two or more pieces have only a few seams, so they are almost as good as the single piece bathtub/shower units. Disadvantages to plastic surrounds include the fact that they can be easily scratched and are susceptible to some minor outgassing. Of the different kinds of plastic surrounds currently on the market, those made from solid countertop material (like Corian) seem to be more inert than fiberglass or acrylic.

Ceramic tile shower surrounds are usually inert from an outgassing standpoint. They can be installed with a cement-based thinset mortar and a low-tox grout as discussed in Chapter 22. Ceramic tile in bathrooms should generally be adhered to a thick mortar bed or to a concrete board (Wonder-Board is a popular brand) for durability. Concrete boards can be fastened to the studs around the tub (instead of drywall or plaster) to provide a moisture-resistant base on which to mount the tile. They are familiar to most tilesetters, are typically a half-inch thick, and there are several different brands on the market. Each brand has a distinctive odor, but it usually isn't detectable once covered with tile. The smell will dissipate somewhat if the boards are stored somewhere for awhile before they are used. The primary disadvantage to ceramic tile surrounds is the fact that each grout line is a potential home for mold.

Porcelainized steel panels can be used as a shower surround to match the color of the bathtub. These are steel panels formed out of sheet metal that have an inert glass-like porcelain coating fused to the surface. They must always be custom-made. I have had this done on two

Figure 24-1.
Stainless-steel shower surround.

occasions in the past. The panels were expensive, there were production delays, and because the panels couldn't be made in very wide widths, I had to use five separate, interlocking sections that resulted in several seams that needed to be caulked. Overall, it made for a difficult installation. They are attractive and durable once installed, but I don't believe I will ever use them again.

Sheets of inert stainless steel can also be used for shower surrounds. There will be a few seams to caulk, but because the sheets can be larger, there won't be as many as with porcelain panels. When the sheets are installed over a backing of drywall or plaster, they can be made of a fairly thin 20-gauge material.

Mold growth occurs primarily in the grout of ceramic tile shower walls or in caulking. If the grout or caulking are not deteriorating and mold is still a problem, it is probably due to the fact that the moisture in the bathroom can't evaporate fast enough—evidence of poor ventilation. An exhaust fan ducted to the outdoors

is vitally important for all bathrooms to remove excess moisture as well as undesirable odors.

Shower Doors

Inert 100% cotton shower curtains are available, but I prefer glass doors. The healthiest doors are called "frameless." Rather than an aluminum frame surrounding each glass panel, they use tempered glass with a clean polished edge. Frameless doors still have an aluminum track that the doors slide in, but the track usually isn't as susceptible to a mold problem as the door frame.

Toilets

For years, our toilets have been guzzling water like our automobiles have guzzled gasoline. Each flush

314

used up to 8 gallons of water. When low-flow toilets first appeared several years ago, they reduced water usage to 3.5 gallons. Today's ultra-low-flow toilets use 1.6 gallons or less per flush. They can save about 20,000 gallons of water in an average household. There are many manufacturers producing ultra-low-flow toilets, but there is a heath-related feature that many don't have—an insulated tank. Without insulation, a toilet tank can sweat in the summer. When this happens, the liquid water can drip onto the floor. The result can easily be mold growth. By insulating the tank, there is no danger of sweating and mold problems are minimized. The insulation is usually expanded polystyrene (beadboard).

Lavatory

For lavatory cabinets, the choices are the same as those for kitchen cabinets (see Chapter 23). Conven-

tional new cabinets are high in formaldehyde emissions, but salvaged, or antique, cabinets can sometimes be acceptable. Custom-made solid wood cabinets are often good choices, but steel cabinets with a baked-on finish are generally the most inert option.

The healthiest bathroom sink tops have no cracks or crevices for mold to grow. While ceramic tile can be inert from an outgassing standpoint, every grout line is a potential breeding ground for mold. Most cultured-marble sink tops are made from plaster or marble dust and a synthetic resin. While they are only minor sources of outgassing, I prefer the inert vitreous-china tops that are made of the same ceramic material as toilets.

Bathrooms in the Model Healthy House

For shower surrounds, I decided to use stainless steel (Figure 24-1). This is by far the most inert, cleanest

Figure 24-2.
"Frameless" shower doors.

solution, and it looks very high-tech. See Sheet 23 of the Plans for the sizes and shapes of the panels. Make sure to double-check all stainless steel dimensions prior to having the panels fabricated because they cannot be stretched if they are cut too small. The panels were adhered to the drywall with several dabs of 100% silicone caulking.

For the shower doors, I chose the frameless Model #340 by **Alumax** (Figure 24-2). I used a silver-colored track with obscure glass, but **Alumax** also produces doors in other colors and glass patterns. This model has an easy-to-clean lower track, so there is no place for mold to grow. I have one in my own house and am very happy with it. The Model #340 is 57" high by 60" wide for use with a bathtub, and **Alumax** has a taller style for a walk-in shower.

I used "tub and tile" caulk to seal the corners of the shower surround, the joint between the surround and the tub, and the track for the glass doors. I prefer tub and tile caulk over 100% silicone caulk indoors wherever water might be present because it is more mold-resistant. It has only a mild odor that it loses after a couple of days. Tub and tile caulk is available from most building supply and hardware stores.

I installed two Model #4098 toilets by **Universal-Rundle Corp.** (Figure 24-3) not only because they use only 1.6 gallons of water per flush, but also because they have insulated tanks. Before setting the toilets in place, I first had to glue the plastic mounting flanges to the under-slab piping that was installed when the floor slab was poured. I used a utility knife to dig away the foam caps that were placed over the pipes in Chapter 5, then glued the mounting flanges to the pipes (with plenty of ventilation). The connections were made airtight by injecting single-component polyurethane aerosol-foam insulation into the space under the flanges (Figure 24-4). When the foam was hard the next day, I trimmed away the excess and installed the toilets in the conventional manner using a wax ring to seal the toilet to the flange.

Figure 24-3.
Low-flow toilet with insulated tank.

316

Figure 24-4.
Sealing toilet flange to concrete floor slab.

Figure 24-5.
Pull-out lavatory faucet.

The lavatory cabinets are Series CRE steel units, just like the kitchen cabinets. They have the same high-quality, long-lasting baked-enamel finish. For these cabinets I elected to have solid wood doors. Wood doors on steel cabinets are an option currently only provided by **Kitchens and Baths by Don Johnson**, and they are available in a variety of woods, styles, and finishes. I chose poplar wood in a simple style, with the same Crystal Aire finish (**Pace Chem Industries, Inc.**) that I used on the rest of the woodwork in the house.

For lavatory faucets, I selected the Model #550 faucets from **Delta Faucet Co.** (Figure 24-5). They have

Figure 24-6.
Completed bathroom.

a unique pull-out spout that makes washing your hair in the sink quite easy. While the flexible hose might impart some minor contaminants into the water, it's doubtful if it would be enough for most people to worry about. For a hypersensitive person who drinks a great deal of water from the bathroom faucet, a simpler style might be in order. In the past, I've used a Model #520 single handle faucet. As I mentioned in Chapter 16, **Delta Faucet Co.** uses machined brass bodies for their valves because of its low-lead content, and all of their single-handle faucets are designed to accommodate the disabled.

I have used the Model #4632 Alexander Style tops made by **Universal-Rundle Corp.** several times in the past and have been quite happy with them. They are made of inert vitreous china and are manufactured in a variety of widths up to 30" and in several colors. To attach the tops to the cabinets, they can be adhered with 100% silicone caulking, but I find that anchoring the lower rear flange to the wall with toggle bolts is usually sufficient. The bathroom fixture installation was finished up by hooking up the sink drains and the water supply lines to the lavatories and toilets. Figure 24-6 shows the completed bathroom.

Update

Something I didn't think about when I decided on stainless-steel shower surrounds is the fact that stainless steel can water spot easily after it gets wet. This may not be a problem with all water supplies, and it won't be noticeable if you wipe down the walls after showering. Also, water spotting will be less noticeable if you use stainless steel with a more textured finish (I used a lightly brushed finish in the Model Healthy House), but textured stainless isn't available in very wide sheets, so it will require more seams. As I mentioned in the "Update" to Chapter 16, my wife and I recently opted for a one-piece fiberglass tub/shower unit to minimize mold growth.

Something else I have done in recent projects is to use one-piece toilets, rather than conventional models that have a separate base and tank. With a one-piece toilet, there are fewer hidden places for mold to grow. They are also available with insulated tanks if you live in a climate where condensation on the toilet's tank can lead to mold growth.

Chapter 25

COMPLETING THE SYSTEMS

■ ■ ■ In Chapters 15-19 the ventilation/filtration, plumbing, central vacuum, electrical, and heating and air-conditioning systems were discussed and roughed in. Then the walls were covered with drywall, finished, and painted, the floors were tiled, and the kitchen and bathrooms were completed. This chapter will cover the finishing touches necessary to complete all the systems of the Model Healthy House that were roughed in earlier.

Ventilation/Filtration

The only things that remained to be done to the ventilation/filtration system were to hook up the controls and the install the grilles. The controls are located in the hallway. There is a crank timer (**Broan Mfg. Co., Inc.** Model #71) and two switches. To avoid any confusion, I had a switch plate engraved to show the functions of the switches (Figure 25-1). See Chapter 15 for a discussion of how to use the controls and information about operating the bath and laundry fans.

The 5" round grilles are adjustable Techgrilles supplied by our HRV manufacturer, **Nutech Energy Systems, Inc.** (Figure 25-2). While they are made from plastic, which could outgas slightly, they are all located on stale air lines so that any air passing through them will be filtered before it returns to the living space. For the small rectangular duct openings in the two closets, I used a standard 4" x 10" return-air grill. It was somewhat larger than the opening, but that shouldn't have an effect on the system operation. The supply air outlet into the living room was fitted with a 12" x 22" grille, and for the two 4" x 12" HRV returns (master bath and kitchen) I used adjustable registers so that the air flows from those rooms could be regulated.

Once all the grilles were in place, I adjusted them so that the air flows were balanced. This was done with the filter on low speed. The kitchen and master bath returns for the HRV were adjusted together, then the remaining returns were balanced to each other. My rather unscientific method involved hanging a narrow strip of tissue paper at each opening and adjusting the grilles until the air flow seemed similar at each opening. By seeing how much the tissue was deflected, I could get a rough idea of the relative air flows. My goal was to have approximately the same amount of stale air flowing into each opening. Many ventilation contractors have air flow measurement instruments that can do this more accu-

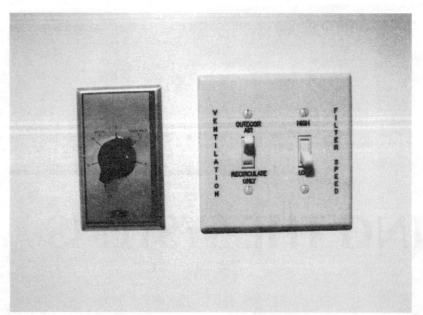

Figure 25-1.
Ventilation/filtration controls in the hallway.

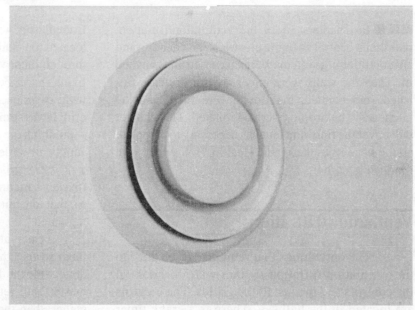

Figure 25-2.
Return air Techgrille for the ventilation/filtration system.

rately, but my method seems to work reasonably well. Air flow testing instruments are available through **Nutech Energy Systems, Inc.**

I installed adjustable dampers at various points in the ductwork to balance the overall air flow into and out of the house. This is extremely important in a

house having a combustion appliance such as a gas furnace. If a heat-recovery ventilator is improperly adjusted, and it results in depressurizing the house, backdrafting or spillage could result. In an airtight, electrically heated house, perfectly balanced air flows aren't as critical. Because of the occasional operation

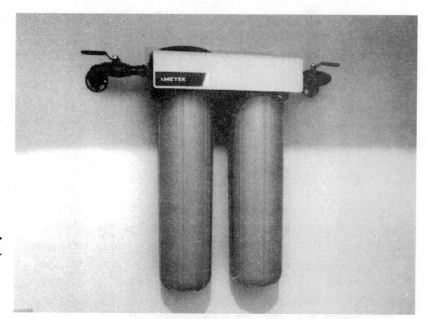

Figure 25-3.
Ametek whole-house water filter.

of bath fans and range hood, and the natural forces of wind and stack effect, a system's balance will be occasionally upset anyway.

Plumbing

The plumbing in the kitchen was finalized by first connecting the sink to both the drain line in the floor and the vent in the wall. I routed the PVC floor drain up through the cabinets and connected to the vent that was stubbed through the wall earlier. The PVC connections were made with 1½" plastic pipe and glue and plenty of ventilation. After the glued connections had aired out several days, I covered all the exposed plastic piping with aluminum foil tape. While the plastic didn't seem to have any noticeable odor, I covered it as a precautionary measure. For the connection between the sink and the drain pipe, I used a P-trap that was made of chrome-plated brass although I doubt if a plastic P-trap would have been much of a problem.

The water lines were connected to the **Asko** dishwasher and the **Delta** single handle faucet, completing the kitchen.

Water Filter

The Model WH-400S water filter by **Ametek** was hung on the wall over the clothes dryer location (Figure 25-3). I installed a ¾" ball valve on each side of the filter to make it easy to periodically change the filter cartridges. For the Model Healthy House, this particular filter is an excellent generic approach because it will clean all the water coming into the house. There will be no need to worry about absorbing chlorine or volatile chemicals while showering or drinking the water. For a water supply with unusual pollutants, or for someone with extreme sensitivities to some specific water contaminants, a different approach may be necessary. This might include an additional under-counter filter in the kitchen that would remove any remaining minor pollutants from the water used for cooking or drinking.

Water Heater

The electric water heater itself is a high-efficiency 50-gallon unit. I obtained it through my

321

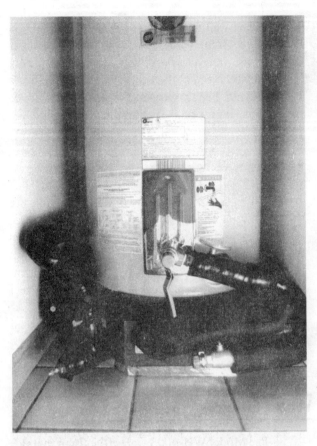

Figure 25-4.
Electric water heater and solar pad installation.

local electric utility. Utilities often have special deals like this for their customers. My utility provides a free high-efficiency water heater for use in a new house, or a discount on a replacement heater for an existing house.

The electric water heater and the Copper Cricket solar water heater (**Sage Advance Corp.**) were hooked up at the same time. First, the solar pad was set on the floor with the electric water heater on top of it. Between the floor and the pad is a layer of foam insulation that was supplied with the solar heater installation package. I wrapped aluminum-foil tape around the perimeter of the insulation to prevent any minor outgassing into the air.

The two ¾" copper lines from the rooftop solar collector were connected to the solar pad, and the two ¾" copper supply lines for the house (one hot, one cold) were connected to the top of the electric water heater. These were all soldered with

lead-free solder. The solar pad and the electric heater were interconnected with piping and valves per the instructions provided by the manufacturer. **Sage Advance Corp.** includes all necessary fittings with their installation package.

To fill the system with solar liquid, I used the equipment supplied with the installation kit. The lines are filled by removing two plugs on the rooftop collector, then a vacuum pump is used to evacuate any air remaining in the ¾" copper lines. Whenever the sun is shining, heat is transferred from the roof collector by means of a solar liquid, to the pad, then from the pad to the electric water heater. The solar liquid contains alcohol and is totally separated from the house's water supply, so there is no danger of contamination—only heat is transferred. The actual connections may look rather complicated, but they are clearly spelled out in the instruction manual (Figure 25-4).

322

Central Vacuum

The Model #189S central vacuum (**Beam Industries**) was hung on the wall in the laundry closet and connected to the suction and exhaust tubing roughed in earlier (Figure 25-5). In Chapter 17 the suction line was connected to the three wall inlets and the exhaust was run to the outdoors.

Two low-voltage control wires (from the wall inlets) are attached to the vacuum, and a power cord is plugged into a 110 volt electric outlet. **Beam Industries** supplies cover plates to attach to the wall inlets. They have two screws on them for connecting the low-voltage control wires.

The vacuum accessory kit comes with a 30'-long hose and a variety of attachments. To use the vacuum, you just plug the hose into a wall inlet, the motor automatically starts, and you begin cleaning. A handy feature on the hose is an on-off switch. You must unplug some manufacturer's hoses to shut off the vacuum, which can prove to be quite inconvenient if you are at the end of the hose and want to answer a nearby phone. I attached a bracket to the wall inside the hall closet on which to store the hose.

Electrical

Most of the electrical work was done during the rough-in in Chapter 18. At this stage the switches, receptacles, and cover plates were installed. Besides the regular electrical components, I also hooked up the telephone and television jacks and the doorbell at this time. Outdoors, at the east end of the house I installed a television antenna and rotor. The Model Healthy House is located between three metropolitan television service areas, so there are a wide number of

Figure 25-5.
Beam central vacuum mounted in laundry closet.

323

channels to choose from. A cable television service also operates in the area, or a future homeowner could elect to install a satellite receiver dish. This could be done through the same wiring that serves the antenna.

I have had people express some concern that the various plastic switches, receptacles, and cover plates could outgas chemicals into the air. Actually, they are made of a hard plastic that is subject to very little outgassing. This type of plastic is a thermosetting material. Thermosetting refers to the fact that when the resins were formed into their final shape, heat was required to cure the material. Once cured, thermosetting plastics cannot be melted down like acrylics, nylons, or vinyls (which are in the thermoplastic class), so they have much less potential for outgassing. In my experience, these components do not seem to be a contributor to indoor air pollution.

I used photoelectric smoke detectors in the Model Healthy House because they contain no radioactive material (Figure 25-6). They were furnished by **Baubiologie Hardware**, a mail-order supplier of healthier building materials, consumer products, and test kits. Smoke detectors need to be located near sleeping areas, so I placed one in the central hallway where it would serve the two bedrooms. I also in-

stalled one in the den/office because that room could possibly be used as a bedroom. The two detectors are wired together so if one goes off, they both do.

There were not any unusual electrical requirements in the healthy kitchen. The range hood, the dishwasher, and the fluorescent light built into the wall cabinet between the range and refrigerator all had electrical wires stubbed in place during the rough-in. The only other wire that was stubbed into the kitchen was for the two receptacles to the left of the sink. These were mounted in the back of one of the 36" high base cabinets so they could be easily accessed from the countertop. The wiring was run within the 36"-high cabinets and was encased in electrical conduit for safety. Connecting these wires completed the kitchen installation.

Heating

I used Intertherm hydronic baseboard heaters (EBH Series by **Nordyne**) in the Model Healthy House because they are the healthiest that I have found (Figure 25-7). **Nordyne** has recently begun using a powder-type paint coating that is baked onto the metal

Figure 25-6.
Radiation-free smoke detector.

324

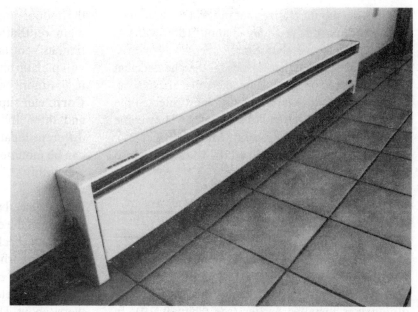

Figure 25-7.
Intertherm self-contained hydronic electric baseboard

Figure 25-8.
Indoor air conditioning unit.

heater cases. This type of paint is quite inert because no solvents are used. I have had trouble with conventional paints used on heaters in the past because they took as long as two or three weeks to burn off the paint smell. **Nordyne's** powder coatings seem very inert almost immediately.

Each of the bedrooms has a 750-watt heater, the kitchen's is 1,000 watts, the living room's is 1,380 watts, and the master bath heater is 500 watts. This is more than enough heat for this particular house in the southern-Indiana climate. To get an idea how little heat is required in a superinsulated house, you should realize that most hand-held hair dryers and toasters are rated at about 1500 watts—enough to heat two bedrooms.

Nordyne has thermostats for their heaters that can be mounted on a wall, and others that are suitable for attaching to the end of the heaters. I selected the ones that mount to the end of the heaters. They come packaged in an installation kit (Model EBK 1-24). **Nordyne** also has kits to add a 110-volt receptacle to the end of a heater.

Air Conditioning

In the Model Healthy House, I used a **Burnham Corp.** 12,000 BTU Model #RAS3128H heat pump for air conditioning. The refrigerant piping was installed earlier (see Chapter 19). In order to hook up the rest of the system, I first hung the indoor unit on the living room wall near the main ventilation duct (Figure 25-8). In this location, as ventilation air moves through the house, it will pick up and carry the cool conditioned air with it. For more complicated house layouts, **Burnham Corp.** can supply a system with one outdoor unit and three indoor units that can be mounted at different locations in the house. The indoor units can be mounted virtually anywhere as long as they are within 33' of the outdoor unit (49' for some models).

Once I mounted the indoor unit on the wall, I connected the electrical wires and the two refrigerant lines to the back. The wires and refrigerant lines were stubbed in earlier (Chapter 18, 19). When you remove the protective caps from the back of the indoor unit, a gas will be released. This is normal and nothing to worry about. The units are shipped with inert nitrogen gas in them. This particular air conditioner has an

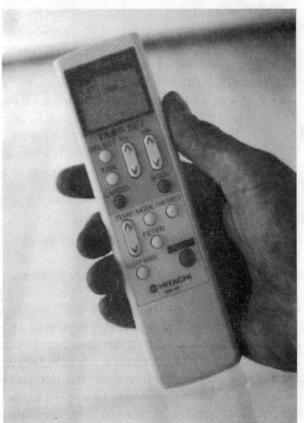

Figure 25-9.
Remote controller for the air conditioner.

Figure 25-10.
Outdoor air conditioning unit.

infrared remote controller that operates similarly to those used on televisions (Figure 25-9). It can be programmed to turn the air conditioner on or off at specific times.

The outdoor unit (Figure 25-30) was bolted to a precast concrete pad outside the house. It is precharged with a refrigerant. Once the refrigerant lines are connected to both units, the air needs to be bled out of the lines. The refrigerant used in air conditioners is capable of damaging the ozone layer, and all air conditioning systems use similar chemicals, but many companies now use a much more benign HCFC material rather than the more damaging CFC refrigerant. New government regulations allow only a small amount of refrigerant to be purged (for 5 seconds) to the atmosphere during installation. The **Burnham Corp.** installation process requires only a short 2-second purge.

Update

While I used an electric water heater in the Model Healthy House, I should mention that there are relatively safe gas water heaters available. They have sealed-combustion chambers like the sealed-combustion furnaces I mentioned in Chapter 19. While I still prefer electric models, in the right situation, a sealed-combustion gas water heater might be acceptable. On the subject of water heating, as I mentioned in the "Update" to Chapter 11, **Sage Advance Corp.** is no longer in business, so the Copper Cricket solar water heater is no longer available. However, this was an energy saving feature—not a health feature—so without it, a house will not have compromised indoor air quality.

If you have a multiple-story house, and install a central vacuum system, it can be very useful to have an extra hose for each level. This is relatively inexpensive, and it is very handy—like having a vacuum on each floor. In some cases it is nice to have a spare shorter hose in one particular room. For example, I've found a 10' hose in a kitchen pantry to be particularly handy.

Baubiologie Hardware, the supplier of our smoke detector, is no longer in business, but photoelectric smoke detectors (those *without* radioactive material) are more readily available than they used to be. I now see them regularly in local department and discount stores.

With baseboard heaters, I've found that a thermostat mounted on the heater itself doesn't regulate the room's temperature as well as having the thermostat mounted on the wall, some distance away. If you decide to do this, electrical boxes for the thermostats should be roughed in prior to the drywall being installed.

As I mentioned in the "Update" to Chapter 19, **Burnham Corp.** no longer offers ductless, split-system air conditioners. However, over the years, I have used units made by three different manufacturers and found them to be very comparable (see Appendix 2). Also, **Nordyne** no longer distributes Intertherm baseboard heaters. They are now called Softheat heaters and are distributed by Cadet Manufacturing Co. Their address and phone number are listed in Appendix 2.

Chapter 26

WOODWORK

■ ■ ■ I decided to use all solid-hardwood trim in the Model Healthy House to avoid the odor of softwoods. When most builders consider hardwood, they automatically think of oak. I believe oak is a beautiful wood, but it certainly isn't the only choice. In fact, some sensitive people are bothered by the smell of oak. Beech, maple, and cherry are other possibilities. My personal choice for woodwork is poplar. It is less expensive than oak and in the Midwest can be less expensive than pine.

I find that, for many sensitive individuals, poplar is more inert than some of the other hardwoods, and I feel it is just as attractive. Some people feel oak is often rather bland, but poplar has both light and dark areas, giving it more character and interest. I think it looks more natural and woody.

Finishing the Woodwork

In Chapter 21 I discussed how I prefinished all of the wood trim and interior doors early in the construction process and stored it in the garage so the finish would have plenty of time to outgas. I used Crystal Aire (**Pace Chem Industries, Inc.**) and coated both sides of the trim with two coats so it would be well-sealed. Using spray equipment makes this job go rather quickly, but I could also have used a brush.

Interior Doors

There are two choices for interior doors in a healthy house—solid wood or metal. Solid wood doors can be custom-made, factory-made, or older salvaged doors can be used. Most interior doors on the market today are made from manufactured wood products and synthetic resins. They should be avoided because of their formaldehyde emissions. Some doors are advertised as being made from solid wood but are actually veneered. When buying wood doors, ask if any components are veneered and find out what kind of glue is used in them. While there isn't very much glue in a solid-wood door, formaldehyde-containing products should be avoided whenever possible.

Metal doors can be quite inert, but they can look very cold and uninviting when used indoors in a residence. Salvaged wood doors can be inexpensive and attractive, but be sure to consider the fact that they may need to be refinished. In the past, I have made my own solid-wood doors from scratch. I thought that by doing so, I could save some money, but as it turned

Figure 26-1.
Solid wood interior door.

out, I could have bought them already made for not much more than I paid for the material. I now prefer factory-made solid-wood doors.

All the interior doors in the Model Healthy House are of the standard 6-panel design and made of poplar (Figure 26-1). The laundry and hall closets have bi-folds (Figure 26-2). The doors were supplied by **Koetter Woodworking, Inc.** in the sizes shown on Sheet 13 of the Plans. In the past, manufacturers assembled doors with wide solid-wood boards, but today they glue boards of various widths together to obtain wider or thicker lumber. One reason for this is to conserve scarce material, but it also helps to reduce warpage. A variety of different glues are used in the industry, but **Koetter Woodworking, Inc.** uses a benign white woodworking glue (similar to Elmer's glue) that many sensitive people find tolerable.

By using 2½" steel studs for most of the interior walls in the Model Healthy House, and covering each side with ½" drywall, the total wall thickness was 3½", the same as a 1x4. As I mentioned earlier, this allowed me to use standard 1x4 poplar material for door jambs. In retrospect, it would have been somewhat easier to use a different stud width that would be compatible with prehung doors. **Koetter Woodworking, Inc.** can also supply doors prehung in several jamb widths, made from poplar, walnut, oak, or cherry.

All the interior doors in the Model Healthy House have a 1" gap between the bottom of the door and the floor for the movement of ventilation air (Figure 26-3). I made my jambs 1" taller than normal to allow for this. When using prehung doors with standard height jambs, it will be necessary to cut 1" off the bottom of the doors.

Hanging a door in a steel-framed wall is similar to hanging a door in a wood-framed wall except that trim screws are used instead of nails. In order to install the screws, the wood must be first predrilled with a pilot hole. This allows the threads (but not the screw's head) to slip through the wood, then bite into the metal. Without a pilot hole, it is very difficult to get the screw to pull the wood tightly against the steel.

A door jamb must be shimmed to get it plumb for proper operation of the door (Figure 26-4). Most shims are made of tapered cedar shingles, but the smell of cedar can often bother sensitive people. In the past, I have painted cedar shims with an environmental sealant, but that can be time-consuming. More recently, I have been cutting my own shims out of scraps of redwood or poplar. Of the two types of wood, redwood is probably slightly less odorous. It didn't take long to make a simple fixture for my table saw, and cutting the shims goes fairly quickly. I have used the homemade redwood shims without painting them and haven't been able to detect any aroma from them.

Wood Trim

For the casing, door stop, and baseboard, I also used poplar, supplied by **Koetter Woodworking, Inc.** While the company offers a wide variety of trim shapes and profiles, I chose a fairly standard Colonial style. (Although there were no stairs in this particular house, **Koetter Woodworking, Inc.** also manufacturers a selection of stair parts.) The trim is attached to the steel framing with the same trim screws used with the door jambs, by first drilling pilot holes in the wood, then driving the screws with a screw gun. This may seem like it takes a little longer than nailing, but because the screw gun countersinks the heads slightly, there is some time saved, compared to sinking nail heads with a hammer and punch.

Where the casing trim was attached to the wood door jamb, I used finish nails in the conven-

Figure 26-2.
Solid wood interior bi-fold doors.

331

Figure 26-3.
One inch air gap for ventilation under interior doors.

Figure 26-4.
Using shims to plumb a door jamb.

tional manner. In the den/office, I decided to use solid-wood wainscoting to give it a warmer, cozier feel (Figure 26-5). Again, I chose poplar and capped it with a chair rail (Figure 26-6). I used the same chair rail material, but without wainscoting, in the dining room (Figure 26-7).

Above the sliding pocket door, I filled the trapezoidal opening with a glass panel. This window gives the area an open, airy feel (Figure 26-8). Because the exterior walls are so thick, the window sills are quite wide. I used wide poplar boards for the window sills and also for the top of the 36"-tall kitchen

Figure 26-5.
Installing wainscoting in the den/office.

Figure 26-6.
Capping the wainscoting with a chair rail.

base cabinets. I used the same poplar door casing trim around the recessed steel kitchen wall cabinet.

The "attic" access hatch in the hallway was made of poplar with a ¾"-thick frame and a panel of wainscoting material, rather than the plywood used in most houses (Figure 26-9).

Built-Ins

I installed three different built-in cabinets in the Model Healthy House: the pantry (Figure 26-10), bookcase (Figure 26-11), and a display case (Figure

333

Figure 26-7.
Installing a chair rail in the dining room.

Figure 26-8.
Pocket door between the kitchen and the living room.

334

Figure 26-9.
Access to the mechanical space above the hallway.

Figure 26-10.
Built-in pantry in the kitchen.

335

Figure 26-11.
Built-in bookcase in the living room.

26-12). The pantry and the bookcase are mounted in the thick wall separating the living room and the kitchen. The display case is located in the thick wall between the entry and the second bedroom.

I like to use built-in cabinets in a healthy house because they can be used to separate bothersome materials from the living space. Sensitive people often react to the residual smell of solvents in printing ink and paper products, so books can be a problem if exposed to the room on open shelves. Older books are often moldy smelling, but behind a glass door, they pose little problem. The pantry can be used for extra storage in the kitchen because you can't have too much storage space. The display case is a nice touch that adds interest to the entry and provides a place to show off the collectibles and other items we all accumulate—without the need for regular dusting.

Once all the woodwork was in place, I filled the recessed screw and nail heads with a putty stick

(Figure 26-13). Putty sticks are sold through building supply and hardware stores. I've used several different brands and found them all to be fairly benign.

Update

As I mentioned in the "Update" to Chapter 21, there are now quite a few manufacturers who offer water-based polyurethane clear finishes. These are typically available locally, and they are often quite well tolerated by hypersensitive people. However, I still always recommend that sensitive people test finishes for personal tolerance. Because we are all biologically unique, we often don't tolerate the same things.

While doors made of solid-poplar or other hardwoods still aren't readily available everywhere, I've been seeing them advertized more and more,

Figure 26-12.
Built-in display case at the entry.

Figure 26-13.
Using a putty stick to fill over nail and screw heads.

337

by both regional and national companies. They typically cost more than the inexpensive hollow-core doors that are widely used, but I've found that solid-wood doors with a clear finish are one of the things that adds a tremendous amount of warmth and beauty to a healthy house. In my mind, they are well worth the extra cost for their aesthetic appeal alone.

Chapter 27

FINISHING TOUCHES

■ ■ ■ For the miscellaneous bathroom accessories in the Model Healthy House, such as towel racks, soap dishes, and toilet paper dispensers, I used chrome-plated metal. Metal with a baked-on finish, ceramic, or glass would have been equally healthy choices.

Light Fixtures

Light fixtures made of metal and glass will be more inert than those having plastic parts because the plastic could be subject to some outgassing when warmed by the light bulb. The fact that not all light fixtures are designed to look good on a sloped ceiling limited my choices somewhat for the Model Healthy House, but I was able to locate models that complemented the interior (Figure 27-1).

Light Bulbs

There are several choices today for healthful lighting. While the standard incandescent light bulb gives off a warm, yellowish light that most people find comfortable, regular fluorescent bulbs can be harshly white by comparison. Both kinds of light are defi-nitely artificial, but full-spectrum fluorescent bulbs and full-spectrum incandescent bulbs are said to produce a healthier light that contain wavelengths similar to those found in natural sunlight. Energy-efficient compact fluorescents can produce a color close to regular incandescent bulbs, have a low life-cycle cost, and save energy. Long-life incandescent light bulbs can mean fewer burned-out bulbs in landfills.

Full-Spectrum Lighting

Several years ago, it was discovered that some people suffer from depression in the winter due to shorter days at that time of the year. For some reason, when certain individuals' are not exposed to enough sunlight, some of the chemicals in their brains get out of balance and depression sets in. This condition is called Seasonal Affective Disorder (SAD). If these people sit in front of a bank of very bright full-spectrum fluorescent light bulbs for several hours a day during the winter, their brain chemistry returns to normal and they're no longer depressed. Research has shown that when these same people are exposed to the same full-spectrum bulbs at normal intensity levels, there is no improvement—there must be enough bulbs so that the

Figure 27-1.
Metal and glass light fixture in the kitchen.

lighting in the room is 5 to 10 times brighter than normal.

While there isn't a great deal of research about the health effects of normal levels of full-spectrum artificial lighting, it certainly sounds like a good idea to live with more natural light if possible. However, most people don't have fixtures in their homes that will accept fluorescent bulbs. An alternative can be to use full-spectrum incandescent bulbs, but they are relatively expensive.

Compact Fluorescent Bulbs

The compact fluorescent bulbs that have come on the market in recent years look nothing like the long, thin fluorescent tubes most of us are familiar with. They have screw bases like standard incandescent bulbs, but that's where the similarity ends. Compact fluorescents also contain a ballast that creates the higher voltage required by the fluorescent bulb. While compact fluorescents can be costly (up to $30), they have a very long life (12 times as long as a standard incandescent bulb) and use only a quarter as much energy for the same brightness. When the extra up-front cost is balanced with the savings, compact fluorescents are indeed a good deal. There is no doubt they will save you both energy and cash. Some electric utilities are selling these bulbs to their customers at a discount because they realize that by saving energy, they will not need to build as many expensive generating plants in the future.

It should also be pointed out that all fluorescent bulbs, compact and standard, contain mercury, a toxic metal. A broken bulb will expose occupants needlessly and eventually place an unnecessary burden on our landfills. In addition, some compact fluorescents contain small amounts of radioactivity and some produce strong electromagnetic fields. In order to select the models that are the most benign, many of the mail-order companies that sell compact fluorescent bulbs compare the different brands side-by-side so that customers can choose intelligently.

Standard Incandescent Bulb Alternatives

A few manufacturers are marketing energy-saving incandescent bulbs. Some are merely selling a lower wattage bulb. A 90-watt bulb will certainly save 10% of the energy used by a 100-watt bulb, but it will also put out 10% less light.

Long-life incandescent light bulbs are simply that—they last much longer than regular bulbs, so you don't need to replace them as often. Even though they cost a little more, this saves money because they last so long. Some long-life bulbs last as much as four times as long as regular bulbs; others are guaranteed to last for a hundred years.

Light Bulbs in the Model Healthy House

When I started researching healthy lighting alternatives, I had a lot of difficulty deciding what to do. I tried a full-spectrum bulb and found it really improved the colors in the room, but the light itself (not having the warm, yellow glow of an incandescent bulb) seemed cold, harsh, uninviting. While others may prefer this type of light, my wife and I didn't like it.

Compact fluorescent bulbs put out a nice comfortable light, but since they are somewhat larger than conventional bulbs, they have a tremendous disadvantage—many won't fit into standard light fixtures. When used in table lamps, compact fluorescents often require a special adapter to move the shade up a little higher. Looking through a ceiling-light-fixture cata-

Figure 27-2.
Enterpriser "life time" light bulbs.

341

log for something that will hold compact fluorescents can be quite frustrating, but some manufacturers are starting to redesign their fixtures to accept them.

By the time I weighed all the advantages and disadvantages, my personal choice was to use long-life incandescent bulbs. They aren't as energy-efficient as compact fluorescents, but they will fit standard fixtures, and I am comfortable with the light they emit. The ones I selected were produced by **Enterpriser Lighting, Inc.** (Figure 27-2). They look like regular bulbs, but they have a small electrical diode attached to the base. The diode converts the alternating house current to a non-alternating current. This gives the bulbs an extremely long life. The only precaution to using **Enterpriser** bulbs is that they should not be screwed in too tightly or the diode could be crushed and damaged. The manufacturer warrants these bulbs against defects for 100 years of normal use, and they are available in dozens of different styles

and sizes. Imagine never having to change a bulb again. I think that is a definite advantage.

Closet Organizers

Many builders use medium-density fiberboard for closet shelving. With its high formaldehyde emissions, it is the worst possible material to use. Not only will you have a polluted closet, your clothes also will absorb formaldehyde and then release it when you wear them. For closet shelves, I recommend either solid wood coated with a low-tox finish or metal with a baked-on finish.

For the Model Healthy House, I chose the all-metal system manufactured by **Lee/Rowan** (Figure 27-3). These have an epoxy finish that I have found to be both durable and inert. This is a powder-coating system that is applied without solvents and baked onto

Figure 27-3.
Ventilated closet storage system.

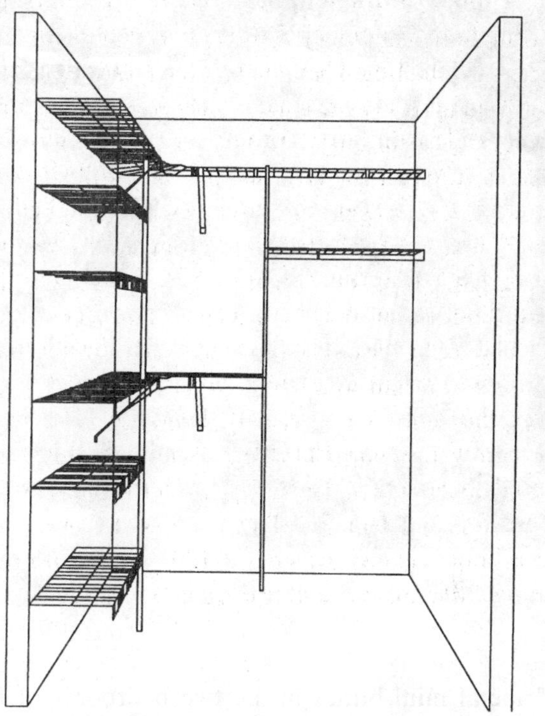

Figure 27-4.
Lee/Rowan computer generated drawing of a closet storage system layout.

the metal. **Lee/Rowan** guarantees the finish on their closet organizers for 15 years of normal use.

Wire shelving of this type is often referred to as ventilated shelving because it allows air to circulate more easily in closets. This results in less stuffiness and fresher smelling clothes. It also means fewer surfaces to collect dust.

Lee/Rowan offers several shelf designs in various sizes for maximum versatility. Shoe and tie racks are also available, as well as several sizes of wire basket drawers. Because the system is so versatile, I used a variety of different layouts in the closets of the Model Healthy House. Ventilated shelving can also be useful in pantries, garages, basements, and offices for storing virtually anything.

Varying kinds of mounting hardware are available for the ventilated shelving, much of which can be attached directly to drywall without needing to be anchored in studs. This makes installation quite easy.

Lee/Rowan also produces a ventilated wire shelving system that has an attractive oak trim, as well as a solid oak ventilated system. Many **Lee/Rowan** dealers can supply computer-generated drawings of closet layouts (Figure 27-4).

Window Coverings

Conventional fabric curtains or draperies can deteriorate when exposed to the sun. As the material breaks down, it can slowly release pollutants into the air that contribute to house dust. If the fabric has been chemically treated with stain resistant or permanent-press coatings, it can be subject to outgassing when heated by the sun. If you want fabric curtains, I recommend untreated cotton and regular cleaning.

Solid wood or metal blinds are a more inert choice than fabric curtains. For privacy, I installed

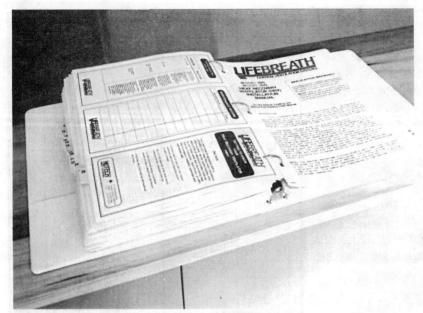

Figure 27-5.
The owner's manuals for the Model Healthy House in a 3-ring binder.

1" metal mini-blinds in the two bedrooms of the Model Healthy House. Although they can be added later, I decided not to install blinds in the south-facing windows in order to preserve the view to the outdoors as much as possible. Because the Model Healthy House is located in a rural wooded area, privacy isn't a major factor.

Owner's Manuals

Nearly every piece of equipment that goes into a house comes with some printed information about the product. The windows are supplied with instructions for adjusting the rollers on the moving panels, the garage door literature tells how to adjust the springs, and the ventilation equipment comes with operating manuals. Unfortunately, these are often discarded by the builder. Sometimes they are left loosely in a kitchen drawer and eventually lost or tossed out by the homeowner.

From the time the first piece of material was delivered for the Model Healthy House, I saved every single scrap of manufacturer's literature, no matter how insignificant. When the house was complete, I put them all into a 3-ring binder that the homeowner could have for future reference (Figure 27-5). A binder is much less likely to be lost than a pile of papers and can be added to if any remodeling is done in the future. It is a good idea for homeowners to sit down and go through their manual after they get settled. That way they will have a better idea of the kind of maintenance their new house requires and how the various components function. Of course, the Model Healthy House has the added advantage of this book as a more detailed owner's manual.

Radon Testing

Once the house was completed, I performed a test to determine the indoor radon level. A short-term radon test kit was opened and placed in the central hall for 48 hours, then sent to a laboratory for analysis. I ran the HRV for 8 hours a day during the test because that is about how long it will be operated once the house is occupied. I wanted the radon test to be an accurate reflection of occupied conditions. The results revealed that the indoor radon level was less than 0.5 pC/l. This is about the same amount of radon that is found in the outdoor air, and it is well below the EPA's action level of 4.0 pC/l.

Because the amount of radon indoors was so low, there was no need to hook up a suction fan to the sub-slab radon removal tube. If I had gambled and not installed the system, then found out that radon levels were high, it would have been much more expensive to install a removal system after the fact. Since there is no accurate way to predict radon levels prior to construction, the sub-slab system should be thought of as something of an insurance policy.

Formaldehyde Testing

Testing for VOCs can be costly, because there are so many different VOCs that could possibly be in the indoor air. It wouldn't be unusual to spend between several hundred and a few thousand dollars to do a complete analysis of the air in a house. Because of the care I took in building the Model Healthy House, I was confident that VOC levels would be quite low indoors; therefore, I couldn't justify the cost of all-out testing to verify what I already knew. At the same time, I was aware that many people would be curious as to what kind of findings an independent testing laboratory would come up with.

Rather than test for all possible VOCs, I decided to test for one of the most common—formaldehyde. Formaldehyde is one of the few pollutants that is said to be ubiquitous, meaning that it is everywhere. Even in an unpolluted area outdoors, it is possible to measure some formaldehyde in the air.

The easiest way to test for formaldehyde is to use a passive monitor. The type I selected looks like a small badge with a clip on it. These monitors are designed to be worn by people to measure the average level of pollutants that they come in contact with

Figure 27-6.
Blower door in place for testing the airtightness of the Model Healthy House.

during the course of their day's activities. Like radon test kits, these are exposed to the air for a certain time period, usually 24-48 hours, then sent to a laboratory for analysis. Passive monitors can be obtained for a variety of different VOCs. The cost depends on the particular pollutant being tested, but it can be as much

as $200 per test. A passive monitor for measuring formaldehyde costs about $60.

I placed formaldehyde monitors in the kitchen and in the master bedroom. I also decided to place one outdoors so I could see how it compared to the indoor level. The results indicated that the outdoor air con-

Figure 27-7.
The completed living room of the Model Healthy House.

Figure 27-8.
The completed living room of the Model Healthy House.

tained 0.01 parts per million (ppm) of formaldehyde. Both indoor tests were also 0.01 ppm, indicating that there is nothing indoors that is releasing formaldehyde. Since formaldehyde is ubiquitous, it can't be avoided completely, but 0.01 ppm is actually extremely low. Formaldehyde expert Thad Godish has recommended that levels need to be below 0.03 ppm for people sensitive to formaldehyde, but he also says that it is often difficult to reach a concentration that low. At 0.01 ppm of formaldehyde, the Model Healthy House has successfully avoided an indoor formaldehyde problem.

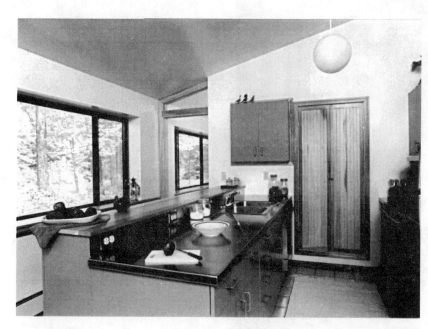

Figure 27-9.
The completed kitchen of the Model Healthy House.

Figure 27-10.
The completed kitchen of the Model Healthy House.

Figure 27-11.
The completed dining room of the Model Healthy House.

Figure 27-12.
The completed den/office of the Model Healthy House.

Airtightness Testing

In order to evaluate how successful I was in making the house airtight, I had a "blower door" test performed. A blower door is a device that fits into an entry door of a house and blows air out of the building in a controlled manner (Figure 27-6). The fan speed is adjustable, and gauges can be calibrated in such a way that you can measure precisely how much air is exhausted when the house is depressurized by a specific amount . With a blower door, it is possible to

348

Figure 27-13.
The completed bedroom of the Model Healthy House.

Figure 27-14.
The completed bathroom of the Model Healthy House.

349

Figure 27-15.
The completed exterior of the Model Healthy House.

measure the tightness of a house accurately under controlled conditions and compare it to other houses.

The standard technique for measuring the tightness of a house is to depressurize the building to 50 pascals (Pa.). A pascal is a unit of pressure measurement. When a house experiences a 50 Pa. depressurization, it is as if every exterior surface of the entire building was feeling the pressure of a 20 mph wind. In other words, at a 50 Pa. depressurization, a house will feel a 20 mph inward wind pressure on all the walls, all the ceilings, and all the floors. Fifty pascals was chosen as a standard testing pressure because most houses are never exposed to that much pressure in the real world.

At 50 Pa., most new houses will have well over 1,000 cubic feet per minute (cfm) of air leakage. That may sound like plenty of fresh air for the occupants, but it isn't. Because 50 Pa. is considerably more pressure than the average house is ever exposed to, the actual infiltration rate of a house having 1,000 cfm leakage at 50 Pa. might be less than 50 cfm under average conditions, and that would be both extremely variable and unreliable. In an older house that is not insulated or weather-stripped, there could be several thousand cfm of leakage at 50 Pa.

When the Model Healthy House was depressurized to 50 Pa. with a blower door, there was only 99 cfm of leakage. This is incredibly tight. It means that, under normal conditions, there is almost no air leaking into (or out of) the structure at all. The Model Healthy House is virtually airtight, so my goal of creating a tight house that would give the occupants maximum control over the indoor air was realized.

Summary

I am very happy with the way the Model Healthy House turned out. It is energy-efficient, cost-effective, airtight, and suitable for most sensitive people. Figures 27-7 thru 27-15 show the completed Model Healthy House. It was sold in early 1993 to a family in which the husband is chemically sensitive. They are quite happy with their new home.

If you are chemically sensitive, you should not use the same products I did in the Model Healthy House without testing for personal tolerance. This is particularly important for materials directly exposed to the living space such as cabinets, paints and clear finishes.

350

Healthy house construction is a growing trend, one whose time has come. Healthy building projects are being featured more and more in magazine and newspaper articles as well as at conferences and workshops catering to builders and designers. As a result, some manufacturers are realizing that health can be a powerful marketing tool in selling merchandise. They will no doubt be offering many new healthy materials in the coming months and years. However, at the same time, there will be products that are advertised as being healthy when in fact they are not. By reading labels carefully, following the concepts described in this book, and comparing different products, you should be able to evaluate the healthfulness of these new materials, and incorporate them into your future projects.

Update

The company that supplied the long-life incandescent light bulbs (**Enterpriser Lighting, Inc.**) is no longer in business. However, for a variety of reasons, I have switched to using compact fluorescent light bulbs in recent projects. First of all, they are now much easier to find locally in hardware stores, discount department stores, and building supply centers. They are also lower in cost than they used to be, and somewhat smaller—so there are now models that will fit into most fixtures. When purchasing them, I recommend the ones with electronic ballasts because magnetic ballasts generally have stronger electromagnetic fields. If you are going to use them in enclosed fixtures (like those in the Model Healthy House) read labels carefully because many manufacturers won't guarantee them if used in either totally enclosed indoor fixtures, or in recessed fixtures. When disposing of compact fluorescent light bulbs, remember that they contain a small amount of toxic mercury, so be careful not to break the glass tubes. Most communities now have drop-off sites for household hazardous waste that accept fluorescent bulbs of all types..

I mentioned that bright full-spectrum lighting was useful in helping to alleviate symptoms of depression in people with SAD (Seasonal Affective Disorder). However, more recent research has shown that virtually any type of bright light will work, that it doesn't need to be full-spectrum light to relieve the symptoms. In fact, there doesn't seem to be any good evidence that full-spectrum lighting is healthier for us than the other forms of lighting we are routinely exposed to. Yes, full-spectrum lighting mimics sunlight, but whether or not you opt for it should be a decision based on your personal preference for the color of the light, rather than on healthfulness.

I continue to believe that an owner's manual is a very important thing for a builder to give to a homeowner. With the Model Healthy House, this book contains numerous photos that were taken at various stages of construction. Such photos can be very useful in the future if the homeowner is interested in doing any remodeling because they will reveal hidden construction details. So, on your next project, I'd like to suggest that after the framing is complete, and the rough-in work has been done, someone walk around indoors and take photos of all the walls. The photos can then be labeled to show their location, and then kept with the owner's manual. The photography can be done by the builder or the homeowner.

The question I posed in the "Preface" about what I would do differently if I were building the Model Healthy House today has been answered throughout this book. In most cases, I would do basically the same things. Of course, where a particular manufacturer's product is no longer available, I would have to substitute a different product. However in some instances, there are now better products on the market—such as duct-sealing mastics and newer low-tox paints and finishes—that I often use. Because all houses are different, in many situations the choice of some materials will depend on the specifics of a particular project. For example, I mentioned how my wife and I used a conventional sheathing on our own new house rather that a foil wind barrier. (For more on our new house, see Chapter 28.) In addition, we built our new house on a pier foundation because our site was quite steep. Most importantly, if I were building a Model Healthy House today, I would continue to stick very

351

carefully to my three healthy house design principles of Eliminate, Separate, and Ventilate. Using these principles means constructing an airtight house with a mechanical ventilation system, and using inert materials exposed to the living space. At its simplest, that is what a healthy house is all about.

Since the completion of the Model Healthy House, there has not been a tremendous growth in interest about improving indoor air quality. However, there has been a slow, but steady, increase in interest. And there are certainly more and more manufacturers who are developing healthier materials. While some of these products were not created primarily with the indoor environment in mind, they have indirectly helped to improve the air in houses. For example, the states that have enacted legislation mandating lower VOC levels in paints and finishes have done so principally to improve the *outdoor* air quality. And manufacturers of sealed-combustion gas appliances brought them out mainly in the name of energy efficiency. Still, both developments also benefit the indoor environment. In the years ahead, I foresee continued steady interest in this field, and look forward to the day when all houses are healthy ones, and books like this are no longer necessary.

Chapter 28

MY OWN NEW HOUSE

■ ■ ■ I built two healthy houses prior to the Model Healthy House project that were similar in many of their construction and design features to the Model Healthy House. For example, while there were certainly differences, all three were single-story ranch houses with concrete slab foundations. My wife, Lynn, and I lived in one of them for about 9 years. In that house, Lynn, who is very chemically sensitive, gained back a great deal of her health, energy, and stamina. It was truly a healthy house, and her personal health benefited a great deal by living in it. It was a small house—just over 1,000 square feet. We also had a detached studio/office of about 360 sq. ft. for our home-based business.

Our small house was well laid out and compact, like a vacation home, and we were quite comfortable in it. However, after the Model Healthy House was completed, we felt like building ourselves a new house. We wanted the new one to be slightly larger, we wanted the office to be attached this time, and we wanted its appearance to be a little different.

To answer the question I posed in the Preface, "If you were going to do it over today, what would you do differently," in this chapter I will cover the construction of our new house. There isn't room to go into the same kind of detail I did with the Model Healthy House, but I don't believe that is necessary because many of the specific construction details are similar. At the same time, our new house doesn't look like the Model Healthy House, and many of the materials we used are different.

We have been quite pleased with our completed new house, however if I were doing a Model Healthy House project again today, I don't think it would look like our new house. That's because I don't think most people would want a house on a pier foundation. So, if I were building a Model Healthy House today, it would probably end up being something between the one shown in the previous chapters, and the one featured in this chapter.

Lynn and I wanted to be able to go into some depth about how we built our new house—without simply documenting all the details in this chapter—so we decided to use a different medium. We chronicled the construction of our new house on video tape, and put together a series of 13 episodes describing the entire design and construction process. For information about the tapes, please see the last few pages of this book.

The Building Site

Our old house was in the middle of a hardwood forest, away from metropolitan areas, on a county road

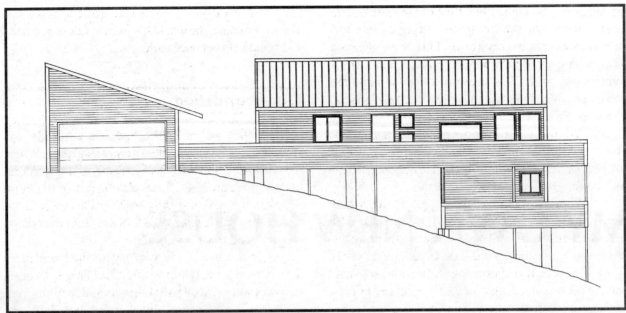

Figure 28-1. *Our own new healthy house.*

that wasn't heavily traveled, so there was little outdoor air pollution in the vicinity. We liked the surroundings, the solitude, and lack of pollution, so we started looking for similar property on which to build our new house.

After several months of searching, we found 15 acres of wooded land with steep hills about 12 miles from where we were living. The land has a fairly level area that we could have built on, but the house would have been relatively close to the road. While it is a dead-end road, and there isn't much traffic, building near the road would have meant more traffic pollution and noise than we wanted, and we would have had less privacy. So, we decided to build on a fairly steep hillside, facing into a wooded ravine that runs down the center of the property.

The house site we decided on is about 200' from the road. There's a small ridge between the house and road, so you can't see the house if you drive by. The nearest neighbor is about 700' away, the utilities are underground, and the driveway is crushed stone.

Because of the terrain, our local Board of Health informed us that we would need a mound-type septic system rather that a more conventional system, where everything is buried. As the name implies, a mound system is built above ground—like a mound. Mounds must be built on relatively flat land, and the only flat place for ours was on top of the ridge. Because our house was

to be down the hill, that meant we would need a pump to get the sewage from our house up to the mound. Because of the lay of the land, there wouldn't be any way to get trucks and excavation equipment down the hill after the foundation was in. With most houses the septic system is one of the last things done, but in our case, some of it had to come first.

After having the trees removed from the immediate area where we were going to build our house, we had a backhoe excavate two holes just below where the house would sit—one for the septic tank and one for the pumping chamber. Then a delivery truck backed down the hill and set one of the concrete tanks in the first hole. It took about an hour for the truck to be pulled back up the hill by the backhoe, go get the second tank, and set it in the second hole. As soon as the backhoe pulled the delivery truck up the hill the second time, it started raining. We barely got the tanks covered before it was too muddy to do any more work.

Our Basic House Design

Like our old house, our new house also contains two bedrooms, one bath, and an eat-in kitchen but, at 1,232 sq. ft., it's slightly larger than our old one. Each of

354

the rooms is a bit bigger, but most of the extra square footage went into storage space—larger closets and built-in cupboards and bookcases. Plus, there's a home office with a small bathroom on a lower level which contains 448 sq. ft. This time we wanted to build the house and office together, rather than as two separate structures. So we have a total of 1,680 sq. ft. under roof for both living space and for our home-based business. This is still smaller than many of the new houses today but, like our old house, we designed it to be both efficient and comfortable—like a vacation home.

We again wanted to superinsulate the house and use the Airtight Drywall Approach (ADA) to build a very tight structure. Lynn is still quite sensitive to many odors most people take for granted—odors that might occasionally be in the office. For example, the strong smelling printing ink on some magazines and brochures, or visitors wearing cologne or perfume will bother her. So we used airtight-construction techniques to separate the home portion from the office. In effect, we created two airtight structures (the main level living space, and the lower level office) that just happened to be attached. There's even a weather-stripped door separating the two spaces, so air from the lower-level office can't leak upstairs into the main level.

We really like the spacious feel of having sloped ceilings throughout the house, so we used them throughout the main level (except for the entry closet and central hallway, where the ventilation equipment is located). The lower-level office has flat 8'-high ceilings.

We have a 2-car garage that is detached. I believe it is possible to build garage attached to a healthy house if you construct it in an airtight manner separate from the living space—just like we separated our lower-level office from the main-level living space. However, we personally like having the garage as a separate structure. That's because, even if the house and garage are tightly constructed, air can still pass from the garage into the living space when the service door connecting the garage and the living space is opened. Figure 28-1 shows a drawing of the south side of the exterior of our new house.

Lynn was able to help quite a bit with the construction of this house. But there were some materials we knew would be bothersome to her—materials she couldn't spend much time around. However, we also knew that once those materials were sealed up inside the airtight structure, she would tolerate the house just fine, and could help out once more.

Our Foundation

When we decided to build on a hillside, we immediately knew we wanted a pier foundation. While it is the least common foundation type, and it won't fit into most subdivisions, it can also be one of the most dramatic. It is also inherently healthier than other foundations because it separates the house from the radon, moisture, and mold in the soil.

It took us a bit longer to lay out the foundation than if we were building on a flat lot. That's because the piers were two different heights and they stepped down the hill. But once everything was laid out accurately, the actual construction went quickly. Bright and early one morning, we had our backhoe dig twelve holes, each 3' square, for the footings. Then we shoveled out the loose soil from each hole by hand and placed reinforcing steel in them. The steel was bent so it would stick up into the piers themselves. Late that afternoon, after the building inspector approved what we had done, the concrete truck arrived, and we placed concrete in each hole.

The next morning the concrete was hard and ready for the piers. We used 18" diameter cardboard tubes for forms. These tubes are wax coated so they won't fall apart when exposed to the wet concrete, and are made just for this purpose. They are widely used in a variety of applications and they make it easy to create cylindrical columns. We first had to cut the tubes to exact height, then slide them over the steel reinforcing that was sticking up out of the footings.

Using 2x4s, we braced each form so it would remain plumb and wouldn't fall over (Figure 28-2). Bracing is extremely important because the concrete in a 4-5' high 18" form will weigh well over 1,000 pounds. Late that afternoon, another concrete truck arrived, and we filled the forms with concrete. Because some of the piers were down the hill, beyond the reach of the concrete truck's delivery chute, I made a long trough by ripping some 8" PVC pipe lengthwise. I then had to support my trough off the ground with

Figure 28-2.
Bracing the cardboard forms with 2x4s.

Figure 28-3.
The plastic trough for getting the concrete down the hill.

2x4 supports so it would reach the top of the piers (Figure 28-3).

On the third morning, we peeled the cardboard forms off the hardened concrete, and started raking out the soil around the piers. In three days, the foundation was complete (Figure 28-4).

Framing

I had already built several steel-framed houses when we decided to build our new house. Once I got used to working with it, I found steel framing quite easy to use.

Of course, I had also built with wood framing in the past too—and enjoyed working with it as well. Because I hadn't framed the bulk of a house with wood for a while, this time I decided to use wood for most of the load-bearing walls, the floor system, and the roof, then use non-load-bearing steel studs for the interior partition walls. I also used load-bearing steel studs for the partition wall that runs down the center of the main level holding up the roof.

While wood framing itself isn't a serious pollution source, Lynn is bothered by very much exposure to the natural aroma of softwood lumber. But we knew from past experience that airtight construction techniques would prevent a variety of odors from migrating into the living space. So we knew we would be able to successfully separate the wood from the indoor air.

The big health disadvantage to framing a house out of wood has always been the inevitable need for toxic termiticides. But there are some less-toxic termite treatments available today that weren't on the market just a few years ago. So, once the framing was complete, and the roof and siding were on, we sprayed all the wood in the house with U.S. Borax's Tim-Bor. Tim-Bor doesn't outgas anything, and it is a permanent termite treatment—as long as it isn't exposed to weather and rain, which can cause it to leech out of the wood.

Since the completion of the Model Healthy House, researchers have confirmed that steel framing can sometimes be very energy-inefficient. Whenever I had built with steel in the past, I used a double-wall system, which is one of the more energy-efficient ways of using steel studs. Because I was using wood framing this time, I decided to use 2x8 studs in order to have superinsulated walls. The 2x8s yield a wall that isn't quite as thick as the double wall system I used in the steel-framed Model Healthy House, but it still gives us nice, wide window sills.

We started by building the lower-level floor system (Figure 28-5) and the lower-level walls. Then we constructed the main-level floor and extended it over the lower level (Figure 28-6). Once it was covered with plywood, there was finally a decent-sized, flat platform to work on. After completing the main-level walls (Figure 28-7) and roof structure (Figure 28-8), we were ready to enclose everything.

The rafters and floor joists are all 2x12s—both for strength, and to give us room for plenty of extra insulation. The subfloor is 3/4" tongue-and-grooved construction-grade plywood. All of the plywood sheets

Figure 28-4.
Our completed foundation.

Figure 28-5.
Building the floor system for the lower level.

are glued to each other, and to the floor joists, with a water-based construction adhesive that outgasses quickly. This results in an airtight, very sturdy, squeak-free floor system. We knew that Lynn would definitely be bothered by plywood, but we also knew that construction-grade plywood had a less-potent glue than some other manufactured wood products. And with our experience using airtight construction techniques, we were confident that we could separate the plywood very well so it wouldn't affect the air in the completed house.

After working with wood framing again, I have mixed feelings about using it. I like using both wood and steel to frame a house, and have gotten used to the fact that steel is always straight. What I regularly seem to forget is that wood is always warped—well not *always*, but it sometimes seems like it. In many instances a slight bow or twist in a wood stud isn't a big deal, but in other cases, it is better to have straight material. In our finished house there are a couple of dips in the floor over bowed floor joists. Many people don't notice the dips, but I do, and it's irritating every time I walk over them.

Another problem with wood framing involves rain. I was continually worried about too much rain warping the plywood, or having the wet framing get

moldy. Fortunately that didn't happen, but it wouldn't have been a concern with steel framing.

The Exterior

On our new house we again used aluminum siding and steel roofing, both of which have baked-on finishes. Now that the house is done, I've noticed a number of small dents in the aluminum siding from where my ladder was leaning against it. This is something others might not notice, but I do. In the future I'll probably consider steel siding.

Because I didn't particularly care for working with the aluminum-foil wind barrier in building the Model Healthy House (see Chapter 8), this time we used more conventional materials for sheathing—a combination of construction-grade plywood and asphalt-impregnated fiberboard. Again, we knew Lynn would be bothered by both these materials if she spent much time around them. But again, based on past experience, we knew they wouldn't affect the indoor air as long as the house was tightly constructed. To avoid a separate wind barrier, I decided to try something new. I used a water-based

Figure 28-6.
The main level floor system under construction.

Figure 28-7.
The main level and the lower level walls completed.

mastic (the same material used to seal ducts that I discussed in the "Update" to Chapter 11) to seal all the seams between the individual sheets of sheathing. It worked just fine, but was a lot of work. I will probably consider using a conventional house wrap as a wind barrier the next time.

We also used aluminum-framed windows once more—with energy-efficient thermal breaks in the frames to minimize sweating in the winter. There have been significant advances in window design in recent years, so we were able to get low-E coatings and argon fill for improved energy efficiency. The slider windows are

359

triple glazed, but our distributor was only able to supply double-glazing for the fixed-glass windows. Most of the windows are positioned to take advantage of solar heat in the winter. We also used insulated-steel entry doors again. I painted the doors with a durable automotive paint early in the construction process, so it was able to outgas for several months before we actually moved in.

Each level of the house has a 6'x17' redwood deck on the east side which reaches out into the woods. There's also an elevated redwood walkway along the south side of each level. The two decks are connected to each other, and to the ground, by a steel spiral stairway, which I painted with the same automotive paint I used on the entry doors. We didn't have the spiral stair on our original plans, but once we started construction, it seemed like the perfect idea, and we are quite happy to have added it. Figure 28-9 shows the completed exterior.

Sealing Up the Structure

As we did in the Model Healthy House, we evaluated a variety of different insulating materials. We considered ease of installation, cost, and availability. Based on past experience, we knew whatever insulation

we picked, it wouldn't be a health problem as long as the house was built in an airtight manner. So we finally settled on fiberglass because I could install it myself, thus saving on installation expenses. We used high-density batts in the 2x8 walls to get an R-value of 30. These high-density batts weren't available a few years ago, so getting this high an R-value in a 2x8 wall wasn't possible until recently. The ceiling and floor are insulated with 12" R-38 batts, so the house is truly superinsulated.

On the interior of all the insulated walls and the ceiling we attached the same thing we used in the Model Healthy House—foil-backed drywall. Then we sealed everything just as we have done in the past—with gaskets, aerosol-foam insulation, airtight electrical boxes, etc. The more I build, the more convinced I am that the Airtight Drywall Approach (ADA) is the only way to go. It helps insure that a house will be healthy, comfortable, energy efficient, and resistant to hidden moisture problems.

On various construction projects over the years, I've tried several approaches to minimize the outgassing from plastic-jacketed wiring and plastic plumbing lines. What seems to work best is to simply buy the materials early in the construction process and let them air out naturally before installing them. So, we had plumbing

Figure 28-8.
The framing is finished.

Figure 28-9.
The completed exterior of our new house.

and wiring materials sitting in the garage for several weeks before we were ready for them in our new house. But, just to be safe, we also used foil-backed drywall for all the non-load-bearing interior partition walls to act as a diffusion retarder. It may not really be necessary, but it doesn't cost much extra.

Interior Finishes

We used the same low-tox joint-finishing compound we used in the past, but there are now a number of additional low-tox paints on the market that weren't available when I built the Model Healthy House. As I've always recommended to other sensitive people, we tested several paints and selected one Lynn could tolerate well.

For interior trim, doors, and woodwork, we've really gotten to like the appearance of unstained poplar wood, so we opted for it again. In our part of the country, poplar is still cheaper than pine. We coated all the poplar with a water-based polyurethane finish.

While ceramic-tile is probably the healthiest floor covering, hardwood is a close second. So for a more varied look in our new house, we used a combination of both. We put ceramic tile in the kitchen, entry, central

hall, and both bathrooms (Figure 28-10). I installed it a bit differently than I did in the Model Healthy House because, in this case, it went on top of plywood rather than a concrete floor slab.

The glazed surface of the ceramic tile acts as a very good diffusion retarder to prevent outgassing from the plywood subfloor from migrating upward into the living space, so there isn't any need to install a separate material to block diffusion. And because I glued the sheets of plywood to each other, the floor system is already airtight. To install the tile, we first troweled a layer of thin-set mortar directly onto the plywood, then bedded 1/2"-thick cementitious boards in the mortar and screwed them down to the plywood. This gave us an excellent base on which to attach the tile. Once the cementitious boards were in place, the rest of the ceramic tile installation was the same as the process used in the Model Healthy House: trowel thinset on the cementitious board, set the tile in the thinset, apply the home-made, additive-free grout, then damp-cure the grout.

For the hardwood floor, we decided against oak because we didn't think its coloring would go very well with the poplar trim. Instead, we opted for beech wood, which we had processed at a local mill. Although beech isn't used as widely as oak, it is some-

361

Figure 28-10.
Ceramic tile floor in our dining room.

what less odorous, a little cheaper, and we think it is very attractive (Figure 28-11).

During installation, most hardwood-floor installers place black, asphalt-impregnated felt paper between the plywood and the hardwood floor, but we didn't. We wanted a more effective diffusion retarder to block any formaldehyde emissions from rising up into the living space, so we used aluminum builder's foil. We simply rolled the foil out onto the plywood, then installed the beech floor on top of it in the conventional manner. Once we had all the beech flooring nailed down, we sanded it in place, then I finished it with a low-tox water-based polyurethane finish that Lynn tolerated once it was cured.

Kitchen, Baths, Built-Ins

I had successfully built solid-wood kitchen and bath cabinets in our old house and I used low-tox steel cabinets in the Model Healthy House. Either approach can be both attractive and healthy. This time we decided on a little of both. I made the cabinets in our new house mostly of solid wood (poplar again) but I had a local sheet-metal shop fold up some sheets of galvanized steel

for the wide shelves in the lower cabinets. The steel won't warp, it is easy to clean, and it won't expand and shrink seasonally like solid wood. We also used galvanized steel for all the drawer bottoms. To simplify the building of the cabinets, we decided not to use any backs on them. So when you look into the back of them, you simply see the painted drywall.

For the cabinet doors, we primarily used solid wood, but to give them an extra special look, Lynn created some door panels for the upper cabinets out of brass. She hand tooled thin sheets of brass foil to create a treetop design that fits in with our location in the middle of the forest (Figure 28-12).

We used stainless-steel countertops again—there was no other choice here because we really love to work on stainless. There are two one-piece countertops, one for each bank of cabinets in our galley kitchen (Figure 28-13). They each have an integral backsplash so there are no places for mold to grow.

As we did in the Model Healthy House, we located the washer and dryer in a closet in the bathroom along with the electric water heater. This keeps the significant moisture sources in the same room. The central vacuum is in the entry closet in our new house—just because it fit there better.

362

Rather than having stainless-steel panels around the shower, we used a one-piece, fiberglass bathtub/shower to minimize caulking and seams where mold might grow. We bought it (on sale) early in the construction process and had it sitting on our porch for about a year, so it was done outgassing by the time we installed it. We also used frameless shower doors similar to those we have used in the past.

For the bathroom vanity we used a marble top. It's a little over 6' long and cost a few hundred dollars. It was one of the areas we decided to spend a little extra money, and it's really beautiful. Although plastic laminate would have been cheaper, the marble actually cost less than a synthetic solid-surfacing material.

As in the Model Healthy House, we installed a glass-doored display cabinet in our foyer (Figure 28-14). It keeps knick-knacks dust-free and prevents minor odors from them from reaching the living space. In our new living room, we built a large floor-to-ceiling bank of glass-doored cabinets and drawers for loads of storage. We added a built-in rolling library ladder to reach the upper book shelves (Figure 28-15).

Mechanical Systems

Because our new house is superinsulated, our heating and cooling requirements are very low, so we used the same non-polluting, hydronic, electric, baseboard heaters. We used a small ductless air conditioner that is similar to the one in the Model Healthy House except for the fact that it has one outdoor unit and two indoor units—one for the main level, and one for the lower-level office.

We used the same heat-recovery ventilator (HRV) we used in the Model Healthy House. The ventilator sits above the dropped hallway ceiling so it is within the conditioned space. Filtration options have expanded a bit in recent years, so we decided to try a packaged filter unit from our HRV manufacturer. It consists of a prefilter, a medium-efficiency particulate filter, and several thin activated carbon filters, and it seems to be working out well, even though it isn't as efficient as a HEPA filter.

The layout of the ventilation ducts is similar to the layout I used in the Model Healthy House. Stale air is pulled from all the upstairs closets, the bathroom, and the kitchen, and fresh air is blown

Figure 28-11.
Beech flooring in our living room.

Figure 28-12.
*Hand tooled brass doors on
upper kitchen cabinets.*

Figure 28-13.
Our Completed galley kitchen.

into the living room. Fresh air is also blown into the office downstairs, and stale air is pulled from the downstairs bathroom. So the entire house is ventilated, but the upstairs air doesn't mix with the downstairs air. In the upstairs bathroom there is a special motorized grille, and a timer control which is located near the bathroom light switch. When the timer is activated, the grille opens, and the HRV bumps up to high speed to air out the bathroom quickly—so we don't need a separate exhaust fan in bathroom. We did put an exhaust fan in the bathroom downstairs, but only for occasional use—when the lower level needs to be aired out quickly. Most of the time the general ventilation system (the HRV) keeps the lower-level bathroom fresh.

Rather than cracking open a window to relieve the depressurization caused by the kitchen range-hood fan, we installed a motorized make-up air inlet under the stove. When the range hood is turned on and blowing air outdoors, the inlet opens automatically to allow fresh air to enter. We put another inlet near the clothes dryer that we open manually to relieve the depressurization caused by the dryer.

Summary

Designing a house as a collection of integrated systems (as I discussed in Chapter 2) is important for several reasons—comfort, energy-efficiency, quietness, and health. It doesn't require a great deal of complexity, but it does require some preplanning, and a little extra work on the part of the designer and the builder. We feel it's well worth it. Because of its energy-efficiency features, our new house has been inspected and certified by the Energy Rated Homes of Indiana program, which makes it easier to qualify for

Figure 28-14.
Our foyer display cabinet.

Figure 28-15.
Our built-in floor-t-ceiling living room cabinetry.

a mortgage. Similar programs exist in many parts of the country, but they weren't as widely available when the Model Healthy House was being built. However, should a future buyer wish to have the Model Healthy House certified, it too would qualify for an energy efficient mortgage.

To find out how and where to apply for an energy-efficient mortgage in your part of the country, contact the Residential Energy Services Network (RESNET) at 760-806-3448 (www.natresnet.org). They have all the information you'll need about the energy saving requirements, the various rating programs across the U.S., as well as mortgage and lender information.

We realize that our new house looks a bit different when compared to most new houses being built today. After all, most houses aren't built on concrete piers, in the middle of the forest, with no lawn. But that part of the design wasn't based so much on health, as it was on aesthetics—an appearance we personally liked. You can build your own healthy house to look like just about anything. It can be large or small, Colonial or French provincial, brown or blue—whatever you want. All you need to do is select the materials and put them together in a way that will enhance your health, not compromise it.

PART 6:
RESOURCES

LIVING IN A HEALTHY HOUSE

■■■ It is possible to build a healthy house and foul the air in it with polluting cleaning products and furnishings. While this subject is quite broad, and is beyond the scope of this book, I felt it important to include a few basic sources of information that would provide guidance in finding healthy products for the interior of the house. The books and organizations below were helpful to my wife and me in furnishing and maintaining our own healthy house.

Books

Berthold-Bond, Annie. *Better Basics for the Home*, New York: Three Rivers Press 1999, 340 pages paperback. A wide variety of formulas for making your own home-maintenance and cleaning products.

Berthold-Bond, Annie. *Clean & Green*, Woodstock, NY: Ceres Press 1990, 163 pages paperback. 485 ways to clean, polish, disinfect, deodorize, launder, remove stains—even wax your car without harming yourself or the environment.

Bower, Lynn Marie. *Creating a Healthy Household: the ultimate guide for healthier, safer, less-toxic living*, Bloomington, IN: The Healthy House Institute 2000, 608 pages paperback. Covers everything indoors, with hundreds of addresses of suppliers.

Dadd, Debra Lynn. *Nontoxic, Natural, & Earthwise*, Los Angeles: Jeremy Tarcher 1990, 360 pages paperback. How to protect yourself and your family from harmful products and live in harmony with the earth. Lists many mail-order catalogs.

Dadd, Debra Lynn. *The Nontoxic Home*, Los Angeles: Jeremy Tarcher 1986, 213 pages paperback. Protecting yourself and your family from everyday toxics and health hazards.

Golos, Natalie, Frances Golos Golbitz and Frances Spatz Leighton. *Coping with Your Allergies*, New York: Simon and Schuster 1979, 351 pages paperback. How to discover what you are allergic to and how to create a safe environment, including diet, clothing and household goods.

Olkowski, William, Sheila Daar and Helga Olkowski. *Common-Sense Pest Control*, Newtown, CT: Taunton Press 1991, 716 pages paperback. Least-toxic solutions for your home, garden, pets, and community.

Raab, Karl H. *Strategies for Healthful Residential Environments*. Ottawa, Ontario: Canada Mortgage and Housing Corporation 1984, (Order from CMHC, 700 Montreal Road, Ottawa, Ontario, Canada, K1A 0P7, 613-748-2003), 121 pages paperback. Covers a wide variety of methods for improving indoor air quality.

Organizations

Human Ecology Action League (HEAL). National support group for individuals with multiple chemical sensitivity (MCS). Membership of $20.00 includes a quarterly subscription to *The Human Ecologist*. HEAL, P.O. Box 29629, Atlanta, GA 30359-1126, (404) 248-1898. http://members.aol.com/HEALNatnl/index.html

The Healthy House Institute. Publishes a variety of books and videos related to healthy construction and life-style, web site offers many articles. The Healthy House Institute, 430 N. Sewell Rd., Bloomington, IN 47408, (812) 332-5073. www.hhinst.com.

The National Center for Environmental Health Strategies (NCEHS). National advocacy and clearinghouse organization for information pertaining to MCS. Membership of $15.00 includes a quarterly subscription to *The Delicate Balance*. NCEHS, 1100 Rural Ave., Voorhees, NJ 08043, (856) 429-5358.

LIST OF SPONSORS

■■■ Having been involved in healthy house construction since 1984, I was generally aware of what kinds of products I wanted to use when I first envisioned this Model Healthy House project. Materials like concrete blocks and framing lumber are pretty much the same throughout the country, so I knew that readers would have no trouble finding them at their local building supply store. However, I felt strongly enough about some particular brand names of other products that I decided to approach a few manufacturers about becoming sponsors of the project by contributing materials. In most cases, these were products that I had used personally in the past with good results.

While the sponsors themselves will certainly benefit from the advertising and publicity generated by the project, I feel that by including them it will also make it much easier for homeowners, builders, and designers to locate healthy materials and products. Also, by working with manufacturers in this way, the concept of healthy construction will spread much faster.

In some model house projects, there is the temptation to obtain as many donations as possible. I decided to only approach certain manufacturers whose products I could stand behind without compromising my own values. For example, I did not approach a producer of fiberglass insulation. Even though I believe it is possible to use a material having some negative health aspects—like fiberglass—in healthy construction, I felt I would lose some of my credibility by having a fiberglass insulation manufacturer as a sponsor.

I made my original list of prospective sponsors based on the healthfulness and quality of their products, without having any idea how many companies would see the merit of a project like this. To my delight, the responses were overwhelmingly positive. All the sponsors of this project are well-aware that healthful construction is a new marketing niche. Their enthusiasm will help to motivate manufacturers of unhealthy products to produce more benign materials in the future. In the long run, homeowners across the country will be the real beneficiaries because their houses will be healthier places in which to raise their families.

In the time since the Model Healthy House was completed, some of the companies who sponsored the project have gone out of business, or no longer handle the products mentioned in the text. However, there are many new companies and products today that didn't exist back then. Yet, I continue to recommend most of the materials I used. Above all, the basic techniques and principles are as valid as ever.

Most of the sponsors listed below sell through distributors across the country. By contacting them, they can direct you to a local supplier. Those marked with an asterisk (*) also sell direct to consumers or residential contractors. If there is no distributor in your area, they can sell to you directly. If you'd like a complete list of healthy construction products, my book, *The Healthy House*, is an excellent companion to this one. It contains a listing of hundreds of additional suppliers with their addresses and phone numbers.

Project Sponsors

Alumax, Magnolia Division
Division of Alcoa
1617 N. Washington
Magnolia, AR 71753
870-234-4260
800-643-1514
www.alumax.com
Frameless shower doors

American Olean Tile Co.
P.O. Box 170130
7834 C.F. Hawn Freeway
Dallas, TX 75217-0130
215-393-2898
888-AOT-TILE
www.aotile.com
Ceramic floor tile

*Ametek
U.S. Filter, Plymouth Products Div.
502 Indiana Ave.
Sheboygan, WI 53081
800-634-1455
www.plymouthwater.com
Central water filter

Asko, Inc.
P.O. Box 851805
Richardson, TX 75085-1805
972-644-8595
www.askousa.com
Energy-efficient dishwasher

Baubiologie Hardware
Radiation-free smoke detectors
(Since the completion of the Model Healthy House, Baubiologie Hardware has gone out of business but you can now generally find radiation-free, photoelectric smoke detectors locally. For gaussmeters, contact LessEMF, Inc. at 888-LESS-EMF.)

*Beam Industries
P.O. Box 788
Webster City, IA 50595-0788
515-832-4620
800-369-2326
www.beamvac.com
Central vacuum system

Broan Manufacturing Co.
P.O. Box 140
Hartford, WI 53027
414-673-4340
800-548-0970
www.broan.com
Ventilation equipment, controls

Burnham Corp.
Split-system air conditioner
(Since the completion of the Model Healthy House, Burnham has quit handling split-system air conditioners, but similar units are available from Sanyo at 818-998-7322 and Mitsubishi at 770-613-5840.)

C-Cure
Division of Custom Building Products
13001 Seal Beach Blvd.
Seal Beach, CA 90740
562-598-8808
800-895-2874
Thinset ceramic tile mortar

Delta Faucet Co.
55 E. 111th St.
Indianapolis, IN 46280
317-848-1812
800-345-DELTA
www.deltafaucet.com
Kitchen and bath faucets

*Denarco, Inc.
301 Industrial Park Drive
Constantine, MI 49042
616-435-8404
Sure-Seal foam sealant tape

Dietrich Industries, Inc.
500 Grant St., #2226
Pittsburgh, PA 15219
412-281-2805
800-873-2443
www.dietrichindustries.com
Steel-stud wall-framing system

Enterpriser Lighting, Inc.
Long-life light bulbs
(Since the completion of the Model Healthy
House, Enterpriser has gone out of business,
however, I now recommend compact fluorescent bulbs that are generally available through
local suppliers.)

*Kitchens and Baths by Don Johnson
Merchandise Mart #1375
Chicago, IL 60654
773-KITCHEN
www.healthycabinets.com
Low-tox steel kitchen and bath cabinets

Koetter Woodworking, Inc.
533 Louis Smith Road
Borden, IN 47106
812-923-8875
www.koetterwoodworking.com
Solid-poplar interior doors and trim

*Lee/Rowan
900 South Highway Dr.
Fenton, MO 63026
636-343-0700
800-325-6150
www.leerowan.com
Wire closet organizers

*Metal Sales Mfg. Corp.
7800 S.R. 60
Sellersburg, IN 47172
812-246-1935
Metal roofing and trim

*Murco Wall Products, Inc.
300 NE 21st St.
Ft. Worth, TX 76106-8528
817-626-1987
800-446-7124
Non-toxic drywall compound

Norandex
Triple-glazed aluminum windows
(Since the completion of the Model Healthy
House, Norandex has discontinued handling
aluminum-framed windows. However, simi-
lar windows are available from MI Home
Products at 717-365-3300 and Milgard at
206-659-0836.)

Nordyne
Nordyne sold their Intertherm heater division to:
Cadet Manufacturing Co.
P.O. Box 1675
Vancouver, WA 98668
360-693-2505
800-442-2338
www.cadetco.com
Intertherm (now"Softheat") baseboard heaters

*Nutech Energy Systems, Inc.
511 McCormick Blvd.
London, ON, Canada N5W 4C8
519-457-1904
www.lifebreath.com
Heat-recovery ventilator

373

Nu-Tek Plastics, Inc.
Distributed by Thomas & Betts
2233 Argentia Rd., Suite 116
Mississauga, ON, Canada L5N 2X7
905-858-1010
Airtight electrical boxes

*Pace Chem Industries, Inc.
3050 Westwood Dr.
Las Vegas, NV 89109
702-369-1424
800-350-2912
Low-toxic paint and clear finish

Polyken Technologies
Division of Tyko Adhesives
15 Hampshire St.
Mansfield, MA 02048
508-261-6200
www.polyken.com
Aluminum-foil sealant tape

*Pure Air Systems
1325 Church St.
Clayton, IN 46118
317-539-4097
800-869-8025
www.pureairsystems.com
Whole-house air filter

Reynolds Metals Co.
8450 S. Bedford Rd.
Macedonia, OH 44056
330-468-2200
800-528-0942
www.reynoldsbp.com
Aluminum siding and trim

Sage Advance Corp.
Solar water heater
(Since the completion of the Model Healthy House, Sage Advance has gone out of business, so that particular solar water heater is no longer available. For more information about various forms of solar heating, you can contact the American Solar Energy Association at 303-433-3130, www.ases.org,, or the Florida Solar Energy Center at 407-638-1000, www.fsec.ucf.edu.)

Stanley Door Systems
480 Myrtle St.
New Britain, CT 06053
860-225-5111
800-521-2752
www.stanleyworks.com
Insulated entry doors

Universal-Rundle Corp.
217 Mill St.
New Castle, PA 16103
724-658-6631
800-955-0316
www.universal-rundle.com
Low flow toilets
(Unfortunately, since the completion of the Model Healthy House, Universal-Rundle has quit handling the one-piece vitreous-china sink tops. On other projects, as an alternative, I've used tops made of solid marble or a synthetic solid sufacing material such as Corian and installed a drop-in sink of vitreous china or porcelainized steel. Although not quite as inert, I sometimes use the molded tops made of plaster and marble dust with an acrylic surface coating.

FOR FURTHER INFORMATION

■ ■ ■ Rather than compile an exhaustive bibliography of hundreds of publications dealing with indoor air pollution, I decided to assemble a list of the resources that I felt would be useful to people who actually plan to design or build a healthy house. The following are some of the best sources of information for both general interest and technical topics. Most of the books can be obtained thru local bookstores. For those not easily available, I have included ordering information. Also listed are periodicals and organizations of interest.

Unfortunately, some of the following books are out-of-print. If your local library doesn't own a copy of a particular book you are interested in, they can often borrow it from another library through their inter-library loan program.

Books

Advanced Energy Corp. *Builder's Field Guide*, (Order from Advanced Energy Corp., 909 Capability Dr., Suite 2100, Raleigh, NC 27606-3870, 919-857-9000) $45.00, 270+ pages spiral bound. Information about state-of-the-art construction practices, airtight construction, duct-sealing, including many construction drawings.

American Iron and Steel Institute. *Residential Steel Framing Manual for Architects, Engineers, and Builders* , (Order from American Iron and Steel Institute, 1101 17th St. NW, Washington, DC, 20036, 202-452-7100) $89.00. 3-ring binder with design, fastener, detail, and reference data.

Anderson, Bruce and Malcom Wells. *Passive Solar Energy*, Andover, MA: Brick House Publishing Co. 1994, 197-page paperback. Concise but comprehensive reference for passive solar design.

Baker, Paula, Erica Elliott, and John Banta. *Prescriptions for a Healthy House: A Practical Guide for Architects, Builders, and Homeowners*, Santa Fe, NM: InWord Press 1998, 259-page paperback. Covers both problems and soultions for all aspects of house construction.

Becker, Robert O. *Cross Currents*, Los Angeles: Jeremy P. Tarcher, Inc. 1990, 336-page hardcover. Covers the electrical nature of the human body and negative health effects resulting from electromagnetic fields.

Beebe, Glenn. *Toxic Carpet III*, 1991, (Order from Glenn Beebe, P.O. Box 53344, Cincinnati, OH 53344) $12.95 + $3.00 shipping, 368-page paperback. Chronicles a family's nightmare after being made ill by new carpeting.

Bonneville Power Administration. *Builder's Field Guide*, 1995, ($13.00 from New Residence Section RMRB, Bonneville Power Administration, P.O. Box 3621, Portland, OR 97208, 503-230-3000) 297-page spiral bound paperback. A guide to various methods of energy-efficient, airtight construction.

Bower, John. *The Healthy House, How to Buy One, How to Build One, How to Cure a Sick One*, Bloomington, IN: The Healthy House Institute 1997 (3rd edition), 672-page paperback. An encyclopedic guide to healthy house construction.

Bower, John. *Understanding Ventilation, How to design, select, and install residential ventilation systems*, Bloomington, IN: The Healthy House Institute 1995, 432-page hardcover. An in-depth discussion of all forms of ventilation.

Bower, John and Lynn Marie Bower. *The Healthy House Answer Book: Answers to the 133 most commonly asked questions*, Bloomington, IN: The Healthy House Institute 1997, 192-page paperback. Short, but complete, answers relating to healthy construction and life-style.

Breecher, Maury and Shirley Linde. *Healthy Homes in a Toxic World*, New York: John Wiley & Sons 1992. Basic information about household allergens and hazards.

Carmody, John, Jeffrey Christian and Kenneth Labs. *Builder's Foundation Handbook*, #ORNL/CON-295, 1991, (Order from National Technical Information Service, 800-553-NTIS) 112-page paperback. A construction manual for various foundation types.

Corman, Rita. *Air Pollution Primer*, New York: American Lung Association 1978, 105-page paperback. Basic technical information for the lay reader.

Davis, Andrew N. and Paul E. Schaffman. *The Home Environmental Sourcebook*. New York: Henry Holt 1996. Fifty environmental hazards to avoid when buying, selling, or maintaining a home.

duPont, Peter, and John Morrill. *Residential Indoor Air Quality and Energy Efficiency*, Washington: ACEEE 1989, (Order from American Council for an Energy Efficient Economy, 1001 Connecticut Ave., Suite 801, Washington, DC 20036, 202-429-0063) 267-page paperback. How energy efficiency and good air quality can be achieved together.

Godish, Thad. *Indoor Air Pollution Control*, Chelsea, MI: Lewis Publishers 1989, 401-page hardcover. Technical background information for understanding and controlling indoor air problems.

Goldbeck, David. *The Smart Kitchen*, Woodstock, NY: Ceres Press 1994, 134-page paperback. Covers various aspects of healthy kitchen design.

Good, Clint. *Healthful Houses*, Bethesda, MD: Guaranty Press 1988. 74-page paperback. Healthful building materials are listed in an architectural format.

Greenfield, Ellen J. *House Dangerous*, New York: Vintage Books 1987, 234-page paperback. General overview of indoor pollution written for homeowners.

Harwood, Barbara. *The Healing House*, Carlsbad, CA: Hay House 1997, 308-page paperback. How living in the right house can heal you spiritually, emotionally, and physically.

Howell, Charles and James Summerville, Eds., *Healthy Building for a Better Earth*, The Proceedings of the First National Conference on Environmental Sensitivity in Construction, 1991, 135-page paperback. Contains summaries of all of the presentations from this ground-breaking conference in Washington, DC.

How to Read a Material Safety Data Sheet, San Diego, CA: American Lung Association of San Diego and Imperial Counties 1988, 6-page flyer (contact your local chapter of the American Lung Association to obtain a copy). A fact sheet containing basic terms, definitions, and information found on Material Data Safety Sheets.

Hunter, Linda Mason. *The Healthy Home*, New York: Pocket Books 1989, 313-page paperback. An attic to basement guide to toxic-free living for homeowners.

Interior Concerns Resource Guide, Mill Valley, CA: Interior Concerns Publications 1992, (Order from Interior Concerns Publications, 131 W. Blithedale Ave., Mill Valley, CA 94941, 415-389-8049) $35.00, 100+ pages in a 3-ring binder. Resource listing for healthier building materials, geared for designers and architects.

Kadulski, Richard. *Heating Systems for Your New Home*, 1998, (Order from Drawing Room Graphics Ltd., Box 866267, North Vancouver, BC, Canada, V7L 4L2, 604-689-1841) 88-page paperback. Good coverage of all the various basic residential heating-system strategies.

Kadulski, Richard. *Residential Ventilation: Achieving Indoor Air Quality*, 1988, (Order from Drawing Room Graphics Ltd., Box 866267, North Vancouver, BC, Canada, V7L 4L2, 604-689-1841) 56-page paperback. Good coverage of basic ventilation strategies.

Labs, Kenneth, et al. *Building Foundation Design Handbook*, #ORNL/Sub/86-72143/1, 1986, 354 page paperback. (Order from National Technical Information Service, 800-553-NTIS) An in-depth design manual for various foundation types in different climate conditions, including many construction drawings.

Leclair, Kin and David Rousseau. *Environmental by Design*, Point Roberts, WA: Hartley & Marcks 1992, 261-page paperback. Covers environmental and health issues of various interior finishing, decorating, and remodeling materials.

Lischkoff, James K. and Joseph Lstiburek. *The Airtight House*, Ames IA: Iowa State University Research Foundation 1985, 84-page paperback. Good reference covering both theory and practical applications of the Airtight Drywall Approach.

Lstiburek, Joseph. *Builder's Guide for Cold (Heating) Climates* (Order from Building Science Corp., 70 Main St., Westford, MA 01886, 978-589-5100) $40.00 + $3.20 shipping, 300+ pages spiral bound. Climate-specific information about moisture control, Airtight Drywall Approach (ADA) to airtight construction, including numerous detailed construction drawings.

Lstiburek, Joseph. *Builder's Guide for Hot-Dry/Mixed-Dry (Cooling) Climates* (Order from Building Science Corp., 70 Main St., Westford, MA 01886, 978-589-5100) $40.00 + $3.20 shipping, 300+ pages spiral bound. Climate-specific information about moisture control, Airtight Drywall Approach (ADA) to airtight construction, including numerous detailed construction drawings.

Lstiburek, Joseph. *Builder's Guide for Hot-Humid (Cooling) Climates* (Order from Building Science Corp., 70 Main St., Westford, MA 01886, 978-589-5100) $40.00 + $3.20 shipping, 300+ pages spiral bound. Climate-specific information about moisture control, Airtight Drywall Approach (ADA) to airtight construction, including numerous detailed construction drawings.

Lstiburek, Joseph. *Builder's Guide for Mixed (Heating and Cooling) Climates* (Order from Building Science Corp., 70 Main St., Westford, MA 01886, 978-589-5100) $40.00 + $3.20 shipping, 300+ pages spiral bound. Climate-specific information about moisture control, Airtight Drywall Approach (ADA) to airtight construction, including numerous detailed construction drawings.

Lstiburek, Joseph and John Carmody. *Moisture Control Handbook*, New York: Van Nostrand Reinhold 1993, 214-page hardcover. A manual containing both theory and practical advice for understanding moisture problems and solutions in all types or residential construction, many detailed drawings.

Marinelli, Janet and Paul Bierman-Lytle. *Your natural Home*, New York: Little Brown 1995, 256-page paperback. Discusses healthy and ungealthy building materials, with sources.

Nisson, J.D. Ned, and Gautam Dutt. *The Superinsulated Home Book*, New York: John Wiley and Sons 1985, 316-page paperback. Covers energy-efficient construction practices, both theory and construction details.

Pearson, David. *The Natural House Book*, New York: Fireside 1989, 281-page paperback. How to use natural materials in healthy construction.

Pearson, David. *The New Natural House Book*, New York: Fireside 1998, 281-page paperback. Creating a healthy, harmonious, and ecologically sound home.

Pearson, David. *The Natural House Catalog*, New York: Fireside 1996, 287-page paperback. Source book for environmentally respomsible building materials.

Pfeiffer, Guy O. and Casimir M. Nikel. *The Household Environment and Chronic Illness*, Springfield, IL: Charles C. Thomas Publisher 1980, 187-pages hardcover. Physician's guide for healthy construction.

Rousseau, David, William Rea and Jean Enwright. *Your Home, Your Health and Well-Being*, Berkeley, CA: Ten Speed Press 1988, 300-page paperback. Room-by-room guidelines for building a healthy house.

Rousseau, David and James Wasley. *Healthy by Design*, Point Roberts, WA: Hartley & Marcks 1997, 290-page paperback. Building and remodeling solutions for creating healthy houses.

Schoemaker, Joyce and Charity Y. Vitale, *Healthy Homes, Healthy Kids*, Washington, DC: Island Press 1991, 180-page paperback. Why children are especially susceptible to indoor pollution, and how to protect them.

Small, Bruce M. *Indoor Air Pollution and Housing Technology*, Ottawa, Ontario: Canada Mortgage and Housing Corp. 1983, (Order from Canada Mortgage and Housing Corp., 700 Montreal Rd., Ottawa, ON, Canada K1A 0P7, 613-748-2003) 295-page paperback. A literature review on indoor pollution and sources.

Sugarman, Ellen. Warning: *The Electricity Around You May Be Hazardous to Your Health*, New York: Fireside 1992. Basic information on understanding electromagneyic fields.

Tile Council of America. *Handbook for Ceramic Tile Installation*, updated annually (Order from TCA, 100 Clemson Research Blvd., Anderson, SC 29625, 864-646-8453) 35-page paperback. Guidelines for most ceramic tile installations.

U.S. Environmental Protection Agency. *Radon-Resistant Residential New Construction*, #EPA/600/8-88/087, 1988, (Order from NTIS at 800-553-NTIS) 67-page paperback. Detailed radon guidelines for the residential builder.

U.S. Environmental Protection Agency. *A Citizen's Guide to Radon*, #402-K92-001, May 1992, (Order from EPA, "M" Street SW, Washington, DC, 202-260-2090, www.epa.gov) 15-page pamphlet. Describes in easy-to-understand language for the lay reader what radon is, how dangerous it is, and what to do about it.

U.S. Environmental Protection Agency. *Electric and Magnetic Fields From 60-Hertz Electric Power*, (Order from EPA, "M" Street SW, Washington, DC, 202-260-2090, www.epa.gov) 22-page paperback. Covers the risk to health; technical information in an easy-to-understand format.

U.S. Environmental Protection Agency. *The Inside Story, A Guide to Indoor Air Quality*, #EPA/400/1-88/004, 1988, (Order from EPA, "M" Street SW, Washington, DC, 202-260-2090, www.epa.gov) 32-page paperback. A very good introduction to the basics of indoor air pollution for the lay reader.

Venolia, Carol. *Healing Environments*, Berkeley, CA: Celestial Arts 1988, 224-page paperback. Health aspects of housing, including indoor air quality, sound, light, color, temperature, plants, etc.

Wilson, Alex. *Consumers Guide to Home Energy Savings*, Washington, DC: ACEEE updated annually, (Order from American Council for an Energy Efficient Economy, 1001 Connecticut Ave., Suite 801, Washington, DC 20036, 202-429-0063) 267-page paperback. Lists efficiencies of home appliances by model number.

Zamm, Alfred V. *Why Your House May Endanger Your Health*, New York: Simon and Schuster 1980, 218-page paperback. Building and maintaining a healthy house from a physician's viewpoint.

Periodicals

Building Concerns Newsletter, for environmentally concerned interior designers, architects and professionals, 131 W. Blithedale Ave., Mill Valley, CA 94941, 415-389-8049, bimonthly subscription $35.00.

Building With Nature Networking Newsletter, "placemaking that supports life," P.O. Box 4417, Santa Rosa, CA 95402, 707-579-2201, bimonthly subscription $35.00.

Environmental Building News, a newsletter on environmentally sustainable and energy efficient design and construction practices, 122 Birge St., Suite 30, Brattleboro, VT 05301, 802-257-7300, www.ebuild.com, monthly subscription $67.00.

Environmental Design & Construction, A magazine for successful building—economically and environmentally, 299 Market St., Suite 320, Saddle Brook, NJ 07663, 201-291-9001, bimonthly subscription, free to qualified individuals.

Solplan Review, the independent journal of energy conservation, building science and construction practice, Box 86627, N. Vancouver, BC, Canada V7L 4L2, 604-689-1841, bimonthly subscription $52.00 (U.S.).

Organizations

Advanced Energy Corp. Provides consulting, testing, and training in various areas related to building science and construction: energy efficiency, sustainablilty, heating-system safety, duct sealing, etc. Advanced Energy Corp., 909 Capability Dr., Suite 2100, Raleigh, NC 27606-3870, (919) 857-9000, www.advancedenergy.org.

American Lung Association. Provides information on their Health House Project to builders, designers, and homeowners about incorporating various healthier approaches in building houses. American Lung Association, Health House Project, 490 Concordia Ave., St. Paul, MN 55103-2441 651-227-8014, www.healthhouse.org.

Energy Efficient Building Association (EEBA). Consists of builders, designers, public utilities, and manufacturers devoted to extremely energy efficient construction thru a quarterly newsletter (*EEBA Excellence*), national conferences, etc. EEBA, 490 Concordia Ave., St. Paul, MN 55103, 651-268-7597, www.eeba.org.

Northwest Eco Building Guild. Has a *Green Pages* directory with a listing of builders, architects, and designers who are members and lists their areas of specialization. Northwest Eco Building Guild, P.O. Box 58530, Seattle, WA 98138-1530, 206-575-2222, www.ecobuilding.org.

Northeast Sustainable Energy Association (NESEA). NESEA members include architects and builders who are dedicated to responsible energy and material use thru a quarterly newsletter (*Northeast Sun*), seminars, and regional conferences. NESEA, 50 Miles St., Greenfield, MA 01301, (413) 774-6051, www.nesea.org.

The Healthy House Institute. Publishes a variety of books and videos on topics related to designing and building healthy houses and creating healthier life-styles, web site contains numerous articles, book descriptions, quiz, etc. The Healthy House Institute, 430 N. Sewell Rd., Bloomington, IN 47408, (812) 332-5073, www.hhinst.com.

Southface Energy Institute. Provides training in various areas related to building science. Publications include *The Southface Journal of Sustainable Building*, *Southface Factsheets*, and *The House Doctor*. Southface Energy Institute, 241 Pine St. NE, Atlanta, GA 30308-3424, 404-872-3549, www.southface.org.

HOUSE PLANS

■■■ The house plans reproduced here were prepared for this particular house. Under no circumstances should they be used "as is" to build a house in another locale. It is imperative that any house plans be reviewed by someone with the proper credentials (engineer, architect, or designer) to insure that they comply with local building regulations and climate conditions. For example, a local building code may require larger bedroom windows for fire egress; colder climates will dictate a deeper foundation in order to be below the frost line; and a location at a different latitude will necessitate a change in the roof overhang for optimal passive solar heating.

It should also be noted that if changes are made to one sheet of the Plans, they could have implications on other sheets. Widening the house from 28' to 30', for example, would mean a change in plumbing rough-in dimensions, and perhaps rafter sizes. Different window sizes could necessitate a different size of window header.

Do not try to use a scale on the Plans. In order to reproduce them so that they would fit into the format of this book, they had to be photographically reduced. Therefore, the scales shown on the Plans, while accurate on the original drawings, are not accurate on the reduced versions.

A SUPERINSULATED MODEL HEALTHY HOUSE

INDEX

1. TITLE AND INDEX
2. SITE PLAN
3. FLOOR PLAN
4. FOUNDATION PLAN
5. FLOOR PLAN, Phase 1
6. FULL HOUSE SECTION, Phase 1
7. WALL SECTION
8. WALL FRAMING DETAILS
9. WALL FRAMING DETAILS
10. STEEL STUD DETAILS
11. ENTRY DETAILS
12. SEALING DETAILS, Phase 1
13. FLOOR PLAN, Phase 2
14. BUILT-IN CABINETRY
15. HOUSE ELEVATIONS
16. HOUSE ELEVATIONS
17. EAVE DETAILS
18. DECK DETAILS
19. ELECTRICAL PLAN
20. PLUMBING SCHEMATICS
21. VENTILATION DETAILS
22. KITCHEN DETAILS
23. STAINLESS STEEL DETAILS
24. GARAGE DETAILS
25. GARAGE ELEVATIONS

NOTES

THIS HOUSE IS DESIGNED TO BE BUILT IN AN AIRTIGHT MANNER WITH A CONTROLLED VENTILATION SYSTEM. THE PLANS ARE SHOWN IN TWO PHASES IN ORDER TO SIMPLIFY THE CONSTRUCTION PROCESS.

ONLY MATERIALS SPECIFIED ARE TO BE USED IN ORDER TO INSURE THE QUALITY OF THE INDOOR AIR. NO SUBSTITUTIONS ALLOWED WITHOUT PRIOR CONSENT.

NO SMOKING ALLOWED ON THE PREMISIS.

THESE PLANS SHOULD NOT BE USED FOR CONSTRUCTION WITHOUT FIRST BEING REVIEWED BY A QUALIFIED PERSON FOR COMPLIANCE WITH LOCAL REGULATIONS AND CLIMATE CONDITIONS.

John Bower
ecologically safe homes

TITLE AND INDEX

COPYRIGHT 1993

SHEET 1 - 25

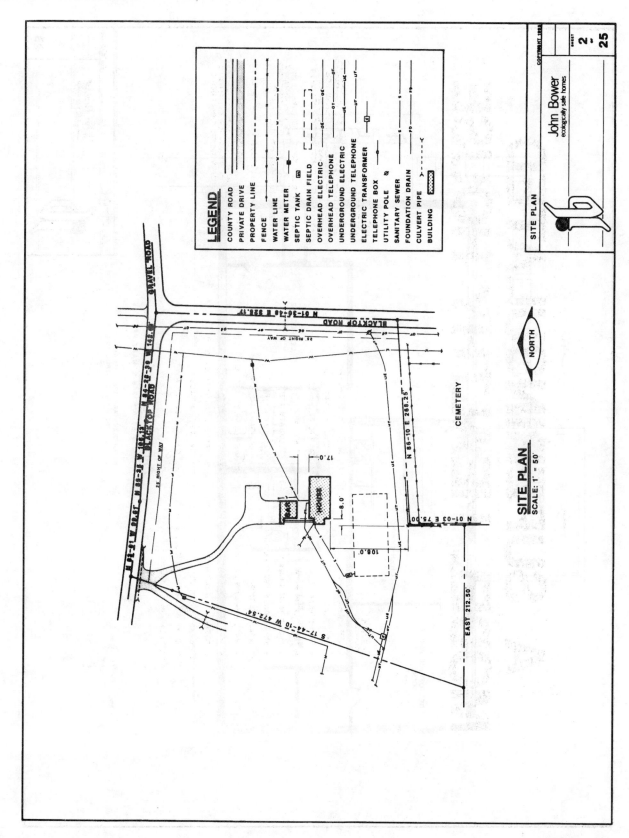

383

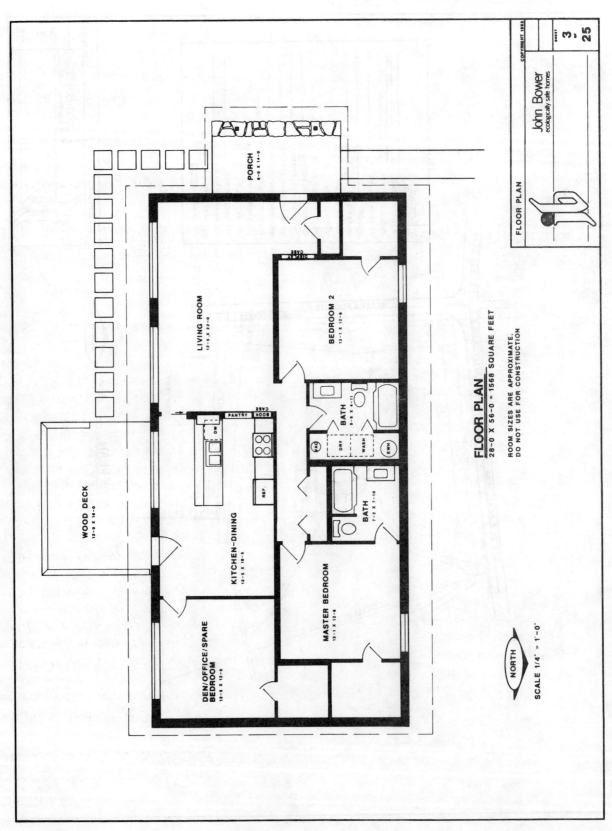

FLOOR PLAN
28-0 X 56-0 = 1568 SQUARE FEET

ROOM SIZES ARE APPROXIMATE.
DO NOT USE FOR CONSTRUCTION

NORTH

SCALE 1/4" = 1'-0"

PORCH
6-0 X 14-0

LIVING ROOM
12-5 X 22-0

BEDROOM 2
13-1 X 12-8

BATH
8-9 X 4-11

DRY

WASH

EWH

BOOK CASE

PANTRY

DW

REF.

WOOD DECK
12-0 X 14-0

KITCHEN-DINING
12-5 X 18-5

BATH
7-2 X 7-10

DEN/OFFICE/SPARE
BEDROOM
12-5 X 12-5

MASTER BEDROOM
13-1 X 12-8

FLOOR PLAN

John Bower
ecologically safe homes

SHEET 3 ~ 25

COPYRIGHT 1993

384

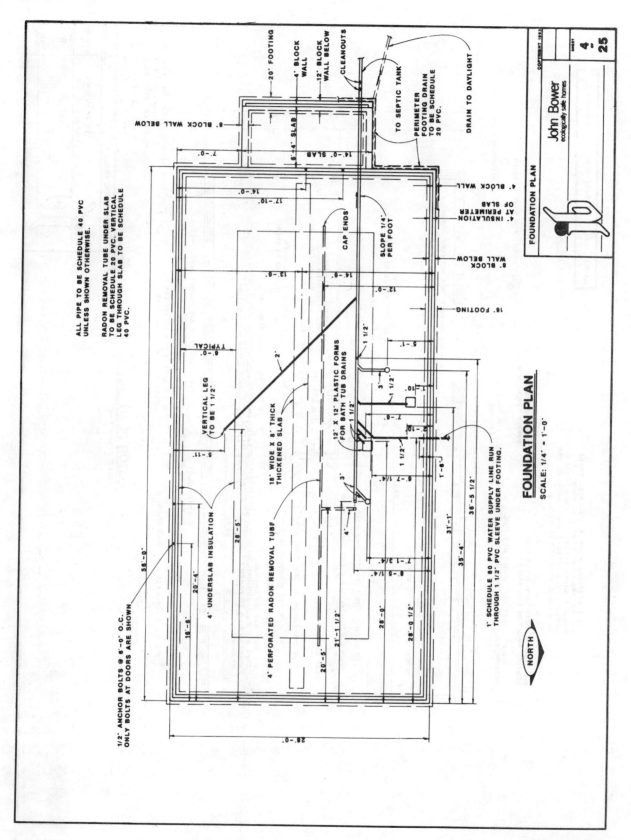

FOUNDATION PLAN

SCALE: 1/4" = 1'-0"

ALL PIPE TO BE SCHEDULE 40 PVC
UNLESS SHOWN OTHERWISE.

RADON REMOVAL TUBE UNDER SLAB
TO BE SCHEDULE 20 PVC. VERTICAL
LEG THROUGH SLAB TO BE SCHEDULE
40 PVC.

1/2" ANCHOR BOLTS @ 6'-0" O.C.
ONLY BOLTS AT DOORS ARE SHOWN

NORTH

20' FOOTING

4" BLOCK WALL

12" BLOCK WALL BELOW

CLEANOUTS

TO SEPTIC TANK

PERIMETER FOOTING DRAIN TO BE SCHEDULE 20 PVC.

DRAIN TO DAYLIGHT

8" BLOCK WALL BELOW

14'-0" SLAB

14'-4" SLAB

4" BLOCK WALL

4" INSULATION AT PERIMETER OF SLAB

SLOPE 1/4" PER FOOT

CAP ENDS

8" BLOCK WALL BELOW

18' FOOTING

VERTICAL LEG TO BE 1 1/2"

TYPICAL

18" WIDE X 8" THICK THICKENED SLAB

4" PERFORATED RADON REMOVAL TUBE

4" UNDERSLAB INSULATION

12' X 12' PLASTIC FORMS FOR BATH TUB DRAINS

1" SCHEDULE 80 PVC WATER SUPPLY LINE RUN THROUGH 1 1/2" PVC SLEEVE UNDER FOOTING.

FOUNDATION PLAN

John Bower
ecologically safe homes

SHEET
4
25

COPYRIGHT 1993

385

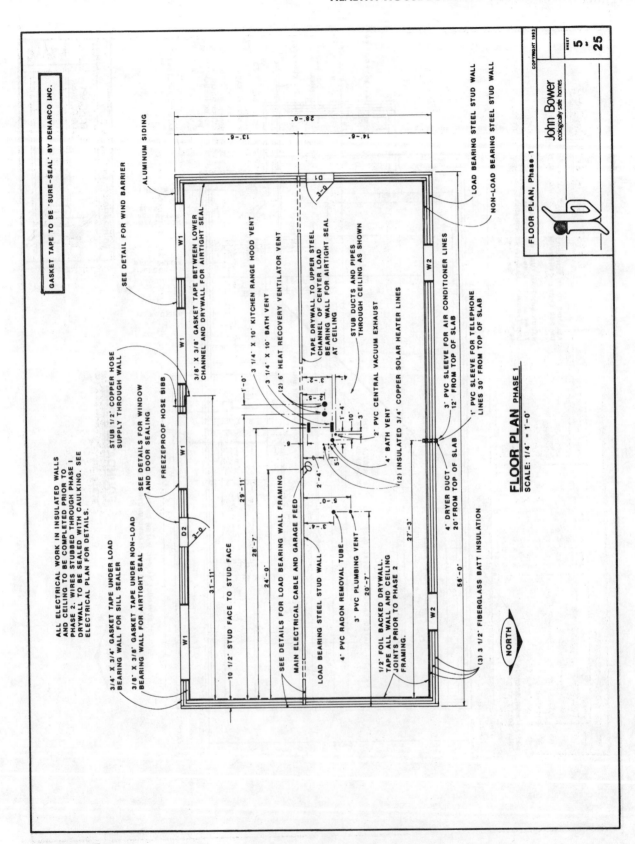

FLOOR PLAN PHASE 1

SCALE: 1/4" = 1'-0"

GASKET TAPE TO BE "SURE-SEAL" BY DENARCO INC.

ALUMINUM SIDING

SEE DETAIL FOR WIND BARRIER

STUB 1/2" COPPER HOSE
SUPPLY THROUGH WALL

FREEZEPROOF HOSE BIBB

SEE DETAILS FOR WINDOW
AND DOOR SEALING

3/8" X 3/8" GASKET TAPE BETWEEN LOWER
CHANNEL AND DRYWALL FOR AIRTIGHT SEAL

3 1/4" X 10" KITCHEN RANGE HOOD VENT

3 1/4" X 10" BATH VENT

(2) 6" HEAT RECOVERY VENTILATOR VENT

TAPE DRYWALL TO UPPER STEEL
CHANNEL OF CENTER LOAD
BEARING WALL FOR AIRTIGHT SEAL
AT CEILING

STUB DUCTS AND PIPES
THROUGH CEILING AS SHOWN

2" PVC CENTRAL VACUUM EXHAUST

4" BATH VENT

(2) INSULATED 3/4" COPPER SOLAR HEATER LINES

3" PVC SLEEVE FOR AIR CONDITIONER LINES
12" FROM TOP OF SLAB

3" PVC SLEEVE FOR TELEPHONE
LINES 30" FROM TOP OF SLAB

1" PVC PLUMBING VENT

4" DRYER DUCT
20" FROM TOP OF SLAB

1/2" FOIL BACKED DRYWALL.
TAPE ALL WALL AND CEILING
JOINTS PRIOR TO PHASE 2
FRAMING.

(3) 3 1/2" FIBERGLASS BATT INSULATION

4" PVC RADON REMOVAL TUBE

MAIN ELECTRICAL CABLE AND GARAGE FEED

SEE DETAILS FOR LOAD BEARING WALL FRAMING

LOAD BEARING STEEL STUD WALL

NON-LOAD BEARING STEEL STUD WALL

LOAD BEARING STEEL STUD WALL

3/4" X 3/4" GASKET TAPE UNDER LOAD
BEARING WALL FOR SILL SEALER

3/8" X 3/8" GASKET TAPE UNDER NON-LOAD
BEARING WALL FOR AIRTIGHT SEAL

ALL ELECTRICAL WORK IN INSULATED WALLS
AND CEILING TO BE COMPLETED PRIOR TO
PHASE 2. WIRES STUBBED THROUGH PHASE I
DRYWALL TO BE SEALED WITH CAULKING. SEE
ELECTRICAL PLAN FOR DETAILS.

NORTH

W1
W2
D1
D2

28'-0"
13'-6"
14'-6"
1'-0"
3'-0"
31'-11"
10 1/2" STUD FACE TO STUD FACE
28'-7"
24'-0"
29'-11"
27'-3"
56'-0"
20'-7"
3'-4"
5'-0"
2'-4"
6"
5"
10"
3'-4"
2'-5"
3'-2"
1'-0"

FLOOR PLAN, Phase 1

John Bower
ecologically safe homes

SHEET
5
~
25

COPYRIGHT 1993

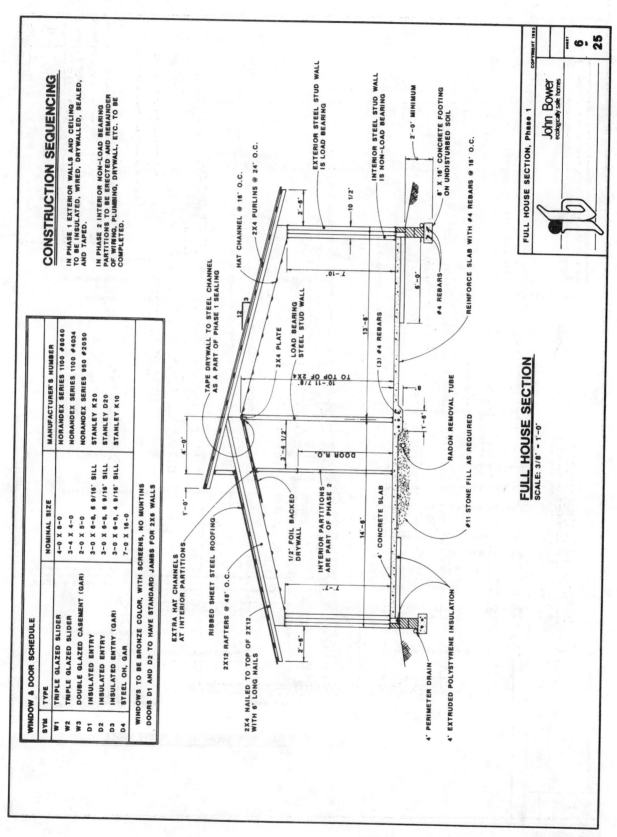

CONSTRUCTION SEQUENCING

IN PHASE 1 EXTERIOR WALLS AND CEILING TO BE INSULATED, WIRED, DRYWALLED, SEALED, AND TAPED.

IN PHASE 2 INTERIOR NON-LOAD BEARING PARTITIONS TO BE ERECTED AND REMAINDER OF WIRING, PLUMBING, DRYWALL, ETC. TO BE COMPLETED.

WINDOW & DOOR SCHEDULE

SYM	TYPE	NOMINAL SIZE	MANUFACTURER'S NUMBER
W1	TRIPLE GLAZED SLIDER	4-0 X 8-0	NORANDEX SERIES 1100 #8040
W2	TRIPLE GLAZED SLIDER	3-4 X 4-0	NORANDEX SERIES 1100 #4034
W3	DOUBLE GLAZED CASEMENT (GAR)	2-0 X 5-0	NORANDEX SERIES 950 #2050
D1	INSULATED ENTRY	3-0 X 6-8, 6 9/16" SILL	STANLEY K20
D2	INSULATED ENTRY	3-0 X 6-8, 6 9/16" SILL	STANLEY D20
D3	INSULATED ENTRY (GAR)	3-0 X 6-8, 4 9/16" SILL	STANLEY K10
D4	STEEL OH, GAR	7-0 X 16-0	

WINDOWS TO BE BRONZE COLOR, WITH SCREENS, NO MUNTINS
DOORS D1 AND D2 TO HAVE STANDARD JAMBS FOR 2X6 WALLS

FULL HOUSE SECTION
SCALE: 3/8" = 1'-0"

John Bower ecologically safe homes

FULL HOUSE SECTION, Phase 1

COPYRIGHT 1993

SHEET
6
–
25

387

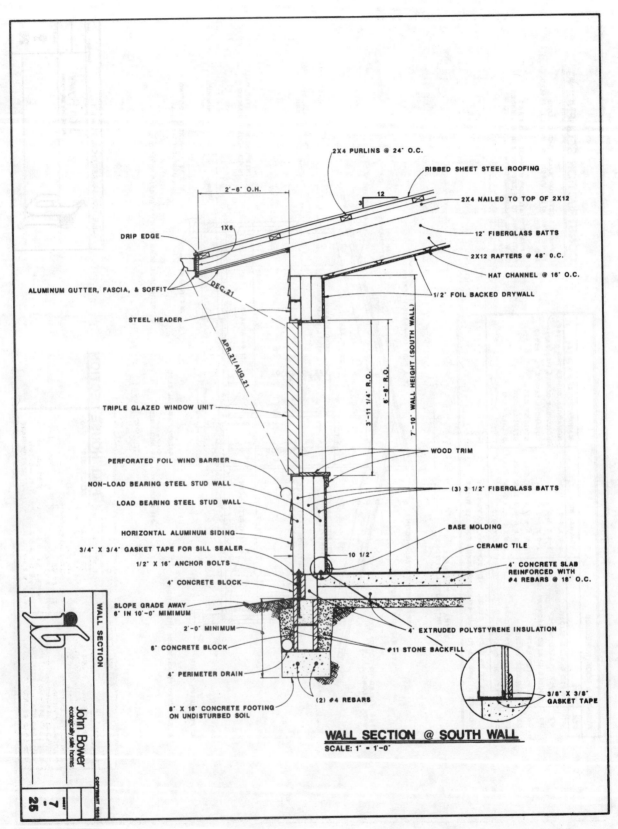

2X4 PURLINS @ 24" O.C.

RIBBED SHEET STEEL ROOFING

2'-6" O.H.

2X4 NAILED TO TOP OF 2X12

DRIP EDGE

1X6

12" FIBERGLASS BATTS

2X12 RAFTERS @ 48" O.C.

HAT CHANNEL @ 16" O.C.

ALUMINUM GUTTER, FASCIA, & SOFFIT

DEC.21

1/2" FOIL BACKED DRYWALL

STEEL HEADER

APR.21/AUG.21

7'-10" WALL HEIGHT (SOUTH WALL)

TRIPLE GLAZED WINDOW UNIT

3'-11 1/4" R.O.

6'-8" R.O.

WOOD TRIM

PERFORATED FOIL WIND BARRIER

NON-LOAD BEARING STEEL STUD WALL

(3) 3 1/2" FIBERGLASS BATTS

LOAD BEARING STEEL STUD WALL

HORIZONTAL ALUMINUM SIDING

BASE MOLDING

3/4" X 3/4" GASKET TAPE FOR SILL SEALER

CERAMIC TILE

1/2" X 16" ANCHOR BOLTS

4" CONCRETE SLAB REINFORCED WITH #4 REBARS @ 18" O.C.

4" CONCRETE BLOCK

10 1/2"

SLOPE GRADE AWAY 6" IN 10'-0" MIMIMUM

2'-0" MINIMUM

4" EXTRUDED POLYSTYRENE INSULATION

6" CONCRETE BLOCK

#11 STONE BACKFILL

4" PERIMETER DRAIN

3/8" X 3/8" GASKET TAPE

8" X 16" CONCRETE FOOTING ON UNDISTURBED SOIL

(2) #4 REBARS

WALL SECTION @ SOUTH WALL
SCALE: 1" = 1'-0"

WALL SECTION

John Bower
ecologically safe homes

COPYRIGHT 1993

SHEET
7
25

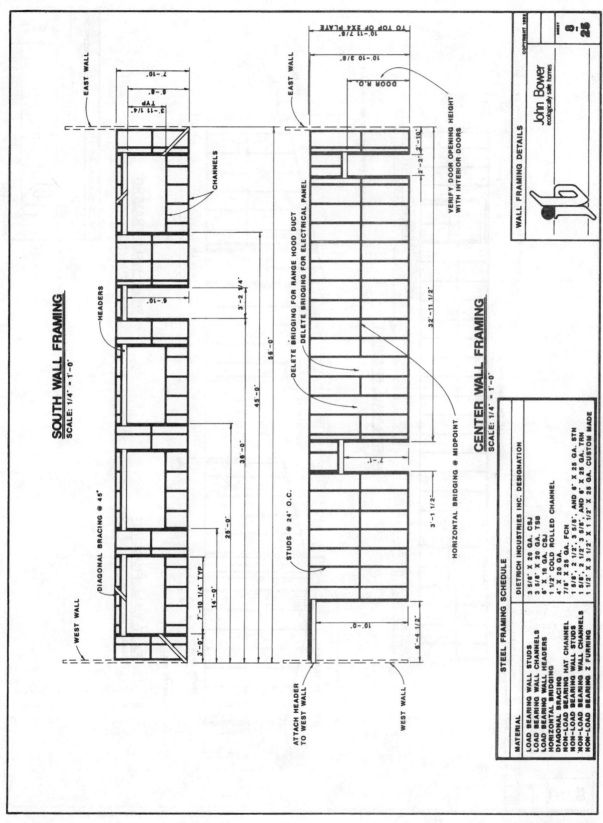

SOUTH WALL FRAMING
SCALE: 1/4" = 1'-0"

CENTER WALL FRAMING
SCALE: 1/4" = 1'-0"

WALL FRAMING DETAILS

John Bower
ecologically safe homes

STEEL FRAMING SCHEDULE	
MATERIAL	DIETRICH INDUSTRIES INC. DESIGNATION
LOAD BEARING WALL STUDS	3 5/8" X 20 GA. CSJ
LOAD BEARING WALL CHANNELS	3 5/8" X 20 GA. TSB
LOAD BEARING WALL HEADERS	6" X 18 GA. CSJ
HORIZONTAL BRIDGING	1 1/2" COLD ROLLED CHANNEL
DIAGONAL BRACING	4" X 20 GA.
NON-LOAD BEARING HAT CHANNEL	7/8" X 25 GA. FCN
NON-LOAD BEARING WALL STUDS	1 5/8", 2 1/2", 3 5/8", AND 6" X 25 GA. STN
NON-LOAD BEARING WALL CHANNELS	1 5/8", 2 1/2", 3 5/8", AND 6" X 25 GA. TRN
NON-LOAD BEARING Z FURRING	1 1/2" X 3 1/2" X 1 1/2" X 25 GA. CUSTOM MADE

389

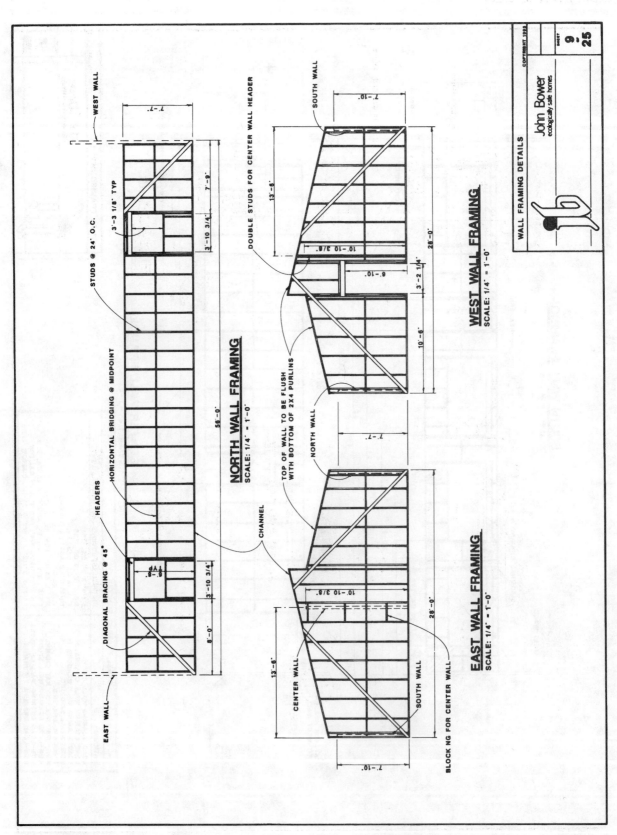

NORTH WALL FRAMING
SCALE: 1/4" = 1'-0"

WEST WALL FRAMING
SCALE: 1/4" = 1'-0"

EAST WALL FRAMING
SCALE: 1/4" = 1'-0"

WALL FRAMING DETAILS

John Bower
ecologically safe homes

390

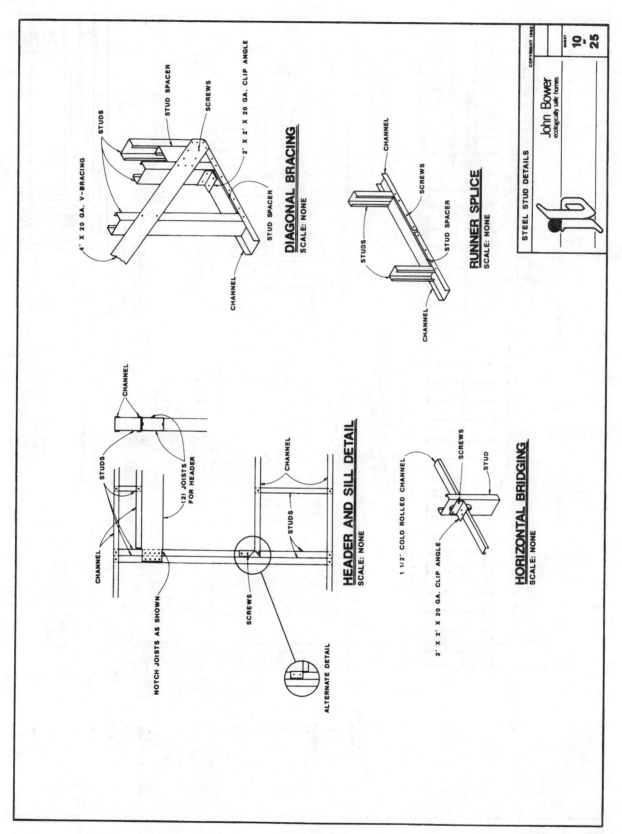

DIAGONAL BRACING
SCALE: NONE

RUNNER SPLICE
SCALE: NONE

HEADER AND SILL DETAIL
SCALE: NONE

HORIZONTAL BRIDGING
SCALE: NONE

STEEL STUD DETAILS

John Bower
ecologically safe homes

SHEET
10
–
25

COPYRIGHT 1993

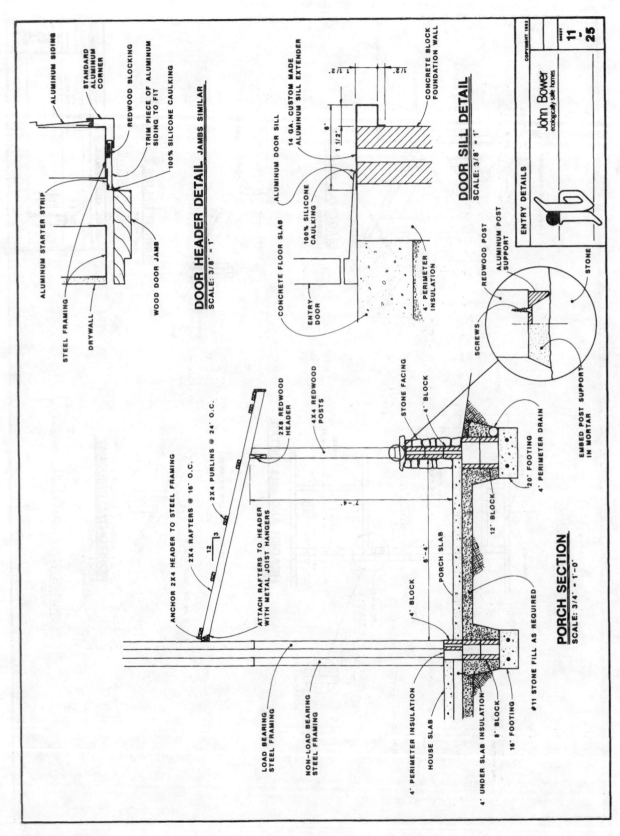

DOOR HEADER DETAIL JAMBS SIMILAR
SCALE: 3/8" = 1"

ALUMINUM SIDING
STANDARD ALUMINUM CORNER
REDWOOD BLOCKING
TRIM PIECE OF ALUMINUM SIDING TO FIT
100% SILICONE CAULKING
ALUMINUM STARTER STRIP
STEEL FRAMING
DRYWALL
WOOD DOOR JAMB

DOOR SILL DETAIL
SCALE: 3/8" = 1"

ALUMINUM DOOR SILL
14 GA. CUSTOM MADE ALUMINUM SILL EXTENDER
CONCRETE BLOCK FOUNDATION WALL
100% SILICONE CAULKING
CONCRETE FLOOR SLAB
ENTRY DOOR
4" PERIMETER INSULATION

PORCH SECTION
SCALE: 3/4" = 1'-0"

2X8 REDWOOD HEADER
4X4 REDWOOD POSTS
2X4 RAFTERS @ 16" O.C.
2X4 PURLINS @ 24" O.C.
ANCHOR 2X4 HEADER TO STEEL FRAMING
ATTACH RAFTERS TO HEADER WITH METAL JOIST HANGERS
STONE FACING
4" BLOCK
SCREWS
REDWOOD POST
ALUMINUM POST SUPPORT
STONE
EMBED POST SUPPORT IN MORTAR
20" FOOTING
12" BLOCK
4" PERIMETER DRAIN
PORCH SLAB
4" BLOCK
LOAD BEARING STEEL FRAMING
NON-LOAD BEARING STEEL FRAMING
4" PERIMETER INSULATION
HOUSE SLAB
4" UNDER SLAB INSULATION
8" BLOCK
16" FOOTING
#11 STONE FILL AS REQUIRED

ENTRY DETAILS

John Bower
ecologically safe homes

COPYRIGHT 1993

SHEET
11
25

392

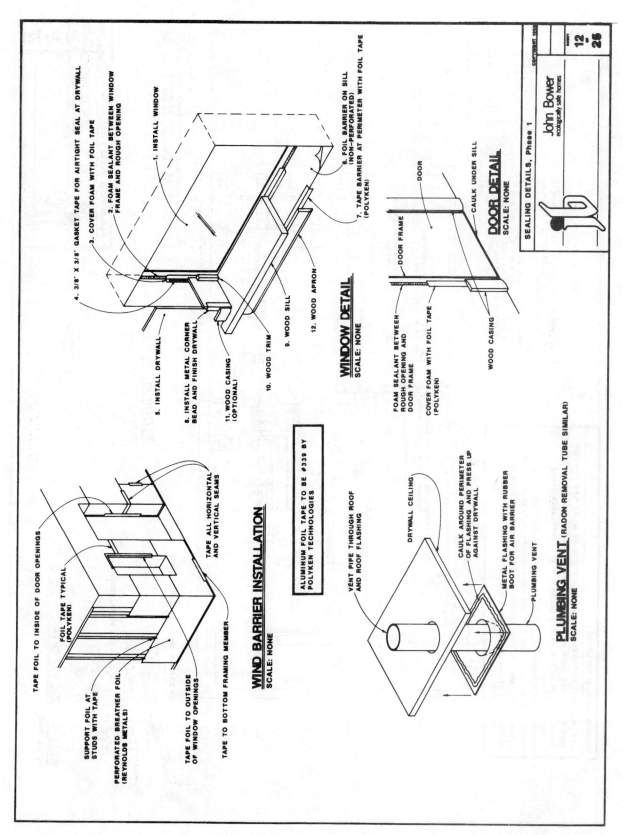

WIND BARRIER INSTALLATION
SCALE: NONE

WINDOW DETAIL
SCALE: NONE

DOOR DETAIL
SCALE: NONE

PLUMBING VENT (RADON REMOVAL TUBE SIMILAR)
SCALE: NONE

John Bower
ecologically safe homes

SEALING DETAILS, Phase 1

393

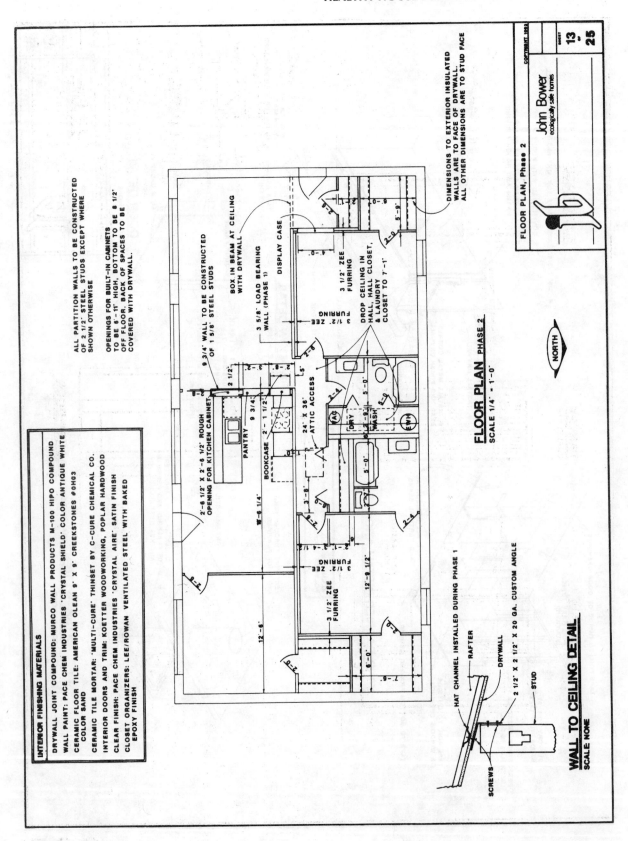

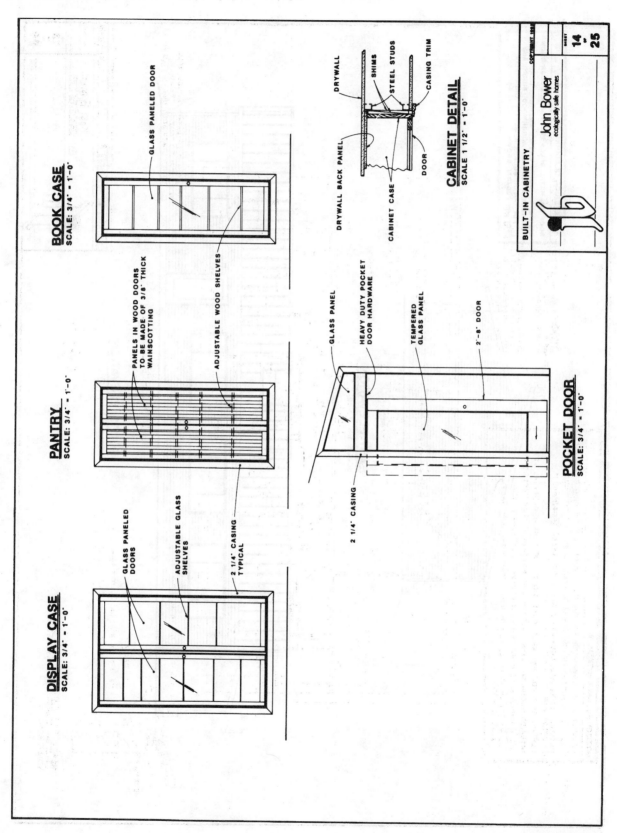

BOOK CASE
SCALE: 3/4" = 1'-0"

GLASS PANELED DOOR

PANTRY
SCALE: 3/4" = 1'-0"

PANELS IN WOOD DOORS
TO BE MADE OF 3/8" THICK
WAINSCOTING

ADJUSTABLE WOOD SHELVES

DISPLAY CASE
SCALE: 3/4" = 1'-0"

GLASS PANELED
DOORS

ADJUSTABLE GLASS
SHELVES

2 1/4" CASING
TYPICAL

CABINET DETAIL
SCALE 1 1/2" = 1'-0"

DRYWALL
SHIMS
STEEL STUDS
CASING TRIM
DRYWALL BACK PANEL
CABINET CASE
DOOR

POCKET DOOR
SCALE: 3/4" = 1'-0"

GLASS PANEL

HEAVY DUTY POCKET
DOOR HARDWARE

TEMPERED
GLASS PANEL

2'-8" DOOR

2 1/4" CASING

BUILT-IN CABINETRY

John Bower
ecologically safe homes

SHEET
14
25

COPYRIGHT 1993

395

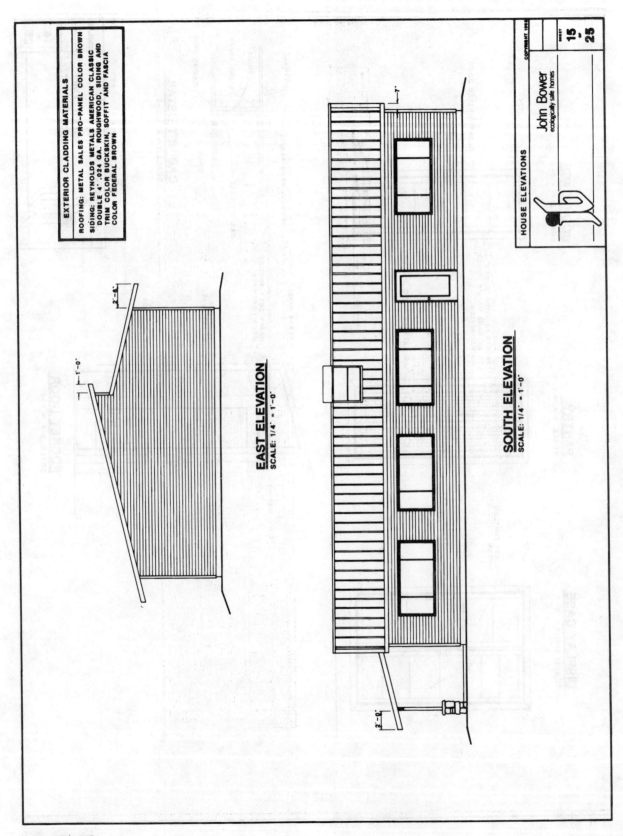

EXTERIOR CLADDING MATERIALS

ROOFING: METAL SALES PRO-PANEL COLOR BROWN

SIDING: REYNOLDS METALS AMERICAN CLASSIC DOUBLE 4" .024 GA. ROUGHWOOD, SIDING AMD TRIM COLOR BUCKSKIN, SOFFIT AND FASCIA COLOR FEDERAL BROWN

EAST ELEVATION
SCALE: 1/4" = 1'-0"

SOUTH ELEVATION
SCALE: 1/4" = 1'-0"

HOUSE ELEVATIONS

John Bower
ecologically safe homes

SHEET
15
—
25

COPYRIGHT 1998

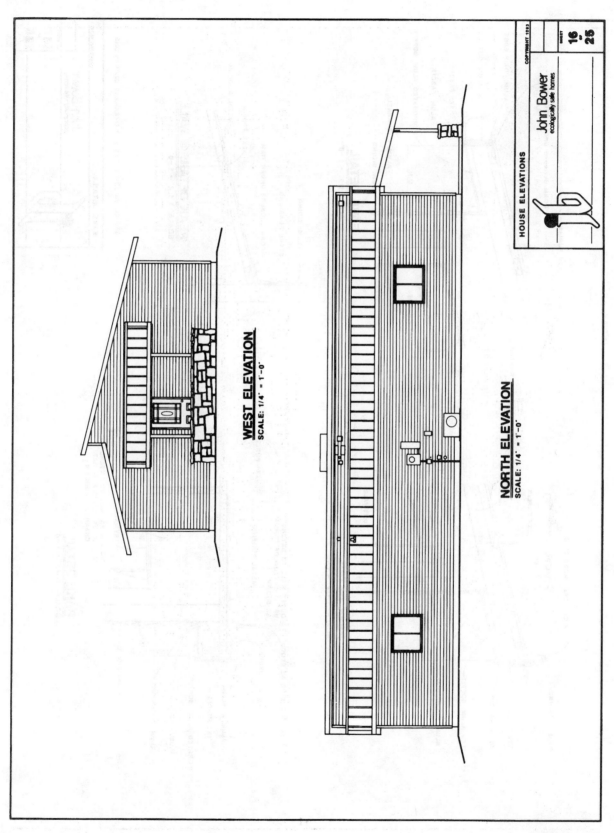

WEST ELEVATION
SCALE: 1/4" = 1'-0"

NORTH ELEVATION
SCALE: 1/4" = 1'-0"

HOUSE ELEVATIONS

John Bower
ecologically safe homes

16
25

COPYRIGHT 1993

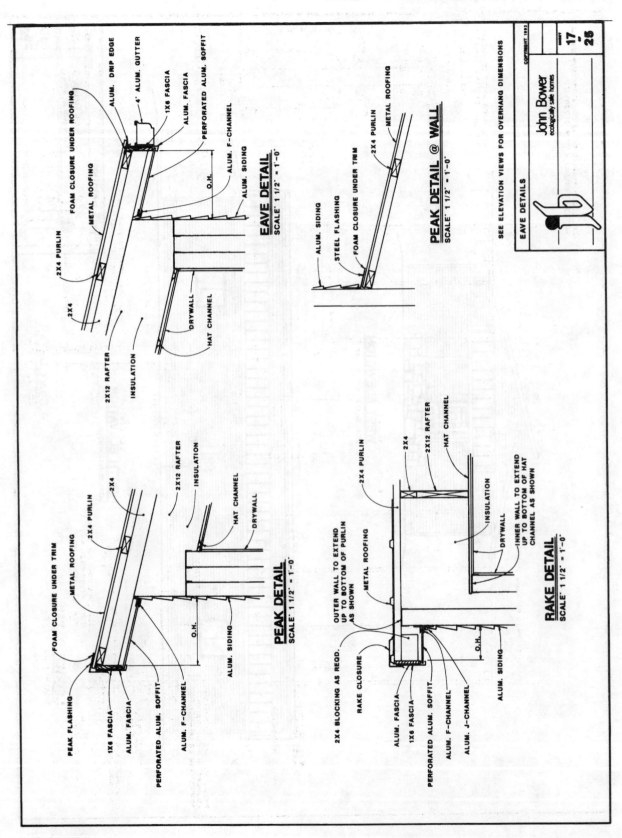

EAVE DETAIL
SCALE: 1 1/2" = 1'-0"

FOAM CLOSURE UNDER ROOFING
ALUM. DRIP EDGE
4" ALUM. GUTTER
1X6 FASCIA
ALUM. FASCIA
PERFORATED ALUM. SOFFIT
ALUM. F-CHANNEL
ALUM. SIDING
METAL ROOFING
2X4 PURLIN
2X4
2X12 RAFTER
INSULATION
DRYWALL
HAT CHANNEL
O.H.

PEAK DETAIL @ WALL
SCALE: 1 1/2" = 1'-0"

ALUM. SIDING
STEEL FLASHING
FOAM CLOSURE UNDER TRIM
2X4 PURLIN
METAL ROOFING

PEAK DETAIL
SCALE: 1 1/2" = 1'-0"

FOAM CLOSURE UNDER TRIM
METAL ROOFING
2X4 PURLIN
2X4
2X12 RAFTER
INSULATION
HAT CHANNEL
DRYWALL
PEAK FLASHING
1X6 FASCIA
ALUM. FASCIA
PERFORATED ALUM. SOFFIT
ALUM. F-CHANNEL
ALUM. SIDING
O.H.

RAKE DETAIL
SCALE: 1 1/2" = 1'-0"

2X4 PURLIN
2X4
2X12 RAFTER
HAT CHANNEL
INSULATION
DRYWALL
INNER WALL TO EXTEND UP TO BOTTOM OF HAT CHANNEL AS SHOWN
OUTER WALL TO EXTEND UP TO BOTTOM OF PURLIN AS SHOWN
2X4 BLOCKING AS REQD.
RAKE CLOSURE
METAL ROOFING
ALUM. FASCIA
1X6 FASCIA
PERFORATED ALUM. SOFFIT
ALUM. F-CHANNEL
ALUM. J-CHANNEL
ALUM. SIDING
O.H.

SEE ELEVATION VIEWS FOR OVERHANG DIMENSIONS

John Bower
ecologically safe homes

EAVE DETAILS

COPYRIGHT 1993

SHEET
17
25

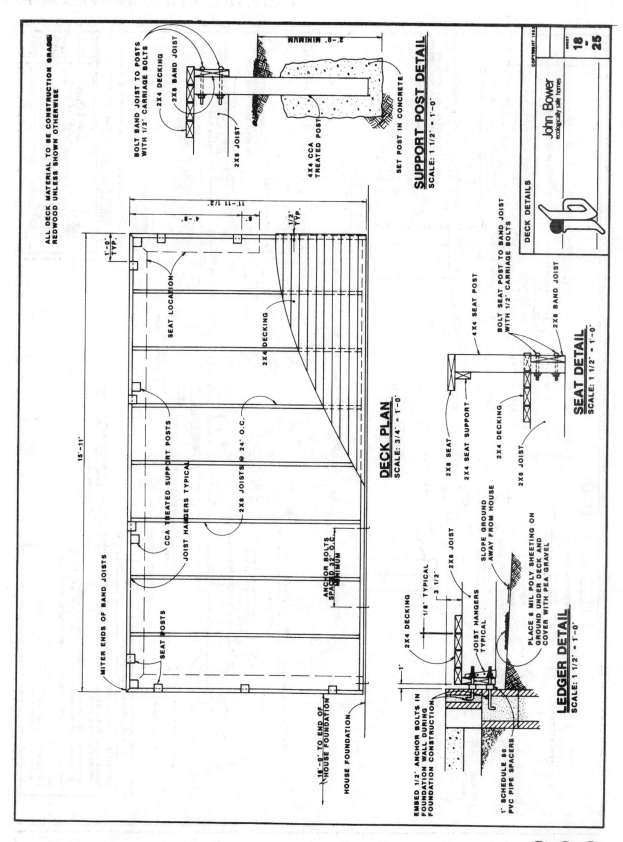

DECK PLAN
SCALE: 3/4" = 1'-0"

SUPPORT POST DETAIL
SCALE: 1 1/2" = 1'-0"

SEAT DETAIL
SCALE: 1 1/2" = 1'-0"

LEDGER DETAIL
SCALE: 1 1/2" = 1'-0"

John Bower
ecologically safe homes

DECK DETAILS

SHEET 18 OF 25

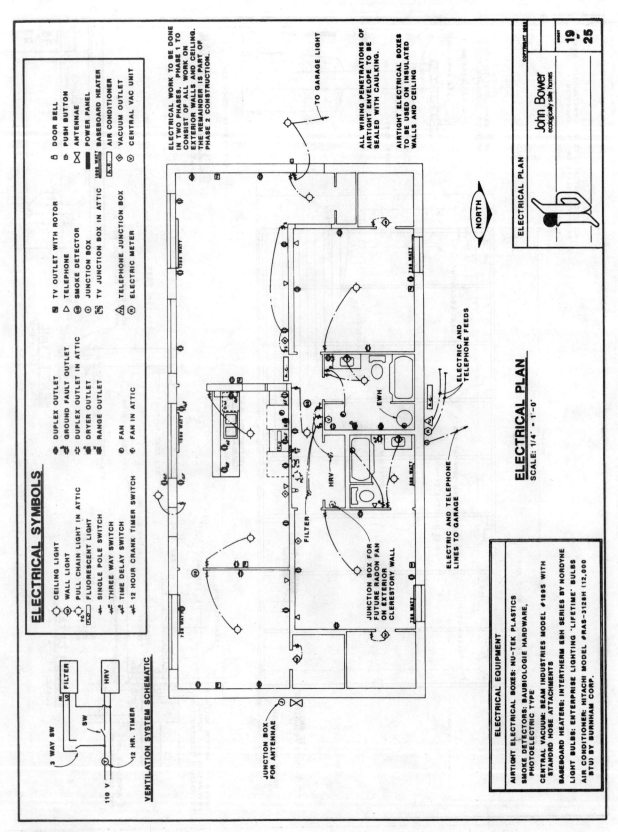

ELECTRICAL SYMBOLS

CEILING LIGHT		TV OUTLET WITH ROTOR	DOOR BELL
WALL LIGHT		TELEPHONE	PUSH BUTTON
PULL CHAIN LIGHT IN ATTIC		SMOKE DETECTOR	ANTENNAE
FLUORESCENT LIGHT		JUNCTION BOX	POWER PANEL
SINGLE POLE SWITCH		TV JUNCTION BOX IN ATTIC	BASEBOARD HEATER
THREE WAY SWITCH		TELEPHONE JUNCTION BOX	AIR CONDITIONER
TIME DELAY SWITCH		ELECTRIC METER	VACUUM OUTLET
12 HOUR CRANK TIMER SWITCH			CENTRAL VAC UNIT
DUPLEX OUTLET			
GROUND FAULT OUTLET			
DUPLEX OUTLET IN ATTIC			
DRYER OUTLET			
RANGE OUTLET			
FAN			
FAN IN ATTIC			

VENTILATION SYSTEM SCHEMATIC

3 WAY SW
FILTER
HRV
SW
110 V
12 HR. TIMER

ELECTRICAL PLAN

SCALE: 1/4" = 1'-0"

NORTH

ELECTRICAL WORK TO BE DONE IN TWO PHASES. PHASE 1 TO CONSIST OF ALL WORK ON EXTERIOR WALLS AND CEILING. THE REMAINDER IS PART OF PHASE 2 CONSTRUCTION.

ALL WIRING PENETRATIONS OF AIRTIGHT ENVELOPE TO BE SEALED WITH CAULKING.

AIRTIGHT ELECTRICAL BOXES TO BE USED ON INSULATED WALLS AND CEILING

TO GARAGE LIGHT

ELECTRIC AND TELEPHONE FEEDS

ELECTRIC AND TELEPHONE LINES TO GARAGE

JUNCTION BOX FOR FUTURE RADON FAN ON EXTERIOR CLERESTORY WALL

JUNCTION BOX FOR ANTENNAE

FILTER
HRV
EWH
A.C.
A.C.

ELECTRICAL EQUIPMENT

AIRTIGHT ELECTRICAL BOXES: NU-TEK PLASTICS

SMOKE DETECTORS: BAUBIOLOGIE HARDWARE, PHOTOELECTRIC TYPE

CENTRAL VACUUM: BEAM INDUSTRIES MODEL #189S WITH STANDRD HOSE ATTACHMENTS

BASEBOARD HEATERS: INTERTHERM EBH SERIES BY NORDYNE

LIGHT BULBS: ENTERPRISE LIGHTING 'LIFETIME' BULBS

AIR CONDITIONER: HITACHI MODEL #RAS-312BH (12,000 BTU) BY BURNHAM CORP.

ELECTRICAL PLAN

John Bower
ecologically safe homes

COPYRIGHT 1993

19
25

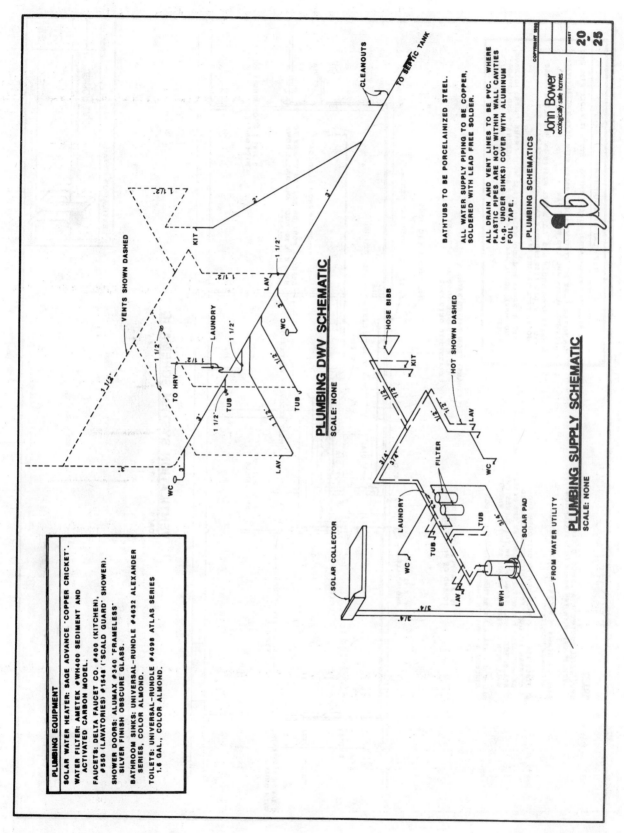

PLUMBING DWV SCHEMATIC
SCALE: NONE

PLUMBING SUPPLY SCHEMATIC
SCALE: NONE

BATHTUBS TO BE PORCELAINIZED STEEL.

ALL WATER SUPPLY PIPING TO BE COPPER, SOLDERED WITH LEAD FREE SOLDER.

ALL DRAIN AND VENT LINES TO BE PVC. WHERE PLASTIC PIPES ARE NOT WITHIN WALL CAVITIES (e.g. UNDER SINKS) COVER WITH ALUMINUM FOIL TAPE.

PLUMBING SCHEMATICS

John Bower
ecologically safe homes

COPYRIGHT 1993

SHEET 20-25

PLUMBING EQUIPMENT

SOLAR WATER HEATER: SAGE ADVANCE 'COPPER CRICKET'.

WATER FILTER: AMETEK #WH400 SEDIMENT AND ACTIVATED CARBON MODEL.

FAUCETS: DELTA FAUCET CO. #400 (KITCHEN), #550 (LAVATORIES) #1548 ('SCALD GUARD' SHOWER).

SHOWER DOORS: ALUMAX #340 'FRAMELESS' SILVER FINISH OBSCURE GLASS.

BATHROOM SINKS: UNIVERSAL-RUNDLE #4632 ALEXANDER SERIES, COLOR ALMOND.

TOILETS: UNIVERSAL-RUNDLE #4098 ATLAS SERIES 1.6 GAL, COLOR ALMOND.

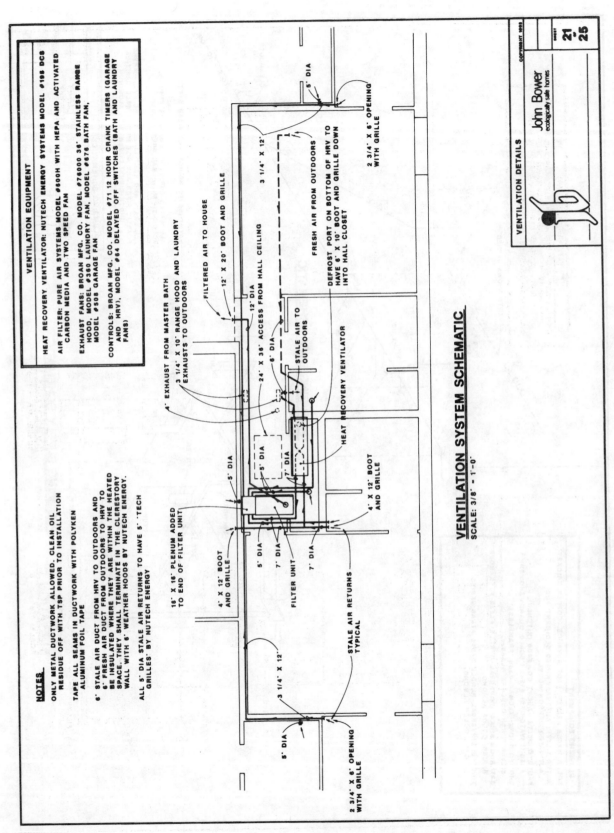

NOTES

ONLY METAL DUCTWORK ALLOWED. CLEAN OIL RESIDUE OFF WITH TSP PRIOR TO INSTALLATION

TAPE ALL SEAMS IN DUCTWORK WITH POLYKEN ALUMINUM FOIL TAPE

6" STALE AIR DUCT FROM HRV TO OUTDOORS AND 6" FRESH AIR DUCT FROM OUTDOORS TO HRV TO BE INSULATED WHERE THEY ARE WITHIN THE HEATED SPACE. THEY SHALL TERMINATE IN THE CLERESTORY WALL WITH 6" WEATHER HOODS BY NUTECH ENERGY.

ALL 5" DIA STALE AIR RETURNS TO HAVE 5" TECH GRILLES BY NUTECH ENERGY

VENTILATION EQUIPMENT

HEAT RECOVERY VENTILATOR: NUTECH ENERGY SYSTEMS MODEL #195 DCS

AIR FILTER: PURE AIR SYSTEMS MODEL #600H WITH HEPA AND ACTIVATED CARBON MEDIA AND TWO SPEED FAN

EXHAUST FANS: BROAN MFG. CO. MODEL #76000 30" STAINLESS RANGE HOOD, MODEL #360 LAUNDRY FAN, MODEL #676 BATH FAN, MODEL #509 GARAGE FAN

CONTROLS: BROAN MFG. CO. MODEL #71 12 HOUR CRANK TIMERS (GARAGE AND HRV), MODEL #64 DELAYED OFF SWITCHES (BATH AND LAUNDRY FANS)

VENTILATION SYSTEM SCHEMATIC
SCALE: 3/8" = 1'-0"

EXHAUST FROM MASTER BATH

3 1/4" X 10" RANGE HOOD AND LAUNDRY EXHAUSTS TO OUTDOORS

FILTERED AIR TO HOUSE

12" X 20" BOOT AND GRILLE

12" DIA

24" X 36" ACCESS FROM HALL CEILING

3 1/4" X 12"

6" DIA

STALE AIR TO OUTDOORS

FRESH AIR FROM OUTDOORS

DEFROST PORT ON BOTTOM OF HRV TO HAVE 6" X 10" BOOT AND GRILLE DOWN INTO HALL CLOSET

HEAT RECOVERY VENTILATOR

2 3/4" X 6" OPENING WITH GRILLE

5" DIA

5" DIA

7" DIA

4" X 12" BOOT AND GRILLE

16" X 16" PLENUM ADDED TO END OF FILTER UNIT

4" X 12" BOOT AND GRILLE

5" DIA

7" DIA

FILTER UNIT

7" DIA

STALE AIR RETURNS TYPICAL

3 1/4" X 12"

5" DIA

2 3/4" X 6" OPENING WITH GRILLE

5" DIA

John Bower
ecologically safe homes

VENTILATION DETAILS

21
25

COPYRIGHT 1993

402

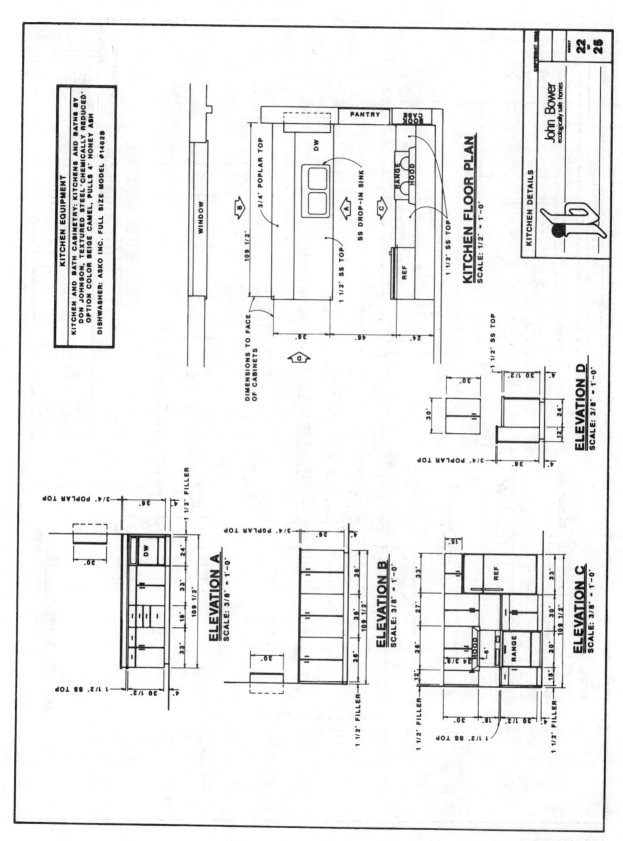

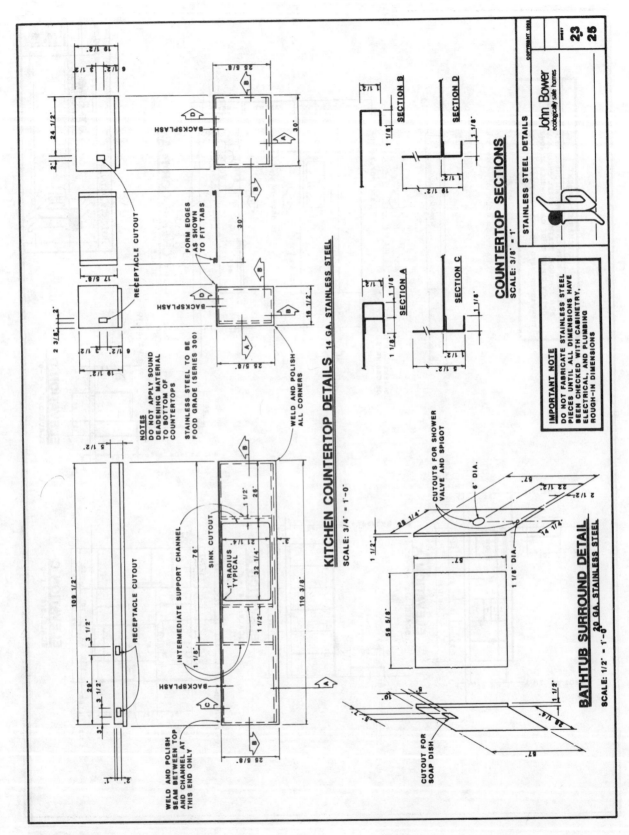

KITCHEN COUNTERTOP DETAILS 14 GA. STAINLESS STEEL

SCALE: 3/4" = 1'-0"

COUNTERTOP SECTIONS

SCALE: 3/8" = 1'

BATHTUB SURROUND DETAIL 20 GA. STAINLESS STEEL

SCALE: 1/2" = 1'-0"

NOTES
DO NOT APPLY SOUND DEADENING MATERIAL TO BOTTOM OF COUNTERTOPS

STAINLESS STEEL TO BE FOOD GRADE (SERIES 300)

IMPORTANT NOTE
DO NOT FABRICATE STAINLESS STEEL PIECES UNTIL ALL DIMENSIONS HAVE BEEN CHECKED WITH CABINETRY, ELECTRICAL, AND PLUMBING ROUGH-IN DIMENSIONS

SECTION A
SECTION B
SECTION C
SECTION D

John Bower
ecologically safe homes

STAINLESS STEEL DETAILS

404

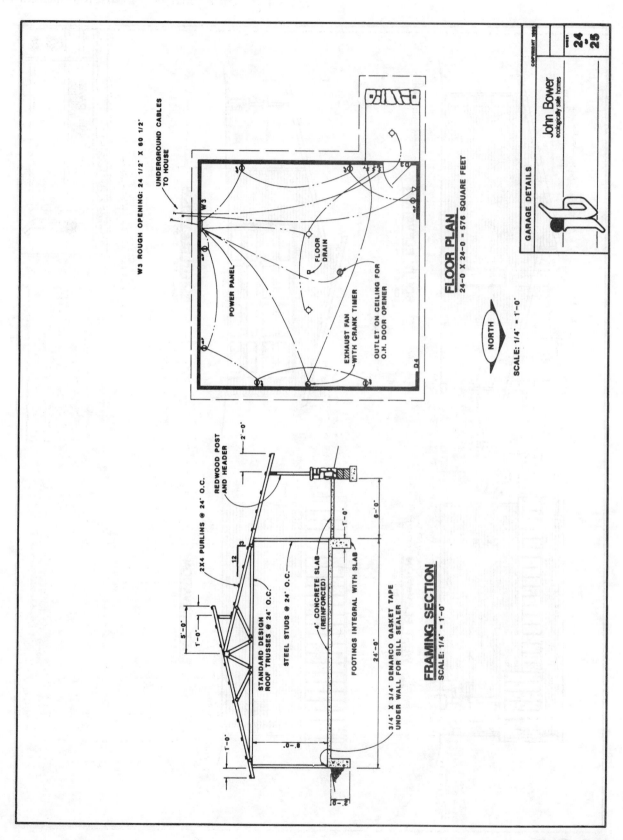

FLOOR PLAN
24-0 X 24-0 = 576 SQUARE FEET

SCALE: 1/4" = 1'-0"

NORTH

W3 ROUGH OPENING: 24 1/2" X 80 1/2"

UNDERGROUND CABLES TO HOUSE

POWER PANEL

FLOOR DRAIN

EXHAUST FAN WITH CRANK TIMER

OUTLET ON CEILING FOR O.H. DOOR OPENER

FRAMING SECTION
SCALE: 1/4" = 1'-0"

REDWOOD POST AND HEADER

2X4 PURLINS @ 24" O.C.

STANDARD DESIGN ROOF TRUSSES @ 24" O.C.

STEEL STUDS @ 24" O.C.

4" CONCRETE SLAB (REINFORCED)

FOOTINGS INTEGRAL WITH SLAB

3/4" X 3/4" DENARCO GASKET TAPE UNDER WALL FOR SILL SEALER

GARAGE DETAILS

John Bower
ecologically safe homes

SHEET 24 of 25

405

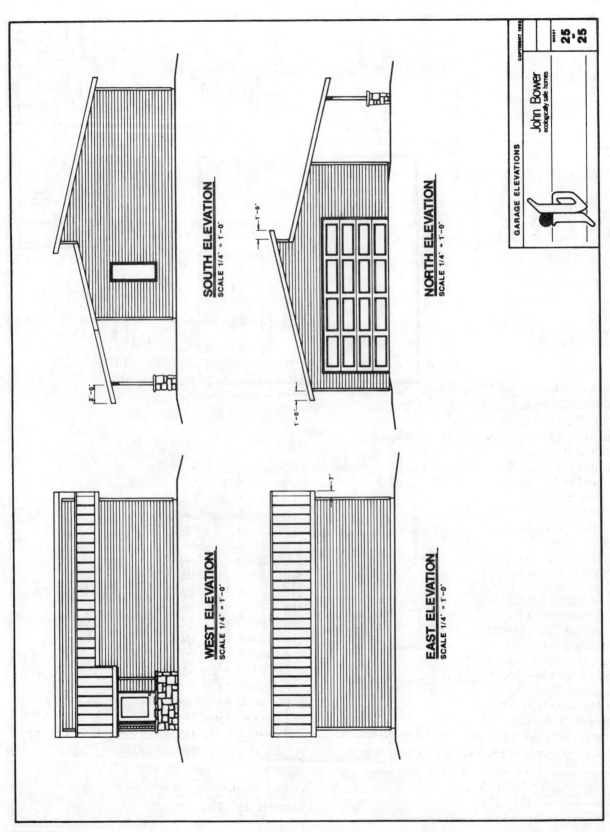

SOUTH ELEVATION
SCALE 1/4" = 1'-0"

NORTH ELEVATION
SCALE 1/4" = 1'-0"

WEST ELEVATION
SCALE 1/4" = 1'-0"

EAST ELEVATION
SCALE 1/4" = 1'-0"

GARAGE ELEVATIONS

John Bower
ecologically safe homes

SHEET
25
25

COPYRIGHT 1993

INDEX

Available from The Healthy House Institute

$23.95

The Healthy House is the most comprehensive guide to healthy construction available. Now in it's third edition, it has been completely revised, reorganized, and updated, and it contains over twice as much information as previous editions. Praised by builders, architects, and homeowners as an essential reference for selecting less-toxic construction materials, it is fully referenced and contains a listing of nearly 500 suppliers of healthier materials. Third edition, trade paperback, 6" x 9", 672 pages.

Creating a Healthy Household offers a wealth of practical suggestions for improving your indoor environment. With chapters devoted to cleaning products, personal-care, clothing, linens, interior decorating, life-style, housekeeping, air and water quality, and electromagnetic radiation, no other book matches its scope. It is an essential reference for anyone interested in their family's health—especially those who are chemically sensitive. Hundreds of product sources including phone numbers, internet addresses, and a comprehensive index. Trade paperback, 6" x 9", 608 pages.

$19.95

$21.95

How a house is put together is just as important as what materials are used. With over 200 photos and illustrations, as well as a complete set of detailed house plans, **Healthy House Building for the New Millennium** takes you step-by-step through the construction of a Model Healthy House. While your house may not look like the one in this book, the important how-to information necessary to build or remodel in a healthy manner is applicable to all houses. This latest edition contains up-to-date construction information and suggestions. Trade paperback, 8½" x 11", 416 pages.

Your House, Your Health is the companion video to *Healthy House Building for the New Millennium.* Author John Bower discusses the basic causes of indoor air pollution and walks you through a Model Healthy House, pointing out all the important design features. This excellent visual introduction takes much of the mystery out of what goes into a healthy house. It helps homeowner's and professionals alike understand fundamental healthy-building concepts. VHS video, 27.5 minutes.

$19.95

Order today from The Healthy House Institute
430 N. Sewell Road • Bloomington, IN 47408
812–332–5073 • Major credit cards accepted • www.hhinst.com

Shipping: $3.00 for the first item, plus $2.00 for each additional item. Indiana residents add 5% sales tax.
Overseas shipping: $5.00 for first item, plus $3.00 for each additional item. Payment must be in U.S. funds.